BASKETBALL

Concepts and Techniques

second edition

BASKETBALL

Concepts and Techniques

Bob Cousy

and

Frank G. Power, Jr.

With additional material by
William E. Warren

ALLYN AND BACON, INC.
Boston, London, Sydney, Toronto

Library of Congress Cataloging in Publication Data

Cousy, Bob, 1928–
  Basketball: concepts and techniques.

  Bibliography: p.
  Includes index.
  1. Basketball. 2. Basketball coaching. I. Power,
Frank G. II. Warren, William E., 1941–   . III. Title.
GV885.C628 1983   796.32'32   82–16420
ISBN 0-205-07819-2

Printed in the United States of America

10 9 8 7 6 5 4 3 2 1 88 87 86 85 84 83

CONTENTS

vii

FOREWORD

No two men are more qualified to write a book on coaching basketball than Bob Cousy and Frank Power. Bob's life has been basketball, and probably no other name in the history of the sport has been so closely identified with it. Frank was both freshman coach and chief scout during Bob's six years at Boston College. For the past twenty years they have been close friends, both on and off the court, a relationship spawned by their mutual love and knowledge of basketball and fostered by reciprocal respect.

Cousy gained national prominence as a Holy Cross All-American and member of an NCAA Championship team, then moved on to a legendary stint in the National Basketball Association that included six NBA championships, and culminated in his election to Basketball's Hall of Fame. In 1963, after retiring as a player, Bob coached for six seasons at Boston College. He quickly built a nationally ranked team that has a six-year record of 117 won and 38 lost—one that was selected for five successive National Tournaments. After leaving the collegiate ranks, Bob worked for five years as head coach of the Cincinnati Royals and Kansas City Kings. In 1973, he coached the USA national team against the USSR that avenged the defeat in the 1972 Olympics. More recently, he has kept his close affiliation with basketball as a television commentator and as the National Fund Raising Chairman for the new Basketball Hall of Fame building.

I have had the privilege of knowing and working with Bob Cousy for a great many years, including thirteen years as his coach with the Boston Celtics. During his great years with the Celtics, he was known as "Mr. Basketball," and in my opinion no player in the history of the game has ever been more deserving of such a title, nor carried it with more dignity and grace.

Bob Cousy is a highly intelligent man, and since his early playing days he has been a keen observer and analyst of the game of basketball. In my judgment, he has as much knowledge and savvy stored up inside him about the game of basketball as any living person today.

Frank Power is the senior Headmaster in the Boston Public Schools currently serving in this capacity at the Boston Business School, a post-secondary institution. His renown as a football, basketball and baseball coach and as a collegiate football official is surpassed only by his stature in the academic world.

Frank's basketball coaching career spans four decades, beginning in the U.S. Navy in 1943. Since then he has coached with outstanding success at every level: high school, prep school, college freshman, college junior varsity and college varsity. His overall head coaching record of 556 wins against 141 losses attests to this. Widely known as an erudite instructor and brilliant technician of basketball, he, therefore, is a natural collaborator for Cousy. (Bob Ryan, the nationally respected basketball writer, calls Frank "the most knowledgeable and caring basketball personality I've ever met.") Having been closely affiliated with Bob both as a fellow coach and friend, he is intimately familiar with—and in complete accord with—the Cousy brand of basketball.

Their first effort was a highly informative and definitive work on the playing and coaching of basketball that has since become a classic. This edition is a worthy sequel—a *must* for every player and coach.

Arnold "Red" Auerbach

PREFACE

In this second edition of *Basketball: Concepts and Techniques,* we have revised many sections and updated several of the offensive and defensive team techniques, eliminating those that have fallen into disuse. As in the first edition, however, we have presented coaches and players with a sound, in-depth compendium of basketball, from its basic individual elements through the complexities of team organization and the strategies of the game. We have endeavored to provide a variety of offensive and defensive alignments, each suited to specific personnel, for use within the framework of the coaches' and players' experience. By using these proven techniques, coaches can improve their team's capabilities.

This second edition is sectioned into four parts for easy reference. Parts Two and Three, Offense and Defense, represent the major portion of the book. Part One discusses essential coaching attributes and the overall operational aspects of the game. Part Four details the principles of complete game organization.

Chapter 4 is extremely valuable to both player and coach. We cannot stress too emphatically the significance of mastering the techniques presented in this chapter. The Boston Celtics fast break is meticulously developed in Chapter 5. Other fast break theories are also outlined here.

Some drills used by the authors over the years are presented next to discussions of the various offensive techniques. More drills are available from many texts listed in the updated bibliography found in the appendix. This section also contains Bob Cousy's own basketball outline as well as sample practice schedules.

The authors wish to express their appreciation to all the athletes in the photographs. Sincere thanks are again extended to Ms. Rowena Dores and others from Allyn and Bacon, Inc. for their cooperation. We are grateful to the staff photographers from *Sub Turri* and to Ken Gorman for allowing us to use selected photographs in our book. Finally, our deep gratitude to Mr. Herman L. Masin, Editor of *Scholastic Coach* magazine, for his years of friendship and encouragement.

KEY FOR DIAGRAMS

A, B, C, D, E Offensive players

X_1, X_2, X_3, X_4, X_5 Defensive players

O_1, O_2, O_3, O_4, O_5 Offensive players in drills

Screen by offensive player

Dribble

Pass

Cut by offensive player

Movement without ball offensively

A● Offensive player with ball

Shooting attempt

Offensive roll by a screener

Foot positioning by a player

Arm and hand position—offense or defense

Movement to new position—offense or defense

Dribble to new position

Depicts three offensive options for A:
  1 & 2. A pass in direction shown
  3. A dribble in direction shown

part one

INTRODUCTION

The Coach

Coaching basketball is not easy. Basketball coaches are highly visible and accessible to spectators packed a scant foot or two behind them in the stands. Adding to the pressure of crowd intimacy and whatever pressures to win the coach faces is the fact that he must assume many roles in the execution of his job: he may be at once a teacher, a leader, a father figure, a psychologist, a counselor, a community role model, a public relations liaison agent, a professional man, and a family man. In these capacities, he has an obligation to basketball and sports in general, to his players, to his fellow coaches, to the opposing participants and game officials, to the school or organization he represents, to the press and other news media, to the community in which he lives and works, and to his family.

CHARACTERISTICS OF A GOOD COACH

The coach is a prime influence on his players during their formative years; therefore, he should be an educated, cultured gentleman with high ideals and firm principles. He must be dignified, serious, businesslike, and even-tempered. He must have understanding, patience, and a personality that inspires confidence in those around him. He must be sincere in his relationships with his players—firm, without being stubborn. He must discipline himself, his players, and his staff within the framework of his moral philosophy. The coach does not necessarily have to have been an outstanding basketball player. However, he should be mentally attuned to the game, and he must be adaptable. Many great coaches were poor players, and many great players make poor coaches.

A coach seeking a job at a certain level should be aware of the duties involved. At the high school or college level he must have a commonsense approach to basketball, keeping it in its proper perspective within the overall institutional administrative policy. At these levels, especially the former, teaching duties may come before coaching, which is merely one facet of the educational process of his players. The basic requirements for a coach are that he be a good teacher, both in the classroom and on the basketball court, and that he have unlimited knowledge of basketball. He must be able to organize his time, he must have patience and fortitude, and he must have a great desire to improve the techniques of his students.

In any school, a pleasant, friendly attitude by the coach can go a long way in helping his relationship with the student body, as well as his players' relationship with the other students. He should be available to students for consultations in his office at specified times. He must also get to know the rest of the faculty and the administrators. They will have a far better understanding of his problems if they are on friendly terms.

A good coach does not enter the coaching profession merely to earn a living. Coaching demands all of one's time and interest almost twelve months a year—usually without regard for social and family obligations. It is impossible to be a clock watcher and still function effectively as a coach. If the coach is not completely dedicated to the team, the players will know it. One of the authors heard his captain comment that the reason he knew the team had the coach's complete interest was that the coach never took long-distance phone calls while practice was going on.

Dedication comes easily to most coaches for a very selfish reason—their ego. Granted we love the game and enjoy teaching it to the youngsters, but the important motive is that the discipline and organization of a team, as well as its success, are a direct reflection of the coach.

The coach's reward is basically intrinsic: he can take pleasure in the travel involved; the meeting of different people; and the loyalty and friendship of the players, the administration, and—perhaps most important—his peers. The financial gain is normally secondary.

The team looks to the coach for organization and leadership, and his ability in these areas is reflected by his players on and off the court. He must have sound judgment and the courage and ability to exercise his judgment when the situation warrants it. Often a coach has the knowledge required but hesitates to act. This weakness will carry over and lead to a similar weakness among his players. A coach should always follow the instincts of his experience and knowledge when the occasion calls for a snap decision. Failure to do so always leads to the second guess and self-recrimination.

The coach must conduct himself ethically, using all practical means to win every contest. He must play every game within the rules and within the spirit of the game, accepting success with humility and failure with grace and restraint. He should never bring discredit on his profession or sport through inexcusable utterances or deeds. Since he is generally the school's most prominent representative, he should follow administrative policy carefully, remembering that his school and community are being judged by his actions.

THE COACH'S BASKETBALL PHILOSOPHY

Every coach should develop his own philosophy concerning basketball, based on his knowledge of the game and his observations. In determining his game plan, he should make use of the observations he has made and all objective material available, such as statistics gathered during games or scrimmage sessions. First, he should select the type of offense and defense he wishes his players to use during the season. Then he must break the offense and defense down into fundamental procedures, designing drills for his players. He must convince them that the offense he has selected will help them win against their opponents.

Planning the Game

The coach must make practice as enjoyable as possible. When practice or playing becomes loathsome, monotonous, or too serious, players lose the proper mental attitude—that of always wanting more—and both the players and the coach suffer. When teaching the fundamentals, the coach must stress perfection. They should be so well learned that they become instinctive in a game situation. The squad should be encouraged to ask questions regarding the fundamentals, and the coach and his assistants should give help before and after practice. Weak fundamentalists will become weak basketball players.

The coach must teach his players to control the pace of a game. If an opposing team wishes to run against them, they should be capable of slowing down the game. If an opponent uses a controlled type of defense, the coach's team must be able to speed it up.

Balance is one of the prime requisites in a team offensive philosophy. Basketball is a team effort: good shooters should take the most shots, and good rebounders should be in position when those shots are taken.

The coach must always think of putting the proper players in each position. The best ball handler should handle the ball most of the time. He is the team quarterback. His duties involve getting the ball to the good shooter when he is in position to shoot and seeing that the good shooter does not get the ball in a poor shooting position if he is the type who insists on taking the shot whenever he gets the ball. He should also be certain that the good rebounders are in position. Having the ball in the hands of the right player will definitely cut down the margin of error for the team offensively. Players should be made aware of what good aggressive defense will do. While aggressive playing may cause them to make more mistakes, it may also give them more scoring opportunities and the victory. The coach should allow players to take advantage of their individual skills and use their initiative, making sure that it conforms to the overall team effort.

Psychological Approach to the Players

The coach should realize that players learn by example, and he should not expect anything from his players that he himself is not capable of giving in his leadership. He must live his philosophy of life and inculcate leadership qualities and a winning attitude in his players.

Each hour, each day, and each week during the season presents a new psychological problem. The coach must maintain a good team spirit as well as a team with good spirits. He should have his players on edge at all times. They should be up for each game. The coach must decide whether a pep talk would be more effective before the game or at half time. He must get the most from each of the players, and he must be aware of the players who need the most understanding. He should also take psychological advantage of lineup changes. He should be cautious in his disciplinary measures and should be aware of team reactions to punitive action.

The coach must occasionally deal with unfortunate happenings during the year, and he should stay on top of any situation that might cause team friction. At the first sign of difficulty, the principals should be called in to talk it out. Any grievances can usually be settled if they are not allowed to fester.

The following are suggestions to the coach:

Hustling is one of the prime prerequisites for an aggressive team. Players should hustle from one place to another, hustle when called by a coach, and hustle entering and leaving the court. They should never sit or sprawl on a court. If they are all listening to an explanation or watching a demonstration, they could rest on one knee, with an arm on the other knee.

For preseason practice, a coach should never select a starting team. He should change personnel constantly; otherwise he will discourage reserves by making them feel unnecessary. By matching his best players against each other in the preseason, he increases their individual ability and effectiveness. Interchanging personnel constantly gives potential starters the feeling of the reserves in competition, and conversely, it allows first-line reserves to coordinate their abilities to the better players during the development of basic offensive and defensive patterns. The late installation of a starting team makes preseason practice much more competitive and allows simulation of actual game conditions.

A coach's criticism should always be constructive. A suggestion made to one player applies to all. Praise a player who makes an outstanding play or makes a suggestion and puts it into practice correctly. Whenever possible, emphasize the importance of the unglamorous defense and rebounding maneuvers that normally get little attention in the press.

A player should understand that criticism is like money— you should worry about the lack of it. The players a coach criticizes are usually the ones he uses. They should realize that they should not blame others for their own shortcomings and that they will learn most from their own mistakes. They shouldn't run away from their problems, but face them and try to overcome them.

Imagination and visualization are important elements not only in coaching the game, but also in dealing with the players' personalities. The coach should be able to project future situations off the court as well as on it. He should be able to make decisions based on sound reasoning, judgment, and imagination.

Injuries should be reported to the coach or the trainer immediately. No injury is so slight it can be completely ignored. Ignoring injuries when they first occur sometimes sidelines the players later.

THE COACH'S RELATIONSHIPS

Staff

A formal staff includes a coach and one, two, or more assistants whose philosophy of basketball coincides with that of the head coach. Assistants must have teaching ability, and they must be energetic and eager to teach. It is the duty of the head coach to create a livable atmosphere for the entire coaching staff. If an assistant is to do a good job, he has to feel that he is a part of the organization and that he is important to the success of the team. He should have a voice in the planning of the team's offensive and defensive systems, and he should be consulted concerning the personnel and the placement of personnel. If the assistants do not feel that their advice is looked for or heeded, they will not be effective in their jobs. A head coach should either accept the advice of an assistant or tell him why he feels the suggestion is not feasible. He should use the pronoun "we" rather than "I" and compliment the assistants in front of a squad.

An assistant should be willing to listen to and consider the ideas of his fellow coaches, accepting or rejecting techniques the others use. He must be able to use what he accepts within the framework of the head coach's pattern, and he must be able to reject what would take more time or energy than he has at his disposal.

Players

The coach's relationship with his players is one of the most important aspects of the coaching situation. He should have individual conferences with each squad member before, during, and after the season to discuss health, studies, outside problems, the player's contributions to the team, and, at high school level, selection of a college.

Players appreciate an interest in their health. A preseason physical examination is prerequisite for a player. During preseason time the coach should be concerned with individual training and conditioning; during the season, he should see that the player avoids a cold whenever possible, takes care of himself when he has a cold, and takes proper care of his feet and legs. Colds and injuries to the feet and legs are major causes of lost practice time. A good relationship with the trainer is important. Each new player should be introduced to him.

The player is in school to learn. A conference with the coach will help him see basketball and education in their proper perspective. The coach should encourage him to value knowledge and apply himself to his studies.

Often a player has outside problems, perhaps involving his family or a girl friend. The outward signs are lack of attention, tiredness at practice, no hustle, and preoccupation. A coach should try to draw the troubled boy out. If he feels the boy's problem is serious, he may seek information from others.

An individual preseason conference should emphasize the coach's philosophy of basketball. It should cover the player's ability, his goals, his ambitions, his weaknesses, his relationship with teammates, his leadership ability, his reliability, his life objectives, and so forth. Topics for discussion during the season include the player's approach to the game, his basketball progress to date, and the current season. In post-season conferences with underclassmen, the coach should discuss weaknesses they should be working on in the off-season, contributions and shortcomings of the season just passed, and next year's objectives. Post-season conferences with high school or college seniors can include advice on the selection of a college or discussion of post-college plans. These conferences will go a long way towards building a rapport with the players, establishing the coach as a leader and as a friendly advisor.

The selection of a college is one of the most important topics at the high school level. The coach should evaluate the boy's ability to play basketball, giving his opinion of how good the boy is capable of becoming and what his correct level of competition will be. If the boy's ability is not great, he should be told that he will have to work harder in order to make a college team. Throughout the conference, the coach should emphasize that basketball is but a means to an end. If a boy is a great player, but a weak student, his choice of colleges will be limited. If he is a great player and a good student, many colleges will be open to him, and the level of basketball competition at each school could be a factor in his choice.

The coach should realize that each player is an individual. His personality, his mental ability, and his basketball ability should be evaluated as separate entities that blend to create the individual. In many cases, background studies help the player evaluation. Information is available from school records, an inventory card by the coach, an autobiography by the college public relations department, and talks with parents and friends. The more the coach understands the player, the easier it is to coach him.

The coach should be friendly with his players, but he must be certain that they maintain the proper respect towards the entire coaching staff. He should be firm without being dictatorial; friendly without being a pal. He should be fair, not ruthless or unyielding in his attitudes. As a teacher, he must impart his knowledge to the players and try to get the most out of them. He must be concerned with their welfare and their moral character.

In theory, it is necessary to treat everyone the same when dealing with a small, close-knit group. However, in practice, that is not possible. A coach must understand his players completely. Some boys need additional stimulus to prepare for competition; others need to be toned down so that they won't get too tight and be unable to relax.

Even at the lower levels, whether he is coaching on a formal or informal basis, the coach should insist on a basic team discipline both on and off the court. (Off-the-court conduct is a true test of whether or not athletics builds character.) At these levels he should allow all of the youngsters to participate as much as possible, and he should try to keep the players abreast of the current trends in the game. Most important, he should teach them respect and fair play. He should be aware of the low level of competition at which he is teaching the game, because at that level the players are generally unsophisticated and unskilled, and they require a great deal of understanding.

The coach should publish and enforce rules of discipline similar to those listed in our basketball outline (see Appendix A), and he should rigidly adhere to scheduled practice times and meetings.

Other Coaches

The coach's relationship with other coaches should always be on a professional level. Each opposing coach should be treated with dignity. If a coach fails to show proper respect for an opposing coach, evidence of his behavior should be delivered to the proper authorities, not to the press.

Basketball Officials

The coach must be aware of his responsibilities to the basketball officials. These men must have complete knowledge of the rules, be in good physical and mental condition, be able to react quickly, and have good judgment. The coach must support them and teach the players to give them the respect they deserve. The exchange of ideas between coaches and officials at rules and interpretation meetings is an important part of the coach-official relationship.

The coach should also have officials work preseason practice and explain new rules and changes to the squad and the coaching staff. Besides improving the squad's knowledge of the game, this official participation will make the players appreciate the officials' position during the game. At games, officials should have a private dressing room, and the coach should not meet with them before the game unless the opposing coach is present.

It is unethical to criticize an official publicly. The coach must never make an uncomplimentary remark or suggestion to excite the players and fans. If anything has to be said, it should be said to the appointing authority by mail.

The Coaching Profession

The coach also has a responsibility to his profession. He should talk with other coaches, observe their techniques, exchange ideas with them, attend clinics, and read current literature in the field. He should experiment with old and new ideas to test their validity and their reliability.

News Media

A coach's relationship with the press, radio, and TV media should be honest at all times. He should never give misleading information. His rule should be either have no comment or give the facts to the press.

THE COACH'S BASIC APPROACH TO THE GAME

At most levels the coach should select the proper offense for the material at hand. If necessary, he can adjust and change annually, but that is not recommended. He must do everything possible to extract the most out of what he has. That is the criterion of a good coach. It is not possible to succeed if a coach is using a shuffle or free-lance offense when a two-three offense is called for. At the upper levels of competition it is possible to fit the material to the coach's offensive philosophy. However, adaptability is essential.

In many cases, the opposition can make a coach change his basic defense to compensate for mismatches in size and speed. Here again it is imperative that the coach adapt his defense to the type of material he has on hand. It is impossible at most levels to stay with the same basic philosophy offensively and defensively season after season.

CHOOSING THE TEAM

Squads vary in size from twelve to fifteen players. They should never be larger than fifteen; nor should they be smaller than twelve, unless there is a B team or Junior Varsity team from which the coach can borrow for daily practice. A twelve-man squad is best. This number can be broken down into two squads for intersquad practice scrimmages, and it allows inclusion of one or two specialists who can be used under certain conditions.

Nothing is more difficult for a coach than determining which of the candidates for the basketball team should be accepted. Cutting the number of candidates to a workable group and selecting a team from this group involves sound judgment, good knowledge of the game, and insight into each candidate.

Factors Involved

Many factors go into the selecting of a squad. At the high school level many candidates will have little experience. The basic physical factors that should be sought are coordination, speed and quickness (both vertical and lateral speed and quickness), balance, aggressiveness, reflexes, good hands, and height. (By height, we mean playing height, not the actual height. A boy six foot two inches may play at the height of six foot four, or a boy who is six foot six may play at six foot three, depending on his jumping ability, his timing, his reflexes, his quickness, and his coordination.) Other desirable characteristics are the ability to learn, desire, good mental attributes, enthusiasm, sound emotional background, and competitive instinct. A coach should not overlook a tall awkward boy if he has good hands, aggressiveness, and jumping ability.

Speed can be evaluated by having the boys run races. Coordination is determined by observing the smoothness of their movements. Desire and aggressiveness, or hustle, are very easy to see when the boys are working one-on-one or two-on-two, or when they are working in a team situation. One of the most important factors is balance. Many boys who are quick and have good speed do not have good body balance or control. They are apt to get themselves into trouble with the ball, bump into other players, change direction slowly, and make aggressive fouls.

At the high school level, a squad can be selected in many ways, depending upon the number of candidates. The pre-practice physical education classes can be used as a basis of selection, and the coach can seek the help of a physical education instructor if he is not one himself. Class tournaments, intramurals, and game practice sessions can be of value. While the final selection of a team belongs with the varsity coach alone, he should not leave all of the evaluative factors to his own judgment. Each candidate should be discussed with other qualified observers who are watching the workout. The coach should also make statistical and analytical charts comparing the attributes of each boy.

In high school, the first game is usually three weeks after the first practice session. This time factor sometimes shortens the evaluative process.

There are two ways to announce cuts. The first method is to post a list on a bulletin board. The second method is to talk to each boy being cut, pointing out his weaknesses and his strong points and telling him that if he can overcome the weaknesses and improve the strong points, he will have a chance to be selected the following year.

Several boys with outstanding ability will stand out immediately. After that, the selection becomes tougher. If a group of eighty tries out for a team, the coach can cut the number substantially by observing the boys in fundamental passing drills and dribbling drills. He should evaluate them on a merit scale, perhaps using 3 for excellent, 2 for above average, 1 for average, and 0 for poor or below average. The coach will know what boys are available from the previous year, so he can know how many of the new group he will have to work with. A word of caution at this time: It is best to announce to the squad that you are not infallible. If any rejected candidate feels that he is better than a player who has been retained, he should be encouraged to discuss his feelings with the coach in private.

The coach should be on the lookout for boys with ability in one area as well as those with all-round good abilities. For example, a boy with exceptional speed and very quick hands might be valuable to the team as an outstanding defensive player even though he is not a good shooter or a good ball handler.

When boys are very close in ability, moral, emotional, and academic factors must be used to help choose the players. The coach should always be on the alert for players who may cause friction. All players on a team must be compatible so that they can work together for their common objective. Boys who are difficult to get along with or who show emotional, mental, or social instability will make poor squad members.

Varsity Captain

Two individuals, the varsity captain and the senior manager, are extremely important to the coach's relations with the squad.

There are two methods for selecting the senior, or varsity, captain. The first method is by election. All squad members or those members who have varsity letters meet after the close of the season, under the supervision of the varsity manager or the coach, and elect a captain for next year by means of a ballot. By the second method, the coach appoints a captain for each game during the season. At the close of the season the squad has a meeting and elects a player the team captain for the past season. We prefer the first method.

Before the election of a captain, the coach discusses with the players the qualities required in a captain. He must be an extremely stable person mentally, morally, and emotionally. He should get along well with all the other players on the team and must have their confidence at all times. He should be a calm and confident leader on and off the court. He should be alert, with great competitive zeal that is a positive influence on his teammates. He does not necessarily have to be the best basketball player on the team, but he has to be a leader in basketball, in the classroom, and on the campus. The captain is a liaison between the coach and the squad, and if he takes his responsibilities seriously, his contribution can be immeasurable.

Senior Manager

The senior manager should also be a valuable asset. A good manager can take over some of the coach's duties, especially at the high school level. The selection of a manager should be the coach's prerogative, but before making his decision he should consult with his staff, the outgoing senior manager, an equipment man, and a trainer (if one is available).

The senior manager helps plan trips and makes many other essential arrangements. Many of his duties are indispensable. On the college level, for example, he handles the financial matters. At a high school level, the senior manager makes sure that his other managers can keep score or run the clocks.

Three of four managers should be at each practice session. They see to it that the gym lights are turned on, that the basketballs and practice shirts are available, and that any mechanical aids that may be used on the court, in the rims, or around the court are in working condition. On game night, six to eight managers are necessary. They should be able to record statistics efficiently, and one manager should take game notes from the coach, sitting next to him on the bench.

Most managers should start at a freshman or sophomore level in high school. We have had success with freshman or sophomore squad members who played junior varsity college basketball but did not make the varsity squad. They became extremely efficient team managers, for they knew the organization and wished to be part of the team. Perhaps that is one of the most important characteristics to look for when selecting a manager: he must wish to be part of the group. Whether he is a basketball player or not is immaterial; compatibility and the amount of work he does are important.

The ideal competitive situation would be to have four managers at a freshman level, cut the number to three in the sophomore year (basing the choice on the work the boys have done during the preceding year), cut to two in the junior year, and select one varsity manager for senior year.

Team Organization and Practice Sessions

2

Team organization is the cornerstone to success in coaching. In Chapter 1 we described the need for a personal coaching philosophy. In that context, organization is the sum total of the coach's efforts to put his philosophy into action in building and maintaining a winning basketball program. Philosophy is theory; organization is the means by which a coach translates theory into practice.

Every team is, to a certain extent, a mirror image of its coach. If a coach's approach to the game is basically conservative, his players are likely to play conservatively. If he prefers a wide open, freewheeling style of offensive attack, his players will normally adjust their thinking to accommodate that style of play even if they were formerly conservative offensively. And if a team's practice sessions are carefully organized to accomplish certain stated objectives on a daily basis within the larger framework of the basketball year, the team's play will reflect the coach's philosophy to a greater extent than when practices are unplanned and apparently scheduled with no specific goals in mind.

The coach should organize each phase of the basketball year to obtain optimum results. This period is divided into three phases.

1. Pre-practice—the period extending from the start of the school year to the date of the first permissible formal practice.
2. Preseason practice—the period from the first permissible formal practice day to the day of the first regularly scheduled game.

3. In-season practice—the period from the first regularly scheduled game to the last game (regularly scheduled or tournament). Planning must include consideration of unavoidable practice breaks for Christmas holidays and midyear exams.

Methodic planning for each area is required for a well-coordinated basketball program. Complete preparation for preseason and in-season practice sessions is imperative.

PRE–PRACTICE ORGANIZATION

In pre-practice, (September–October), the coaching staff should meet formally every day, or at least several times a week. On the college level, the meetings should start at least at the beginning of the official school year. On the high school level, they should start at least six weeks before the official start of practice. All of the planning for the preseason should be done at these meetings. Other coaches (naturally not those of opponents) who are interested in discussion and an exchange of ideas can sit in on the meetings, which should be intense brainstorming sessions, with magnetic board, projector, screen, movies, diagram material, etc., on hand.

The time of the first allowable preseason practice in relation to the time of the first game is the most important single consideration. On the junior high school and high school levels, the State Principals' Association usually determines when practice can start. Some states do not allow basketball practice to start until the close of the football season. Other states allow practice to begin in the middle of November, still others allow it on the first of November, and some have no restrictions.

The limit on the number of games played is also determined by the State Principals' Association. Twenty games (exclusive of tournaments) is the limit at a high school level in most states, and no more than two games a week may be scheduled. Three to five weeks of practice at most are usually available to the high school coach before his first game.

For colleges, the National Collegiate Athletic Association decides on the number of games—27 (exclusive of post-season tournaments), including outside scrimmages and regularly scheduled games. Practice cannot begin until October 15.

On a school-year calendar, the coach should mark the first day of practice, the first game, and the home games to be played during the season. He should mark the away games in a different color. (Travel plans and practice away from home must be taken into consideration in an overall master plan.) Next, in a third color, he should write in the schedule for scouting opponents and the name of the scout (either a member of the coaching staff or an expert who knows the team). The days when practice will not be held should be x'd out.

Practice goals must be decided during the formal coaches' meetings, and a checklist should be made. The coach should also make a master preseason schedule, listing what he hopes to accomplish on offense and defense before the first game, then work within this program of operation to make up weekly and daily schedules and to determine the fundamental drills he wishes to incorporate. He should develop and use daily drills. The master plan should include the amount of time planned for each activity, and after practice starts the coach should keep a written record of time actually spent for each in the daily sessions and in the weekly sessions.

When the outline of the preseason practice schedule is complete, the coaching staff should determine the quickest method of selecting the team. The most important single task for a coach is to screen the candidates until he has a group that is a workable size and then make a team of the individuals in the group. The coaches know which squad members are returning. They also know what the abilities of other players who are trying out have been. But they should remember that youngsters with initiative who were rejected the previous year may have practiced during the off-season and become more coordinated and physically mature so that they may become valuable squad members. This is especially true of some tall high school boys who were not squad members previously because of lack of coordination.

Next, the coach must select the proper offensive and defensive alignments for the personnel available and condition the players. Pre-practice conditioning must be supervised by the captain or captains and the team manager, as the coach is not allowed to participate before an established date.

The coaches should review the previous season analytically, discussing the high and the low points during the season and determining why they were high points or low points. If movies of the previous year's games are available they should be reviewed. Any areas of uncertainty by the players or of good teamwork should be marked on the film. Later, these areas can be shown to the players as points for improvement or duplication. Previous post-game reports should be analyzed, and current comments should be added by the coach.

The coaches should decide whether practice sessions will be open to visitors or limited to players, managers, and coach. Open practice sessions make for goodwill and added school interest in the team. Coaches should plan an occasional open practice session, perhaps during routine drills or fundamentals sessions or during full scrimmages, when the likelihood of criticism of players is minimal. Open practice sessions when the team is being selected indicates a democratic attitude by the coach.

As a general practice, however, closed sessions are best for players and coach. Many youngsters feel that a coach who is critical in front of their friends is downgrading them. Also, some coaches, in deference to players' feelings, don't criticize objectively in open practice sessions. This attitude, while understandable, is bad for correct team functioning. Closed sessions should be indicated by notices posted on doors to the gym, and the sessions should be policed by managers.

When school starts in the fall, the captain and the manager should be in charge of all returning players and new players who wish to work out until the formal practice begins. The captain and the manager should insist that players follow the conditioning regulations prescribed by the coach. Group running, calisthenics, and weight lifting are good not only for the physical condition of the squad but also for squad spirit and cohesiveness. Playing two-on-two or three-on-three in free gymnasium time will also be helpful if the players do so within the framework of the drills that the coach has outlined in previous years. However, players must not form cliques in these informal sessions. All players must enjoy them so that the whole team will benefit.

PRESEASON PRACTICE

Preseason is the most important time of the year for coaches; therefore, efficient master-planning and good use of the time are imperative. Efficient preseason planning can result in a winning team. The coach should arrange the schedule so that each player may participate daily in all functions. He should use effective teaching methods in practice, and he must allocate enough time for salient requirements. He must also analyze all practice sessions.

The time allotted to practice sessions must be determined by the amount of time a coach has from the first practice session to the first scheduled game. Even experienced coaches should make a written weekly time chart and a daily schedule and distribute copies to all coaches and managers; otherwise they will always leave something uncovered. The daily plan should be broken down into a practice outline, and it should be checked against the master plan.

Many coaches tend to practice too long early in the season. A practice session should be only as long as players can work at their optimum physical ability. It should rarely be more than two hours long. First, players cannot absorb information after working for two hours; second, players will put less effort into the practice in order to conserve energy for the finish; and third, the players have time limitations, since they have other obligations.

When an item has been covered during a preseason practice session, it should be checked off on the list of objectives.

Organizing Practice

There are many training problems in basketball, and all areas must be covered. Therefore, it is important to record the time spent on each activity: conditioning, lectures, training rules, rules discussion, chalk talks, movies, staff meetings, regular drills, and pregame drills.

Practice for the entire season should be generally outlined before the squad reports so that coaches and players can schedule their time. The coach and his staff should make up the weekly preseason practice schedules in advance. Weekly practice schedules during the season are determined by travel schedules, scouting reports, and the squad's physical condition.

Making out a practice schedule before and during the season is tedious. Usually a practice schedule should be made no more than one week in advance—and sometimes a schedule must be revised during the week, occasionally on the day of practice. A sound practice schedule makes best possible use of the practice time.

Daily practice plans should be charted and posted so that players can report to specified areas for specific drills without delay.

Appendix B is a sample of our weekly preseason practice schedule with objectives. Samples of daily practice schedules evolved from the weekly objectives are in Appendix C. At the college level, preseason weekly practices cover six weeks. Each week must be outlined objectively, and each of the six weeks' objectives must be listed. Daily schedules list the number of minutes allowed to each drill and to each area and the type of work expected each day. The weekly objectives are kept on a master schedule plan so that the coaches can tell at a glance what has been accomplished and what has yet to be done. These are all kept within the framework of an overall philosophy.

Player Selection

On the opening day of practice, the coach should give a get-acquainted talk to the entire group, both former squad members and new candidates, outlining what will be expected of them during the entire season. Formulating plans at this time will take care of any differences of opinion among squad members. A coach should attempt to keep players' morale high. Everyone must feel that it is possible for him to contribute something during the season.

The boys must have a desire to play the game. An aggressive team is always a dangerous team. The boys should be willing to pay the price for the opportunity to play. They should report in good physical condition and practice diligently so that they improve every day. The team's success is based on unity and self-lessness. Loyalty to the school, the coaches, and the teammates is expected at all times.

Practice should be businesslike. The basketball court is a workshop, not a social hall. All players are expected to work towards maximum possible improvement. They either improve daily or they regress; therefore, practice must be designed to bring out the best in every player.

In many high schools, it is important to select the varsity squad in as short a time as is reasonable. To save time, returning varsity players may help screen new candidates, and the coach can screen potential players during physical education periods. The first practice session is usually devoted to a discussion of the rules of the game and the regulations that the team must follow. Then, as quickly as possible, the coach should reduce his squad to about twenty-five players. It is almost impossible to do any effective group work with a larger squad.

When sizing up candidates in early preseason practice, the coach should remember that players want to show to their best advantage in order to make the team or to make the starting five. If blisters or ankle turns occur, players normally are reluctant to tell the coach for fear he may feel they are malingering or their chances for making the team may be hurt. The coach must allay his players' apprehension in this regard.

The coach should never do on the court what can be done off the court. He should never work with only one or two players during the team practice time. Individualized instruction should be given before or after daily practice.

Too much explanation is bad. Basketball players learn mainly by doing and understanding why they are doing, not by simply listening.

Teaching Techniques

The coach should not over-teach in the early preseason practice sessions or make them so strenuous that players lose their ability to retain what is being taught. Players can and should work when physically tired, but they can't learn when they are tired, so coaches should not introduce new material at that time.

The most significant point to stress at all times is the importance of possession of the ball. The player should be told never to pass to a voice. He should also be warned that bad shots are detrimental to the team, and that short passes are safer from interception than long passes. After an incorrect or extraneous maneuver, the coach should always ask the players, "why?" replacing them in scrimmage momentarily, if necessary, for brief, individual conferences. Coaches should do this frequently during practice scrimmages, because the players should know the reason for everything they do on the court. A coach should criticize softly and encourage loudly, informing the team often that practice makes playing habits permanent. Players who are practicing bad habits should be corrected immediately. Even in a drill on passing, the coach should correct a player who makes a poor or improper cut, briefly explaining the proper technique. The coach should strive constantly for mental anticipation, instinctive reaction, and intelligent aggressiveness on the part of all players. These intangibles make a good player a great one.

After determining the best offensive and defensive patterns for the material at hand, the coach should be positive in their installation, helping players to develop confidence in them. First, a strategy should be explained and diagramed. Second, the skills involved should be demonstrated, by the coach or a skilled player or shown on a film or videotape. Third, the players should walk through the various parts of the offense or defense, run through it at half speed, then do it full speed, with no opponents. Fourth, the strategy should be implemented full speed with defenders. At this stage, the defenders usually are junior varsity or freshmen who are the weakest players. This enables the team to practice their strategy successfully, thus developing a positive attitude about their ability. The coach thereby negates any doubts the players may have. He should use as a motto, "Better learn a little a lot, than a lot a little."

Coaches should take advantage of individual abilities, without letting individual abilities take over to the disadvantage of the team. They should also allow for free-lance patterns that won't hurt the team. The style of play that a coach incorporates offensively should blend with the material at hand and be based on good offensive floor balance and movement, proper execution of play patterns, and good timing.

The Coach's Daily Duties

For all daily practice sessions, the coach should arrive on the court dressed for practice at least a half hour before the beginning of practice. He should review the day's schedule to familiarize himself with the routine of the practice. The coach should be sure that the necessary materials are available. These include basketballs, scrimmage shirts, training aids, extra shoelaces, tape, and towels to be used for obstacles in drill. (We prefer to use towels as obstacles rather than chairs or other players. Chairs are bulky, and stationary players are not taking part in the drills. Managers can carry an armful of towels and place them in the proper spot easily and quickly.)

Before practice begins, the coach can give individual attention to players, discussing shortcomings observed in the previous practice session, praising good playing, or working with one or two players. In early preseason, before cutting the squad down to workable size, a coach should give time to new candidates for on-the-spot evaluation, making players who are in the questionable category feel that he has given them sufficient time. This attitude and attention by the coach makes the selection process much less painful for both the coach and the candidates who are dropped.

The coach should be sure that the players begin before-practice workouts as soon as they arrive.

He should make certain that all players are on time and that the practice starts at the prescribed time. The organized practice time, in which the timing by the manager is all-important, should begin with a whistle. The manager or assistant manager should check the time allotted for each part of the practice session and inform the coach when the time is up for each segment.

Drilling

Drilling is the secret of good performance at critical times in a ball game. It is essential for game pressure. Early preseason practice should stress conditioning and fundamentals, for the team must be in excellent condition before the first game. A player, preferably a captain, should lead the conditioning drills, which should be executed at top speed and at intervals to maintain full interest. Complete coordination of eye, mind, and muscles should be taught, first slowly, then increasing in tempo to full speed. Players must be warmed up before strenuous work begins.

The importance of carefully conceived and skillfully organized and executed drills cannot be overemphasized. The players should devote about 20 percent of the time to shooting and foul shooting, and drills should incorporate the ingredients of the team's planned defenses and offenses. However, do not drill initiative and motivation out of a good basketball player. The best players can drill themselves to perfection.

Drills for fundamentals, simulating game conditions whenever possible, should be organized early in the preseason, when they are most important. An experienced coach will know what drills will be best for his team, both for teaching his offense and defense and for conditioning his players; a new coach must decide what drills to use and how long to spend on them. Drills should be simple and competitive, and they should cover as many techniques as possible. They should also be selective. Don't use too many drills or too complicated a drill, and don't use a drill just because somebody else has used it.

Drills are good only when they are completely assimilated by the squad. The coach must give the reason for each operation and explain the correct technique. First, an explanation gives the players confidence; second, it shows them that there is a reason for everything. The coach should analyze any mistakes that the players are making and compliment those players who are doing the drills well.

Drills allow for concentrated practice in specific areas. Preseason conditioning drills must be utilitarian; therefore, whenever possible, they should include fundamental techniques. Early in the year, many necessary conditioning drills use running without involving the ball or defensive techniques.

Drills serve as a change of pace in the daily practice routine. They are excellent for before practice or pregame warm-up.

They should be simple, of short duration, and interesting. A variety of drills keeps players interested in seeking perfection in fundamentals, preventing boredom and complacency. Too little time on drills, leaving the desire for more, is much more effective than too much time in drills. When they become drudgery and there is a lack of enthusiasm and desire, incorrect habits and improper techniques will be formed. Drills should be spirited, evoking constant chatter and desire for perfection.

Drills should be readily applicable to the team's offensive and defensive pattern. In fact, coaches should devise their own drills. Too many of today's drills have been adapted from ones that were handed down from coaches of generations ago. The adaptable, inventive coach is generally the successful coach.

There are three steps to learning. First, the student must be interested and ready to learn. A competent coach who has the full attention of a receptive student can teach him the proper fundamentals of the game, stressing the acquisition of accuracy before speed. The second step is practice. Once the player understands the techniques involved, he practices willingly for hours on end. The final step is the examination—in the case of basketball, the actual playing of the game itself.

To properly inculcate basic team concepts early in the preseason, the coach should use skeleton teams offensively and defensively. The concepts should be broken down and practiced in drills involving two-on-two and three-on-three groupings. Much of the offense and defense to be used in the season should be broken down into drills. Man-to-man attack and defense, zone attack and defense, pressure attack and defense, and combination attack and defense must be skeletonized if they are to be used. Coaches should also discuss how they want special situations to be handled. Drills should be repetitive so that proper reaction becomes instinctive. Players should not have to think about what they are going to do.

Every drill must demand perfect or near perfect performance from every player. Coaches must be constantly observant and highly critical, making corrections immediately. They must overcome a tendency to ignore or overlook slight irregularities or imperfections in a player's form or habits. Coaches should remember that practicing something incorrectly is just as habit forming as practicing something correctly. Perhaps the most important motto for drills is practice makes permanent.

Competitive drills hold players' interest, and the use of rewards for winners and penalties for the losers creates incentive and enthusiasm. Winners could be given a pair of sweat socks, and losers could be made to run laps or do extra wind sprints.

Most drills should be performed under as much pressure as possible. The more game conditions are simulated in practice, the more beneficial the drills are.

All drills should have short, definitive names so that players know exactly what to do as soon as the name is called. Through drills, teams develop unity. Players become accustomed to the movements, attitudes, habits, and idiosyncrasies of teammates.

New drills can be explained during a brief practice break one day then incorporated into the practice for the next day. Drills should be scheduled so that a physically strenuous drill is followed by one that is easier. Several small groups in which all players work strenuously are more beneficial than one large group in which several players are not working. The coach should plan to use all his players in drill activities every day in early season.

At the end of a hard practice, the coaches should incorporate a drill that the players enjoy. This implementation will leave the players in a good frame of mind, anticipating the following day's practice.

The selected drills found in this book are some that we have used to advantage. Hundreds of other excellent drills are available to the discerning coach.

Selecting and Evaluating Players

Early preseason scrimmaging should be done in order to help select the squad. At this time, coaches should plan scrimmage teams for balance, with good players scattered evenly among the teams used. Daily evaluations of each scrimmage should be made. Many coaches today tend to drill too much and scrimmage too little. The right amount of scrimmage for a team depends on the experience and physical and psychological condition of the players.

After the squad has been selected in the early season, scrimmage sessions should involve five-man teams of varying ability. In selecting squads for early preseason scrimmage practice, coaches should allow designated players of equal ability to pick the other members of their teams. A different selection order should be used each round until each designated player has made four choices. A manager should record the selections and give the list to the coaches. The selectors should be varied as often as possible. Allowing the players to select their teams enables the coach to see how the players rate each other. He also gains insight into personality clashes or cliques within the squad.

If there are three teams, they should scrimmage for approximately five to eight minutes, with the winning team staying on. With four teams, play a round robin tournament, winners playing winners, losers playing losers. This procedure should be followed until each player has run approximately twenty minutes of full-court scrimmage. These scrimmage practice sessions should be interrupted for criticism and analysis when necessary, using the double whistle procedure outlined in our team offense drill section at the end of Chapter 5.

We feel that teammate evaluation sheets should be used. Filling these out takes approximately five minutes during a practice session. They should be issued to the squad without warning. Be certain that a manager has an adequate supply of sharpened pencils on hand.

Following is an outline of the factors to be evaluated:

I. Positive
   A. Three players who always take good shots
   B. Three best shooters
   C. Three best rebounders
   D. Three best drivers
   E. Three best passers
   F. Three best defensive players
   G. Three best team players offensively
   H. Three best team players defensively
   I. Three best hustlers
   J. Three quickest players
   K. Three players with best straightaway speed
   L. Four players you most like to play with
       (Naturally, the evaluator cannot include himself in any
       of these categories.)

II. Negative
   A. Three players who habitually take bad shots
   B. Three poorest shooters
   C. Three poorest rebounders
   D. Three poorest drivers
   E. Three poorest passers
   F. Three poorest defenders
   G. Three poorest team players offensively
   H. Three poorest team players defensively
   I. Three poorest hustlers
   J. Three players who are least quick
   K. Three players with least speed
   L. Four players you least like to play with

The coaches should collect the unsigned evaluation sheets, transfer the information to a master sheet, and destroy the individual sheets. It is best to destroy them with the manager present, so that he can assure the squad that the sheets are not kept. The coach and assistant coaches should also fill out evaluation sheets, keeping the results confidential. The coaches should then assess the player-evaluation results against their own evaluations. Many times it will be obvious to the coaches that there are possible discrepancies or inadequacies in their own thinking. Also, personality clashes or conflicts may be festering, so evaluations by the involved players should not be taken seriously in the master evaluation. However, for harmonious team relationship the coach should try to resolve any conflicts. A good coach should be able to meet any contingency, and flexibility is an asset. Therefore, coaches should be prepared to learn from these eval-

uations. The use of teammate evaluation sheets and player selection of teams for early season scrimmage contributes a great
deal toward development of team spirit and understanding of the
squad.

A self-evaluation sheet is also important to players. This
sheet should cover the intangibles as well as the qualities that
coaches can observe. The qualities that should be included are
basketball instinct, attention, ability to follow the coach's instructions, alertness, aggressiveness, coordination, relative speed,
team defensive abilities, individual defensive abilities, team offensive abilities, and individual offensive ability.

Ratings of 4 for excellent, 3 for good, 2 for fair and 1 for poor
should be given. Many times a coach will find that players are
downgrading themselves. Other players may have an exaggerated opinion of themselves. Through individual talks, the coach
may be able to help the players evaluate themselves realistically.
Self-evaluation sheets should be destroyed after they have served
their purpose.

Scrimmaging in Early Preseason

Scrimmaging is important all during the preseason. While we do
not scrimmage much during the first week, we allow candidates
of dubious ability to scrimmage full court, as often as feasible,
with some of the better players so that they will feel they were
given every opportunity to become members of the squad. Coaches
should remember that scrimmaging is ten teaching situations at
once; by scrimmaging, players learn to react under game conditions.

All scrimmages must be properly officiated. During early
preseason scrimmages clocks must be available, as well as all the
statistical sheets that are used in scheduled games. The assistant
coaches should record positive and negative factors during a
scrimmage so that constructive changes can be made in the practices that follow. The head coach should be on the court, using
the double-whistle technique to stop practice when something is
fundamentally wrong. All aspects of each scrimmage should be
charted and recorded so that individual player analysis is complete. All preseason scrimmage statistics should be recorded on
a master copy for dissemination and use with the squad. Shooting
percentages, foul shooting percentages, and all other statistical
information should be available to the squad as a result of these
scrimmages.

If there are enough players for four balanced five-man
teams, run a tournament type of competitive scrimmage allowing
two teams to play approximately eight minutes, then the next

two to play for eight minutes. The winners then play for first and second place, and the losers play for third and fourth place. This brings an element of competition into the practice, motivating the players to play well in the early preseason to reach a visible goal. Scrimmaging in early preseason enables the players to work under the pressure they will be under in actual games. This type of scrimmaging should not take place until the team has learned the necessary offensive and defensive fundamentals.

These early scrimmages should be handled by officials. An experienced basketball official should be present at the first early scrimmage to explain the rule changes and the rule emphasis for the forthcoming season.

PRESEASON ESSENTIALS

At the close of each practice session, there should be a post-practice coaches' meeting, twenty minutes to one half hour long. At this meeting the coaches should analyze the practice session and decide if it accomplished what they planned. The coaches should also analyze each player's basketball progress, attentiveness, and attitude. Each player should be rated on a *4*-excellent, *3*-good, *2*-fair, *1*-poor scale. A record of this analysis should be kept. At the end of the second week, the coaches can discuss any apparent weaknesses with the players in a before-practice session. It is imperative that the coaches cover the following areas thoroughly so that the players are completely prepared by the first game:

Offense

Fast-break; basic patterns against man-to-man and zone defenses, pressing defenses, and combination defenses

Out-of-bounds plays, both from the side and under the basket, first for possession of the ball and second for a basket

A free-throw alignment for a possible fast break

Semi-freeze and stall situations

A one-shot play for late in the game

Rebounding fundamentals for the individual and the team

Last minute and late game situations when behind, with the score tied, and when ahead

Defense

Team defense in a man-to-man situation

The methods of stopping the fast break at the defensive backboard, cutting off the outlet or delaying the break

Zone defense (aggressive, loose or pressing)

Pressure defenses

The defensive rebounding pattern for both individual and team

Last minute situations and late game situations when behind, with the score tied, or when ahead

The pregame warm-up drills to be used for a twenty-minute period should be properly practiced so that players know what to do when they come on the court before a game. Naturally the team must be well-conditioned for the first game. The coach must explain all details, even those that seem minor—for instance, how a substitute should enter a game (he should report to the scorer's table and wait there until an official beckons him onto the court) or signals that can be used from the bench to change the team's offense or defense. These areas must be completely covered in preseason practice and then checked off the preseason master plan. Even after an item has been checked it should be reviewed constantly.

Coaches often feel that players will get enough shooting before daily practice, but this is not necessarily true; therefore, shooting drills should take up approximately 20 percent of the total preseason practice time. The coach should put the number of minutes actually spent in each area of practice on his master sheet weekly, and the time should be totaled each preseason week so that none of the fundamentals are left uncovered. The coach must control the offense and defense used by the scrimmaging teams in preseason practice sessions. For example, in a fifteen-minute scrimmage, Team A may use the stack offense for the first eight minutes and a two-one-two offense for seven minutes. Team B may use man-to-man loose defense for the first five minutes, a two-three zone for the next five minutes, and a press defense for the last five minutes. Similar assignments are made for A on defense and B on offense.

A manager should keep an offense pattern chart for such scrimmages, noting the number of possessions, the number of shots, and the baskets scored for each team from the offense used. For example:

Team A
1. Stack offense   33 possessions   31 shots   14 baskets
2. 2-1-2 offense   24 possessions   17 shots   6 baskets
3. Fast-break   17 possessions   16 shots   10 baskets

Using statistics like these will indicate the effectiveness of the offenses and defenses used when assessed against the offensive-defensive time allotments.

IN–SEASON PRACTICE SESSIONS

Once the regular season has started, practice time should be shortened. As most teams play two games a week, two or three days prior to a game the on-court practice session should be approximately an hour and three quarters long. Game plans should be part of the practice session on the days preceding most games.

On pre-game days, sessions should be limited to an hour and a half or less. Before practice the coach might review a scouting report with the squad. If games fall on consecutive days, usually the complete scouting report for the second game should not be given until after the game with the first scouted opponent has been completed. A partial report may be presented on the second opponent, however, if a strategy requires on-court practice for implementation against the second opponent. Looking ahead, beyond any game, is bad. After reviewing a scouting report in a session before the practice, the coach should go over it on the floor, with the junior varsity, or the lower men in the squad simulating the opponents. The coach should also review post-game analyses with the assembled squad for glaring errors and mistakes. At this time, he should praise the positive aspects of the game just completed, if possible injecting some humor into the meeting.

Coaches should include remedial and developmental fundamental skill drills in practice sessions to correct obvious weaknesses that have been noted in games. Again, they should use a time schedule and follow it. The amount of time spent in each aspect should be recorded and summarized on a master sheet.

The scrimmage time for reserves should be all important on the day after a game has been played. If possible, all reserves who have had little playing time should be given a full thirty- to thirty-five-minute scrimmage session, because they must be kept in the best possible condition. If they are not in condition, the overall team ability will suffer.

The coach should keep a record of each practice session, which can be consulted and analyzed during and after the season.

part two

THE OFFENSE

Individual-Player Offense

3

The skills involved in individual-player offense are harder to perform than they look. While many players nowadays routinely perform shooting, ball handling, passing, and footwork skills that once were the domain of a select few individuals in the game, these skills—shooting a jump shot, spin-dribbling without carrying the ball, and threading passes accurately through and around the defense, to name three examples—are not easily obtained. They are perfected through countless hours of practice, and players who aspire to the highest levels of individual offensive achievement will put in the hours necessary to develop proper shooting form, passing skills, and footwork and dribbling techniques. The only known shortcut to success in individual-player offense is to be a superbly coordinated seven-footer with excellent vertical jumping ability. Even then, however, the player must have a degree of mobility to free himself from defensive pressure long enough to get the ball, he must be able to hold onto the ball when faced with double-teaming or overplaying, he must be able to dribble into position to shoot, and he must possess at least enough shooting touch to make an acceptable percentage of his shots.

All of which brings us back to our original contention that becoming an effective individual offensive player is more difficult than it looks. If it were otherwise, everyone who played the game would be a good shooter and ball handler. Still, several factors work in favor of the player who wants to become a high scorer or skillful ball handler. First, while offensive skills are normally acquired over a longer period of time than defensive skills, they require less physical exertion, or hustle, to succeed. Offensive skills such as shooting and dribbling involve finely tuned neuromuscular coordinations that operate independently of the amount of work expended. No amount of hustle is going to make an errant shot fall through the hoop, or an errant pass reach its target.

Second, a person doesn't need a partner (or an opponent) to learn the basic offensive skills of basketball. All he needs in order to learn how to shoot is a ball and a goal. All he needs to learn how to dribble correctly is a ball and a surface to dribble on. All he needs to learn how to execute the basic passes in basketball is a ball and a wall. Basic footwork patterns can be practiced anywhere. Eventually, of course, a player will need teammates and opponents to put his newfound skills into perspective, but first he should spend time practicing basic offensive skills alone. (We hardly need stress, on the other hand, that learning individual defensive skills requires at least one other person, since a player cannot block a shot if there is no shooter or steal the ball from a nonexistent dribbler.)

A third factor favoring offensive players is that while the defender has an initial advantage of sorts in being positioned more or less between his man and the ball (or the basket), this advantage tends to diminish greatly when he is guarding a player who does not have the ball: if the defender remains between his man and the ball, he is vulnerable to back-door cuts and lay-ups, and if he protects the basket by playing between his man and the basket, he cannot deny passes to his man. Additionally, the offensive player with or without the ball has the advantage of directly initiating scoring situations, while the defender must usually be content to react to offensive movement. And even in reacting he is liable to place his team in jeopardy by misreading the offensive player's movements and fakes.

Finally, once a player becomes an effective shooter, he is likely to have a lasting advantage over most defenders. With the advent over the past thirty years of shots such as the jump shot and the sky hook, basketball has become a shooter's game. Many coaches feel, and with some justification, that good shooters simply cannot be stopped from scoring. The best that defenders can do in most cases is try to keep the ball away from their men or force the men to alter their shots enough to affect their timing. Still, the defender's role is basically reactive, and many of today's players are so quick offensively that a shooter can get up in the air and release his shot before the defender can stop, set himself, and jump to deflect the shot or disturb the shooter's concentration.

In this chapter we describe the proven techniques for successfully executing the offensive tasks performed by individual members of a basketball team: shooting, passing, dribbling, and footwork. Since we believe that each player should be allowed as much latitude as possible in perfecting his own most effective style, in our descriptions we emphasize the underlying principles that make a given technique work. Although at first any technique seems mechanical, even unnatural, hours of practicing it, together with a thorough understanding of the principles involved, should lead to each player's evolving the variations that best realize his own natural potential.

SHOOTING

Fundamental Principles

In basketball, the objective of offense is accurate shooting—to throw the ball through the basket defended by the opponent. All basketball players recognize this, of course, and most practice their shooting year round. Since most of his practice is not in the presence of a coach, each player should become his own severest critic, which means he must clearly understand the principles affecting the success or failure of every shot.

This does not mean that there is no room for experimentation. In basketball, as in golf, baseball, or boxing, there is considerable latitude for the participant to develop a style of his own. In fact, experimentation, rather than a slavish imitation of a player whose strengths and weaknesses may be entirely different, should be encouraged. However, fundamental principles underly the success of every great player, regardless of stylistic variation, and these principles must be mastered and constantly practiced by every serious shooter.

Therefore, before examining the specific techniques associated with the various kinds of shots an accomplished basketball player is expected to have in his repertory, we present in some detail those fundamental principles that we believe are at work in every scoring shot from every basketball floor. For convenience, these are divided into two categories: (1) Mental, comprising concentration, the ability to relax, and confidence; and (2) Physical, comprising sighting, body balance, force, timing, coordination, and follow-through.

1. Mental Principles. There is probably no arguing the fact that the game of basketball is to a great degree mental; at no time is psychological conditioning more critical than when shooting. Knowing when to shoot and being able to do so effectively under pressure are, ultimately, what distinguishes the

great shooter from the passable. Fortunately, although it is sometimes ignored, a player's ability to improve the mental aspects of
his shooting is often far less limited than his ability to improve
the physical aspects. Regardless of how much he practices or how
well he conditions himself physically, only a modest amount of
improvement is possible in speed, reflexes, strength, or height;
however, the history of basketball, like that of other sports, affords many examples of players who were able to achieve great-
ness despite relatively mediocre physical talent. Usually, such
successes are attributed to determination, which is really too general a term. We believe the determined player will find *concentration*, the *ability to relax*, and *confidence* to be the essential
mental principles that, when mastered, will take him at least
halfway toward becoming a great shooter.

Concentration. Concentration might be called mental discipline. It is the fixing of attention on the job at hand and is an
ability characteristic of every great athlete. Through continuous
practice, good shooters develop their concentration to the extent
that they are oblivious to every distraction—in fact, they frequently become more accurate when under pressure than when
not—whether the distraction is a clutch situation or an opponent's waving, shouting, or even fouling. To develop a high order
of concentration, the shooter should practice under conditions as
near as possible to those of an actual contest and should discipline
himself to be constantly critical of every aspect of his technique.
At first, this will require a conscious effort, but in time it will
become as reflexive as "feeling" the ball.

Ability to relax. The *ability to relax* is closely related to concentration. It is a cliché that great clutch players have ice water
in their veins, but we are convinced that the seemingly super-
human coolness that some players have under pressure is nothing
more than a kind of practiced absentmindedness regarding everything but the immediate task. Watch a great foul shooter as he
reaches the foul line and begins the ritual of adjusting his feet
and bouncing the ball—nearly always a set number of times. As
his eyes open wide in sighting the basket, his trance-like concentration is so intense, there is little wonder that he is undis-
turbed by the crowd or game pressures. In fact, a smart defensive
player, realizing this, will try to break the shooter's concentration, either by engaging him in conversation or by saying something intended to upset him. Again, the best counter is an
absentminded, or singleminded, preoccupation with the task
at hand.

Confidence. Every shot must be made with *confidence*—a gut certainty that the ball will drop through the basket without touching the rim. Confidence, however, is not probability. In truth, the two are at odds. Although a good shooter never takes a shot that he is not confident he will make, he often misses; therefore, the probability of his making any given shot is somewhat less than the 100 percent that his confidence leads him to expect. Clearly, then, when we say, "Don't shoot when in doubt," we have something different in mind than we do when we say, "Don't take a low-percentage shot except in desperate circumstances." In fact, a player may be confident of making a low-percentage shot and not at all confident of making what should be for him a high-percentage shot. There is no problem in the first instance, since the shooter simply makes a rational decision not to shoot unless the situation is dire, in which case confidence is appropriate—even essential. The second instance, however, is a problem, since high-percentage shots should neither be wasted nor passed up.

There are several reasons why a player might lack confidence when confronted with a shooting opportunity having a good statistical probability of success: he may be off balance; he may have had his confidence shaken by a string of misses; he may be overly tense or tired; or he may have a lapse in concentration. None of these are mutually exclusive; in fact, one often contributes to the other.

Probably every player experiences off nights when nothing works, but an equally familiar phenomenon is that of a player's returning to peak form in the second half after a miserable first half. This ability to make a mental recovery is like the ability some players have of recovering in mid-air after an off-balance take-off: each is the mark of a superbly trained athlete.

2. Physical Principles. Shooting a ball and connecting with the target involve six factors. These are (1) *sighting*, or locating a target whose position relative to the attacker is to some extent constantly changing; (2) maintaining a *body balance* that allows a coordinate effort of leg, trunk, and arm muscles; (3) *generating the force;* (4) *timing* the attack so that each event in its development occurs at the right instant in the sequence; (5) *coordinating hand and eye* to effect a desired trajectory; and (6) effecting *follow-through* and recovery. The following is a brief discussion of each of the problems as they pertain to shooting baskets. With few modifications, however, they would apply to any game in which muscles are used to strike, or throw at, a target.

Figure 3-1. Sighting for a shot.

Sighting, or locating the target. The difference between *sighting* and *aiming* is that in aiming, a device (for example, a gun) is visually aligned with a target; thus, visual attention is equally divided between the pointer and the target. In sighting, however, the eyes are used merely to locate, or fix, the target in space, and the computing of an intercept trajectory is left for the brain to do automatically.

To demonstrate the brain's ability to determine a trajectory to a known location, close your eyes and touch either your nose or your ear lobe with a forefinger. To convince yourself of this ability in relation to a visually fixed target, focus your eyes on a nearby object and, without aiming, point your finger at the object. Notice that there is a strong tendency for your attention to shift from the object to your finger and that considerable concentration is required in order to remain focused on the object. (Notice, too, that when concentrating on the object your eyes open quite wide, as in Figure 3-1.) The reason it is so important for the eyes to remain focused on the target is that they, too, are a kind of computer, continuously updating a three-dimensional fix on whatever is being held in focus. Naturally, the smaller the area focused upon, the smaller the fix, and the greater the potential accuracy.

This brings us to the problem facing a basketball player of having as his *real* target not a concrete object, but an open area inside the rim of the basket. Since his eyes cannot focus on empty space, the best he can do is to select a sighting point as nearly on line with the intended trajectory and as near the real target as possible. When making a bank shot, the shooter solves the problem by focusing on a spot related to the painted rectangle above the basket. For all other shots, however, he must decide upon a sighting point somewhere on the rim. Personal preference determines whether the point selected is on the front or the back rim, but he should decide upon one or the other and stick with that sighting point for all similar shots. Also, remembering that the eye computes distance by comparing texture, converging lines, etc., against past experience, the basketball player intent upon improving the accuracy of his shooting should determine, for the longest shot that he would normally attempt, the smallest number of rim cords upon which he can focus his eyes. Then, for every shot, he should fix upon the same number of cords, while conscious that he wishes to drop the ball either just beyond (front rim) or just before (back rim) the point sighted. *The sighting point must be held in constant and clear focus from the moment the shot is begun to the completion of follow-through.*

Body balance. When properly balanced, a shooter can co-ordinate the efforts of each muscle to produce a net force in the direction of the basket, although the degree of balance may vary from the near perfect stance of a two-hand set shot to the last-effort recovery of an aggressive drive-in (see Figure 3–2). The

Figure 3–2. Recovery of balance on drive-in shots.

shooter's ability to control the trajectory of the ball is directly dependent upon his ability to control the acceleration forces generated by his own body; it is doubtful whether a shot ever succeeds unless, at the moment of release, the shooter has enough control to complete a smooth, continuous follow-through. Some players have such exceptional body control they can shoot successfully from positions that would be awkward and unmanageable for another player. Each player must develop his ability to judge whether or not he is in a position to initiate a shot and complete a follow-through that will leave him poised for a possible rebound.

Generating the force. From physics, we know that when several forces act upon an object, the effect is the same as that of a single force equal to the vectorial sum of the force components; that is, the more horses pulling in the same direction, the greater the horsepower. To a weightlifter, this means that it is possible to synchronize the efforts of leg, back, shoulder, and arm muscles to lift a considerably heavier weight above the head (as in a *jerk*) than is possible with the arms alone (as in a *press*). To a basketball player, it means that the force he can impart to the ball ranges from that required for a long *two-hand set shot* to that required for a *tip-in* a few inches from the basket. Thus, beginning at the ball, each of the following adds to the total force imparted: (1) a forward, supple action of the wrist and fingers; (2) a sudden extension of the arm, snapping the shoulder and elbow; and (3) a sharp, knee-locking thrust with the legs while (4) rising to the balls of the feet. Since the force imparted by a muscle under strain is difficult to control, best results are obtained when all muscles can be brought into a smooth, coordinated effort that is well within individual limitations. In a jump shot, obviously, much of the energy generated is converted to altitude, from which the remaining force required to reach the basket must be provided by the arms, wrists, and fingers.

Timing, or rhythm. The *timing* of a shot begins with getting the correct foot down for takeoff (jump shot) and ends with follow-through and recovery. In a set shot, perfect timing results in a smooth, continuous thrust from the floor upward, developing a peak force at the fingertips the instant before, and sustained through, fingertip release. In a jump shot, body momentum decreases rapidly to zero, and the shot must be timed so that fingertip release occurs at the highest point of the jump, when the only forces imparted to the ball are those of the arm, fingers, and wrist. When this is done perfectly, an illusion is created of the shooter's hanging momentarily in space while he gets the shot away. Any nonsynchronized acceleration of the body or its members (for example, jerking the head) will directly affect the trajectory of the ball.

Hand-eye coordination and fingertip control. All forces imparted to the ball by the shooter should pass through the fingertips. This technique allows the fingers to make fine trajectory adjustments at release and provides a soft, natural backspin. (By stating that the optimum trajectory is that which results in the ball's entering the basket at the highest possible angle commensurate with the lowest possible velocity, we shall have said all that can be said dogmatically about trajectory. Many good shooters use a low trajectory, for it allows somewhat better control of velocity and accuracy. However, the ball "sees" a smaller rim opening and is easier to block using a low trajectory. The disadvantages of a high trajectory are the increased velocity and decreased accuracy, despite the larger apparent target. The best rule is to follow the natural inclination to "just drop the ball over the rim." Combined with a natural backspin, a medium [or optimum] trajectory results in the "soft touch" kind of shot that, even if slightly off target, will either drop in or hang on the rim for an easy tip-in.)

In the section on sighting, we alluded to the exceptional directional sensitivity of the forefinger. Combined with a supple, sure wrist action, this dexterity, or *feel*, becomes the ultimate factor in determining shooting accuracy. In adjusting his hands preparatory to shooting, the shooter should space his fingers comfortably to hold the ball firmly in his fingertips and on the heels of both hands—the palms held slightly clear and the three middle fingers aligned perpendicular to the seams. Players should practice their feel until this adjustment becomes reflexive as soon as they receive the ball.

Follow-through. Throughout the act of shooting, as in any other sport involving hand-eye coordination, the brain continues to compute the precise amount and direction of the force needed to reach the target (the basket). Although these computations continue automatically in what computer people call *real time*, there is, nevertheless, sufficient lag to make compensations impossible for any abrupt accelerations at, or just before, the instant of release. Success, then, depends upon constant sighting and a smooth, continuous build-up of a propelling force that reaches its peak at the instant the ball leaves the fingertips, which means that a follow-through period in which the forces generated are allowed to diminish is an *essential* part of the shooting sequence.

Fundamental Techniques for Specific Shots

Before describing the specific techniques associated with the various shots a player might have in his offensive repertory, we again emphasize the importance of improvisation to the particular style of each player. Basketball has changed drastically in recent years, largely as a result of the innovations of individual players whose experimenting with accepted techniques led to the development and recognition of revolutionary new techniques. For example, dunks, behind-the-back passes, jump shots, shot-blocking, and one-hand set shots were once considered ineffectual showboating. What accounts for their present respectability is utilitarianism, the criterion against which every technique or individual refinement must be considered. As every innovator knows, however, success in experimenting comes after one has mastered the basics.

The Basic Shots. Virtually every shot required can be adapted from a mastery of six basic techniques: (1) one-hand underhand, (2) two-hand set, (3) one-hand set, (4) jump, (5) hook, and (6) lay-up. Although specific adjustments are necessary for various ranges and purposes (for example, free throws, drive-ins, tip-ins, lay-ups, pivots, turn-arounds, and step-aways), the basic six shots will provide the nucleus of a repertory for exploiting any situation.

Priority, however, should be given to mastering the shots that are likely to be most useful to a given player for a given position. For example, there would be little advantage in a seven-foot center's practicing two-hand set shots from 30 feet out, or a six-foot guard's practicing close-in pivots. As a rule, centers should perfect a versatile repertory of close-in (within 12 feet of the basket), right- and left-hand hooks, jumps, turn-around jumps, and overhead sets, adapting this repertory to the various pivots, lay-ups, tip-ins, etc. Forwards, on the other hand, should spend considerable time practicing medium-range (13 to 20 feet) jumps, drives, sets, and hooks, particularly from the sides, and proportionately less time practicing the close-in pivots and long-range sets. The essential shots for a guard are long-range (beyond 20 feet) sets, medium-range jumps, and a variety of overhand and underhand shots for quick drive-ins and lay-ups.

1. One-hand underhand shot. Except in theory, the *one-hand underhand* is probably never used from a set position. However, the usefulness of this technique for such special-purpose shots as underhand lay-ups and pivots will compensate generously for time spent in mastering it. Its advantage is the additional reach possible when only one arm is extended toward the basket.

From an initial position with both hands holding the ball, the shooter reaches toward the basket with one hand under the ball, allowing the off hand to fall away. With his shooting arm fully extended and his eyes focused on the sighting spot, the shooter lifts the ball toward either the basket or a spot on the backboard by raising his arm and adding a soft flick of his wrist and fingers. Follow-through is with the palm upward and the arm bending slightly at the elbow. Executed as described, the shot will carry with a minimum forward rotation. Any side rotation of the hand position at release, however, culminating in a follow-through with the hand edgewise and the wrist cocked upward, will impart a sidespin, or *English*, that must be compensated for when sighting.

2. *Two-hand set shot.* Although not widely used in modern basketball, the two-hand set shot from the chest position (Figure 3–3) has one advantage in that it has the longest accurate range. It is not, however, readily adaptable to the fast-break offense used by many teams.

In the set position, the feet are spaced and aligned for balance and comfort. Each player should determine the foot position that gives him the most confidence and then use that position for all similar shots. The important thing is that the shooter feel relaxed and mobile. The weight is on the balls of the feet, with the heels resting lightly on the floor; both knees are flexed; and the upper body is bent forward slightly from the waist, with the back straight. With the fingers spread wide, the thumbs and little fingers on the same line, and the thumbs close together in the rear, the ball is held comfortably in the fingertips of both hands, about a foot in front of the body and just below chin level. The elbows are held fairly close to the body, the head is stationary and erect, and the eyes are fixed on the sighting point.

Execution is a simultaneous thrust with arms and legs—rising from the heels and locking the knees and elbows—and a flick with the wrists and fingers in the direction of the basket, imparting a soft backspin to the ball. Follow-through is a continuation of the inward and downward rotation of the thumbs, leaving the hands declined slightly at the wrists, the palms turned outward. Eye concentration throughout is essential.

Figure 3–3. Two-hand set shot.

3. One-hand set shot. The *one-hand set* (Figure 3–4) retains much of the balance, range, and accuracy of the *two-hand set* while realizing a substantial increase in speed and flexibility. Because its techniques are essentially the same as those for all other nonhooking, one-hand overhead shots, including the jump shot, it should be the basic shot in the repertory of every player.

For the one-hand set, the position of the feet is a matter of personal choice, although most players prefer the foot under the shooting hand to be slightly forward. The level that the ball is carried when in the set position also varies with the player, one preferring to shoot from the chest, another from the shoulder. As a rule, however, the higher the ball is carried in the set position, the closer the shooter can be to a defender and still get the shot away. The starting point also affects the range—the higher the ball the shorter the range.

Figure 3–4. One-hand set shot.

The shooting hand is positioned on the low-back side of the ball, the fingers spread comfortably wide, with the palm facing the basket and held clear of the ball by the fingertips and the heel of the hand. The off hand is on the low-forward side, palm away from the basket. The function of the off hand is to provide additional balance and control. The off hand falls away the instant before release, and the impetus to the ball is transmitted solely by the shooting hand. Otherwise, shot execution is the same as for a two-hand set: as the shooter rises to his toes and thrusts with his legs, he simultaneously thrusts his shooting arm to full extension, his hand and fingers flexing downward smoothly at the wrist in order to impart a soft backspin as the ball is released.

A variation of the one-hand set from the shoulder or chest position is the one-hand set from the hip. In this instance, the ball is started at hip level from the shooting side and is brought up for a release directly above the shooter's line of sight. (A release from the shoulder or chest position is slightly to one side of the line of sight.) In a crouch, as though to dribble, and holding the ball in both hands, the shooter steps forward with the foot *opposite* his shooting hand at the same time that he starts the ball up and toward the basket. Revolving his hands so that his shooting hand is hindmost, he times the thrust off his *opposite* foot to occur simultaneously with the extension of his shooting hand. Release and follow-through are the same as for all other one-hand shots.

4. *Jump Shot.* The *jump shot* is one of the most effective offensive weapons. Although it is possible to become a good, even great, offensive player without it, no other shot puts quite so much pressure on a defense. When preceded by a fake, a fast, accurate jump shot is virtually impossible to block. The fake, in fact, is essential to the jump shot's effectiveness. To guard against the jump, the defender (unless he has a considerable height advantage) must be able to synchronize his own jump perfectly with that of the shooter—a task made extremely difficult by even the simplest fake.

If movement is toward the basket, from the shoulders up, shot execution is essentially the same as for a one-hand set shot; therefore, once the techniques of set shooting have been perfected, it should prove relatively easy to expand one's shooting arsenal to include a versatile assortment of jump shots for any reasonable range. Since the propelling force must be supplied almost solely by the arm, wrist, and fingers, usefulness of the shot is limited primarily to the short-to-medium range although some jump shooters are consistently successful as far out as 26 feet.

Takeoff can be either from a stationary position, facing any direction, or from a position on the move after dribbling, pivoting, or receiving a pass. Although highly individualized, takeoff from a stationary position is generally from both feet (see Figure 3–5); when moving, it is usually from the foot opposite the shooting hand. The position of the legs once the shooter is in the air is determined by what feels comfortable and natural: some great

Figure 3–5. Jump shot at takeoff.

shooters tuck their legs, others leave them extended and spread, and others keep them extended and together. Depending upon balance, distance from the basket, and defensive pressure, the jump can be either straight up, inclined toward the basket, or falling away. In all instances, however, the objective is to arrive at a near-stationary, balanced shooting position, above the floor and facing the basket, with the shooting arm cocked and poised to shoot. When perfectly timed, the jump presents an illusion of the shooter's hanging in mid-air for the instant required to get the shot away. When the jump is improperly timed or poorly executed, the result is an awkward, off-balance shot having very little chance of entering the basket. Regardless of individual style, the following techniques are essentially the same for all jump shots, whether stationary or moving (see Figure 3–6).

As he begins his crouch the shooter carries the ball in both hands to a *preliminary position* near the shoulder of his shooting side. If the player is moving, the crouch occurs on count two of a two-count stop and is initiated by the foot opposite the shooting

Figure 3–6. Jump shot techniques.

hand; if he is stationary, the crouch is with both legs, the weight evenly distributed on the balls of both feet. The elbows are held slightly forward and under the ball, and the hands are positioned with the off hand leading and the shooting hand trailing, the fingers spread comfortably as for a one-hand set shot. While sighting the target and as the legs unflex at the start of the jump, the shooter raises the ball with both hands to a *shooting position* slightly forward and either straight above, or above and to the shooting side of, his head. (Taller players tend to prefer a more overhead position than do shorter players.) Approaching the apex of the jump, with the elbow of his shooting arm pointed at the basket, the shooter cocks the wrist of his shooting hand so that the palm faces up and forward and his off hand rides high and in front. Considerable concentration is necessary to ensure continuous sighting as the shooter's hands and forearms cross his line of vision. Reaching the apex of the jump, he uncocks the forearm and wrist of his shooting hand in a quick, supple motion, allowing his off hand to fall away, and imparts with his fingertips a soft, natural backspin to the ball. Follow-through is completed with

Figure 3–7. Hook shot.

the shooting arm fully extended and the hand and fingers declined at the wrist as though to dip inside the basket.

    5. *Hook shot.* The *hook* is an extremely versatile and effective shot in the close-in–to–medium range. Centers and forwards in particular should begin early in their careers to master its techniques, with both the left and the right hand.

    The hook shot can be executed after dribbling to either side, after receiving a pass-in and pivoting, or after rebounding and pivoting. In each instance, the shot is taken off the foot opposite the shooting hand. As described here, the hook is initiated from a back-to-the-basket pivot.

    For a right-hand hook, the shooter pivots to the left, pushing off his right foot and turning his body and head to pick up the sighting point while his right hand, palm up, extends out parallel to the floor. Taking off from his left foot, he completes a continuous, sweeping overhead arc toward the basket (see Figure 3–7). As in every other shot in basketball, success depends upon effective sighting, a soft wrist, fingertip control, and a smooth continuous follow-through. Other checkpoints include high knee lift, two-hand raising of the ball for added control before extending the ball away from the body, and extension of the weak-hand elbow to a position parallel to the floor (and toward the defender) to keep the defender at a distance. A correctly executed follow-through will leave the shooter facing the basket and in good position for a rebound. (See Figure 3–8.)

6. *Lay-ups.* A *lay-up* shot is used in the following situations: (1) a player receives a pass, close in, while cutting toward the basket; (2) a player dribbles past defenders and under the basket.

Approaching from the right (technique reverses from the left), the shooter grasps the ball strongly in both hands as his

Figure 3–8. Hook shot follow-through.

a.   b.

Figure 3–9. Start of lay-ups: *a*, from left; *b*, from right.

right foot hits the floor. Keeping his body between the ball and
the defender (see Figure 3–9a), coming down hard on his left foot,
and thrusting sharply upward with his right knee (as in a *high
jump*), he carries the ball in both hands as high as possible, with
the right hand behind the ball, wrist cocked and facing the basket,
and the left hand in front, wrist away from the basket (as for a
one-hand set or jump shot) (see Figure 3–9b). This last step is a
shorter step that enables the shooter to convert his forward momentum into vertical jumping thrust. At the top of the high jump,
with both arms above his head (erect, with eyes fixed on a spot
above and to the right of the basket), he allows his left hand to
fall away as his right arm, wrist, and fingers extend to "place"
the ball against the sighting point in a motion similar to that of
trying to grasp the basket rim from a running start without the
ball. (The backboard should be used for lay-ups approached from
the side.) After completing his follow-through, the shooter alights
with hips down, knees bent, and body-weight low, ready to move
immediately into position for a rebound or to go on defense. (When
approaching the basket from the left, the player should use his
left hand, and all direction considerations should be reversed.)

A modified lay-up shot (preferred by many players because
of better control of the ball and a softer touch when laying it
against the backboard) is done with the hand positions reversed.

Figure 3–10. Right-hand lay-ups with hand under.

The approach and takeoff are the same as before, but the ball is carried with the right hand in front, palm facing slightly upward (as for a one-hand underhand shot). As the left hand falls away, the right arm extends, and the ball is laid up by a soft flick of the wrist and fingers.

Little or no spin, or English, should be used for either shot, since the softness depends upon a minimum of wrist and finger action. Therefore, the shooter must select a sighting point from which the ball should touch off and fall, with very little momentum, into the basket. (See Figure 3–10.)

Adaptations and Variations. After a player has mastered the fundamental techniques of hook shooting from various distances within his own optimum-percentage area, he should begin to elaborate upon this technique by incorporating the specialized fakes, pivots, turns, etc., that apply to the play situations most often developing from his team position. Informal practice to perfect close-in shots with either hand will significantly add to a player's value as an offensive threat.

Special purpose lay-ups. Although one of the two variations described above should be used in most lay-up situations, the exceptionally talented player may find that two additional lay-up shots will significantly increase his scoring opportunities: the *floating two-hand underhand lay-up* and the *driving one-hand underhand lay-up*.

The floating two-hand underhand lay-up (see Figure 3–11) can be used by a hard-driving guard coming down the lane in front of a closely defended basket. Instead of the high jump of the conventional lay-up, a broad jump is begun toward the basket, from six to nine feet out, with a takeoff from either foot. After

Figure 3–11. Two-hand underhand lay-ups.

Figure 3–12. Floating one-hand lay-up with hand under ball.

takeoff (the feet may be tucked under the thighs), the shooter floats toward the basket, the ball held between both hands. Release is timed for the apex of the jump and is effected by extending both arms forward and flipping the ball up with wrists and fingers.

The driving one-hand underhand lay-up is useful either for a miscalculated takeoff too far from the basket or as a calculated tactic to counter pressure from a defender in position to block a conventional overhead shot. Again, the shot is made from a broad jump, but in this instance the takeoff foot is the same as for a conventional lay-up—left foot for right-hand shot, right foot for left-hand shot. The ball is initially held in both hands, the body between it and the defender. After takeoff, however, the hand nearer the defender falls away, and the shot is accomplished by a reaching motion—the arm extends forward at shoulder level, the shooting hand under the ball, and the wrist and fingers flick the ball toward a sighting spot on the backboard, slightly above and to the shooter's side of the basket. (See One-hand underhand shot.) Some rotation of the wrist may be required in order to impart a slight carrying spin.

Under-the-basket shots. Frequently, a player cutting under the basket finds himself with the ball, too close in for any form of a lay-up. In this situation, he has two alternatives for a high-percentage shot: the first is either a *semi-hook* or a *short-hook*, taken from the approach side of the basket; the second is a *lay-back*, or *reverse lay-up*, taken from the side opposite the approach.

Semi-hook and short hook. Takeoff for both the semi-hook and the short hook is from the foot opposite the shooting hand, with the ball held high and in both hands. In the semi-hook, however, as the shooter rises from the floor he turns to face the basket, allowing his off hand to fall away, and hooking over-head and toward the basket with his shooting arm, the elbow and wrist inclined in a shallow arch. (See Figure 3–13.) For a short

Figure 3–13. Semi-hook shot.

Figure 3–14. Short-hook shot.

hook, the shooter does not turn toward the basket. Instead, he gets the ball away by a full overhead hook, with the arm relaxed and extended, and a soft flick of the wrist and fingers. (See Figure 3–14.)

Layback, or reverse lay-up. The layback, or reverse lay-up, is initiated from the side opposite the side from which the basket is approached. Actually, approach can be either from a side or from the rear, utilizing the four-foot area between the backboard and the end line. Takeoff is from the foot opposite the strong hand. The head is tilted backward to see the sighting point, and the ball is carried upward in both hands. At full extension, the off hand falls away, and the shooting hand rotates inward toward the little finger. The ball is released by a soft flick of wrist and fingers. (See Figure 3–15.) This is a difficult shot to master, and the ambidextrous shooter might consider the advantage of using his weak hand, instead, for an almost conventional lay-up.

Figure 3–15. Reverse lay-ups.

Figure 3–16. Drive-in hooks.

Drive-in hook. A very important weapon in the repertory of smaller backcourt players is a *drive-in hook shot* to be used when a taller defender switches to block a direct drive to the basket. (See Figure 3–16.) While still in motion, the shooter begins with the same takeoff as for a conventional lay-up, but when the ball is level with his shoulders, it is extended out, held in the shooting hand, away from the defender. A high-trajectory shot is then effected by an overhead hook with the arm fully extended.

Close-in jump shot. Following a quick stop and fake, a *close-in jump shot* can often be executed before the defender can react. The attacker moves from his weak to his strong side, stops, fakes, and takes off from his strong foot. Turning in mid-air toward the basket, he shoots quickly, with one hand, at the apex of his jump. The attacker uses the same technique when moving from his strong side, except a slight fall away may be necessary in turning toward the basket.

Close-in pivot shots. Most close-in scoring opportunities come either to the medium- or low-pivot man or to a forward when his back is toward the basket. Therefore, players in these positions must master the following: *right-* and *left-hand hooks; turn-arounds; step-in pivots; underhand pivots; step-aways;* and *jump-turns.*

Hooks. Properly executed, a close-in, back-to-the-basket hook shot is almost impossible to block. Because of the three-second time restriction in the foul-lane area, however, speed in getting the shot away is essential. Ideally, the pass-in should be received shoulder height, with the feet in position for a pivot in either direction. However, should pass reception require establishing one foot as the pivot by taking a step in the direction of the pass, then the step should be taken with the foot nearest the basket. Upon receiving the ball, the shooter should execute a head-and-shoulder fake while bringing the ball to shoulder level. (Obviously, the shooter must be capable of shooting with either hand if a fake is to be convincing.) Depending upon opportunity and ability, the shooter follows his fake with a quick pivot

Figure 3–17. Left-hand hook shot: *a,* preliminary fake to left, then step with right foot; *b,* step away from basket.

a.   b.

obliquely toward, parallel to, or away from, the end line. Figure 3–17 illustrates a left-hand hook shot.

Turn-around. The *turn-around* is a simple pivot shot to master. Its successful execution requires that a step, pivot, take-off, and shot be effected in one continuous motion. The ball is received with both hands, with the weight evenly distributed on both feet so that a turn may be made in either direction. For a right-hand shot, a head-shoulder fake to the right is quickly followed by a step to the left with the left, or non-pivot, foot; a simultaneous pivot to face the basket; an upward thrust with the right knee; and a left-foot takeoff. During the execution of the turn, the ball is brought with both hands up to a shooting position above the head.

Step-in pivot. From a close-in pivot position, it is sometimes possible to take advantage of a defensive lapse by following a fake with a pivot directly toward the basket. If he sees that the defender is moving in the direction of the fake, the pivot man, synchronizing his movements with the defender's lapse, can drop his non-pivot foot straight back, pivot quickly toward the basket, and trap the defender behind him. The object is to maneuver into the position of a fulcrum around which the pivot is executed. The shot can be either a hook, a turn-around, an underhand pivot, or a lay-up.

Underhand pivot. When a pivot man is in a close-in, back-to-the-basket position and feels pressure from a defender behind him, he can fake to the side of the pressure, execute a *step-in pivot* in the opposite direction, and shoot under the defender's arm with

Figure 3–18. Underhand pivot.

an underhand, upward motion. The ball is released toward the basket with a lifting rotation of the forearm and wrist of the shooting hand, imparting a soft carrying spin. (See Figure 3–18.) Sighting must take into account both the spin and the lower arc. Rhythm and follow-through are essential.

Step-away. The *step-away shot* is useful when the back-to-the-basket pivot player has the ball but is not closely guarded because of a lapse by the pivot defender; for instance, when the defender reacts to a pivot fake by moving away from the shooter and toward the basket. The shot is executed by stepping away from the basket with the non-pivot foot, pivoting on this foot to face the basket, and simultaneously thrusting upward with the other knee for a rear-foot takeoff, using a one-hand shot to the basket. Since this shot is easily blocked by a close defender, the fake, pivot, and shot must be perfectly timed.

Jump-turn. Many pivot players consider the *jump-turn shot* to be their best back-to-the-basket offensive weapon. Its success is largely due to its simplicity and to the effectiveness of an easily executed fake. In making the shot, the back-to-the-basket pivot brings the ball up to the shooting position while simultaneously executing a straight-up jump-turn to face the basket, timing the one-hand release for the apex of the jump. The fake is accomplished by a quick straightening of the knees and upward motion that simulates the beginning of a takeoff, making it impossible for the defender to synchronize his jump with that of the shooter.

Tip-in. The *tip-in* is not just a lucky slap at the ball. It should be practiced as a regular shot in the repertory of any tall player. An offensive rebounder should be ready to make a *tip-in shot* of any rebound in his area and within five feet of the basket.

Facing the basket, with knees flexed, hands up, and elbows shoulder high, the tip-in shooter times his takeoff to make fingertip contact just as he is reaching the top of his jump. (See Figure 3–19.) With the fingers spread and the wrist flexible, the shooting hand first controls the ball and then flicks it upward with a soft trajectory to the basket. Even if control is not possible, some kind of contact, such as a slap, should be made with the ball. Sighting, fingertip control, and follow-through are the same as for any other one-hand shot. (Although some players prefer to go up for the ball with both hands in order to be in better position for a rebound should a tip-in prove not feasible, most players can jump quicker and higher with only one hand up, which is the recommended technique whenever a tip-in opportunity is likely.)

The free throw. Free-throw shooting should be a regular part of every practice session and should take place under as near

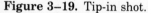

Figure 3-19. Tip-in shot.

game conditions as possible. Every player must determine his best-percentage medium- or long-range shot and use that shot for all free throws. (To be proficient, a shooter should make at least 75 percent of his free throws in practice.) If, however, a player is not particularly proficient in any one medium- or long-range shot, he should be taught to master the two-hand underhand shot for free throws. (Although the jump shot is used for free throws by many outstanding players who feel more confident with it than with any other shot, the shooter must take special care not to step on the foul line and thus nullify a successful throw.) The following fundamentals should be practiced until they become second nature for any free throw, regardless of style:

1. Dry hands and fingers before entering the free-throw circle; shake the arms, wrists, and fingers to relieve any tenseness.
2. Before accepting the ball from the official, look to both sides and behind to check opponents' offensive alignment and teammates' positions.
3. Receive the ball from the official before positioning yourself at the free-throw line.

4. Move up to the line, and set feet in the exact position that you always use for free throws.

5. Spin the ball in your hands to acquire proper feel; bounce the ball on the floor a few times to relax your arms and body and to accentuate feel.

6. After assuming final hand placement, inhale and exhale slowly.

7. Shoot.

The free throw should become as mechanical and reflexive as possible. Therefore, preliminary actions and foot positions should be the same for every shot.

PASSING

Passing is the foundation for all scoring plays; its importance is second only to shooting. Left alone, however, most players would spend a great deal of their time perfecting their shooting technique, and little on their passing. Therefore, during formal practice, coaches must balance the training by reversing the emphasis.

Fundamental Principles

Many of the principles and techniques of shooting apply equally to passing, and the reader would do well to review the beginning of this chapter before proceeding. Just as a shooter does not take a shot he is not confident of making, a passer does not attempt a pass unless he feels certain that it will be completed.

Every basketball pass must be, in precisely the right proportions, *accurate, well-timed, quick, deceptive,* and *relevant.* Although an excellent shooter may make only 50 percent of his attempts, a good passer must approach 100 percent effectiveness. To do so, he must develop the following perceptual abilities to the point that they become instinctive—even when he does not have the ball.

1. Court Awareness. The accomplished passer must be constantly aware of the positions and the relative physical and mental capabilities of every player on the court. This includes each player's speed, ball-handling ability, aggressiveness (both on offense and on defense), reaction to fakes, rebounding ability, and shooting ability.

2. Peripheral Vision. Since it is neither possible nor desirable that the passer always look directly at each potential receiver and each defender, he must develop his peripheral vision to the point that he can see everything that takes place within 90 degrees on either side of the direction he is facing. This means that with practice he will be able to encompass a 360-degree field of vision by simply turning his head 90 degrees right and left. Generally, the player's primary focus is toward the basket, where he can read the defense and observe his teammates' actions.

3. Anticipation. The accomplished passer knows the best opening and how a play might develop, even before he has the ball. Anticipating the movements of receivers and defenders, he can react with a well-timed pass that arrives at his receiver's best reception zone at the optimum moment for offensive advantage.

4. Judgment. This is the perceptual attribute of knowing when a fake is or is not necessary; whether to use a lob, bounce, or straight pass; what receiver is in the best offensive position; who not to pass to because of poor position, exceptionally strong defender, etc; what the maxim "not too fast, not too slow, not too high, not too low" means for a given receiver; and, finally, how to make each pass relevant to the objective of scoring.

Obviously, judgment is related to the other attributes of perception. Court awareness, peripheral vision, and anticipation provide the passer with a four-dimensional frame of reference in which to operate; the ultimate measure of his judgment and his excellence as a passer is his ability to pull all factors together and execute, within his own limitations, an accurate and meaningful pass, with just the right amount of deception and crispness.

Basic Two-Hand Passes

This section describes the more conventional passes that a player will have an opportunity to use. It should be remembered, however, that any pass is a good one if it meets the criteria of accuracy, timing, quickness, deception, and relevance. Although a poor passer will usually improve his effectiveness by staying with the simpler passes, a gifted passer should not feel limited by arbitrary or standard techniques, but should use whatever methods are at his disposal to successfully complete the play. Of course, each passer must remember not only his own passing limitations, but also the reception limitations of each team member. A player may be a valuable member of the team because of his rebounding, shooting, or defensive abilities, yet be unable to handle certain

Figure 3–20. Lob pass to cutter.

kinds of passes. It is the passer's responsibility to throw him a pass that he *can* handle.

Other considerations of judgment are the inherent advantages and disadvantages of lob passes and bounce passes. Since both of these are slower than a pass thrown parallel to the floor, they should be used only when there is a compelling reason for doing so. A lob pass, for example, might be used with good advantage to throw over a defender to a pivot man going in to the basket; to lead a fast-breaking cutter (Figure 3–20); to throw an easy-to-handle pass over a defensive man to a teammate coming into a high pivot; to exploit a distinct height advantage under the offensive basket; or to complete an out-of-bounds play. A bounce pass, on the other hand, can be used to get the ball past tall or high-hand-guarding defenders; to penetrate a zone; or to exploit any situation in which a side, carrying, or reverse spin can be used with advantage.

It should be kept in mind, too, that it is difficult to pass through or around a defender playing off the ball. If the ball handler is not planning to make a lob pass, he should close the distance between himself and his man before passing and then use fakes to get the defender's hands out of position to intercept or deflect the pass.

Although almost any pass can be completed from a jump, it is best to attempt such a pass only in rare instances—for example, when it is impossible to complete a jump shot or when double-teamed by a pressing or zone defense.

Two-Hand Chest Pass. This pass is used from any position on the court, primarily for short, fast passing of distances up to twenty feet. The basic foot and body position is the same as that for a two-hand set shot from the chest. Feet are spread comfortably, knees are flexed, body is bent slightly forward from the waist, and the ball is held comfortably, chest high, in both hands. Fingers are widespread. The pass is executed by stepping in the direction of the receiver, preferably with the foot closest to the receiver, and coordinating this movement with a full extension

Figure 3–21. Two-hand chest pass.

of the arms and a quick snap of the wrist and fingers as the weight shifts forward to the extended foot. (See Figure 3–21.) If the receiver is closely guarded, the target should be a hand held in the clear, away from the defender; otherwise, the target should be the receiver's chest. Often, this pass can be used to fake a two-hand chest shot that becomes a lob pass over the head of the defenders. A natural, easy-to-handle backspin is imparted at fingertip release.

Two-Hand Bounce Pass. Except for the release, the two-hand bounce pass is the same as a regular two-hand chest pass. Depending upon the circumstance, the ball can be released with a top spin, a backspin, or little or no spin. Normally, the ball should strike the floor two-thirds of the way to the receiver and bounce high enough to be caught at the waist. *The ball should always strike the floor closer to the receiver than to the passer.*

Top spin. Top spin is used to give a bounce greater distance. Initially, the ball is held as for a two-hand set, but the wrists are cocked upward just before execution. From a deeper crouch and off a more exaggerated forward step than for a regular two-hand pass, the passer fully extends both arms down and away, and as the stepping foot hits the floor, he releases the ball with a powerful, forward and downward flip of the wrists, forcing the ball out over the index fingers. Follow-through is with the thumbs pointing in the direction of the pass and with the fingers pointing downward.

The top-spin pass should strike the floor somewhat farther from the receiver than would a no-spin pass. Because it tends to take off, the top spin is the most difficult of the bounce passes to handle.

Backspin. Backspin is used when the passer wishes to blunt the rebound, as when leading a cutter or making a sharp, quick pass that bounces close to a pivot player. Execution is the same as for a top spin except that the wrists and fingers flick inward and down and the arms do not fully extend. (See Figure 3–22.) Last contact is with the thumbs, and follow-through is with both hands and forearms rotated inward, palms facing outward, and thumbs downward.

The backspin pass should strike the floor somewhat closer than normal to the receiver. Because it tends to come up, it is the easiest bounce pass to handle when the receiver is moving in to the pass.

Figure 3–22. Two-hand bounce pass with back spin.

Normal or little spin. The normal bounce pass, with little or no spin, is a change-of-pace pass that can be used by a guard or forward for feeding a pivot man, for passing through a zone, for out-of-bounds plays, or for passing off at the end of a fast break. Execution is similar to a two-hand chest pass except that the step in the direction of the pass is slightly larger and the body crouch is more exaggerated. The arms and hands move forward and downward, with a natural, quick flick of the wrists and fingers. (See Figure 3–23.)

It is also possible to impart a left- or right-carry action in order to pass around a defender to a teammate. For a left carry,

Figure 3–23. Two-hand bounce pass with no spin.

the hands are rotated sharply counterclockwise at release, causing the ball to veer to the left after striking the floor. For a right
carry, the hands are rotated clockwise. Through practice and experimentation, each player will be able to anticipate the correct
amount of carry for a variety of situations.

Two-Hand Pass from Over the Shoulder. Stance and the
initial position of the hands for this pass are the same as for the
chest pass. To begin a shoulder pass, however, the passer brings
the ball back over his left or right shoulder, keeping both hands
in their relative positions but with the outside hand lower and
more to rear, the palm more under the ball, and the fingers pointing up. The inside hand rides forward and up. (See Figure 3–24.)
The pass is executed by stepping in the direction of the receiver
with the foot opposite the ball, and extending the arms with a
quick inward flick of the wrists and fingers.

Although this pass is not notably efficient, the initial two-
hand-over-the-shoulder position frequently occurs when the ball

Figure 3–24. Two-hand over-the-shoulder pass.

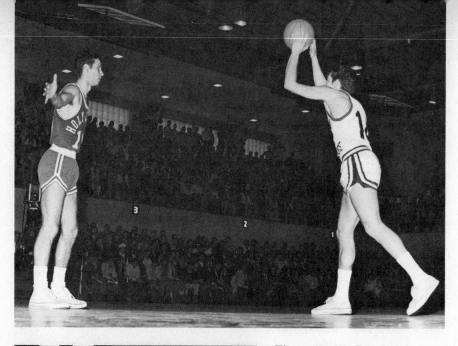

Figure 3–25. Two-hand overhead pass.

is being protected from a defender and allows the passer to take advantage of a quick opening. Possible variations are bounce passes, one-hand passes (allowing the inside hand to fall away as for a one-hand set shot), or an over-the-shoulder drop to a man either standing or cutting behind the passer. Since a one-hand pass from this position is usually more effective than the two-hand pass, it should be used when there is an alternative.

Two-Hand Overhead Pass. The two-hand overhead is one of the most effective passes. It can be used from all parts of the court, although it is most commonly used by forwards passing either in to the pivot or in to a guard cutting to the basket. It is especially useful to players when feeding the pivot, when closely guarded, or when initiating a fast break after a defensive rebound.

Stance is the same as for a two-hand set shot. The ball is held on each side and toward the back with widespread fingers, the thumbs pointed toward each other, and the pass is initiated from a position directly overhead, with the player's arms partially extended. (See Figure 3–25.) Taking a quick, short step in the direction of the receiver, the passer rises on his toes and shifts his weight onto his forward foot as he releases the ball by extending his arms and flicking his wrists and fingers downward. The target area for this pass should never be lower than shoulder level, as the downward force makes lower passes difficult to handle. The follow-through rotates the thumbs inward and downward. Very little body movement is required.

Two-Hand Underhand Pass from the Hip. This pass has a number of variations and can be made from either hip. It is

Figure 3–26. Two-hand underhand pass from hip.

primarily used for short, soft, easily handled passing in close areas and is generally handled at waist level or a little lower.

From a crouched position, with weight evenly distributed on both feet and with the head forward, the player passes from either the right or the left hip, with the opposite foot forward. The ball is held in the fingertips, with one hand on either side of the ball. The fingers are spread wide and pointing downward, and the thumbs are pointed toward each other. The inside hand is close to the hip; the outside upper arm is parallel to the floor, with the elbow pointing rearward, and the lower arm is parallel to the body. (See Figure 3–26.) If passing for distance (twelve feet maximum), the passer releases the ball with a short step off the opposite foot, a full extension of both arms, and an under-and-forward flick with the wrists and fingers. Follow-through leaves the fingers and arms fully extended and the thumbs pointed upward and slightly outward.

On lateral, guard-to-guard crosses or longitudinal, forward-to-guard exchanges, this pass is executed by stepping with the foot nearest the defender and the basket, raising the ball slightly, and squeezing it out of the hands so that it pops up about six to eight inches to be easily handled by the receiver. A shovel-pass variation is used by pivot men to flip the ball to cutters, from the front or from either side, as a short pass or a close hand-off. Another variation is a two-hand, backward, underhand pass, either to a stationary teammate behind the passer or to a guard cutting outside. This is effected by flipping the wrists and fingers backward and upward, allowing the hands to follow through. For any backward pass, however, the passer must first turn his head in order to make certain of the receiver's position.

Because of the frequency with which they occur and because of the natural tendency to let attention relax, close passes must be rigorously emphasized during formal practice. Coaches must constantly stress the importance of such fundamentals as timing and the height and softness of the exchange. To avoid fumbles and interceptions, the passer must lay the ball up waist high so that it hangs, hands off, for the receiver to catch easily without danger of colliding with the passer's hands, feet, or body.

Basic One-Hand Passes

As a rule, one-hand passes can be used for longer distances than two-hand passes, but a one-hand pass (for example, a baseball pass or a hook pass) is somewhat more difficult to control and often requires more time to execute. Within twenty-five feet, therefore, a two-hand pass is generally more appropriate, although the ruling factor is opportunity, which may require a one-hand pass at any distance.

The techniques described below are for right-hand passes; the techniques for the left hand are simply the mirror image of those for the right.

One-Hand Baseball Pass. The one-hand baseball pass can be used as a long pass from any position on the court and is often used to inbound the ball quickly after a score or to initiate a fast break.

From a well-balanced stance, feet spread, weight evenly distributed, the player brings the ball with both hands (fingertip control) to a point above the right shoulder and just behind the right ear. In this passing position the right hand is behind the ball, a little to the outside, with the fingers pointing upward and the palm toward the target; the left hand is on the front side and helps guide the ball into position. Facing the right sideline and with both feet on a line to the target, the passer reaches back with the ball, his weight shifting onto his rear foot, and releases the pass by stepping forward on the opposite foot and throwing the ball with a quick snap of the elbow, wrist, and fingers. At reach-back, the left hand moves off the ball, and at shoulder level it moves in the direction of the pass. At release, the weight shifts to the opposite foot, and follow-through is completed with an inward and downward rotation of forearm and wrist, arm extended and thumb pointed at the floor. Body weight pivots around the front foot so that the passer ends up facing the receiver, his toes pointing in the direction of the pass. It is important that the follow-through of fingers be an exaggerated rotation inward toward the thumb. Should the wrist rotate outward, in the direction of the little finger, the ball will tend to curve and will have a hard-to-handle spin.

Although some passers can impart a backspin in order to throw the ball over the heads of defenders and hold up the bounce to lead a break-away man, the one-hand baseball pass is extremely difficult to control and should not be attempted by the average passer, who will usually be more effective with a moving, two-hand chest pass.

Hook Pass. The hook pass is used as follows: to initiate a fast break when defensive pressure from one side negates the use of a baseball pass; to feed the pivot when defensive pressure negates the use of a two-hand overhead pass; and (by a pivot man) to pass off to a cutter. The techniques are essentially the same as those for a hook shot and can be executed either with or without a jump.

The pass is made with the hand farthest from the defender. Stepping away with his outside foot and protecting the ball with his inside elbow and arm, the passer releases the ball with an arm-extended hook and a flick of the wrist and fingers, taking care neither to impart more force than is absolutely necessary nor to propel the ball on a downward trajectory. For greater quickness, the pass can be made with the passing arm not fully extended, but compensated by more wrist and finger action. Follow-through is the same as for a hook shot.

One-Hand Underhand Pass. This pass is used when the passer is moving at great speed in one direction and a cutter is breaking toward him from the opposite direction. It is a very difficult pass to control and should only be attempted by good passers when no other alternative is practicable.

Off the front foot, left or right, the pass is released underhand with a stiff wrist and the passing arm fully extended, the impetus coming from the snap of the elbow, the fingertips providing direction and control.

One-Hand Cross-Body Pass. This pass is similar to the baseball pass. It is used for shorter distances when quickness is essential. From a baseball passing position, the ball is released with a quick extension of the arm across the body and with a powerful snap of the elbow and wrist. The thumb and fingers rotate inward, toward the body, with the thumb pointing at the feet during follow-through.

One-Hand Push Pass (after a lateral fake). The one-hand push pass to one side, after faking a two-hand chest pass in the opposite direction, can be used either to feed a cutter or a pivot man or as a safety pass when a defensive man must be moved away from the passing lane. It can be either a straight pass or a bounce pass and is essentially the same as a two-hand pass, except one hand is used only to help control the ball, the impetus being supplied solely by the hand and arm on the side from which the pass is released. (See Figure 3–27.) As the defender moves with the fake, the pass is released to the opposite side by a full extension of the arm and a brisk snap of the wrist and fingers and a balance step in the direction of the pass. Follow-through is with the arm and hand only—parallel to the floor for a straight pass, declined slightly toward the target spot for a bounce pass.

Figure 3–27. One-hand push pass.

One-Hand Bounce Pass. This is an excellent pass to use off a dribble when a long, quick, and accurate pass to a cutter is needed. The passing motion is similar to that of a baseball pass except that the release is made off a dribble and the arm is not drawn back. As the ball comes off the floor on the last dribble, it is caught and controlled by the passing (dribbling) hand. In one long passing motion, the passer extends his arm with the ball and releases (as the opposite foot strikes the floor) with a strong elbow, wrist, and finger action. Follow-through will be determined by the spin imparted. (See Two-Hand Chest Pass.) The pass should be timed to bounce up to the waist of the cutter in full stride.

When thrown hard enough to reach a receiver even though it is partially deflected, the bounce pass should reach its target. It requires a longer windup and, consequently, more time to execute. Therefore, it should be used with discretion. Normally it is most effective against a tall defender.

One-Hand Behind-the-Back Pass. This pass should never be used except as a short flip pass to a teammate coming

Figure 3–28. Behind-the-back pass.

behind for a screen or when it is the only pass possible to a free cutter—as at the end of a two-on-one break. It can be either a straight pass or a bounce pass.

The passer either turns his head slightly or uses peripheral vision to pick up the receiver. Cupping the ball in his passing hand, inclined at a right angle to his forearm, the passer carries the ball behind his back and releases with a back-hand flip of his wrist. His fingers point at the receiver, and his body pivots on the right foot (right-hand pass), away from the path of the pass. (See Figure 3–28.)

One-Hand Tap Pass. This pass is used to deflect a ball in flight to send it to a teammate who is in a better position to control it and possibly score. The pass is effected by a supple action of the wrist and fingers and is essentially the same as a tip-in shot. When two hands can be used, somewhat better control is possible.

DRIBBLING

Dribbling is an integral part of basketball offense. Along with passing and shooting, it is one of three methods used to advance the ball. It is the only method for moving with the ball. Inexperienced players, however, tend to waste their dribble by bouncing the ball purposelessly as soon as they obtain possession. By doing so, they lose their mobility, thus one third of their offensive potential. A player who has not used his dribble is *alive* (mobile). A player who has used his dribble is *dead* (immobile).

There are four reasons to dribble:

1. To penetrate a defense in order to gain a scoring opportunity
2. To protect the ball when pressured defensively
3. To move the ball into offensive territory when the defense is in a good protective position or when the offense is re-forming after initial penetration is unsuccessful
4. To protect the ball in the closing moments of a game

Fundamental Principles

The three most important concerns when dribbling are *posture, ball control,* and *field of vision.*

1. Posture. The basic body position for dribbling is as follows: The knees are flexed, the hips are lowered slightly, and the weight is balanced and flowing forward onto the back of the front foot; the upper torso is bent forward at the waist, and the head and shoulders are held erect for balance and control; the free hand is available for protection if necessary. Different types of dribbling call for varying degrees of crouch, but body control must be such that the player retains all the options of a dribbler in motion: to shoot, pass, change direction, or stop.

2. Ball Control. The ball is controlled by the fingers, with the wrist, elbow, and arm coordinating to regulate the height and speed of the bounce and to cause the desired lateral and longitudinal displacement. With the palm cupped and never contacting the ball, the fingers are spread comfortably, and the dribble is initiated by a supple wrist action that tosses the ball lightly floorward. As the ball rebounds, it is caught for an infinitesimal moment in the inverted cup formed by the fingers, the wrist yielding to absorb the upward force, and is again tapped to the floor. The cycle is repeated as many times as the dribbler wishes so long as his wrist is kept facing the floor and there is no perceptible stopping of the ball.

No player is a proficient dribbler until he can perform equally well with either hand.

3. Field of Vision. Peripheral vision is as important to the dribbler as it is to the passer. With his head held erect and facing to the front, the dribbler should have a field of view that encompasses everything forward of an imaginary line drawn through his shoulders and extended to the court perimeter. Although he should never consciously look at the ball, it should be continuously within his vision, as should all the other players, the officials, the court markings, and the basket.

With practice, a player's peripheral vision can be improved until he can take in, at a glance, everything within a 180 degree arc; by swiveling his head 90 degrees right and left, he can get a picture of the entire court in less time than it takes to complete one dribble. This ability is especially valuable to key playmakers. Coaches can demonstrate the method by having a player face away from a lamp placed approximately ten feet to his rear and then having him turn his head quickly 90 degrees right and left. Normal peripheral vision should enable him to see the lamp from either side without turning his shoulders.

Basic Forms of Dribbling

High (Speed) Dribble. When speed is essential and defensive pressure allows, the high, or speed, dribble should be used; for example, when driving to the basket, when leading a fast

Figure 3–29. High-speed dribble drives.

break, or when bringing the ball into offensive territory without opposition. The body is almost erect, with only a very slight forward crouch for balance, as the dribbler moves in a full stride limited only by his ability to control the ball. (See Figure 3–29.) For a proficient dribbler, this limit should be very near his top running speed. The dribbling arm is almost at full extension, pushing the ball forward and slightly to the dribbling side. The height of the balance is above the waist and below the shoulders, varying with the individual player, but must be such that it allows maximum running speed. The ball is continually tossed floorward with a pumping motion.

Low (Protective) Dribble. The low dribble is used when it is necessary to protect the ball from a defender; for instance, when closely guarded in a drive to the basket; when clearing the ball from a crowded area, without the possibility of a pass; or when protectively dribbling in position in order to remain alive while waiting for offensive balance after an unsuccessful play attempt. The dribble is approximately knee high; the body is in an extreme crouch; and, on the dribbling side, the upper arm and elbow are held close in (see Figure 3–30). The ball is controlled by the usual method.

Against extreme defensive pressure, the dribbling height can be farther lowered, and the body can be positioned completely between the defender and the ball. In this situation, the dribbler continuously pivots around the foot closest to the defender and combines head and body feints to upset the defender's timing. The free arm is used for balance and protection; the head is erect; the eyes are alert; and the elbow of the dribbling arm is held close to the side.

Figure 3–30. Dribbler protecting the ball.

Change-of-Pace Dribble. The change-of-pace dribble is used to fake the defender into relaxing his guard during an apparent routine dribble. It is an excellent driving maneuver when using a screen or when driving in for a basket against a defender in good position. The change of pace is effected by changing the dribbling speed. For example, a change from slow to fast can be used after deceiving a guard into expecting a routine move. A change from fast to slow to fast can be used, dribbling fast into the basket; slowing to deceive a close defender into expecting a stop, change of direction, or cross-over; and then suddenly continuing with the original move to the basket.

Methods of Changing Direction and Hands while Dribbling

1. Simple Change of Direction. When a defender is retreating and not too close (four to five feet away), but on the dribbling-hand side, the dribbler should change hands, using a minimum of body turn. Execution is simply pushing the ball across for the opposite hand to pick up the dribble as the foot on the original dribbling-hand side contacts the floor. Little change of direction is necessary, since the dribbler is now between the ball and the defender. (See Figure 3–31.)

Figure 3–31. Change-of-direction dribble.

Figure 3–32. Cross-over dribble.

2. **Cross-over.** This method should be used when a more evasive tactic than a simple change of direction is called for. As the foot on the dribbling side contacts the floor, a hard push-off is initiated toward the opposite foot, the dribbling hand lowering slightly to the outside of the ball and angling it across the body for the opposite hand to pick up the dribble. (See Figure 3–32.) If the defender is close, extreme caution must be used to prevent him from intercepting or deflecting the ball. The maneuver is completed with a long cross-over step by the foot on the original side of dribble. The change of direction must be emphatic, with an exchange of dribbling hands, in order to throw the defender off pace and to protect the ball as he recovers.

3. **Reverse (Pivot) Dribble.** This maneuver is very effective during a one-on-one drive to the basket when the defender has good position on the ball side. (See Figure 3–33.) It is also useful in a congested area when trying to protect the ball and

Figure 3–33. Drive-in—
protecting ball with body.

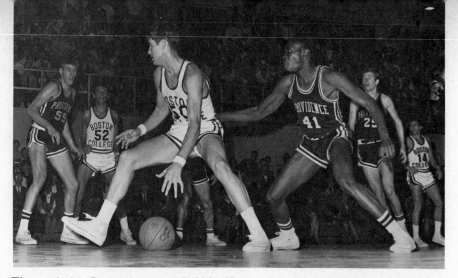

Figure 3–34. Protective pivot dribble. Notice that the dribbler's head is up.

out-maneuver the defensive guard. (See Figure 3–34.) Less foot action is required in the latter instance, and the feet may be kept closer together to afford greater body protection for the ball. The following procedure is reversed when starting from a left-hand dribble.

As the right foot contacts the floor, the dribble action is moved back to a position outside the right heel. A stride step is taken with the left foot while the ball is bounced progressively to the left and behind the right foot. Executing a pivot on the left foot and turning his back to the defender, the dribbler picks up the dribble with his left hand. A push off the right foot increases the pivoting speed. At all times, the dribbler's body must be kept between the ball and the defender.

4. Behind-the-Back Dribble. For the exceptional ball handler, this maneuver is safer than the cross-over and quicker than the reverse, with the same end result. With his right hand, the dribbler bounces the ball even with his left foot as his right leg comes forward in stride. As his right foot contacts the floor and his left leg is moving forward and out of the way, the dribbler adroitly angles the ball behind his back, causing the ball to bounce up under his left hand, which picks up the dribble.

FOOTWORK AND MISCELLANEOUS OFFENSIVE SKILLS

This section comprises the additional skills that the individual player must command on offense. Included in this category are *starting, stopping, turning and pivoting, faking or feinting, jumping, cutting, pass receiving, and moving without the ball.*

Starting

At the start of a dribble, the pivot foot cannot leave the floor until the ball leaves the hand. For shooting or passing, the pivot foot can leave the floor, but it cannot return before the ball is released.

Players must always be balanced for a step in any direction. In the normal offensive stance, the feet are spaced approximately the width of the shoulders; the hips, knees, and ankles are comfortably flexed in a semi-crouch; the weight is forward on the balls of the feet, the heels slightly off the floor; and the head is erect and centered. The start is initiated by shifting the weight to the stepping foot and pushing off with a strong thrust of the trailing foot. Without the ball, the upper arms are at the sides, close to the body, with the elbows pointing downward. The forearms are parallel to the floor, and the hands are above the waist and ready for receiving a pass.

Stopping

Basketball players must learn to stop quickly with perfect balance. (See Figure 3–35.) In addition, a player having ball possession must stop within the limits specified by the rules. When

Figure 3–35. Defender stops after wheel-and-guard. Dribbler stops, maintaining dribble.

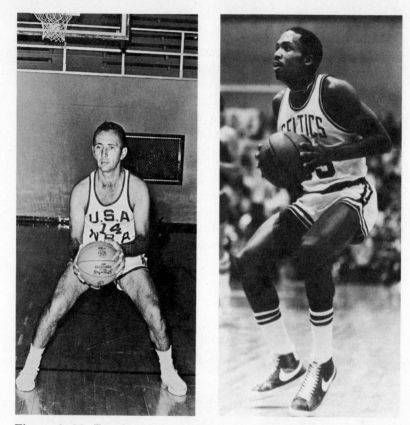

Figure 3–36. Two-foot jump stop.

the ball is caught while both feet are off the floor, and the player lands on both feet simultaneously, the rules are the same as for receiving a pass while standing: either foot may be used as the pivot. When the ball is caught while one foot is on the floor (*one count*), that foot becomes the pivot foot, and the other foot becomes the stepping foot (*two count*). There is no pivot foot when the ball is caught on one foot and the player jumps and lands on both feet simultaneously.

Of the two methods of stopping with the ball, the *two-foot jump stop* (Figure 3–36) and the *stride stop* (Figure 3–37), we have found the latter to be more natural and easier to teach. When stopping in stride, the player, running in a slight crouch, lowers his hips as his pivot foot contacts the floor (*one count*), flexing his pivot-foot knee until it almost touches the floor as the stepping foot makes contact (*two count*). The stepping foot strides longer than normally, the entire foot slapping the floor to gain maximum traction. Instantly, the forward leg thrusts back to regain body

Figure 3–37. Stride stop.

balance. The player must protect the ball by holding it in both hands, keeping his body between it and the defender.

For those who can master it, the two-foot jump stop has the advantage of allowing either foot to be used as the pivot. This stop is performed by catching the ball while both feet are in the air and landing with both feet parallel, body weight very low, and the entire bottom surface of the shoes in contact with the floor. There is danger that the body weight will be too far forward, however, resulting in an extra step and a travelling violation.

Turning and Pivoting

For our definition, a *turn* can be considered any change in the direction that a player is facing, with or without the ball, whether moving or stationary. Cross-overs and simple changes of direction are examples of turns when moving with the ball; jump turns, pivots, and facing movements, in the last instance without par-

ticular regard to foot position, are examples of turns when stationary. Of the last category, only pivots and jump turns with an
aerial release are legal when having ball possession. Without ball
possession, the only requirement of a turn is that proper balance
and offensive poise be maintained; with possession, care must be
taken to observe the rules governing the pivot foot. (See Starting
and Stopping.)

A *pivot* is a legal maneuver for changing, without dribbling,
the direction that a player is facing when in possession of the ball.
The *pivot foot* is as defined under *Stopping*. Using the ball of his
pivot foot as a swivel point, a player is free to rotate his body so
long as he does not permit his pivot foot to move from its position
or to break contact with the floor. The force of rotation is supplied
by the outside, or *stepping*, foot, which the ball handler is permitted to move in an arc around the pivot foot as freely as he
chooses—either left or right, forward or backward.

Pivoting is one of the most fundamental movements in basketball. It is most often used following a stop after dribbling or
receiving a pass, and, within the compass of a player's pivoting
range, it is an effective means of moving vigorously with the ball
for any offensive advantage, such as gaining a better position for
shooting or passing or for protecting the ball from an aggressive
defender.

There are three basic pivots: the rear pivot, the front pivot,
and the reverse pivot.

1. Rear Pivot. When forced by a defender to stop near a
sideline, a dribbler must quickly reorient his body to protect the
ball and to face into the court for a pass-off. Since the sideline
and the defender prevent a forward movement, a rear pivot is
called for. Using the foot away from the sideline as his pivot foot,
the ball handler crouches, moves the ball with both hands to a
position behind his hip and away from the defender, and thrusts
hard with his stepping foot (nearest the sideline), rotating his
body backward around the pivot foot until he has a view of mid-
court or is able to pass off to a teammate. (See Figure 3–38.)

To maintain proper balance, the stepping foot remains close
to the floor during the pivot, and the weight alternates smoothly
between the pivot foot and the stepping foot. Between pivots, with
his back to the defender, the man with the ball may reach outward
with it to avoid being tied up. For the actual pivot, however,
pulling the ball close to his body, elbows wide, both protects the
ball from a defender and minimizes the rotational arm of inertia
to be overcome.

Figure 3–38. Rear pivot.

a.

b.

c.

2. Front Pivot. When a man with the ball is not being pressed and has stopped while facing a sideline or away from the basket, he can shift his weight to his pivot foot and swing his stepping foot forward and around, pivoting to face the desired direction. Upon completing the pivot, the player resumes a two-foot balance and carries the ball from its pivot position, close to his chest, to a position suitable for passing, shooting, or protecting.

From the high-post position, when either foot is eligible for the pivot, most players prefer to initiate the front pivot by swinging the leg closest to the sideline and pivoting on the other foot. After receiving a pass, the high-post player pulls the ball in to a position in front of his pivot hip, drops his opposite shoulder, crouches slightly, pivots 180 degrees, and initiates a shot, pass, or drive.

3. Reverse Pivot. The reverse pivot differs from the pivots above in that it is executed on the balls of both feet simultaneously. (See Figure 3–39.) Following a stride stop, his body still in a crouch and his weight forward, the player pulls the ball to his waist, rises to the balls of both feet, thrusts his weight back, and pivots 180 degrees toward the trailing foot. Completing the pivot, still on the balls of both feet, the player then takes a full step in the new direction with the original forward foot. During the course of this maneuver, body weight, which is kept low throughout, moves from the forward foot to the trailing foot and back to the forward foot as it steps out in the new direction.

This pivot is frequently used to protect the ball from a defender who is directly in front of a player stopping while facing the basket. Except that it is much more vigorous, the movement is similar to a military *face to the rear while marching.*

Faking or Feinting

As used here, *faking* and *feinting* are near-synonymous terms for movements intended to confuse or mislead a defender so as to upset his timing or balance or to rob him of a positional advantage. Faking with ball possession, for example, can be used to obtain passing or shooting room or to open a passing or driving lane. Faking without possession can be used to keep a defender away from a play situation or to free a teammate for a pass or

---

Figure 3–39. Reverse pivot: *a*, stride stop; *b*, pivot on balls of both feet; *c*, full step away.

shot. The accomplished player has an assortment of deceptive moves for every play situation.

Ball Fakes. A short, quick movement of the ball in one direction, followed quickly and in the same motion by a pass, pivot, shot, or dribble in another direction, is an extremely effective and simple means of gaining an advantage over a defender. The diversionary movement should be such as to allow the intended action to follow, not drawing back but as a sudden redirection. For example, a forward may fake a two-hand chest pass to a guard and, from full arm extension, execute a two-hand bounce pass under the arms of the defender and into the pivot.

Foot Fakes. All change-of-pace and change-of-direction maneuvers, with or without the ball, are preceded by a foot or leg fake. Since a step transfers some weight to the extended foot, however, a faking step must be short enough to allow an immediate thrust back onto the other foot as it steps off in the intended direction. For dribble fakes, the feinting movement of the non-pivot foot must be slight and without a transfer of weight, since the pivot foot is not permitted to leave the floor until the ball leaves the dribbling hand, and the step off in the intended direction must be with the non-pivot foot.

Other foot fakes are as follows: (1) a quick step forward and back, followed by either a set shot or a fake set shot and a drive to the basket; (2) a quick bending of the knees to fake a jump shot, followed by a drive to the basket (if the defender jumps) or a continuation of the jump shot (if the defender does not jump).

Head-and-Shoulder Fakes. Many pivot men use quick head-and-shoulder fakes in one direction and move in the opposite direction for a shot. Success depends upon sharp, concise movements for momentary deception without compromising balance. Head-and-shoulder fakes are also used before a change-of-direction cut, a reverse cut from a stationary position, and most dribble fakes.

Eye Fakes. Many good defensive players watch the eyes of their opponents. An alert player on offense can turn this against a defender by the use of misleading or deceptive eye movements. The most effective eye fakes are those using peripheral vision to conceal the true path of a pass, whether the faking is by the passer or the receiver.

Arm-and-Hand Fakes. The best example of an arm-and-hand fake on offense is the pass receiver's keeping his arms at his side, watching the ball with his peripheral vision, and raising his hands at the last instant to catch the pass over the head of a defender. The opposite technique, faking a catch, can be used to draw a defender out of position.

Combinations. Most faking maneuvers are really combinations of deceptive movements using the ball, eyes, head, shoulders, arms, hands, legs, and feet. Basketball is a game of advantage, and the intelligent player, with or without the ball, is constantly working to place the defender at a disadvantage by using whatever combination of fakes and feints necessary to disguise the offense. Purposeless or irrelevant faking, however, works only to the disadvantage of the player himself, causing misplays, needless turn-overs, and early tiring.

Special Faking Techniques

The following are faking techniques for specialized situations when in scoring areas with the ball. Each should be mastered for use when facing the basket, when facing away from the basket, and after recovering an offensive rebound.

Up and Under. Upon receiving a pass, the player brings the ball up quickly to the shooting position for a set shot. If the defender moves in and up to defend against the shot, the player steps long toward the basket, pushing off his pivot foot but making certain to release the ball for the dribble before the pivot foot leaves the floor. (See Figure 3–40.) The initial step must be directly into the basket, to either side of the defender, preferably to the side of an uplifted or stepping foot. Driving by a defender's uplifted foot puts him at a disadvantage, since regaining position will require that he first return the foot to the floor and then push off the opposite foot for a move that is defensively relevant.

In the pivot area, the *up-and-under* move calls for faking an above-the-head pivot shot and executing a step-in underhand shot under the upstretched hands of the defender. A similar move can be used by a player after making an offensive rebound with a defensive rebounder between him and the basket: a quick, upward head-and-shoulder fake from a crouched position, *with the ball well protected*, forces the defender up; the shooter then steps in under the defender and lunges to the basket, holding the ball in both hands until laying it up.

Figure 3–40. Up-and-under fake.

Rocker Step. The *rocker-step* drive is similar to the up-and-under movement. After receiving a pass, the player steps toward the basket as though to drive. As the defender retreats protectively (if the defender does not retreat, the driver should continue into the basket), the player draws back his stepping foot, straightens upright, and brings the ball up as though to shoot. Should the defender advance, the player thrusts his stepping foot toward the basket and dribbles by the defender. (See Figure 3–41.) Some players bring the stepping foot back behind the pivot foot after the first fake. The most effective rocker movement, however, is with little or no drawback of the foot: a quick back-straightening motion, followed by a second, short extending of the out-thrust foot, quickens the move without losing any of the faking effectiveness.

Jumping

A player's ability to jump can be improved by practicing technique and by daily exercise. Drills such as jumping up and touching the rim several times a day provide the player with both the means

Figure 3–41. Rocker step.

and the incentive for improving. If he cannot jump and touch the rim from a standing position, he should jump to touch either the net or the backboard, striving for higher jumps at each practice. Other means of improving are stretching exercises and skipping rope.

In addition to jump shooting, which has been discussed, another situation in which jumping is fundamental is rebounding.

Offensive Rebounding. Although there is some overlapping, the techniques and starting positions for offensive and defensive rebounding are essentially different.

Rebounding technique. The two most important principles of rebounding technique are balance and timing. To maintain his balance in the congested area under the basket, the player must establish a wide, strong base in which to operate. His feet should be spaced as widely as comfort will allow. His knees are slightly bent, his hips lowered, and his body braced. His elbows are held wide at shoulder level, his upper arms parallel to the floor, and his forearms and hands are held high and parallel to his body. His fingers are widespread, his palms facing the basket. His body should be balanced slightly forward, with the weight on the balls of his feet.

In rebounding, the timing of the jump is even more critical than its height. The factors governing timing are the height and direction of the rebound, which, in turn, are determined by such factors as shot trajectory and distance; whether the ball hits the backboard or the rim; their resiliency; and the amount of spin on the ball. Considering each of these factors when timing his jump, the rebounder springs into the ball, attempting a tip-in, a tap-off, or a two-hand retrieval. Should he elect to retrieve the ball, he should do so at the highest point of his jump, with his legs and elbows spread wide and his buttocks extended rearward for maximum protection. Turning the ball over while he is still in the air, so that one hand is below and one above, the offensive rebounder lands with feet and elbows wide, hips low, and buttocks extended. (A taller rebounder might elect to come down more upright, with the ball held high, to effect more quickly either a second shot or a pass-off.) Bringing the ball strongly to his chest, the rebounder avoids a held ball by quick fakes and pivots, if necessary, in combination with a drive, shot, or pass-off. He should not make the mistake of shooting hurriedly or off balance, but should treat the rebound as he would the retrieval of a loose ball: if a shot opportunity presents itself, it should be taken immediately; otherwise the ball should be cleared to back-court, and the play pattern resumed.

Offensive rebounding tactics. Many coaches spend much time teaching defensive rebounding but little on the offensive phase. Since few teams make as many as half of their shots, however, the probability of losing the ball upon shooting can become greater than that of scoring a basket. Obviously, rebounding on

Figure 3–42. Offensive rebounding. Teammates of shooters getting good rebound position.

offense cannot be left to hustle and chance, but must be given the same emphasis as is rebounding on defense.

Although the defense generally has the inside position, the offense has several means by which it can neutralize this positional advantage. First, knowing when a teammate is likely to shoot, the player on offense can gain a split-second advantage in maneuvering time and thus prevent his being blocked out for the rebound. The defender cannot look for rebounding positions until the shot is released, since turning too soon makes him susceptible to a fake and cut to the basket; however, teammates of the shooter should know his shooting habits well enough to move instinctively into a favorable position as soon as a play begins to develop that is likely to produce a shot. (See Figure 3–42.)

Second, teammates of the shooter should have a better feel for how his shots typically behave when coming off the rim or backboard: the rebounds of missed shots attempted by a given player tend to follow a definite pattern, depending upon spin, use of backboard, trajectory, etc. Teammates, as well as the shooter himself, should be alert to those characteristics and adjust for them when moving into position.

A third means of neutralizing a defender's advantage of inside position is to crowd him with body pressure to affect his timing and balance. Should the offensive rebounder detect that the defender is leaning back when crowded, he can maintain or increase the pressure and then suddenly slide around, causing the opponent to lose his balance.

Effective use of body, leg, shoulder, and elbow pressure can upset an opponent's mental poise as well as his physical poise. The congested rebounding area is the scene of much allowable or overlooked body contact. So long as he does not use his hands or jump over a positioned defender, an aggressive and combative rebounder can do much to make up for whatever disadvantage he may have in height or initial position.

The rebounder on offense also has the advantage of not having to strive always for two-hand control. Therefore, he can seek a closer position to the basket, from which he can attempt a tip-in. Even if the tip is unsuccessful, he or a teammate will get a second opportunity to recover the ball, tip it for a score, or bat it to one of (generally) two offensive guards standing outside the top of the free-throw circle, ready either to retreat on defense or to retrieve a ball batted over his head. Success under the offensive boards often depends upon the offensive team's ability to keep the ball in play until either a score is made or a team member gains possession. After each jump, a rebounder on offense should

Figure 3–43. Offense timing jump, going up as defensive man inside (boxing out) comes down, to steal rebound.

land on the balls of his feet, his hips low and his arms and hands high, ready for a second, third, fourth, or fifth effort if necessary. Extra determination is in itself an advantage.

Often the play pattern will cause a defender to leave his man while a shot is being attempted by another player. For example, a back-court shot from the opposite side may cause a defender guarding a forward away from the ball to drop off toward the free-throw area in order to help his teammates in defense. The freed offensive forward should then be able to move into a good rebound position without being blocked off the backboards. Even if he is unable to get inside the guard, he should at least manage a side-by-side situation. If the pivot man can also gain a positional advantage in such instances, which he should do easily when his defender plays him in front, the offensive team will be in an excellent position to control its own rebound.

When all of the above tactics fail and an offensive player is completely blocked out, he can delay his jump until the blocker is descending, then time his jump with this descent to tip the ball from the outstretched arms of the opponent (see Figure 3–43).

Cutting

Cutting to the basket is a tactic to elude a guard when a teammate has the ball. Cutting successfully requires the use, either individually or in combination, of such maneuvers as change of direction, change of pace, pivots, fakes, stops, starts, and turns (see applicable sections in this chapter). Many players, unfortunately, know neither when nor how to cut. They simply run at top speed, hoping to outdistance the defender.

Although speed is the greatest natural asset a basketball player can have, without finesse it is wasted: when the cutter uses sheer speed, without deception, the defensive guard can adjust for it and neutralize its effectiveness. Timing his movements with the position of the ball, however, the cutter can use whatever methods necessary to gain a step advantage, at which time he can open his stride and attempt to outrun his adversary. If he is open when he approaches the basket, the cutter should raise a hand as a target and shout to catch the passer's attention. Should the cutter be unable to gain a step, he may still gain the advantage by stopping suddenly and facing the passer.

Cuts should always be either in a straight line or in a series of straight lines (broken line), and each fake, feint, change of direction, or change of pace must be quick and sharp. A curved or rounded path allows the defender to cut inside and regain position.

It may be necessary to use many preliminary cuts before loosening a defense sufficiently for a scoring attempt. Often, the passer cannot complete a play to the cutter because of a shift by the defense, poor timing by the cutter, or loss of ball control by the passer. If the cutter does not receive the pass, he should not become discouraged or disgusted but should continue to move.

Although any cut that loosens the defense is effective, purposeless movement is tiring and can interfere with offensive patterns. Good cutting opportunities occur in situations such as when a defender turns his head and momentarily loses sight of the man he is guarding, allowing the man to cut behind him.

Cutting is also purposeful when a player finds himself and his guard so close to a teammate in possession there is danger that the guard will be able to double-up on the teammate and force a held ball. In this instance, the purpose of cutting is to relieve the pressure on the ball.

Often, two cutters will start their movement simultaneously: the player cutting off the ball, using the passer as a screen, is primary; the player starting farthest from the ball is secondary. In this instance, the secondary cutter must watch in the direction

Figure 3–44. Back-door cut.

of the primary cutter and pull off if there is danger of interference. If the secondary cutter and not the primary gets clear, however, the secondary should continue to the basket and shout to draw the passer's attention. A *cut off the ball* is a cut initiated when a player finds himself and his defender on the outside of a teammate in possession of the ball. Unless the teammate is in a pivot position and maneuvering for a shot, the player without possession can use him as a screen to wipe off the defender and cut for the basket.

A *back-door* cut can be used when a player without possession is being overplayed by his guard, between him and the ball. The cut is initiated with a good feint toward the ball, followed by a change of direction—pushing off hard on the foot opposite the direction of the cut. (See Figure 3–44.)

One of the best times to cut is immediately after passing, when the defender tends either to relax, his man having relinquished possession, or to concentrate on intercepting the pass. Either defensive error will open the way for a cut, a quick return pass, and a good scoring opportunity.

When an offensive player discovers early in the game that the man guarding him is weak in defending a particular movement, he should use discretion in exploiting his discovery in order that the opposing coach does not immediately replace the man. By using the move sparingly, while probing for other weaknesses, the cutter will ensure that the play will be available should the need arise for a high-percentage shot late in the game.

Pass Receiving

The way a pass is caught is determined by such factors as the flight path and velocity of the ball, the movement of the receiver, the proximity of defensive players, and the kind of offensive move to be made with the ball after it is received. There are, however, certain fundamental techniques that apply equally to the receiving of any pass. The first of these is *seeing* the ball into the hands. Fumbles, when not caused by the passer, are inevitably the result of the receiver's taking his eye off the ball before it is securely in his hands. The alert player on offense has the ball in constant vision, even though it may be his peripheral vision, whenever his proximity to a teammate having possession is such that a pass between them is likely or possible. Once the ball is in the air, the receiver continues to track it with his peripheral or direct vision until the instant before reception, when he must begin to focus directly on the ball and continue doing so until he has positive, two-hand control. Only then does he divert his attention to the task of dribbling, passing, or shooting.

The principles of hand-eye coordination were discussed at some length in the section on shooting, at the beginning of this chapter. The same principles apply to catching a pass that apply to shooting, though the techniques are reversed. Instead of sighting a stationary target and coordinating the hands to impart an intercept trajectory to a ball, as in shooting, the pass receiver tracks a moving target and coordinates his hands to do the actual intercepting. Catching the ball requires that the kinetic energy associated with its flight be quickly and completely absorbed by the fingers, wrists, and arms of the receiver. With practice, this can be accomplished consistently by focusing the eyes on the surface of the ball as it nears, while consciously anticipating the objective of grabbing and holding it. As a consequence, the hands should move instinctively at the right instant to grasp the ball firmly in the fingertips, spaced comfortably to absorb the spin, the wrists and arms recoiling naturally to absorb the momentum.

Whenever possible, a pass should be caught in both hands, the receiver stepping toward the ball. When the situation demands a one-hand catch, the off hand must be immediately brought up to assist in protection and control. A retreating catch should occur only as the result of a bad pass.

The mental attributes of a pass receiver are alertness for the unexpected pass, relaxed confidence in the sureness of his hands, and disciplined eye concentration.

Receiving Straight Passes. When catching a straight pass in an outside area and with no defensive pressure, the receiver, his eyes on the ball, steps toward the passer with either foot, extending both hands chest high in front of his body, his palms facing each other with fingers widespread. The ball is caught in the fingertips, and the arms recoil naturally toward the chest.

When catching a straight pass in an outside area and with defensive pressure, the receiver steps back with one foot to the side of the defender, blocking him from the ball, extends an arm to the side of the step, and makes a one-hand catch. The fingers of the catching hand are widespread and slightly cupped; the hand and arm yield with the ball, cushioning the force of the pass; the body turns slightly toward the catching hand as the other hand goes up quickly for control; and the ball is grasped firmly in the fingertips of both hands.

Receiving a straight pass while moving away from the passer can be accomplished with either one or both hands, although both hands should be used whenever possible.

A one-hand reception is usually made when cutting at full stride with the defender in pursuit. In this situation, the hand away from the defender is held up as a target, and the off hand comes up for control after the one-hand catch. The timing of passer and receiver should be such that, without breaking stride or lowering the ball, the receiver can follow through for a shot. Should it be necessary to pull the ball in before releasing the shot, the defender may be able to flick the ball out of the receiver's grasp.

Receiving a Pass in the Pivot Area. Receiving a pass in the pivot area requires either that the receiver be moving strongly toward the ball or that he catch the ball with the hand away from the defender. If the pivot man is sure of the defender's position, he may hold up a hand to the opposite side as a target for the passer; otherwise, the passer must himself decide where to put the ball so that it is best received and protected. The techniques for catching the ball are the same as described for receiving a pass in an open area—the fingers widespread, the wrists and forearms recoiling naturally to absorb the force. Pivot men must practice at great length their ability to handle, when under defensive pressure, the various straight, lob, and bounce passes used to feed a pivot. Since bounce passes tend to be low and with a spin, they should always be caught with both hands, the palms facing each other, and the spin absorbed by supple, widespread fingertips. The pivot player must learn to catch lob passes with either hand or both hands and shoot or pass in one motion. A quick pass back to the first passer often produces a score when his defender drops off with the pass-in.

Receiving a Hand-off, or Flip Pass. Players on offense must be able to receive a hand-off perfectly when moving at top speed. (See Figure 3–45.) They must be especially alert when crossing in a congested area with a teammate in possession, since the hand-off is often preceded by a fake and may be hurried by defensive pressure.

Normally, the hand-off, or flip pass, is with little or no spin, and the ball is received, waist high, by a deft, two-hand grab, the

Figure 3–45. Receiving a hand-off pass.

receiver immediately following through with a pass, dribble, or shot. In the pivot area, however, the receiver must be alert for an over-the-shoulder drop pass, a quick bounce pass, or a simple hand-off that may be poorly timed and hurriedly executed.

Individual Offense without the Ball

The ability of a player to function within the framework of the offense when he does not have the ball is as important as his ability to pass, shoot, and dribble. A player without possession must move in such a way as to advance the offense, either by getting open to receive a pass or by drawing the defense away from the ball or a play. Continual evasive maneuvers consisting of stops, starts, and feints in order to get free for a pass, even if unsuccessful, put pressure on the defender and keep him from sagging away from his man to help out inside or double-team the man with the ball. Since, however, an unplanned move is useless and may even interfere with the play action, each player without possession must maneuver intelligently, coordinating his moves with the actions of the player having possession.

In a planned attack, the man with the ball determines the pattern within which the other offensive players regulate their movements. For example, consider a situation in which the team is in a two-three alignment, with a guard dribbling toward the right corner man and with a pivot man in the right, medium pivot area. When the guard passes to the right corner and follows his pass toward the corner man's defender, his movement signals the four other players on offense that the guard intends either to set a screen for the corner man or to attempt a change-of-pace or change-of-direction cut to the basket for a return pass. Therefore, the forward receiving the pass should be prepared to return a pass to the cutter, to take advantage of the screening maneuver, or, if his defender reacts to a fake, to drive along the end line to the basket. The pivot man should move away from the area, using fakes and pivots to draw his defender's attention away from the point of attack. Should the pivot defender remain in the area, however, the pivot man must immediately assume a favorable offensive position, either at the free-throw line or in the low-pivot area on the ball side.

The uninvolved guard should start toward the corner on the opposite side, as if to screen for the opposite-side forward. The move should be timed to cause the guard's defender to turn his attention away from the play. The guard may fake the move-in, however, and then abruptly pull back toward the side of the ball, close enough either to be a safety release for the man in possession, should the play attempt be shut off, or to be in good position to retreat quickly on defense should there be an interception or a lost rebound after a missed shot.

The movements of the far-side forward complement those of the far-side guard; he may either fake an interchange with the guard or feint toward the foul line as if to receive a pass in the middle. Since he is the key rebounder on the side away from the ball, his movements have the dual function of drawing the attention of his defender away from the point of attack and placing himself in the best rebound position, as determined by the rebound position assumed by the pivot man: one of the two should be under the basket, on the side away from the shot; the other, in the free-throw lane about ten feet in front of the basket.

The play of the two or three team members not involved in the principal action is the most difficult of individual-player offensive techniques to teach. Much depends upon the intelligence and self-discipline of the player himself. Not only must he synchronize his actions with those of the other uninvolved team members to decoy defenders away from the play, but he must also be alert to a sudden change in the play's development that calls for his own direct involvement. The following are some of the offensive moves available to a player without the ball:

1. A cut to the ball or basket, at the proper time and without interfering with the play action
2. A screen for a teammate, whether with or away from the ball
3. A properly timed cut off of a teammate's screen, whether the teammate does or does not have possession
4. Maneuvers that will result in best rebound position when a teammate shoots
5. Feints and faking maneuvers that exploit the weaknesses of an individual defender, decoying him to the team's advantage and distracting his attention from the point of attack
6. A quick defensive retreat should the opponents gain possession
7. A move into position for an outlet pass should a teammate have to relinquish possession because of defensive pressure
8. Individually assigned moves for special situations (jump balls, out of bounds, free throws)
9. Countermoves should the defensive team change its tactics; for example, a change from a man-to-man to a press or a zone defense.

The player on offense should constantly remember that even when he does not have the ball his every move has an impact, either negative or positive, on the success or failure of a scoring attempt. Attuning his thinking to that of his teammatses and being aware of the offensive and defensive capabilities of every man on the floor, the accomplished player is involved, directly or indirectly, in the score of every basket.

Coordinating Individual Offensive Techniques into Play Patterns

4

In addition to teaching individual offensive techniques, the coach must coordinate all offensive movements into patterns of play that enhance the effectiveness of those individual skills. Most successful basketball plays involve only two or three offensive players in the play structure at any given time, with the remaining players maneuvering and decoying opponents away from the point of attack.

If a team can outnumber its opponents at the offensive end (one offensive player unopposed, two offensive players against a single defender, three offensive players against two defenders, etc.), it will be successful in scoring a basket most of the time. These opportunities, however, are not always available. The best offensive patterns when an outnumbering advantage is unobtainable are two-on-two and three-on-three. All offensive players must become so well versed in these play patterns that their movement to counter defensive measures is intuitive and reflexive. When more than three offensive players are involved in one pattern, the timing, movement, and ball handling become complex, and the chance for errors increases. The greater the number of players involved, the greater the chances for defensive double-teaming, deflections, or interceptions.

Two-man patterns involve guard with guard, guard with forward, and forward with center. Three-man patterns involve guards and forward; guard, forward, and center; and guards and center. (In alternate terminology, two-man patterns involve point guard and wing, point guard and post, and wing and post; and three-man patterns involve point guard, wing, and post.) All play-ers should be versatile enough to maneuver from more than one position or section of the court, and they must recognize the pattern potential in all areas in order that they may involve themselves, if conditions warrant, or move away with decoy-ing maneuvers to lure their defenders from the attacking area.

Much practice time must be given to two-on-two and three-on-three situations, using a limited court area. Game conditions can be simulated best by using no more than half of the front court.

PLAYS NOT INVOLVING A SCREEN

Most play patterns include a screen, which is a legal maneuver by an offensive player who, without causing contact, delays or prevents an opponent from reaching a desired floor position. The following plays are the only ones that do not require a screen.

Pass-and-Cut. The pass-and-cut, or give-and-go, is a basic offensive play in which a player simply passes (gives) to a team-mate and cuts (goes) to the basket, attempting to break free of his guard and expecting a return pass from his teammate. If the defender moves with the first pass or turns his head, the ensuing cut should be fast and straight. However, a fake, feint, change of direction, or change of pace may be necessary in order to draw a reaction from the guard. When they see the pass-and-cut maneu-ver initiated, other offensive players must decoy their guards away from the basket area and passing lane. If free to receive a pass, the cutter should raise his hand nearest the basket as a passing signal and target. The pass can be a straight pass, a bounce pass, or a lob pass, as the situation warrants.

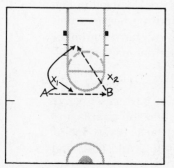

Diagram 4–1. Pass-and-Cut, or Give-and-Go. A passes to B, faking in B's direction to move his own defender, X_1. As X_1 moves towards B, A pushes off his right foot around X_1, cutting di-rectly to the basket. B returns the pass.

DIAGRAM 4–1

Change of Direction. A change of direction (reverse, back-door) cut is used when one guard brings the ball toward the other guard or the forward on his side of the floor when they are closely guarded. As the guard dribbles toward the forward, the man guarding the forward on the left side of the floor will be over-playing him on the ball side to prevent an easy ball exchange. As the guard approaches, the forward will step with his right foot toward the dribbler, decoying the defender toward the ball with him. As the right foot contacts the floor, with the body weight on this foot, the forward pushes hard off this foot and quickly turns toward the basket, shifting the weight and stepping with a short step on the left foot, then crossing with the right foot in full stride to the basket. The body weight is low to facilitate a quick start on the direction change. To lure the defender into overplaying, the dribbler should fake a pass as the right foot of the forward hits the floor. Usually, a bounce pass or high lead pass to the outstretched left hand is used.

Diagram 4–2. Change of Direction, or Reverse Cut. A has the ball; B is on the left sideline. B steps towards A with his right foot. As his foot is coming down, A fakes the pass. X_1 moves out. B pushes off the right foot, takes a short step with his left foot, crosses long with the right foot, and receives a pass behind X_1 from A.

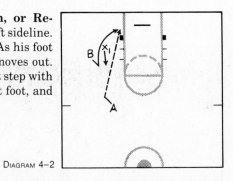

DIAGRAM 4–2

Diagram 4–3. Change of Direction, Inside Cut. B fakes toward the basket, stepping with his left foot and drawing X_1's attention. B pushes off the left foot, takes a short step with the right foot and a long step with the left foot, cutting inside X_1, and receives a pass from A.

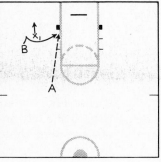

DIAGRAM 4–3

Dummy. The dummy play is a deceptive, nonfake reception of a pass when a cutter or a stationary offensive player near the basket is closely guarded by a defender who is face-guarding or has lost sight of the ball in order to concentrate on his man. The passer should pass the ball over the head of the defender, using either a straight two-hand pass or a lob pass. The receiver must be relaxed and unconcerned, as though he is out of the play. He must make no movement that will alert the defender. As a concentrating defender may be intent on the eyes of the receiver, the dummy must pick up the flight of the ball *without eye movement*, using peripheral vision. When the ball is almost on the defender, the receiver reaches up quickly and catches the ball at the last instant. This maneuver is excellent in out-of-bounds situations.

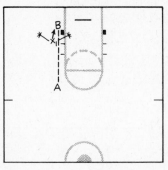

Diagram 4–4. Dummy Play. B is being guarded by X_1. B is in a low-pivot position facing A. X_1 cannot see the ball, since he is looking directly at B with his arms extended or up. B must dummy X_1 into thinking that he is not going to receive the ball. He must remain expressionless, making no movements and not looking directly at the ball. A passes to B. As the ball passes over X_1's head, B must move his arms quickly to catch the ball and shoot in one motion.

DIAGRAM 4–4

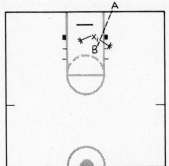

Diagram 4–5. Dummy Play from Out-of-Bounds. This is an excellent out-of-bounds play for big man who is guarded by a smaller opponent.

DIAGRAM 4–5

Making a V to Obtain the Ball. This movement begins with a fake toward the basket and a push off the far foot back toward the ball in order to receive a pass. This maneuver is the basic method that any potential pass receiver must use from any location on the court to free himself from a close-guarding defender. (Diagram 4–6[1]).

Receiving an Inside Hand-off. Play situations can be determined by the man guarding the potential pass receiver. If the guard allows for passage between him and the offensive man, the passer should nod as he passes to indicate that he wishes the ball

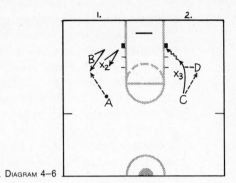

DIAGRAM 4-6

back (Diagram 4-6[2]). If the guard closes, the offense can use an inside screen. All players should be alert to good cuts by teammates towards the basket or towards good shooting areas when their defensive opponents are in poor position with respect to the ball. Any time an offensive player can cut inside his defender and receive a pass within fifteen feet of the basket, he is in excellent shooting area and should be given the ball. This play may be made at the strong side guard to forward (Diagram 4-7[1]) or forward to guard (Diagram 4-7[2]), or it may be made to a forward on the weak side when the ball is in possession of a guard on the opposite side, if the keyhole area is open.

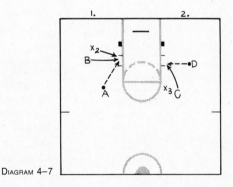

DIAGRAM 4-7

PLAYS INVOLVING A SCREEN

Screens are involved in all other play patterns. A screen can be set as close to an opponent as desired, short of contact, so long as the screening player is in the normal field of vision of the opponent and the opponent can avoid contact. Outside the field of vision, a screener must be far enough away from the opponent to allow him a normal step. Screens can be stationary or moving, with or without the ball, inside a defender (between the defender and the basket), outside a defender (between the defender and the offensive teammate that he is guarding), or to either side of a defender. If a screener is moving, he must be moving in the same direction as the defensive player he is screening. It is important that all players know how to screen and how to cut or dribble off a screen, because when offensive balance and defensive balance are equal, screening is the best way to obtain an offensive advantage. The primary function of a screen is to free the cutter or dribbler for a good shooting opportunity. The secondary purpose is to beat a switching maneuver by defense by taking advantage of inside position resulting from the exchange in defensive responsibility.

Inside Screen. When the defender is close to the offensive player being screened for, the screener should be inside the defender, closer to the basket.

Diagram 4–8. Inside Screen. A has passed to B and has moved into position between B's guard, X_1, and the basket. He is setting an inside screen for B.

DIAGRAM 4–8 _____

Diagram 4–9. Inside Hand-off. A has passed to B. He moves between B and X_2 (B's defender), receives an inside hand-off, and dribbles into the basket. A must always signal the intent for an inside hand-off, perhaps by nodding his head as he passes the ball to B.

DIAGRAM 4–9 _____

Outside Screen. When the defender is loose, the screener should be outside the defender, between the defender and the teammate he is guarding.

Diagram 4–10. Outside Screen. A passes to B. Since X_2, B's guard, has dropped back, playing B loosely, A screens outside X_2 between him and B.

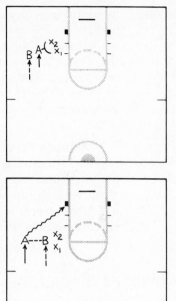

Diagram 4–10

Diagram 4–11. Outside Hand-off. A has passed to B and has cut behind him. A receives a hand-off pass outside B. (A hand-off is the normal procedure whenever an offensive player passes to a teammate and cuts behind him.) A may dribble in to the basket or shoot a set shot.

Diagram 4–11

Lateral Screen. When the defender is guarding an offensive player in such a way that lateral screening, or side screening, may open the offensive player for a jump shot, a set shot, or a drive or cut to the basket, the screener stops on either side of the teammate's guard. An advantage to the lateral screen is that it comes in the field of vision of the defender, so it can be set very close to him with a widespread foot base, making it very difficult for him to avoid being screened legally.

Back Screen. When an offensive player moves behind a stationary teammate who has the ball, or dribbles behind a teammate, a back screen is being set up. Both defenders will be inside, closer to the basket than the offensive men.

Rear Screen. When a forward or pivot player moves behind a defender from a position out of the visual field of that defender, he sets up a rear screen. It is an inside screen that is set by a player moving from a close-to-the-basket position to the rear of the opponent. An excellent rear-screen maneuver is to have the pivot player break from his position toward the ball possessor, who passes to him. The pass is usually high, so the pivot man jumps and catches it in the air. He must be well in front of his guard as he moves into the ball from directly behind the passer's defender. As the pivot player contacts the floor, he pivots toward the basket, holding the ball over his head. The passer-in cuts off the pivot man, to either side, running his guard into the pivot's rear screen. The pivot man passes to the cutter if no switch is made or dribbles in for an easy lay-up himself if his defender switches to the cutter.

Double Screen. A double screen is set when two offensive players stop in a shoulder-to-shoulder position, parallel to, perpendicular to, or oblique to, the end line, anywhere within shooting distance of the basket. Many set offensive patterns use a double-screen maneuver to obtain good jump shooting and cutting opportunities.

OFFENSIVE ROLL

If an offensive player is not facing the basket when he sets an inside, double, or lateral screen, either stationary or moving, he must know the techniques of the offensive roll, a pivoting maneuver used by a screener after the teammate he screened for cuts off the screen. The screener pivots on the left foot taking a long step toward the basket with his right, when the cutter goes to the screener's right side; he pivots on the right foot, taking a long step toward the basket with his left, when the cutter has cut to the screener's left side. The pivoting foot should slide imperceptibly toward the screened opponent for body balance and to initiate and facilitate this rolling action. This foot movement should be simultaneous with the cutting action of the teammate screened for. The push is off the pivot foot, with the arm and shoulder of the stepping-foot side swinging hard in the direction of the pivot to speed up the turning action. This foot steps directly toward the basket before contacting the floor. Body balance must be maintained through a low center of gravity while in motion, therefore the knees are flexed and the hips lowered to effect proper weight control. The screener must anticipate defensive pressure during this maneuver and counteract its force by keeping the body balance centered above the foot spread, using the opponent's force to accentuate his own into-the-basket movement to beat the switch. When a lateral screen is made facing the end line, the pivot is made on the inside foot (right foot on the left side, left foot on the right side), rolling into the basket as the cutter comes off the screen, with the screener looking for a return pass if the defense switches or for inside rebounding position if the cutter shoots.

The offensive roll allows the screener to pivot and face toward his original position and the ball to receive a pass for a jump shot if both defenders concentrate on the cutter or to become a trailer if the cutter is moving into the basket with the ball. The roll also prevents a blocking foul on the screener if the cutter's guard is moving backward toward the screener without room to avoid contact.

SCREENING PRINCIPLES

If possible, players should adhere to the principles that apply to player movement when a cutter or dribbler is screened for.

When an inside or lateral screen is made, the cutter or dribbler should always move off the screener toward the direction from which the screen came. If a guard on the left screens for a forward on that side, the guard moving from the outside toward the end line, the forward should cut behind the screener to the outside. When a rear screen or a double screen is set, the cutter or dribbler may cut to either side of the screen. The screener determines the type of screen he will position for; the cutter or dribbler must cut closely off the screen, timing his movement so that the defender is in fact impeded by the screen.

The position of the defensive opponent guarding the player being screened for dictates the screening maneuver. When the defender is close, the screener may pass to the teammate if possible, or dribble in and set an inside screen or a lateral screen. The inside screen should be used whenever practicable, preferably with the screener facing the basket. While the screen can be set with the screener facing any direction, facing toward the basket allows the greatest visual field for the screener, and it allows quick movement toward the basket without pivoting.

When the defender is playing loose (three to four feet or more away) an outside screen should be used. As a shot over the screen is the first offensive option in this situation, the player being screened for must be within his accurate shooting range. Should the defender close in on the player being screened for as the screener is moving into position, the screener must change to an inside or lateral screen. He may also go behind this teammate and set a back screen for himself, if this position is within his accurate set-shooting range.

Whenever a screen is set for an offensive player, he must cut off the screen, unless defensive adjustments make a different maneuver more practical. For example, if a forward has received a pass from the guard on his side who follows the pass to set an inside screen, and the forward's defender shifts toward the screen to neutralize its effectiveness, the defender leaves the end line open for a drive. The forward does not cut off the screen, because the defensive adjustment gives the forward a better-percentage offensive maneuver.

Whenever the man being screened for does not have the ball, a cut must be made. If the screener has the ball, the cut will relieve defensive pressure at the point of attack. If the ball is not in the possession of either the screener or the cutter, the cut will open a congested area and perhaps clear this area for an optional offensive play.

Any time a defender picks up his man in the back court or near the mid-court line, and the ball is closer to the offensive basket than this defender and the offensive player he is guarding, the player in possession should dribble into a position between the defensive man and the basket. The guarded teammate should move slowly up-court, delaying his forward progress until the dribbler is in position. Then he should cut as close off the dribbler as possible, so that the defensive guard cannot slide through. The dribbler must maintain his dribble, because he will be able to drive into the basket if his guard switches. If there is no switch, the dribbler can pass to the free cutter. All other offensive teammates must move their defenders away from the direct cutting, passing, or dribbling lane to the basket.

This principle (cutting off the ball whenever the ball's position is between any offensive player's guard and the basket) applies at all times except when a low or medium pivot is in possession and maneuvering for a close-in shot. When an inside screener has the ball and a defensive switch to the cutter takes place, the screener is open for a shot, or if dribbling, he may drive.

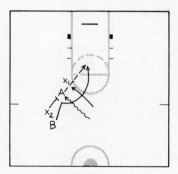

Diagram 4–12. Cutting off the Ball, or a Runaround. A dribbles directly in line between B's defender (X_2) and the basket. B moves X_2 into A and cuts close off A toward the basket, receiving a pass if open.

DIAGRAM 4–12 _____

When the player cutting off an inside screen is in possession and a defensive switch is made, the screener, if facing the basket, should step toward the basket with the foot opposite the side the cutter comes over. If his back is to the basket, he should use the offensive roll. The player in possession should pass to the screener as soon as the defensive switch maneuver takes place. At that instant, the passing lane is widest, because the switching defender is intent on stopping the dribbler, and the screened defender has not had time to readjust his defensive position inside to protect against the screener. The best pass to use in this situation is a quick bounce pass, although a lead two-hand pass (chest or overhead) or lob pass can be used also.

Diagram 4–13. Passing to the Screener on a Switch. A has passed to B and screened inside B's defender, X_2. B dribbles off the screen to his right, the direction from which the screen came. X_1, A's guard, switches to B as B dribble drives for the basket. At X_1's switch, B passes immediately to A. It is important that the ball be passed as the switch is made, since that is when the opening is the widest and both defenders are generally intent on the driver.

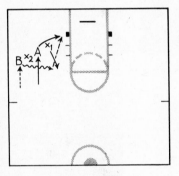

DIAGRAM 4–13

When a screen is set, the player using it must follow proper cutting procedure. He must determine where the best screening spot will be and maneuver effectively, using fakes and feints if necessary, to gain time and position before moving off the screen. The cutter may, for example, take his defender below the screen and change direction, coming back hard toward the screen, running as close to the screener as possible to prevent the defender from sliding between the offensive players.

Diagram 4–14. Screening Away from the Ball Position. C, at the head and to the right of the key, has the ball. A has set an inside screen for B. B cuts tightly off A's screen. If there is no switch, B is free underneath for a basket. If X_1 switches, B should go straight across the foul lane and A should make an offensive roll to the basket. C would pass to A on the offensive roll.

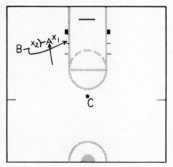

DIAGRAM 4–14

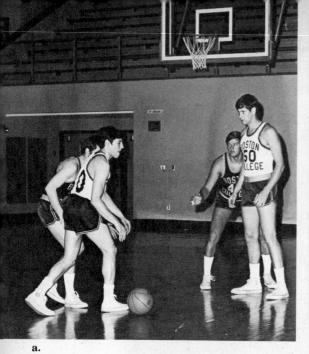

a.

b.

c.

d.

Diagram 4–15. Taking Advantage of a Switch. B, the tall forward, has set a lateral screen for A, the guard. A dribbles off B's lateral screen. X_2 switches to pick up A, the dangerous offensive player. B uses an offensive roll into the basket. He now has the smaller defender, X_1, guarding him. He assumes a pivot position, taking advantage of the usual mismatch in size, and anticipates a pass from A. The option here will be to allow A to go one-on-one with the bigger defender, X_2, outmaneuvering this defender while B draws X_1 away. —————————

——— DIAGRAM 4–15

When two offensive players cut off a teammate in any pivot position, the player who passes into the pivot man is always the first cutter, moving in the direction the first cutter comes from to set the moving screen. The first cutter can stop to set a stationary screen for the second cutter, hesitating long enough to free the teammate, then continue with his cut if open, fall back for defensive protection, or assume rebound position if a shot is taken. Defensive realignment determines the offensive techniques.

All players should anticipate defensive switching maneuvers and take advantage of the offensive benefits that can result. When a guard and forward or center combine in a two-on-two offensive pattern, and a defensive switch is made, a big defender will usually be guarding the smaller offensive player while the smaller defender guards the taller offensive man. The smaller offensive player should pass into the pivot area, to a taller teammate who has a shorter opponent. (See Figure 4–1.) The taller offensive player in the pivot area should also realize that his shorter teammate will probably have quicker maneuvering ability than his taller defender and be ready to clear the pivot area if no play is made into the pivot mismatch (short defender guarding taller offensive player). The better play in this mismatch situation is usually to make the play into the pivot area, because if the taller offensive player has position, an excellent scoring possibility is present with the probability of a three-point play resulting as well.

Figure 4–1. Taking advantage of a switch: *a*, guard dribbles off forward's lateral screen; *b*, guard's close dribble necessitates switch; *c*, forward uses offensive roll, taking smaller defender in close to basket; *d*, guard passes in to take advantage of mismatch (note two-hand overhead pass).

TWO-ON-TWO PLAY PATTERN TECHNIQUES

The most common play patterns in two-on-two situations are guard-and-guard plays, guard-and-forward plays, guard-and-center plays, and forward-and-center plays. The techniques are similar in the guard-to-guard and guard-to-forward combinations, but in the latter, as in the guard- or forward-to-center combination, the probability exists that a switch will result in a short man defending a taller offensive man, and vice versa.

Outside-Screen or Back-Screen Plays

These are among the most important two-on-two maneuvers in basketball. The outside-screen or back-screen play maneuvers are used when two offensive players, the one farther out in possession of the ball, are one behind the other, farther from the basket than their defenders.

These screening positions are most common when guards cross laterally, the guard closer to the basket hands off to the other guard crossing behind him, and both stop and turn to face the basket, or when a guard passes to the forward on his side of the court who is being played loose and follows his pass to set up behind a stationary outside screen. The guard can also dribble in and hand-off to the forward, who is behind him.

The player in possession after the pass should always remain alive and be within his accurate set-shot range. If neither defender forces over the screen, the player in possession takes a set shot. If one defender moves toward the ball over one side of the stationary screen (see Figure 4–2), the man in possession should drive to the opposite side, and the screener should step toward the basket, stepping first with the foot closest to the defender who is moving toward the handler, keeping the defender behind him while breaking to the basket. (This first step with the correct foot is all important. If the far foot steps first, a quick-reacting defensive player may regain good defensive position on the screener.) The dribbler should continue to the basket or to a good shooting position unless the other defender attacks him. If that happens, he should pass immediately to the screener. The best passing lane opens as soon as the second defender moves into his path to play him, as that defender has now committed himself, and the screener, who has position on the first defender, is moving into the basket. Both offensive players should be alert for defensive switches that result in mismatches in size if the defenders regain good defensive positions.

a.

b.

Figure 4–2. Two-on-two outside screen: *a*, no.
43 sets screen; *b*, screener's guard steps toward
ball while screener steps to basket with right
foot; *c*, dribbler passes to cutting screener.

c.

The forward's approximate position should be between
twelve and fifteen feet from the end line and between six and nine
feet from the sideline when he receives the pass-in from the guard
on his side. This general location can be approximated quickly
by establishing the catching position at two or three steps from
the sideline tangent to the front half of the free-throw circle. Correct positioning is important, because the forward must be able
to drive either left or right. If placement is too close to the end

line, there may not be enough room to drive in that direction. If the defensive man guarding the forward moves in to a close-guarding position, the guard can adjust his position while moving in, using an inside screen or going behind the forward to set up a back screen for himself. The forward uses a hand-off pass or flip pass to the guard behind him, and the same offensive procedure described above is followed, reversing the positions. The guard-to-forward play pattern is one of the basic two-on-two plays in basketball. It must be practiced at length by all players so that correct movement becomes instinctive and can be executed rapidly and precisely before defensive assistance can be deployed by the opponents.

DIAGRAM 4–16

Diagram 4–16. Outside-Screen Play. (This is also applicable if A goes behind B, setting a back screen, with B handing the ball to A.) A passes to B. X_2 is playing B loosely, providing an opportunity for an outside screen. A sets the outside screen, facing the basket. The defenders, X_1 and X_2, are side by side guarding A and B. The options: (1) B may set shoot over A's outside screen if the screen is set within B's percentage shooting range. (2) If X_2 moves around A on the baseline side, B drives opposite, to his right. As X_2 comes around, A will step toward the basket with his left foot, pinning X_2 behind him. Then he will step with his right foot as B is dribbling. If X_1 picks up B on his movement right, B passes immediately to A, who is inside X_2. (3) If X_1 moves around A on the outside, B will start his dribble to the left. A will step toward the basket with his right foot, to keep X_1 behind him, and then step with the left, expecting a pass from B. (4) B may make a jump shot if the defensive pickup of X_1 or X_2 is slow. (5) B may drive into the basket if he is free.

Lateral Screens

Lateral screens are used in guard and guard, guard and forward, forward and center, and guard and high-pivot center situations when an outside screen or inside screen is not expedient, or when a lateral screen will open a teammate for a good close-in or medium jump-shot opportunity. A lateral screen is set with the screener's body perpendicular to that of the opponent being screened.

Guard-to-Guard. In the guard-to-guard play, the man with the ball may hand off to his teammate crossing behind him

Figure 4–3. Lateral screen: *a*, no. 43 sets screen; *b*, ball handler dribbles off screen; *c*, lateral screener slides right foot and rolls on switch; *d*, dribbler passes to screener after his offensive roll.

and set a lateral screen, or a player can set a lateral screen for the dribbler as the dribbler crosses behind him. In either case, the screener can stop close to the defender, because the defender can see the screening movement. (See Figure 4–3.)

When the man with the ball hands off or passes to the dribbler and sets a lateral screen, he should stop and use an offensive roll immediately after the teammate moves by him. Stepping imperceptibly toward the second opponent, in the direction of the end line, with the foot nearest the end line he pivots on that foot, away from the opponent he has screened. With this move he avoids causing any contact and obtains and holds an inside advantage on that opponent if there is a defensive switch. His non-pivot foot steps directly toward the basket. He should continue toward the basket quickly with his inside hand up as a target for a pass if defense exchanges assignments. If a defensive switch occurs, the best passing lane opens immediately after the defensive exchange is made.

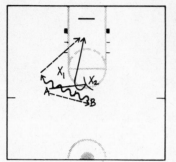

DIAGRAM 4–17

Diagram 4–17. Lateral Screen, Guard for Guard. A has passed to B, then moved into position setting a lateral screen on guard X_2, B's defender. B, on receiving the ball, dribbles hard to his left off the screen. Just as B begins his movement, A slides his left foot imperceptibly toward the left corner. It is a very slight adjustment. As he makes this slide, X_2, moving to stay with B, bumps into A, causing him to pivot on his left foot. A then takes a long 180-degree-arc swing with his right foot so that he steps directly toward the basket. He is now in front of X_2. B makes a return pass to A if X_1 switches. The lateral screen is set with A's body perpendicular to the direction of X_2's body.

Guard-to-Forward. The guard-to-forward lateral screen is an excellent method of forcing a defensive switch that will put a smaller defender on the taller forward, who can take advantage of pivot maneuvers in close to the basket. The guard may pass in and screen for the forward or he may dribble in and use a hand-off or flip pass to the forward, who cuts behind him. If the forward has the ball, he may pass back to the guard and come out of the corner position to lateral screen for the guard. A dribble out and lateral screen utilizing the hand-off or flip pass to the guard may also be used.

When the guard lateral screens for the forward, the guard is generally facing the end line. As the forward cuts behind him, the guard should step slightly toward the end line with his inside foot and pivot, or pivot immediately without the step, depending on which alternative is most likely to keep the forward's defender behind him in case of a switch. The pivot is on the inside foot, the outside foot and leg turning through a greater-than-180-degree arc before contacting the floor, facing the body toward the opposite sideline and into the basket. Quick movement toward the basket following this pivot turn is essential. The shielding of the defender through the pivot maneuver and the resultant pressure of the defender in attempting to regain defensive position will accentuate this starting speed. If a defensive switch is made,

and a good shooting opportunity is not available to guard or forward during the play pattern, the guard should quickly back out
to the forward's original position to receive a pass out from the
forward, who now has the smaller defender guarding him. Either
a fake-and-drive maneuver by the guard, with the forward clearing the area, or a return pass to the forward in good pivot position
should be attempted. Teammates of these offensive players must
recognize the play potential at the attack point and steer their
opponents accordingly.

**Diagram 4–18. Lateral Screen, Guard for For-
ward.** B is in the forward position; A is a guard.
A has set a lateral screen for B. B dribbles off,
anticipating a switch by X_1, A's defender. A, as
B starts his movement, slides his right foot imperceptibly toward the left corner as X_2 moves to
guard B. X_2 bumps A. A's left foot now makes a
180-degree arc, he pivots on right foot, and ends
up facing the basket. B passes to A on the switch.
A's facing position is perpendicular to X_2's position.

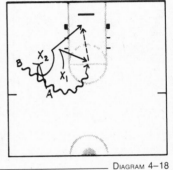

DIAGRAM 4–18

**Diagram 4–19. Lateral Screen, Forward for
Guard.** The forward, B, has passed to Guard A
and set a lateral screen for A. As A starts his
dribble to the left, tightly off the screen so that
X_1 can't slide through, B slides his left foot
slightly forward toward the foul lane. As X_1
moves to stay with A, he bumps B. B makes a
180-degree-arc swing, pivoting on the left foot
and swinging the right foot and leg, stepping toward the basket with this foot. As A comes off the
screen, X_2, B's defender, switches; therefore, A
passes to B, who moved inside X_1 on the offensive
roll.

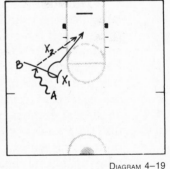

DIAGRAM 4–19

Forward-to-Center. Many times a pass in to the pivot man
from the forward and a protective return pass to the forward necessitated by defensive pressure in the pivot area leaves the forward fairly deep in the corner. A pass out to the guard may be
impractical because his defender is overplaying at an intercepting
angle and the guard's reverse, or back-door, cut doesn't open him
for a pass. A rear screen by the pivot man is impractical, as the
forward is too close to the end line. In such a situation, the pivot
man should take a lateral screening position on the outside of the

forward's defensive opponent, permitting the forward to drive to the middle or into the outer free-throw area. The pivot will be facing into the near corner when he lateral screens. As the forward drives off the screen, the pivot man should pivot on the foot nearer the basket and raise the hand nearer the basket as a target for the forward in case a defensive switch is made. This is excellent territory for a quick lob pass to the center, or possibly a bounce pass if there is no congestion in the area.

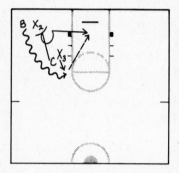

Diagram 4–20. Lateral Screen, Center for Forward. The center cannot use a rear screen in this case, because B has only one direction in which to drive. C is facing into the left corner of the court. B drives toward the middle, outside C. As B starts his movement, C slides his right foot slightly toward the corner, and X_2 bumps C, accentuating his pivot movement on the right foot so that the left foot swings 180 degrees. As X_3, C's defender, switches, B passes in to C.

DIAGRAM 4–20 _____

Guard-to-Center. An opportunity for a guard-to-center lateral screen usually appears when the center is in a high-pivot position and the guard has received a pass out from the forward on his side. The screening area for the center is to the side-center, left or right, between an imaginary extension of the free-throw line and the top of the free-throw circle. As the guard receives the outlet pass from the forward, the center positions himself close on the side of the guard's defender. The guard drives off the screen into the free-throw-line area. If no switch is made, the guard can take the fifteen-foot jump shot or he can drive into the basket for a lay-up, but he should anticipate either forward's defender stepping into his dribbling path. If that occurs, the pass-off should be made to the side the pressure comes from, because if either forward's defender moves into the free-throw line in anticipation of the driving move, that forward should be moving into the open under-the-basket area expecting the pass-off from the guard. If a switch is made, the guard should make a short lob pass to the center, who should have pivoted into the free-throw lane toward the basket. The center should expect the high lob pass, because on the switch he is picked up by a much shorter opponent whose stature negates a bounce pass. The passer must see a clear passing lane, however, because a defender guarding a forward will probably move into the area.

In all lateral screening situations the screener must know how to execute the offensive roll for full advantage in case of a defensive switch. The screener can never pivot prematurely, as moving too soon will allow the defender to fight over the top of the screen and nullify its effectiveness. If the lateral position is held too long, the opponent being screened can regain position and destroy the inside position advantage the screener should secure.

When a lateral screen is used with a third offensive teammate in possession of the ball, the cutter should take a switching defensive player away from the point of attack if he is not clear in order to open a passing lane and allow the screener to receive a pass from the teammate in possession. Many times the switching defender picking up the offensive player cutting off the screen will anticipate a pass-in to the screener after the switch, therefore the cutter should maneuver to attract the complete attention of his guard. If the guard leaves him, the cutter must position himself quickly for the best offensive advantage, as he will be free for a shot.

Diagram 4–21. Lateral Screen with the Ball Away from the Screening Area. B has passed to A, then moved in to set a lateral screen for D. Defenders X_2 and X_4 are concentrating on the cutter, D. B's initial position was low, near X_4. D cuts to the right off the screen. (He always cuts in the direction from which the screen came.) X_2 switches and moves with D on his cut. X_4 also moves with D. B pivots slightly on the left foot and swings the right foot 180 degrees back toward the ball. B's new position is facing the ball. A passes to B. B, on his roll back toward the ball, gets the ball for a short jump shot.

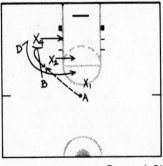

DIAGRAM 4–21

Inside Screen and Rear Screen

All set offensive play patterns use the inside screen as a basic technique in attempting to provide open shooting opportunities. The inside screen and the rear screen are the best methods of impeding the defense for a cutter in order to gain an advantage when a third offensive player has the ball. They are also excellent screens for out-of-bounds plays.

In setting the inside screen, the screener must take a position that will place him in the direct line between the defender

Figure 4-4. Inside screen: *a*, player with ball dribbles; *b*, defenders switch (note open passing lane).

being screened and the basket. The screen can be either stationary or moving; with the ball at the screening area or away from it. The onus is on the screener to position himself so that the cutter, using deploying or delaying fakes and feints, can cut close to the screen quickly, preventing his defender from remaining in good defensive position. Proper timing of the cut, considering the status and position of the ball and the location of the screen, is the responsibility of the cutter. If the defenders switch, the cutter must continue along his path to open the passing lane into the screener, who has the inside path to the basket since the screened defender is behind him. (See Figure 4-4.)

When a player has set an inside screen from fifteen to twenty feet out from the basket and away from the ball, he should execute

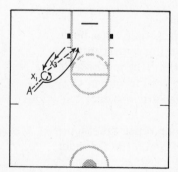

Diagram 4-22. Rear Screen. C, in a medium-pivot position, has moved up quickly from behind X_1, A's defender. A passes to C. C catches the ball in the air, lands, and pivots immediately to face the basket. He must be far enough from X_1 to act as a rear screen out of X_1's sight. A moves X_1 into C, then cuts to the basket. C passes to A. If there is a switch, C does not pass to A, and C is open for a shot or a one-bounce drive into the basket.

DIAGRAM 4-22

an offensive roll toward the ball position after the cutter has gone by. The defenders of both the screener and the cutter are usually intent on minimizing the effectiveness of the cutter, and they underestimate the potential of the screener. Using the roll, the screener can maneuver himself into excellent medium-range shooting territory and usually be free for a shot without extreme defensive pressure.

When executing an inside or rear screen the screener should face the basket whenever possible, because if defense switches, the screened opponent will bump the screener toward the basket in his effort to regain defensive position as the cutter goes by. The dribbler can use a change-of-pace dribble to advantage when setting an inside screen against a switching defensive team by maintaining his dribble, hesitating, anticipating a switch or movement by his defender to delay the cutter when the cutter uses the screen, and quickly resuming a fast driving dribble into the basket to outmaneuver his defender.

When using an inside or rear screen, the screener must be careful to allow room for a normal step by the opponent being screened. Since these screens are set out of the visual field of the screened defender, the responsibility for ensuing contact rests with the screener. Because the screener must be cautious in positioning for the inside screen, the cutter must maneuver his defender into the screen. (See Figure 4–5.) If the defender is playing close, the cutter should take his man below, or even with, the screen, using change-of-pace or change-of-direction maneuvers to position the defender so that the cutter can cut hard and tight off the screen. If the defender is playing loose, the cutter should back

Figure 4–5. Drive off a screen.

the man into the screen by moving directly toward it and using head and shoulder fakes to disguise his final movement off the screen.

THREE-ON-THREE PLAY PATTERN TECHNIQUES

The most common type of three-on-three play in basketball is *splitting the post*, or *scissoring off the post*. It utilizes an inside screen and a rear screen and involves the high-pivot man and both guards or a medium-pivot man and the forward and guard on the ball side.

The high-pivot man moves into a position in the outer half of the free-throw circle. As he reaches position, the ball is passed in from either guard. The pivot man is facing mid-court, his back to the basket, with a well-balanced foot spread. He must be extremely protective of the ball, as there will be much congestion in the area. The passer-in cuts first, hesitating slightly then following his pass, from left to right or right to left, cutting close off the pivot man. The second guard cuts closely behind the moving first cutter in the opposite direction, timing his cut so that his defender is impeded in the crossing maneuver.

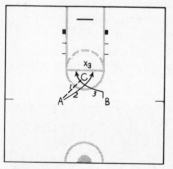

Diagram 4–23. Scissor Movement, Basic. This play involves two guards, A and B, and the center. A passes to C, the pivot man, and cuts to the right. B fakes a step, then cuts to the left. The passer is always the first cutter, going to the outside of the pivot. The other cutter cuts behind the first cutter in a scissor movement.

DIAGRAM 4–23 _____

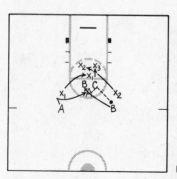

Diagram 4–24. Scissor Movement Used with Shot over Double Screen. C receives a pass from B, who moves in his original scissor movement to the outside of his pass. A fakes and completes the scissor. X_1, A's defender, slides back behind B and C to negate the effectiveness of A's cut. A stops, receives a pass from C, and shoots an 18-foot jump shot over the double screen set by B and C.

DIAGRAM 4–24 _____

The pivot man must quickly assess the defensive reactions to determine whether the first cutter or the second cutter will be in the more advantageous scoring position. He must also be aware of his own defender's reaction. After handing off to either guard, the pivot man should step toward the basket with the foot to the side he handed off on and move in quickly toward the basket. This step opens his body position toward the ball side, allowing for a quick return pass (generally a high lob pass) if his defender switches to the cutter and bringing him into good rebounding position in case the man in possession shoots.

Defensive tactics used to upset the scissoring action can be neutralized easily by using optional splitting-the-post maneuvers. Some defensive pivot players will overplay to the side where the play initiated, expecting the second cutter, who will come this way, to receive the pass. The post defender can step in and draw the offensive charge. The pivot man should observe this defensive shift, using a slight head turn and peripheral vision. A good fake hand-off and a step to the basket with the foot opposite the post defender's position, a pivot, and a one-bounce dribble will free the pivot man for a lay-up. The pivot man may also take a medium turn-around one-hand shot.

Diagram 4–25. Scissor Movement–Pivot Technique. B has passed to C and started his cut. The pivot man, C, observes his defender, X_3, move to the right in anticipation of B's cut. A delays his cut on seeing the defensive deployment. C pivots on the right foot and steps toward the basket with a long left stride. C may (1) dribble to the basket or (2) take a jump shot.

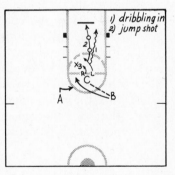

DIAGRAM 4–25

Many guard defenders in a split-the-post attack drop back to about a step in front of the pivot and automatically switch on the crossing guards. To negate this defensive tactic, the second cutter can change direction immediately after starting his cut behind his teammate and go through on the same side as the first cutter; or the first cutter can stop in front of a defender on the same side that he passed in from instead of crossing, and the second guard can stop behind the pivot-and-guard double screen for a medium-range shot.

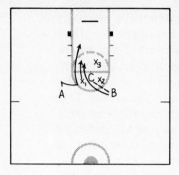

Diagram 4–26. Scissor Movement When Defenders Anticipate the Scissor and Switch Prematurely. B passes to C and cuts. A starts his cut behind B. He observes that X_2 has stopped following B and that his own guard, X_1, will pick up B. A changes direction immediately and cuts to the same side of the pivot as B.

DIAGRAM 4–26 _____

The splitting-the-post maneuver can also be used by a medium pivot and the forward and guard on the ball side. Usually the forward makes the pass in to the pivot and cuts first, with the guard timing his cut behind the forward. Many good shooting opportunities open up in this maneuver. If the forward receives the hand-off pass as the first cutter, he is in excellent range for a short fake-and-jump-shot. The guard, cutting behind the forward, is also in good short jump-shooting range if the defense drops back, and the guard can also continue into the basket for a lay-up if the defense is screened. The pivot man should step to the basket and open to the side of the hand-off, as he will have inside position if his defender switches. Many shooting opportunities for step-away one-handers, hook shots, or turn-around jump shots may be available to the pivot player. It is important that the two offensive teammates not involved in these play patterns lure their defenders away from the point of attack and retreat so that they give good defensive balance if the ball is intercepted or possession is lost in the rebounding action.

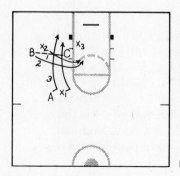

Diagram 4–27. Scissor Movement Using the Center, Forward, and Guard. (1) Forward, B, passes into pivot, C. (2) B cuts to the outside of his pass. (3) A, the guard, fakes and cuts off B's movement.

DIAGRAM 4–27 _____

THREE-OUT–TWO-IN SCREENING MANEUVERS

Many excellent medium-range shooting opportunities can be obtained from a three-out–two-in pattern when three players coordinate their movements using inside screens. It is especially effective in obtaining a good medium-range jump-shot for an outstanding shooter. Any of the five players can be set up for this shot. To set up the left corner man, the left outside man passes to the outside middle man and follows the pass, setting an inside screen. The middle man dribbles close off the screen to the left, causing his defender to slide through between the screener and the screener's defender. The left corner man, alerted for and anticipating the movement, starts away from the screening area toward the basket. The middle man, dribbling with the ball, inside (or lateral) screens close to the left end of the free-throw lane or closer to the basket if possible. The left corner man, who has changed direction, comes back hard behind the screen for a medium-range shot. (If the middle man cuts free off the first screen, the left corner man can continue on under the basket to open the left side for the driver.)

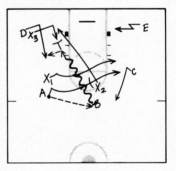

Diagram 4–28. Three-Man Screen Weave (Medium Jump Shot for a Good Shooter). A, in possession of the ball, passes to B, then moves across the lane to set an inside screen for B. B dribbles off the inside screen. A moves away, decoying X_1 away from the ball area with him. D fakes to the baseline and cuts back behind B's dribble screen. This is now an outside screen. D gets a hand-back or drop-back pass from B and shoots a jumper over the screen.

DIAGRAM 4–28

This maneuver can be used to set up a shot for any offensive player (except a pivot man) from any offensive alignment. We call the maneuver *Get One For*. It obtains a medium jumper after a fast three-man weave.

In this weave, or figure eight, a player sets up a shot for a designated teammate. The passer or dribbler who initiates the movement should be adjacent to the player to be set up. He passes or hands off to a player on his right to get one for a designated teammate to his left and vice versa. After his pass, he screens for the receiver, who passes to, or dribbles and hands off to, the teammate the team wishes to get one for. This potential shooter receives the ball and shoots over his passer's screen. This type of tight, cutting, screening weave is applicable to any type of offense.

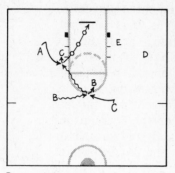

DIAGRAM 4-29

Diagram 4–29. Get-One-For Weave from a Two-Three Offensive Alignment. In this offense we are getting one for A, the left forward. B starts the movement by passing or dribbling away from A. C fakes, changes direction, receives a hand-off and a screen from B, and continues laterally toward the left corner. A fakes to the baseline, comes behind C's dribble move, and receives a hand-off pass. He takes one or two bounces and shoots if the defensive deployment permits.

DIAGRAM 4-30

Diagram 4–30. Get-One-For Weave from the Tandem Alignment. In this offense, A is at the point, B and C are at the right lane, and D and E are at the left lane. While we only need three men, we are using the other two players on the court to show offensive balance and deployment. We are getting one for D. A dribbles to the right side, and C comes behind him. A hands-off and holds the screen, and C dribbles across the lane. D comes behind E and C and receives the ball. He dribbles and takes an intermediate jump shot at the basket. The timing of D's initial move is crucial. (This weave can also be implemented using passing only.)

TWO-OUT–THREE-IN SCREENING MANEUVERS

A series of inside and rear screens can be set from a two-out–three-in offensive pattern without the ball. The guards can control the ball in the backcourt, and as it is passed to the right, the low-pivot or medium-pivot man can use a rear screen for the right forward, who cuts to the basket. If the defense does not switch, the forward may be open for a shot; if they do switch, the pivot will be inside his defender for a shot. If nothing materializes, the right forward continues to his left and screens to the inside for the left forward, the pivot man moving to a position in the right corner. The ball passes from the right guard outside to the left guard. The left forward cuts off the right forward's screen into the basket, and the right forward rolls, anticipating a pass if the defense switches. If no good shooting opening appears, the left forward continues to the right to screen for the pivot man as the ball is passed from left guard to right guard. The movement can continue indefinitely as long as the guards can retain positive control of the ball in good passing position.

DOUBLE SCREENS

Double screens are incorporated into many set offenses, both as primary plays and as optional maneuvers after the initial pattern is executed. A double screen is set by two offensive men standing shoulder to shoulder within shooting range, facing the basket or facing away from it. A third offensive player attempts to run his defender into this block. Usually, the cut off a double screen can be to either side, going toward the basket for a close-in shot or away from the basket for a medium-range shot. If the defense switches, one of the players setting the double screen may be open. The open screener should employ either the offensive roll technique or step away from the basket, whichever is applicable.

As the play involves at least four offensive players—the cutter, the two screeners, and the passer—proper timing is difficult. When properly timed, however, double screens offer a variety of options that result in excellent scoring opportunities. This type of screen is especially effective in setting up good medium-range shots for an outstanding shooter who is not a good ball handler.

The offensive roll is an integral part of maneuvers involving a double screen, for many double screens are set with the screeners facing away from the basket. When a defensive switch is made, the screener whose opponent switches must roll to the basket to take full advantage of his position inside the screened defender.

Diagram 4–31. Double Screen, Guard and Center for the Forward on a Cut to the Basket. A passes to B. A moves in as though to get a return pass and sets a double screen next to the low pivot, C. D fakes to the baseline and cuts around A and C's double screen into the foul lane area for a pass from B. X₄ is screened by the double screen of C and A.

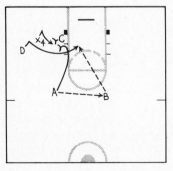

DIAGRAM 4–31

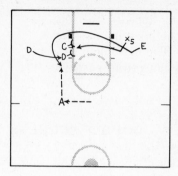

Diagram 4–32. Double Screen, Forward and Center on a Cut Away from the Basket. C, the low pivot, and D, the forward, set a double screen low along the left foul lane. E, the right forward, cuts to the baseline side and comes behind the double screen, cutting away from the basket. He receives a pass from A for a short jump shot behind C and D's double screen.

DIAGRAM 4–32 _____

INCORPORATING FUNDAMENTAL TECHNIQUES INTO SCREENING PATTERNS

In practice sessions, the coach must emphasize the individual offensive tactics that precede and follow the screening maneuver: passing, cutting, opening to receive a pass, faking, pivoting, and rebounding. The ability of all players to recognize and execute basic play patterns quickly, utilizing the correct fundamental techniques of offensive basketball, is the cornerstone to success in competition. The proper mental approach has to be an integral part of all individual and team effort. Some players are better shooters than others, some better passers, some better rebounders, some stronger, some more aggressive, but all must be unselfish. Selflessness must be the predominant characteristic in all players to guarantee team success. No one player—not even a super-star—can carry a team without the coordinated mental and physical endeavors of his teammates.

Knowing when to shoot requires a completely disciplined attitude on the part of every player. A player should shoot whenever he has confidence that the shot he is taking will score; when defense cannot block the shot; when there is no open teammate in a better percentage area; and when teammates are in position to rebound (except on a close-in or lay-up shot). Game factors may alter these determinants. All players must recognize the strengths and shortcomings of themselves and their teammates. They should play to the strong points of their teammates and to the weak points of their opponents.

In the execution of all play patterns, offensive players must constantly be aware of defensive deployment as well as their teammates' positions. The ability to generate and take advantage of defensive commitment is the prime essential in the success of any offensive play pattern.

Guard with Guard

Two guards must work together on the following techniques: advancing the ball against pressure; screening for each other off the high post; reading the intent of a guard who passes and moves away; setting up a defender to properly time a cut off a guard's screen; moving their opponents away from the attack point; returning to that area as a safety outlet at the proper time; dropping back as possible defenders in case possession is lost; getting open to receive a pass in the most advantageous attacking area, properly timing one guard's movement with the status and position of the other guard; and coordinating their movements so that they function as a smooth working unit, complementing each other at all times.

Guards with Forward

Guards must work with a forward in properly timing the forward's pass reception by gauging defensive deployment, the forward's feinting maneuvers, the guards' deceptive fakes, and the use of the correct pass to the correct spot. Guards must always move after a pass is made. The guards must recognize when forwards will change direction (reverse) and execute the play using deception, timing, and the proper pass (usually a bounce or lob pass). A guard must coordinate his screening maneuvers with the forward's. Both must recognize the defensive positions that dictate the type of screen to employ, and they must react to defensive commitment by taking maximum offensive advantage of the play situation.

Guard with Center

Guards should work with the center under pressure. A guard should pass to the center, who has come out from under the basket after using evasive action against a defender to receive a pass, generally in the high pivot. They must both learn proper timing, with the center jumping into the high pass or stepping forward with body crouched and balanced for reception of a bounce pass. Many types of passes and passing postures must be utilized, with the passer maintaining positive attacking control of the ball until the proper passing moment.

   Guards and centers should practice the rear-screen turn-around play. (Center breaks toward guard's defender, receives high pass in air, and turns around after reception. Guard, cutting tight, runs his defender into the center. Both utilize options determined by defensive tactics.)

Guards and centers must perfect the placement and timing of the lob pass, used when an aggressive defender maintains a fronting position on the center as he attempts to obtain a high-pivot position. Some guards can pass off the backboard in this situation, but that procedure is not generally recommended.

Guards should practice passing to the center in the medium-pivot area, as some occasions demand that the guard make the pass-in. (The forward pass-in to this area is preferable in most play situations.)

The guard and center must coordinate their movements in setting a double screen for a guard or a forward.

Centers must practice with all guards to recognize backcourt shooting opportunities so that they can establish rebound position before the defenders can out-position them.

Forward with Forward or Center

A forward must team with another forward or a center to coordinate movement and timing in passing into the medium- or low-pivot areas when the most advantageous position is taken by a teammate. (Players passing into pivot areas must pass to the hand of the pivot man away from his defender. This is the safest pass, as it is farthest from the defender. It also indicates the defender's position to the pivot man and forces the pivot man to move into the pass.)

Forwards must perfect the lob pass to the center, used when defense overplays in front as the center attempts to obtain low- or medium-pivot position. (This pass is extremely effective, but it is also dangerous, because the far forward's defender may sag deep into the free-throw lane. If this sag is too far in, the possibility of a cross-court pass to the far forward exists.)

Forwards and centers should practice the rear-screen turn-around play outlined for guards and centers. They must also practice getting open for the diverse shots that are available close in to the basket, utilizing individual feints and fakes, a teammate's screen, or an unwary defender's screen of his teammate to obtain a quick advantage before shooting.

Forwards must work with centers on movements when the ball is in the pivot area, cutting, screening, reversing direction, pivoting, and rolling to get free for a shooting opportunity. Pass execution and reception must be emphasized because of congestion in the area.

Forwards must be alert for guards cutting free from the weak side. The forwards must be ready to decoy their defenders away from the play area, and they must watch for shooting opportunities that open for teammates in order to get an advantage in starting for rebound position. If they are removed from the rebound area, or if the rebound bounces away from their position, they must be ready for instant transition from offense to defense. Each forward must be alert to opportunities for double-screening plays for the guards or the other forward and for good screening position for a guard, especially away from the ball.

Forwards and centers must be constantly aware that they are functioning in a tight, limited area, and that control and possession of the ball is imperative. They must assess the defensive positions, the play possibilities, the proximity to sideline or end line, their ball-handling shortcomings (if any), the degree of difficulty in passing to a teammate in an advantageous position, and his weaknesses (if any) in pass reception, and they must always be prepared for an unexpected defensive maneuver. They must always know the best safety release area for an outlet pass.

All play patterns diagramed in this chapter *must* be incorporated into the drilling procedures at all levels for maximum efficiency of team offense. These drills will inculcate teammates with instinctive knowledge of each other's probable movement in any play situation.

Team Offense

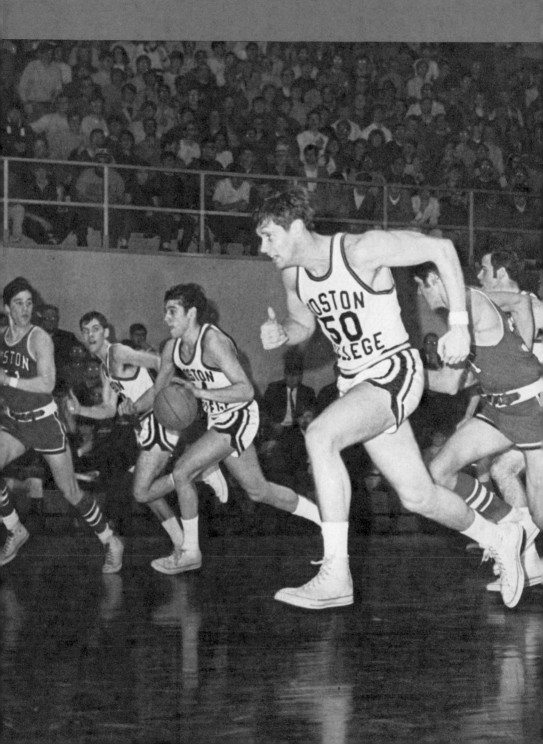

5

Successful offenses are as many and as varied as the successful coaches who use them. To be successful, an offensive pattern must create high-percentage scoring situations from the basic play pattern and secondary variations while maintaining adequate rebound coverage and defensive balance. Those involved in the primary aspect must attack the defense to immobilize it, while the remaining men must use deploying tactics to concentrate their opponents' attention away from the focal point of attack, at the same time remaining prepared to carry out their other team functions—rebounding, defensive balance, secondary shooting, and so forth.

Many different approaches to offense may be used. Each should be carefully thought out and skillfully executed, based on unified movement by players with properly ingrained individual fundamental techniques.

SELECTING AN OFFENSE

The coach chooses the offense to be used by his team, basing his decision on his own philosophy and his players' abilities. He should adapt the good parts of any system to his own philosophy, striving for maximum efficiency within the framework of the total abilities of the players involved.

Seldom do all players on a starting team possess similar abilities. Therefore, the coach should use the positive attributes of each in his offensive planning, blending these talents into the team pattern and taking measures to protect players who lack talent in certain areas. He should assign individual duties that best utilize the personal abilities of each player. Good ball handlers should handle the ball most of the time, and good cutters should be exploited. The good rebounders should be in position to rebound, and the good shooters should be constantly screened for by knowledgeable teammates. The types of shots each player takes should be determined by his basic shooting ability. Perfection of the offense comes from constant practice of correct techniques, first in small groups of two or three, then in team groups using drills incorporating various aspects of the team offense. Speed, timing, and deception of movement are the important factors in the effectiveness of the offense.

A coach should be learning constantly—reading books and magazines on basketball, attending clinics, and swapping ideas with other coaches—integrating into his own offense any new tactics that are suitable for his personnel. Offenses are seldom entirely new. Chances are that one used ten years from now will be an adaptation of something that was in common use five years ago.

The coach should know his material before installing a system. If he is new and doesn't know his material, his preseason practice will be essential in determining the system. The success of a system is due more to the personnel than to the coach. If it is the wrong system, regardless of the coach's ability, it cannot succeed. For example, if a coach has slow players, they cannot fast break effectively; if he has tall, uncoordinated players, he cannot use a four- or five-man weave offense effectively.

As a rule, coaches should not change their offense in midstream. When change is essential, they should adapt from the existing structure so that the change will not be too radical. All offenses should be adaptable for use against the three types of defense—man-to-man, zone, and combination.

PERSONNEL

While coaches should try to have the best combination of personnel as quickly as possible, they should not be too hasty in their selection. It's best to keep players on their toes and unsure of their position for a while so as to obtain maximum potential from each man.

The best teams have set starting combinations; therefore, coaches should practice their five best players together as a unit as soon as their superior ability is evident. The more compatible the players are off the court the better they will function on the court. Through bull sessions, they will obtain a better understanding of their individual characteristics.

Necessary changes must be made decisively. The team will probably know before the coach that changes should be made. Coaches normally need two or three replacements at most—in the center position, in the forward position, and in the guard position. If there are only two replacements, the change might be to a forward-center combination or guard-forward combination. Starters may be moved to new positions, but it is not advisable.

Replacements must have as much practice time and game time as possible so that they coordinate their movements with those of the starters. Coaches should never wait until pressure situations to insert a first-line sub.

TYPE OF OFFENSE

There are two types of offense—free-lance and control. In a free-lance type of offense, players make their own patterns, depending on the defensive deployment and the ability of the opponents. Free-lance is not as free or uncontrolled as the term implies, because all two-on-two and three-on-three plays should be drilled completely. Control basketball is a system in which a team maintains control of the ball until one player is in an unguarded high-percentage area. Any basic system can be used to implement a control-type of basketball.

There are several basic offensive systems that teams may use in attempting to obtain high-percentage shots. All must fall into one of the following classifications, based on the position of the offensive players in relation to the basket and to the defensive players guarding them.

1. Five Offensive Players Outside. If five offensive players are eighteen to twenty feet from the basket, all defensive players are closer to the basket than the closest offensive player is. Offenses that begin from this structure are a three-two (wide) and a five-man weave.

2. Four Offensive Players Outside and One Inside. Four offensive players are farther out than their four opponents, and one player is nearer the basket. Normally this is a four-man weave system or a single pivot type of offense in which the corner men are approximately eighteen or nineteen feet from the basket.

3. Three Offensive Players Outside and Two Inside. Three offenses start from this structure. (1) A double pivot places the two larger

men in closer to the basket than the other three. A three-two offense may have three front men moving while the two inside men are stationary in close to the basket. (2) A one-three-one offense uses a tandem pivot, one high, one low. (3) An overload offense overloads one side of the court, passing the ball to the side that has only one player and having a teammate who was away from the ball cut off a post man toward the ball.

4. Two Offensive Players Outside and Three Inside. This is a standard two-three offense in which the forwards are within eighteen feet of the basket.

5. One Offensive Player Outside and Four Inside. We use this as a primary offense. Designated the stack offense, it has four players in close to the basket.

Physical Makeup

The type of offense to be used is determined by the physical makeup of the team. Each team fits into one of the following categories.

Five Tall Men. This type of team should not use the fast break unless more than two players are fast and one of the five is an exceptional ball handler. The team should use a definite set offense, shooting over screens. If they have one good ball handler, we would recommend the stack offense. If they have two good ball handlers, they could use a two-three offense, with the low men screening for each other and watching for the easy inside shot.

Four Big Men and One Small Man. Assuming that the small man has good or better-than-average speed and ball handling ability, this team should attempt to use the fast break with the small man as the middle man. Their set offense can be a two-three if one of the taller men can handle the ball. It could also be a stack offense or an unorthodox offense devised by the coach, taking advantage of overall team size and using low double screens for the bigger players.

Three Big Men and Two Small Men. This is normally the ideal type of basketball team. The team can use the fast break or a set two-three offense in which the three big men stay in close for the offensive rebounds.

Two Big Men and Three Small Men. We recommend the fast break for this team, possibly using a three-two offense with the two big men as a double pivot, side by side or in tandem. They could also use a one-three-one set offense.

One Big Man and Four Small Men. This team could use a controlled fast break. A good set offense for them is a four-man weave, using the one big man as a moving pivot. They can also use a one-three-one offense with the big man as the high pivot and the next tallest man as an inside man moving toward the corners. Another good offense for them is a three-two with flash pivots (men moving into the pivot area quickly and moving out as plays develop).

Five Small Men. In high school, the five men would be six feet or under; in college they would be six feet three inches or under. This team's offense should incorporate aggressive defensive tactics as an offensive weapon, depending on the players' speed and ball handling ability to penetrate toward the basket as quickly as possible. They can use a three-two moving offense or a five-man weave offense. The players should only take good high-percentage shots from within the eighteen-to-twenty-foot area.

BALANCE AND PROTECTION

All players must be deployed to provide balance and protection to the offense. At least one player (preferably one and one-half players) should play defense in every offensive pattern to protect against offensive mistakes.

The offense must keep the floor balanced with continuous designed movement, meanwhile, never allowing the defense time to regroup or think. Of course, players must maintain team organization, always knowing their position with relation to teammates. One man must always be moving to, or away from, each offensive station. Such positioning is essential for good offensive rebounding opportunities. Offensive rebounding positions must be organized within the framework of the team structure on each pattern. The team must be balanced so that it can use both inside and outside scoring threats. Movement by a screener is important, as an alert screener may be able to take a quick shot unopposed if he is left open momentarily while his defender concentrates on the cutter.

Coaches must determine the type of pivot they wish to use. If the defense is playing in a zone-structure, the offense must pressure it. A high pivot forces the defense to concentrate on this area. However if the high-pivot man is uncoordinated and not quick, the defense may easily block him out on the rebound. Players must be situated to spread the defense as much as possible to allow more space for offensive maneuvering. It is possible to have an overloaded offense with four men on one side of the court, but it limits the direction of movement.

Primary receivers who are close to the man with the ball must not be so close that one defender can play two or that two defenders can double-team the ball. A primary receiver must use offensive faking and footwork to clear himself to receive the pass. He must be cognizant at all times of his location on the court with respect to the deep corners, the hash marks, the sidelines, and the mid-court line, as these are restrictive barriers. Timing is an intricate and essential ingredient in floor balance, for players must know when they should move toward the ball and when they should move away from it.

Primarily, a team's offensive movements are determined by the opposing defenders' movements. Good offense requires overall balance—offensive balance in the area of the basket for shooting and rebounding, defensive balance in case of a mistake or misplay, strong-side movement on the side of the ball, and weak-side movement away from the ball. Players should understand and be aware of the movement of teammates in every situation. They must be able to move with the ball and without the ball. Moving without the ball is necessary because a man guarding a standstill offensive player can guard others at the same time. Of course, players must always move with a purpose.

COMPONENTS OF A TEAM OFFENSE

The following eight factors are essential for every team offense.

1. It must be synchronized. Each player must understand his part in relation to the movements of the others. All players must understand the movement required of each of the five offensive positions.
2. It must have a smooth transition from one phase of offense to another, coordinating ball and player movement.
3. There must be three offensive rebounders, one player who is half offensive rebounder and half on defense, and one player moving back to play defense at all times.
4. It must have continuity, moving efficiently from the fast break, or penetrating aspect, to the pattern aspect.
5. It must be uncomplicated.
6. Each aspect should be easy to learn.
7. The coach should resist a natural tendency to adopt additional patterns.
8. Players must have patience in obtaining the good shot.

OFFENSIVE PHILOSOPHY AND PRINCIPLES

There are two types of offensive attacks: the aggressive, fast, penetrating type and the slowdown, or ball-control, type. In each type, offensive pressure should constantly be exerted upon the opposing defense.

Using an aggressive offense, the team should get the ball upcourt as quickly as possible, taking the good-percentage shot when it appears. High percentage shots after quick penetration improve the offensive rebound recovery chances, as the defense is moving and is not in good blocking-out position or in good team position for getting the rebound. This offense also weakens the opponents' offensive rebounding structure, as they are thinking in terms of retreat on defense and a slowdown offense that is more susceptible to aggressive defensive pressure.

In the second type of offense, the team slows down the attack or changes the tempo of the game. This offense is essential when a team is out-personneled, when the opponents are an excellent running team, when a team is leading late in the game, and when the opponents' defensive posture is set. You cannot attack a set defense with a fast, penetrating attack.

Teams that use a penetrating attack are generally in the superb condition so essential for late game strength in close ball games. Their object is to score by the most direct method. Attacking aggressively and with pressure each time upsets opponents. Such attack eliminates unnecessary ball handling and offensive movement. It develops individual and team aggressiveness, allows for the frequent use of substitutes, keeps the players alert, and confuses and disorganizes the defense. It increases the defensive rebounding strength of the attacked fast-break team. All offensive players have the opportunity to score if they are hustling, so the penetrating attack is enjoyable for the team to play and for the spectators to watch. With this attack, it is possible to employ sneak-away tactics—one man sneaks when the opponent shoots.

Coaches must be aware of the negative aspects of the penetrating offense and make sure their players do not take foolish chances. They should teach the men the value of ball possession. Teams that penetrate aggressively are sometimes prone to excessive fouling, and they get themselves into forcing situations. Players may expend their energy needlessly. Sometimes players break too soon, or they break when the defenders are set defensively, thus making for a poor type of attack.

For best results a team should use the fast break and an aggressive ball-penetration offense combined with a set-play theory of attack. If it is to be a well-balanced team offensively, it must be able to play fast and slow.

In the attack, a team must always be able to function against man-to-man, zone, press, and combination defenses and be able to play control basketball, using stalls and freezes. (Control pattern does not necessarily mean slow movement. It implies the proper execution of fundamentals to ensure the efficiency of a given pattern.) The team must also be able to implement last-second plays, patterned plays, and all offensive out-of-bounds plays with maximum efficiency.

For the following reasons, teams should strive for short jump shots rather than penetration all the way to the basket. First, the defense places bigger men near the basket so that they can block shots of small men penetrating too deeply. Second, the short jump is a maximum efficiency shot, as players are better shooters today than in the past. Third, according to the offensive charge rule, the man driving to the basket is responsible for contact when a defender moves into his path.

The following factors are *musts* for an effective offense. The players must believe that the coach has selected the best possible offense for the existing situation. Each player must know his own strengths and weaknesses and the strengths and weaknesses of his teammates. Players must be selfless, subjugating their individual wills to the best interest of the team. The "we won" "we lost" attitude is important.

In the team effort every man is important. Therefore, the coach must praise those who are in secondary roles, decoying men away from the focal point of attack. The coach should give the players a critique on the offensive opportunities they missed, telling them if they passed up a good shot; if they took a bad shot; if they missed a cutting teammate, or if they did not decoy their men away from the focal point of attack.

IMPORTANT OFFENSIVE CONSIDERATIONS

In offensive planning, the following important principles must be adhered to.

1. All players must take the high-percentage shot. This is perhaps the most important single offensive principle. The shot should be a lay-up, if possible, or a medium jumper within the player's good shooting range, and it should never be forced or hurried. Teammates must be in rebounding position unless the shot is a lay-up or within six feet of the basket. The shooter must be in better shooting position than any of his teammates.

With proper ball movement and proper player movement, a player never has to be told when he has the shot. If a player is coming off a screen unopposed and the ball is passed to him within the good shooting area, we say the shot has come to him. If the man cutting off the screen continues his movement on a switch, the screener is open, and the ball is passed to the screener without defensive opposition and within the eighteen-foot area, the shot has come to him.

2. All offenses must be based on the margin-of-error theory. The ball should always be in the hands of the player most unlikely to make a mistake at that juncture; for instance, the same middle man should have the ball whenever the offense attempts a fast-break. When the team is using a set pattern, the best ball handler should have the ball until the pattern moves into offensive shooting position. Then he should give the ball to a teammate who has the ability to make a good shot or pass. Normally, guards make longer passes; centers and forwards, shorter passes.

We want our ball handler to have maneuvering room at all times without being double-teamed; therefore we use the *stack offense*, in which one player controls the ball until the shooters and rebounders deploy into advantageous offensive position. This play usually necessitates only one pass for a good shot—or at most, two. If you do not obtain the shot you are looking for within this framework, return the ball to the best ball handler, who will then proceed to a different play within the structure of the stack offense.

3. The best defense is possession of the ball, and to obtain the maximum efficiency from possession, all team members must be completely aware of its value. The loss of the ball offensively without a shot is the most serious failure in team basketball. It is essential that a team obtain a good shot every time it has the ball.

Many teams talk about a shooting percentage, which is based on the number of shots made divided by the number of shots taken. If a team takes sixty shots and makes thirty shots, it has a shooting percentage of fifty percent. However, the true norm is not the shooting percentage but the possession percentage. That is based on the number of times a team has possession of the ball divided into the number of points a team has scored, taking into consideration the number of times the team loses a ball by a bad pass, a tie-up for a held-ball, or an offensive foul.

4. Players should know how to play without the ball and when to come to the ball from either the ball side or the weak side. They must also know how to come to the ball—by V'ing in, V'ing out, changing pace, or changing direction. They should take

advantage of every opening, being careful never to clog the pivot area. All players must see the ball, know the offensive keys for their team, and understand their teammates' reactions. If a player has screened with his back to the basket or the ball, he should use an offensive roll to open to the ball. Correct timing is imperative. The coach should make the players aware of the weaknesses in the offensive set system so that they can guard against mistakes.

5. Each player should know his own shooting ability and the position from which he makes the highest percentage of shots. In addition, he must know the shooting abilities and ball-handling abilities of his teammates, making certain that they receive the ball where they can take advantage of their positive attributes and do not receive it where their weaknesses will hurt the team effort. If players know when they have a shot and when they do not, they will lessen the number of bad shots.

A player expecting to receive a pass must decoy his defender away so that when he gets the ball he is not under pressure and does not have to force or hurry the shot. The game plan should include special plays for good spot shooters, and the coach should correct those who pass up good shots. The coach should control the type of shot taken by each player. Many times great shooters take a high percentage of the shots.

6. Players must see the total offensive picture: both the offensive deployment of their teammates and the defensive alignment of the opponents. Except for a low-pivot man with the ball, players should be facing the basket and the greater part of the playing court area when they receive the ball. Therefore, there should be no pass to a man moving away from the basket unless it is necessary for possession and protection. The player who receives a ball when he is not facing the basket should immediately front pivot.

7. The offense must control the defensive alignment. This is both a team function and an individual function. Each player must control his own defensive man. By maneuvering the defender, the player can anticipate the defender's moves and decoy him away from the point of attack or take advantage of a defensive weakness to obtain an offensive advantage. A basic offensive principle is that the defender tells an offensive player what he should do—to control a defender, the offensive man must know how the defender is playing. If the defense is playing zone, each offensive player must attempt to control the man in whose area he is located, keeping the defender occupied with offensive movement. If an opponent guarding man-to-man is a good defensive player, it is best to keep him away from the ball as much as possible by

deploying to the weak side or by cutting off teammates away from the ball.

8. Teams should eliminate mistakes and never force a play. The elimination of mistakes means complete protection of the ball at all times. Players should never take unnecessary chances when they have possession of the ball, nor should they force a pass or shot. However, many players do, for several reasons. First, they accept the challenge of a good opponent. Second, they want the first offensive move to result in a good shot. (In most offensive movement this is not possible, and players should not force the shot if it does not appear with the first pass.) Third, they try to rectify an error by making an immediate good offensive play. (People who make bad passes are inclined to follow the ball in an effort to retrieve it. Rather than following the ball, they should retreat.) Fourth, a player may make a bad defensive error that gives his opponent an easy basket then try to rectify it immediately by making a basket himself with a forced or hurried shot.

Normally, the best method of overcoming a bad play is intelligent reaction. For example, if an opponent intercepts the ball and breaks for the basket, the player who lost the ball should get back in good defensive position immediately. Even if the opponents score, if the erring player follows the ball and inbounds it immediately, there may be a chance to get the basket back quickly, as the opponents may have weakened their defensive structure by a fast, aggressive rush at the basket to take advantage of the mistake.

9. The offense must be flexible, changing structure repeatedly during the offensive thrusts. It should be able to adjust to any style of defense instantaneously, incorporating elements of individual or dual free-lance possibilities.

10. The offense should have good timing; continuous movement must be coordinated. Opportunities for scoring maneuvers at the ball and away from the ball must be staggered. To make sure that he will be at the right place at the right time, a player should use stops, starts, changes of pace, and changes of direction. Timing requires accurate steps in definite direction from each player, especially by those at the focal point of attack.

11. The offense must be able to adapt to any defense. For example, a smaller team may work one-on-one on bigger men, a faster team opposing a slower team may speed up the game, a larger team should work to its big men, and every team should play to opponents who are weak defensively if there are any. If there is a good offensive opponent, a player should concentrate his attention defensively in hopes that it will affect his offensive ability or discourage him defensively. Essentially, all offensive

players are forwards working for the best possible shot and best scoring opportunity, and all five defenders are guards, protecting the basket against the scoring thrusts of the opponents. Within the team offensive structure the importance of transition from the defensive to the offensive posture is extremely important. The calling of the word *ball* indicates that a team has the ball and that members should go quickly to the best offensive position.

THE SET PATTERN AFTER THE OPPONENT'S DEFENSIVE ALIGNMENT IS SET

A number of offensive systems are adaptable for any team, and the plays that can be devised within each structure are unlimited. The coach should build his own offense rather than copy another's, expending a great deal of time in its development. He must have confidence in it, yet know its limitations. The players must be able to visualize it and understand it completely.

Each pattern should entail options of different men moving to the basket at various times, with one player (not necessarily the same player each time) in defensive posture ready to go back if the ball is lost. For best offensive results, players should normally move at moderate speed, varying the speed up or down. Variation is essential for body control and for setting up the defender. The offense must be able to reverse the direction of the ball, moving it from one side of the court to the other rapidly, and in a concerted movement, in order to keep defenses honest to prevent double-teaming by the opponents. The coach must keep the players in a set pattern moving, because it is harder for defense to guard an opponent in motion.

Team set patterns must have definitive cutting movement— weak-side cutting, baseline cutting, lateral cutting, and cuts out front for defensive protection and for the outside set shot. Only one cutter should move to the basket at a time. If two cutters are cutting to the basket from opposite directions, the least advantageous cutter should stop or deploy. Normally, the first cutter is given preference. However, if the second cutter is moving in from a position away from the ball and he is open, the first cutter should give way to him.

Teams should not congest the keyhole area, as they place too many defensive hands around the ball in a confined area, and the pivot player may be tied up with the ball. The coach should plan combinations that strengthen the offense, using free-lance or instinctive patterns for two or three players. He should utilize all his offensive threats but concentrate on the two or three best players, if possible. He should take advantage of team offensive ability so that all players may have scoring opportunities. This prevents double-teaming on the best scorers, and it is good for team morale.

The coach and the team must determine the defensive point of attack and the opponent's defensive philosophy in order to better attack this defense. They should find the defensive weaknesses and move the offense into patterns that will take advantage of it.

The coach should be certain that offensive rebounding coverage is adequate and defined in all patterns. The team must be prepared for all defensive possibilities.

SIGNALS

Both audible and visual signals can be used by players to regulate the type of play to be used. An audible signal is usually the calling of the name or number of the alignment or pattern. Some teams name their plays for colleges or great players.

A visual key can be (1) an arm or finger signal to designate the number of a certain play; (2) ball movement or ball location; and (3) player movement. Normally, the player with the ball determines offensive movement. If he passes and moves in a certain direction, it is a signal. Players must be aware of the initiating offensive moves so as to obtain good timing in all plays.

METHODS OF DETERMINING THE OPPONENT'S DEFENSE

The ability to determine whether an opposing team is in a man-to-man, zone, or combination alignment is extremely important. Definite probing offensive movement must be made in order to predetermine the types of offensive thrusts that must be made against the defense. The first movement is a diagonal cut through the defense by an offensive guard as the ball is moving upcourt. If his opponent does not go through with him, it is a zone, match-up, or combination defense. Second is a vertical cut in which a player passes and cuts directly to the basket. Again, if his opponent does not go through with him, the defense is probably a zone or combination. The third movement may be a lateral cut to further check the opponent's defense. It is possible to incorporate all three movements into one play to recognize the opponent's defense quickly. Determining the defense is important, as the basic principle of attack is different for each type. Some defenses will follow the man through initially to deceive the offensive team. However, after two or three passes, the true defense should be obvious.

THE FAST BREAK

The fast break is the ultimate offensive weapon. It affords maximum penetration on many occasions and penetration to within a fifteen-foot radius of the basket on all occasions. In a three-on-two or a four-on-three situation the tactic often results in a lay-up shot. Even if the defense responds quickly enough to get back into position, the fast-breaking unit is still within a fifteen- or sixteen-foot radius of the basket, so the player, with one pass or one pivot, can set up either a wing man or the middle man or take advantage of a jump-shooting opportunity.

Running a fast break combats the numerous changes in defense that one sees today on the college level and even, occasionally, on the high school level. Such changes can be very confusing, regardless of how well the team or individual is coached or drilled. Few high school or college teams have players who can adjust quickly enough to a different defense on three or four occasions and who know immediately what offense to employ. They might, even though it is extreme, call for time out to get instructions from the coach. This is not a practical solution. It is better to get downfloor quickly to eliminate the necessity of worrying about what particular defense the opposing team has changed to.

Running an effective fast break puts extreme pressure on the opponents, affecting their offensive tempo and causing their coach to have to adjust his defenses. The break may force the defenders to play a slow and deliberate style of basketball that will affect their own game adversely. Through a fear of being caught upfloor, rebounders may drop off the offensive backboard too soon, to the advantage of the fast-breaking team. Conversely, they may stay too long, in an effort to slow down a break. Another positive psychological factor is that running the fast break effectively invariably leads to better defense on the part of the fast-breaking team. A successful break stimulates the players' aggressive defensive play so that they come up with many more loose balls, violations, and aggressive rebounds.

If a team is known for its fast break, the opponents (unless they feel they have a decided advantage and do not have to change strategy before the game) will do everything possible to get the team to play a slowdown or deliberate game rather than the other way around, so the fast-break team will attempt to get the opponents to accelerate their attack as much as possible. If the fast break is being run properly—if the defensive board is being controlled and the men are getting downfloor quickly the majority of times—it will make the opponents play more of a running game—eventually a wide-open game.

Kids shoot well today. In order to capitalize on this talent, the offense should get downfloor more quickly than the defense. If the best ball handler gets downcourt quickly, before the defense sets up, with a minimum of ball handling, he can achieve with one pass and a fifteen-foot jump shot or a lay-up shot what it would take three, four, five, or more passes to achieve in any kind of pattern situation.

Another important advantage of the fast break is that it makes every player a potential scorer. The mediocre scorer, who would get no more than half a dozen scoring opportunities a game when running patterns, can pick up two, three, or four easy baskets a game if he hustles on a fast break.

Lastly, the fast break adds to the game, making it more colorful, interesting, and fast-moving—the kind of game spectators prefer.

Positions for the Fast Break

When used selectively, the fast break takes advantage of the varying skills of all players on the team. The men should be in the positions in which they function to the utmost of their abilities. The best ball handler, best dribbler, and quickest man is in the middle position. The lanemen—the shooters—have the most speed and know how to penetrate on a movement to the basket. Normally, the guard who makes the pass to the middle man (or the other guard who is defensively stationed in the front-court area) is in the best position to fill the second lane. The opposite forward is usually the man who fills the third lane. In order to have a successful fast break, these men have to get into their positions as quickly as possible, taking the shortest path downfloor. Instant transition from a defensive posture to an offensive posture is essential. The fourth man down the floor fills the trailer position. The fifth man is the first defender back downfloor. (See Figure 5–1.) The option is almost not to take the fast break if the situation doesn't develop this way. The margin of error must be cut down to the nth degree. It does no good to run three successful breaks out of five if the other two result in loss of the ball through a violation.

Figure 5–1. The classic fast break—middle man with ball, lanes filled, trailer and safety men in position.

This system allows all the men more freedom to free-lance at the end of the fast break, capitalizing on individual initiative, and makes it a bit more fun for the players, instead of putting them in a completely patterned, disciplined situation. We feel that we strike a happy medium, offensively, in that if the fast-break opportunity shows itself, the players are able to take it and exercise their initiative. If it does not show itself, they continue in a disciplined pattern.

To run an effective fast break, a team has to exert extreme and aggressive defensive pressure—getting into position quickly, forcing the opponents to violation, stealing the ball, etc. The fast break allows for the close-in baskets—the lay-up baskets—cheap baskets compared to the ones that require a lot of work in a pattern.

Starting the Fast Break

There are several ways to start the fast break. To implement a fast offense, possibly the most important thing is to get everyone on a team thinking fast break in the sense of an instantaneous transition from defense to offense. A pressure man-to-man defense lends itself to the starting of an immediate fast break, because all the men are in ready position, on their toes, playing aggressive defense. This makes the mental, as well as the physical, transition to the necessary positions easier. Every man must be thinking fast break at all times. The man must be prepared to give the signal as soon as he gets possession of the ball. Most teams probably use the vocal signal "ball" to indicate to four of the men, who possibly do not see the ball, that one of their team-mates has it and they should get into position.

Most of the time, the fast break begins by the rebound being taken off the defensive board, and its success depends on how quickly the rebound can be cleared out. To execute a suc-cessful fast break it is necessary to have good positioning on the defensive backboard. The men have to be certain of their respon-sibilities.

Before the game, the forwards should be told whether they are to go to the board strong to acquire the rebound, box and hold the man off the board without going for the rebound, or box and then go to the basket. The primary rebounder, perhaps the center, should also have explicit instructions. The chances are that he would be given the responsibility of making an attempt at the rebound almost every time, rather than boxing out his own man, assuming that he has the inside position and the quickness to get to the board before his defender.

The two outside men should also be given alternatives, de-pending on who they are guarding and what the men are doing. If one of the guards is guarding a good back-court rebounder who is in the habit of going to the basket, the coach may want the guard to box him out before clearing to the outlet area. Alter-natively, he may allow the man to break to his basket to be ready for a long pass, knowing that the big men on his own team are closer to the basket and probably will get the rebound most of the time. The coach may prefer a third alternative—having the guards position themselves on a seventeen- or eighteen-foot ra-dius of the basket. If the ball is tapped out, they have a good opportunity to gain control of the ball, because they are inside the opponent's small men and quicker than their big men. The middle man should be told to get to the side of the floor that the rebound will probably come off to.

When the defensive rebound is acquired, the rebounder should signal as quickly as possible so that the other four men know he has possession of the ball. He must guard against making the signal before he has possession. If he anticipates possession and hollers "ball," four men abandon their rebounding and de-fensive responsibilities and start downfloor, while the offensive rebounder gets the ball or keeps it in play.

Of course, there is a split second to be gained on the fast break if players can react as soon as they are certain that a man on their team will get possession of the ball. Such knowledge

Figure 5–2. Rebounder, still in air, looks for outlet pass to start fast break.

comes with timing and getting accustomed to each other—knowing, for instance, who the primary rebounder is. If the best rebounder is going up clearly for a rebound with no aggressive pressure on his back, a wing man or even a guard may be able to start down on the break. However, it is important that he does not leave too soon.

Ideally, the rebounder should release the ball to the outlet before he has even hit the ground. (See Figure 5–2.) However, this move may be too advanced for boys on a college level and certainly at a high school level. Once the rebounder has the ball, he must try to pivot to his outside, on the same side the rebound came off on, in order to make the outlet pass. Assuming that he is one of the bigger men, he should raise the ball over his head as quickly as possible to eliminate the possibility of a guard's stealing or deflecting it. (In our fast breaking style, he does not look for the middle man; instead, he looks for the man he can clear the ball to, because this move is the one that starts a successful fast break.)

Whenever possible, the middle man should receive the outlet pass. The middle man and the primary rebounder must establish such a rapport they will be able to anticipate each other's reactions without an actual signal, thus increasing the speed and effectiveness of the fast break. If the middle man does not have to box out when the ball goes up, he should try to position himself on the side where the rebound comes off, get out to the side where he is clear of pressure, and make his position known by vocal

Figure 5–3. Middle man penetrating under control, moving defense to their right to feed his right wing man. Both wings are wide in full stride, turned to ball.

signals or hand signals. If he can do this and receive the outlet pass, he can assume the middle position immediately, saving a little time and the need for an additional pass. (See Figure 5–3.) If the outlet pass comes to a guard the coach does not want in the middle, that guard will have to make a second pass to the opposite guard designated to be in the middle. The longer the rebounder holds the ball, the less chance the break has of being successful, or even starting.

The rebounder should never dribble unless it is an extreme situation. If the ball is stolen here, close to the dribbler's own basket, it usually results in an easy two points for the opponent. Usually, the rebounder should protect the ball rather than dribble. If he is getting a sense of pressure on the outside, however, the player can protect the ball along the baseline side, take one dribble to clear himself of the pressure. If he is being overplayed to that side to the point where a dribble will not do the job, he may pivot to the middle, still trying to make his outlet pass to the same side as the rebound came off. (We do not, except in rare instances, advocate clearing the ball up the middle of the floor, because the retreating defensive men usually position themselves up the middle.)

The pass must be made aggressively; it should not be a lob pass, since that pass gives the defense time to move in to steal or deflect it. When the player turns outside or inside to get the ball to the outlet man on the same side, he must be aware of the defensive alignment. If the outlet man is under excessive pressure, the player with the ball may reverse his position in a backdoor move. The outlet man must be prepared to adjust to this maneuver.

The primary responsibility of the rebounder is to start the fast break without throwing the ball away. If he is going to sacrifice safety for the sake of starting the break a little more quickly, he is better off not starting the break.

The fast break can also be started from interceptions of one kind or another and from violations. In the case of a violation, the official handles the ball, which may slow down the start of the break. However, there is still an advantage to be gained if a violation is called. The new offensive team may get over to the sidelines or jump on the ball so that they can get it into the hands of the official, get it back as quickly as possible, and take advantage of the fast break before the defense sets up. Knowing that the official must handle the ball, the opponents may not get back on the defense as quickly as they should.

Another way to start a fast break is from an out-of-bounds play. The coach may assign the closest man or specific men to take the ball out-of-bounds as quickly as possible after a basket. Occasionally, a coach will prefer not to have certain men take the ball out-of-bounds at any time.

After a foul shot is a fourth time to start a fast break. Certain teams are primarily geared to develop a play, and there is an advantage to be gained in starting it off a foul shot rather than off a basket, since the men can be positioned advantageously on a foul shot.

A fast break can also start from a fumbled ball, a bad pass, a loose ball, or a missed free-throw.

Passes Used

The length of the pass and the type of pass that will be used to clear the rebound to the outlet man will depend on the defensive pressure on the rebounder and the middle man. If the pressure on a rebounder is negligible, he can use either the two-hand-over-the-head snap pass or the one-hand baseball pass. The first is the safest, quickest pass. It is the most common pass in a fast-break situation, since the guards or the outlet men are usually no more than fifteen to eighteen feet away from the rebounder at the time of the rebound. As the player gets the rebound, the ball is almost always over his head, since his arms are completely extended. As he comes down, he just has to pivot and release the ball.

Opportunity to use the baseball pass does not present itself often. There are relatively few players who throw that pass accurately, but when a player does have good control of it he can throw the ball harder and farther, and the farther he can throw it the quicker he can start the fast break. He can throw to an outlet man downcourt, perhaps at the half-court line. If the passer must rely on a two-hand overhead pass, the outlet man will normally have to retreat and come much closer.

To make the baseball pass, the player has to get the ball in position and wind up. While he is winding up, two things happen: (1) the man closest to him has an opportunity to adjust and perhaps deflect the pass, and (2) the time it takes him to get the arm back enables the defensive men to get in defensive position on him and on the receiver. The rebound is valueless if the pass to the outlet man is not a good pass. If the outlet man is under pressure, the pass must be on the outside shoulder away from the pressure. If he is not under pressure, it should be a lead pass that will get the outlet man started in the direction downfloor that he must take in order to start the fast break a bit more quickly. If he has to come back for the pass, or if he has to stand momentarily and wait for the pass to get to him, it will delay the play.

Laning the Fast Break

To standardize the fast break as much as possible, reduce error, and ensure that the best ball handlers control the ball as much as possible, many coaches have gone to a style of fast-breaking known as laning. In laning the fast break, the coach first assigns letters or numbers to the lanes to be used in fast-breaking and then assigns corresponding letters or numbers to the players. Under strictest laning techniques, the same players always fill the same lanes downcourt (except on unopposed, breakaway lay-ups), regardless of their court position when the fast break began. For example, the lane down the center of the court may be designated Lane A, and the team's best ball handler may be Player A. The sideline lanes and the players filling them may be designated B and C, and the intermediate lanes between the sidelines and middle may be designated D and E. The latter are normally reserved for the team's big men who get the defensive rebounds, make the outlet pass, and serve as trailers on the fast break. At first glance, this style of fast-breaking may seem to be slower than the older technique of allowing the players to fill the passing lanes randomly on a first-come, first-served basis, but two factors tend to make strict laning as fast as, or faster than, other methods: First, having the same players fill the same lanes reduces confusion regarding who fills which lane and permits players to practice spot shooting from areas they know they'll be shooting from at the end of the break. Second, strict laning virtually guarantees that the best ball handler will be handling the ball every time fast-breaking situations arise.

Still, some coaches, particularly those with more than one good ball handler, prefer to give their teams greater latitude in forming the fast break by providing two outlet pass receivers and primary ball handlers, depending upon which side of the court the outlet pass can be made from most quickly. If, for example, Player A (the team's best ball handler) is on one side of the court and transition occurs on the other side of the court, or a defensive rebound is taken, it may be more expedient to have Player B, the team's second best ball handler, move to the outlet passing area on that side of the court and take the ball downcourt, with A filling B's lane, than to wait for the other offensive and defensive players to clear the area in order to pass to Player A.

Many variations of this style of laning exist. The simplest is for both A and B to serve as outlet pass receivers on their respective sides of the court. If A receives the outlet pass, B cuts to the middle and takes the ball down, and A fills B's sideline lane after he passes to B in the middle. The reverse is true, of course, if B receives the outlet pass.

The principal benefit of laning the fast break is that since the same players fill the same lanes every time they head downcourt, no delay is involved in their moving quickly to their assigned areas. Constant repetition in practice and in games teaches players to find their lanes quickly in all kinds of situations. Too, the fact that the best ball handlers are controlling the ball throughout the fast break from the time the outlet pass is made until the final pass at the end of the break tends to drastically

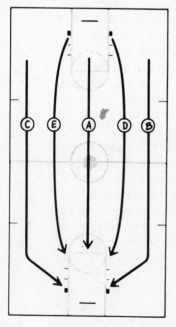

Diagram 5–1. Laning the Fast Break. The letters or numbers may differ among coaches, depending upon individual preferences, but the direction of the lanes is largely invariable: the middle, usually designated A or 1; the left wing, designated B or 2; the right wing, C or 3; the left intermediate, or trailer, wing, designated D or 4; and the right intermediate wing, E or 5. Unless told otherwise by the coach, players should follow their own lanes every time they come downcourt. Two points should be made here: first, some systems of fast-breaking require that Wings B and C stop at the free-throw line extended (or the baseline) rather than going all the way to the basket as shown; and second, the *sideline fast break* pattern does not follow the lanes shown here.

DIAGRAM 5–1

Diagram 5–2. Laned Fast Break after Score or Rebound. When E gets the ball after the opponents' score, he steps out-of-bounds and looks for A clearing toward the sideline (not toward the ball) for a pass. B and C fill the sideline lanes. D will move downcourt as shown. If he is fast enough, he may be ahead of B and C, in which case E may be able to make the long pass to D for an easy score. (Most coaches prefer that Player E not attempt the long pass to the wings because of the danger of throwing the ball out-of-bounds.) If D doesn't receive E's pass, he may set up at low post.

As an alternative to A's dribbling all the way downcourt, he may be able to pass the ball ahead to B or C to speed up the fast break. (He will not throw to D, however, since any defenders dropping back to stop the fast break will be in the middle of the court by the time A gets the ball and turns to throw.)

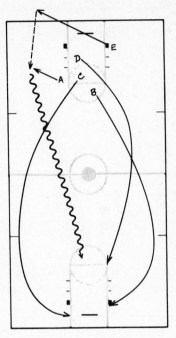

DIAGRAM 5–2

Diagram 5–3. Laning the Fast Break, Two-Pass Variation. When D claims the rebound, B clears toward the sideline for D's pass. A slides to the middle and receives B's pass. B and C fill their lanes as before.

It is not advisable to have A clear to the baseline or the sideline on D's side to receive D's pass, since players on both teams will be moving downcourt ahead of the ball while A is clearing.

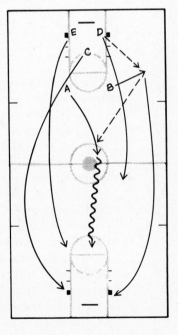

DIAGRAM 5–3

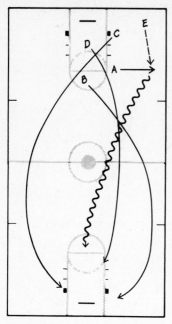

DIAGRAM 5–4

Diagram 5–4. Laning the Fast Break after Transition. The difference between laned and free-lance fast-breaking may be seen clearly in the movements after transition. E has stolen the ball from his man. A clears to the sideline to receive a pass from E. It would seem that B should either move up the middle of the court to receive A's pass or follow the right sideline, since he is nearer to it than C. Since A is the designated ball handler on the break, however, B follows his usual route and C (not D) fills Lane C along the right sideline.

Thus, we can see that in strict laning, it does not matter where a player is when transition occurs: he is expected to follow his normal fast-breaking route. If he is covered, someone else will be open. The only exception to this rule arises when transition yields an open breakaway possibility—say, if B steals the ball with nothing but daylight between him and the basket, or if D steals the ball and spots a teammate other than A in the clear beyond his man. In such cases, regular laning techniques would give the defenders time to get back and stop the breakaway threat. In the first case, B will drive all the way to the basket, using the shortest route possible; in the second case, D will pass downcourt to his open teammate regardless of where that player is on the court.

reduce the turnovers and ball-handling mistakes that sometimes make coaches leery of fast breaking.

So many variations of fast-break laning exist that it is impossible to describe the player characteristics for each of the lanes. Using the system described, we might say that Player A should be a quick, confident ball handler and capable dribbler, capable of spotting open players downcourt and making accurate passes under pressure. B should be a good ball handler, since he may have to bring the ball down when A has to give it up, and B should be able to hit the open shot at the end of the break, whether it be a lay-up or a twelve-to-fifteen-foot shot. (Many times, if C is used as a streaker downcourt, one opponent will be able to get back to cover C, the first man down on the break, and a second defender will take Ball Handler A, leaving no one to cover B.) Many coaches assign Lane C to their fastest player, hoping to catch the opponents off guard for a long pass and subsequent lay-

Diagram 5–5. Laning the Fast Break to the Baseline. In this version of the laning technique, B and C continue to the baseline rather than stopping at the free-throw line extended or cutting to the basket, and D and E continue to the basket instead of stopping at the corners of the free-throw line. This technique is intended either to spread the defensive coverage at the end of the break to permit D or E to slip inside for a lay-up, or to guarantee an open shot along the baseline. It is seen most often among teams with excellent corner shooting or big men capable of filling the lanes to the basket on the fast break.

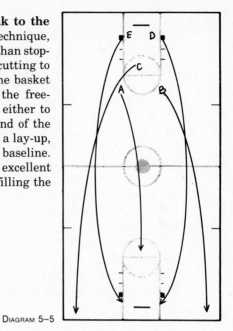

DIAGRAM 5–5

up. Players D and E are generally the team's best rebounders and serve as outlet passers and trailers in the ensuing fast break. If, for example, D inbounds the ball after scores, he trails the play and E fills his own lane as a trailer.

The chief weakness associated with laning is that when substitutes have been drilled in following one lane downcourt, they may become confused if they have to play other positions involving different passing lanes. Too, some offensive patterns are not conducive to players' moving out of their lanes and into a set offense quickly when the break does not yield a high-percentage scoring opportunity; still, this problem can usually be solved by modifying the offense slightly. Finally, when a team has only one capable ball handler, the opponents may overplay or double-team him to deny the outlet pass that begins the fast break. The team hoping to fast break more often than occasionally should have either a secondary ball handler or an inbounds passer (or preferably both) capable of making the long pass downcourt.

Moving Downfloor

There are conflicting theories on the best way to handle a fast break. Some coaches believe that the ball can move downfloor more quickly if it is passed back and forth from the center to the lanes. Advocates of this technique feel that in a standard three-on-two fast-break situation, it is more difficult for the two defense men to adjust their position if the ball is moving quickly from middle to lane than if it is moving down the middle. However, the ball must be passed back and forth to men running at top speed, and the lane men are very often big men who are not as agile as the middle men and tend to be a little more clumsy with the ball. They would have to make two or three perfect passes to the inside, leading the man and being careful of the defense.

We advocate that the middle man keep the ball. When he gets the ball in the center position and starts downfloor he maintains possession of the ball (in theory) all the way to the opposite foul line and makes the play. The ball is in the hands of the best ball handler, who can advance it downfloor as quickly as if it were being passed back and forth. No time is lost in starting the break as a result of this. However, if seconds were lost, it would be preferable to pay that penalty rather than running in a helter-skelter fashion or taking the increased possibility of throwing the ball away.

The middle position is the most critical position on the fast break, since the middle man develops the play, brings the ball downfloor, and decides what has to be done with it when it gets into the penetrating area. The lanemen simply have to get downfloor as quickly as they can in the most advantageous positions, depending on the defensive deployment. The wing men must get downfloor to the basket as quickly as possible, not waiting for the ball. If the middle man is going to release the ball early, it is his responsibility to make sure that the ball gets to them. They should get a step or two in front of their defensive men or lag a bit behind so that they will be open for a pass. The trailer man must also beat his man down the floor. The fifth man down floor will be several seconds behind the play. If a shot is taken and missed by either the wing or the trailer, the fifth man may be in an excellent position to knife through the middle and make a rebounding shot. If the opponents have regained possession of the ball, he must realize that he is the first man who must get back on defense and do so as quickly as possible. By placing men—not merely allowing the closest man to take the middle position—you cut down the margin of error, since you always have the ball in the hands of the best ball handler.

Once the middle man gets the ball in a center position (see Figure 5–4), he maintains control of the ball with a dribble all the way down the floor until he gets into penetrating area, at which time he must decide what he should do with it—whether to continue on to the basket or whether to throw to the lane man.

Figure 5–4. Rebounder finding middle man in center court.

The pass he makes must, in theory, lead directly to the score. If he passes to either of the lane positions or to a trailer position, he must try to make the play so that the man who receives the ball does not have to put the ball to the floor before he takes the shot. If a big man is in the lane position or in the trailer position, giving him the ball a bit too early and forcing him to take even one dribble increases the margin of error. The entire thinking on the fast break should be geared to cutting down errors or the opportunity for errors whenever possible.

Players must get the ball to the middle man behind the mid-court line as quickly as possible. If the middle man receives the outlet pass, he simply dribbles into the middle, after receiving the outlet pass facing into the middle of the court, if there is no defensive pressure. If he is not the man who receives the outlet, he must come to the ball as quickly as possible, taking a route determined by where the defense is stationed. If there is a defensive man between him and the ball, he has to move laterally toward the other guard, who has received the outlet pass, staying between the defense and the ball so that there is no question of an interception. If there is no defensive pressure and the defensive men are getting back downcourt quickly, he can move in a more diagonal path downcourt. Thus he can receive the secondary pass

Figure 5–5. Middle man moves defender to his left, opening his left wing man.

or the pass into the middle so that it always leads him into a position where he doesn't have to be concerned about defensive pressure or anyone stealing the ball. He is the one, once the first outlet pass has been made, who is going to make or break the fast break.

To develop the play properly, an alert middle man must be aware of who the lane men are, who his trailer man is, if possible, and what the defensive deployment in front of him is. As he approaches the head of the offensive key and the beginning of penetrating area, he must be under complete control, thinking about how he is going to develop the break, how he is going to move the defense, and what lane he is going to go to with the pass. (See Figure 5–5.) If a slower defensive man has taken a position against him in a three-on-two situation and is attempting to delay the advancement of the ball, the middle man can usually get around him very quickly. If they are matched off or the opponent is quicker, the middle man should release the ball to one of the wing men, even at a half-court position, thus developing a two-on-one situation by taking himself more or less out of the play rather than delaying the continuation of the fast break.

He should also consider getting the ball up a bit earlier if the wing man who is the best shooter has a step or two on his defender and if a lay-up situation can develop before he reaches the foul-line area.

Middle Man's Tactics

A number of alternatives are open to the middle man when he reaches a position within a radius of about fifteen feet from the basket. In unbalanced situations, he may, depending on the defensive adjustment, continue to the basket himself for a shot (see Figure 5–6), pass to his right wing or his left wing in the classic three-on-two situation (see Figure 5–7), or execute a trailer play if the trailer man (usually a big man) is in position. If the defense is balanced off, he again has the option of trying to effect the shot by passing to either wing and screening for the opposite wing, or he may dribble the ball toward either wing and simply set a lateral screen for a short jumper over his screen after a hand-off to that wing man.

In theory, if an overbalanced situation is present at the end of the court, the middle man, a wing man, or the trailer should

Figure 5–6. Middle-man tactic: split of defenders when they fall off to wing men.

a.

b.

Figure 5–7. Middle-man tactic: *a*, in three-on-two, he moves defense to his left; *b*, he passes to right wing.

be able to make a driving lay-up—the last two without dribbling. Sometimes both defenders may face back, guarding both wing men as the middle man picks up his dribble. If he can penetrate to the foul line, he may shoot. (See Figure 5–8.) Actually, this result will depend on two factors:

1. The middle man's timing in moving the defense and releasing the ball must be such that the receiver never has to dribble.

a.

b.

Figure 5–8. Middle-man tactic: *a*, fake to right wing; *b*, shot at foul line as defender falls back.

2. Once the receiver (a wing man) gets the ball, he must continue directly to the basket. If the low defensive man on that side picks him up, he may have to pass back to the middle man, who must remain at the foul line for this purpose. If the wing man drives for a basket himself, in spite of the guard, he may make a three-point play.

When the overbalance situation is not present, the middle man must immediately take alternative steps to effect a shot,

a.

b.

c.

Figure 5–9. Three-on-three: *a*, no fast break advantage; *b*, middle man dribble-screens for left wing; *c*, left wing cuts off middle man for jump shot or drive.

without slowing down the fast-break momentum. He should go into the three-on-three (Figure 5–9) or the two-on-two situation, either screening for a teammate or passing to one wing and screening for the opposite wing. The third alternative, the trailer play, is normally initiated by one of the two forwards or the center who is not involved in the initial fast break. He beats his man down the floor, alerting the middle man to his presence by calling out "right" or "left," indicating the side to which he is coming. This is an excellent alternative to exercise if your middle man is mobile. The middle man moves the defense to one side so that the trailer can come through. If the ball is given to the trailer at the proper time, it is almost impossible for the defense to adjust back in time to stop him. A three-point play will probably result.

If the middle man cannot make the play himself when he hears the trailer's call, he may pass to the opposite wing man and clear to the other side; in theory, opening up the middle. The wing man must then pass to the trailer. The problem with this alternative is that it necessitates two passes, raising the margin of error. We would prefer that the middle man keep the ball, knife off to his right or left as he reaches the middle, hopefully drawing the defensive man with him, and pass off to the trailer. The pass would be either a backward flip as he veers to the side without turning to look at the trailer or a two-hand underhand pass after he pivots quickly and protectively back to the middle.

Coaches differ in their beliefs on what the wing men should do if they reach the basket area and have not received a pass from the middle man. Some coaches have the men go completely under the basket; others have them step aside. We advocate button-hooking and coming back to the ball in case the middle man has been delayed or prevented from making the pass. However, if the trailer is following the wing man in, the wing man should not buttonhook back. He must continue under the basket to the opposite side in order to lure his guard along with him, leaving the lane wide open for the trailer. If the guard does not go with him, this wing man will be free under. The opposite wing man must be mentally alert for this alternative and decoy his defender. If the defender retreats, the opposite wing man may stop quickly, opening himself for a short jumper.

The middle man may have to waste some time around the middle area if one wing is a little behind the other. He should use lateral movement and a lot of movement toward the basket to make the defense think he is going into the basket himself, so that the pass to the wing will be more effective.

He should also attempt to pass, whenever possible, with the outside hand. If the passer is right-handed and he wishes to go to his left lane, he is going to be passing across the defender if he uses his right hand. To cut down the chances of a deflection or an interception, he should strengthen his other hand. If he doesn't have the power in his left hand to make this play, he must use a two-handed pass and step toward the receiver, keeping his body between the defender and the ball. When the middle man gets in the fifteen-foot area, the best pass to use 90 percent of the time is the bounce pass, because an aggressive bounce pass is almost impossible to intercept; even if it is deflected, it can get through the hands of a deflector and still reach its target. If the wing man cannot take the shot himself, he should pass back to the middle man, not to the opposite wing. The wing man may seem to be clear, but his defender has only about eight to ten feet to get back into position to deflect or intercept the ball.

Two-on-One and Five-on-Four Situations

We have explained the principles of the classic three-on-two and trailer (four-on-three) situations that develop most of the time in a fast break. Most of these principles also apply in a two-on-one situation. It is obviously a more simplified situation. The two offensive men must keep spread as much as possible in the front court while moving in to the basket. We do not advocate passing the ball back and forth. If the ball is in the hands of a guard, he should drive into the basket, looking for the lay-up shot and forcing the lone defender to jump to try to block the anticipated shot. The guard must dribble all the way into the basket. If he stops prematurely, he will not force the defender to commit himself, and that commitment is essential. If the driver feels he has the advantage when the defender jumps, he can attempt the lay-up. If not, he can drop the ball back down to the remaining man.

The five-on-four situation is really a trailer situation in that the fifth man must hang on the periphery of the action, possibly fifteen or so feet from the basket on the side away from the trailer, where he can receive a pass if his defensive man switches to the trailer. If the fifth man draws his defensive man with him, the trailer man will be clear for a pass. Depending on the reaction of the defensive man, the middle man can pass to the trailer or the fourth man.

Options Prior to a Pattern Offense

Even if the defense has evened off in a two-on-two or three-on-three or four-on-four situation when a fast break reaches the pen-

a.

b.

c.

Figure 5–10. Three-on-three: *a*, middle man passes left; *b*, middle man screens right; *c*, left wing passes to cutter (right wing).

etration area, the offense should carry this opportunity one step further and look for the short fifteen-foot jump shot. This action takes advantage of the fact that the offensive players have gotten downfloor before the defense has completely set. If no shot is possible, however, the offense may have to fall back on a pattern offense. The following three-on-three situation was developed in case a fast break does not show when the third defensive man gets back in position. The middle man uses a simple pass-and-pick-away movement. Its purpose is to free the opposite wing man for a short jump shot with an option of a pass to the screener, depending on the defensive adjustment. (See Figure 5–10.)

No team can depend on a fast break exclusively, so it must have a pattern it can fall back into, whether it is two-one-two or three-two or two-three. However, in some games the fast break can be used almost exclusively.

Sideline Fast Break

Sideline fast-breaking provides extremely quick ball movement downcourt. Instead of taking time to center the ball as teammates fill the passing lanes on either side of the court, as in traditional fast-breaking, the sideline fast break features a series of passes to players cutting along the sideline to free a superior wing or corner shooter for an open twelve-to-eighteen-foot shot before the opponents can organize their defense.

The strength of sideline fast-breaking lies primarily in the speed with which an open shot can be taken: after an opponent's score, the fast-breaking team can make three quick passes and have the ball in the hands of a superior shooter at the wing or in the corner inside four seconds—and after a defensive rebound, that time can be reduced by as much as a full second, since the outlet passer merely has to pivot and pass rather than jump out-of-bounds before passing. A second positive aspect of sideline fast-breaking is the ease with which weak-side rebounding is established, since the two or three players filling the passing lanes tend to draw most of the defenders' attention.

Finally, the sideline fast-breaking pattern is likely to be difficult for defenders because they almost invariably retreat in a straight line toward their own basket and gather their forces near their defensive basket to stop the most obvious threat, the lay-up. Since the fast-breaking team is using the sideline rather than the middle of the court to advance the ball, the offensive players are away from the defensive flow as the ball is moved downcourt.

There are only two weaknesses associated with the sideline fast-breaking technique. First, the designated shooter must be an outstanding shooter for the pattern to pay maximum dividends. (With an outstanding shooter, however, the pattern can add hundreds of points to a team's offensive output over the course of a season.) Second, the outlet pass receiver and the relay passer must be able to catch the ball and take no more than one dribble before finding the cutter ahead of them and passing the ball, all at full speed.

Diagram 5–6. Laning the Sideline Fast Break.
A is the inbound pass receiver after scores and
the outlet pass receiver after defensive rebounds.
(Most teams that use the sideline fast-break pattern always use the same side of the court; still,
the pattern could, with little difficulty, be
adapted for use on the other side by switching A
and B as outlet pass receiver and relay passer on
the left side of the court.) B is the second guard.
(Many coaches use their point guard at the B position, since he can always take the ball to the
middle for a normal three-on-two fast break if C
is guarded.) C is the designated shooter. D and E
are interchangeable: if one rebounds at the defensive end, the other fills the weak-side rebounding lane at the offensive end.

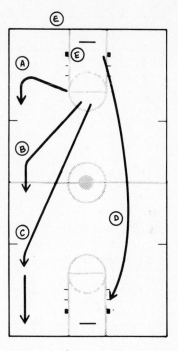

DIAGRAM 5–6

Diagram 5–7. Sideline Fast Break. E rebounds
the ball and pivots away from the basket, looking
for A cutting to the area of the free-throw line
extended. E passes to A, who turns and dribbles
once to give himself time to control the ball, check
the defense, and find B cutting toward the sideline in the midcourt area. A passes to B, who repeats the process, looking for C at the wing or the
corner. Meanwhile, D is breaking downcourt on
the weak side. B passes to C, who shoots if he is
open. D rebounds on the weak side, and B (or A,
whoever gets there first) rebounds in the middle.
C may also pass to A or B cutting toward the basket, which in turn may drawn defensive attention
to the cutter and leave D open under the basket.

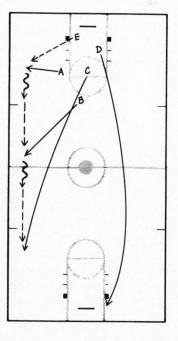

DIAGRAM 5–7

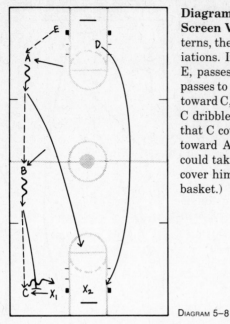

Diagram 5–8. Sideline Fast Break, Corner Screen Variation. Like all other fast-break patterns, the basic sideline fast break has many variations. In this example, A receives a pass from E, passes to B, and breaks down the middle. B passes to C and, seeing that the defense is playing toward C, moves to the baseline to screen C's man. C dribbles around the screen for the shot. (Note that C could also pass to A or continue dribbling toward A to set up a weave-like pattern. Or C could take the ball inside, forcing defender X_2 to cover him, and dump the ball off to D under the basket.)

DIAGRAM 5–8

Combating a Fast Break

The coach has two choices in combating an effective fast-breaking unit. One is to sustain as much pressure on the offensive board as possible, thereby delaying the defensive rebound and the outlet pass and subsequently the fast break. In that case he has to hold two or three men under the offensive board. The alternative is to concede the offensive rebound and tell the men to drop back as quickly as possible in order to assume a defensive posture or delay or stop the fast break.

Drilling

The fast break options must be practiced repeatedly so that the players react instinctively and the middle man knows the characteristics of his teammates—their speed, shooting ability, mobility, psychological reaction to the fast break, etc.

The following drill is particularly effective. One J.V. or weaker varsity team comes down the floor with the ball and takes a shot. (This team remains on the floor throughout the drill.)

When the opposing varsity team gets the ball, it immediately starts a fast break. The coach has two or three fast-break units alternating as the attacking team. This attacking unit must retreat defensively to beyond mid-court when it loses the ball. It is then replaced by another attacking unit, and the drill is repeated.

This drill serves many purposes. Initially, the weaker team practices working out of a stationary offensive pattern. The members of the team that is on defense initially, besides getting defensive practice, prepare themselves mentally for the instant transition to offense necessary for the fast break. They become defensively aggressive and alert so that they can get the ball more quickly and force the opposing team into mistakes or violations. They rebound more aggressively, positioning the men properly for the fast break. This drill also serves as a conditioning drill because it can be repeated over and over, shuttling as many as twenty men into it.

Fast-break Drills

Diagrams 5–9 through 5–13 on pages 181–185 are fundamental drills for incorporating the fast break into a team offense. We feel that the fast break is the most important single offensive attack that a team may have; therefore, players should perfect the fundamentals in early season practice.

A primary drill is a simple rebound drill.

Diagram 5–9. "Ball" Drill. A rebounder stands on either side of the basket. The coach shoots the ball, and the rebounder who rebounds it calls "Ball" as he obtains possession. Calling "Ball" to alert teammates is the first fundamental on obtaining the ball off the defensive board. Managers are stationed near the twenty-eight-foot hash marks in outlet position, and the rebounders must look for them and make the toss out as quickly as possible in good pass form, using a two-hand overhead, hook, or baseball pass. After the pass, rebounders should change positions. At first, no opposition should be on the court. However, once rebounders are used to calling "Ball," a defender should be placed against each rebounder to make the drill more realistic.

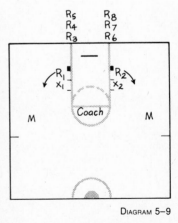

DIAGRAM 5–9

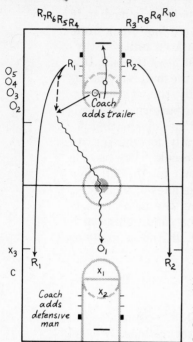

DIAGRAM 5–10

Diagram 5–10. Basic Three-on-Two Drill. This is one of the most important drills in teaching the fast break. One coach stands near the head of the circle at one end; another coach stands on the side of the court at the far end, at the foul line extended. Two defenders, X_1 and X_2, position at the far end. At the near end are two rebounders, R_1 and R_2, and an outlet man, O_1. The coach shoots, and the player who rebounds calls "Ball." The outlet man goes to the side of the court the rebounder is on, as close to the hash mark as he can get. Because he is always coming from behind the rebounder, the rebounder has to pick him up visually before making the outlet pass. The rebounder must *see* the outlet man before throwing; he cannot throw to a voice. O_1, the middle man on the break, receives the outlet pass and dribbles toward the center circle as R_1 and R_2 fill in the wing lanes, running in a straight line. The dribbler should use a high dribble as long as he does not meet any opposition. Occasionally, X_1 should dart out to challenge O_1. When O_1 comes into penetrating area near the top of the key, he must control his dribble and be under complete control himself. He should move the defenders, X_1 and X_2, so that he may pass off to either R_1 or R_2 without the receiver's having to make another pass or dribble.

Initially, this drill is used with just the three attackers against the two defenders. After the players become familiar with the movements, the coach at the defensive end adds a third defensive player. When he is added, the three fast-break men must immediately recognize that the defense is matched man-to-man and can play a man-to-man defense. The middle man must make a two-on-two or three-on-three play, either dribble in and screen for either side man, pass to his left and screen to his right or vice versa. He should not wait until the other two offensive players and the other two defenders can get into the play.

The third defensive man should be sent in before O_1 approaches the head of the free-throw circle so that all offensive players can recognize that they are matched defensively and go into some type of simple play pattern. It is much easier to get a good shot under three-on-three half-court conditions than it is when the defense is back and balanced in the five-on-five situation.

The coach at the initiating end will occasionally add a fourth man as a trailer during this three-on-three situation, calling a player by name from the group underneath the basket or the group on the side. Since the trailer comes up completely blind on the middle man, the trailer must give O_1 a verbal signal so that he can move the defenders to give the trailer a clear path to the basket. From this drill, coaches learn which players intuitively know how to move the defensive players to set up the trailer or to pass to a wing man in such a way that he does not have to dribble or make another pass. Occasionally, use all guards at the O_1 position, not only designated middle men. This drill helps to evaluate their potential. _____

TYPES OF OFFENSES AGAINST MAN-TO-MAN DEFENSE

The following principles must be incorporated into all basic man-to-man offenses, whether they be set pattern or free-lance play. The offense should keep the middle open. If a pivot man is being used, he should play opposite the ball side as much as possible. If a double pivot is being used, cutters should be able to move toward the basket without moving into the pivot area.

INSTALLING THE OFFENSIVE SYSTEM

The offensive system from a set pattern should be installed by diagraming each play on a blackboard, breaking down the options on each play, and explaining them thoroughly. (Each player should be given a copy of the diagram for reference.) The best method is to outline the play on a movable blackboard on the court. Then the coach should have five players walk through the set play on the court, without opposition. If necessary, the coach can lead the players through the play initially during this walk-through period. After each aspect of the play has been completely covered, the coach should leave the five players at one end of the court, then walk a second group through the play at the other

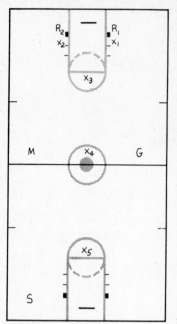

DIAGRAM 5–11

Diagram 5–11. Fast-Break Drill, Foul-Line Play. When the opponents are shooting a free-throw, the best rebounder-passer, R_1, should be stationed in the right offensive lane. R_2, the second-best rebounder, should be in the left lane. M, the designated middle man, should be at midcourt on the side opposite R_1. The best-shooting big man, S, should be in the deep corner on the same side as the middle man, and the other guard, G should be at mid-court.

The purpose of this drill is to initiate a fast break by beating the foul shooter, X_3, downcourt or to obtain a good jump shot for S. As soon as the ball reaches S, he should take any shot that he can take from twenty feet in.

Probably 70 percent of the shots that the foul shooter takes will go in. Therefore, the first fundamental this drill teaches is quick retrieval of the ball by the best rebounder-passer, who must step out-of-bounds and get the ball in to M. R_1, as the best passer-rebounder, will be the pass-in man. He must take the ball out-of-bounds immediately and throw it in to M, taking into consideration the position of X_4. If X_4 has moved toward M, R_1, who is normally the strongest passer and best long passer, should look for G cutting downcourt and may throw the ball long to him beyond half-court. (If the foul shot is missed and R_1 is the rebounder, he will pivot to the outside and pass immediately up to G.) G looks downcourt for S, who moves to the ball side. G passes to S if he is open. If S is not free, G may assume the middle man's role. However, in most situations M should be given the ball.

All the important ingredients of fast-break basketball are involved in this foul-line play. Therefore, we teach it as a drill in skeleton form first, later put a defensive team in to passively resist, then put in a team that will actively and aggressively attempt to stop the break.

end. The first group, led by an assistant coach or a captain, should be going through the play pattern slowly as the coach is working with the second group. The coach must insist on correct movement initially, since proper implementation of the play depends on accurate movement and timing. The coach should hold a player if he is going too soon or tap him lightly to start him on his way at the correct juncture.

On the first day that a play pattern is given to a team, the coach should identify it by a number, a name, or a recognizable key signal. He should use this name, number, or key signal repeatedly during his explanation of the play in the walk-through and slow-motion period.

On the second day, the coach should repeat the procedure explaining the play to the assembled squad, outlining it schematically on a blackboard on the court, going over the play repeatedly in the walk-through and slow-movement procedures (again doing it at both ends), and at all times referring to the play by name, by number, or by the recognizable key. On the third day, the coach should use passive defense against this play pattern. The defensive players should usually be the weaker players on the team, and they should be told to maintain passive defensive positions on their men. They should not use their hands, and they should not switch. It is imperative that the team gain confidence in the play; therefore, coaches should not defense their offense out of existence early in practice. Aggressive defense at this time may make the players lose confidence in the play.

The fourth day, the players should move more aggressively. Timing should be checked as the pattern movement speeds up, and constant constructive criticism should be offered. Once the players understand the play and the options completely, the coach should break the play down into its fundamental ingredients, for drilling. (Of course, the coach will probably inaugurate other play patterns periodically during these four days.)

The following tactics will help offensive teams maintain the proper deployment, or spread, against man-to-man defense. First, try to beat the opponent's weakest player one-on-one. Second, if the opponents adjust defensively to help this weaker defender, work through the weakened area after a feint towards the weak defender. Third, use inside screens to cut men free for a close-in shot, screening away from the ball or at the ball. Fourth, use beat-the-switch tactics and offensive rolls to negate the effectiveness of switches. Fifth, to obtain good shots for good shooters, use outside screens in the set shot area, especially against teams that use sloughing or sagging principles in their man-to-man defense.

The following are suggestions for offensive players in specific situations.

When playing against an opponent who is playing closely man-to-man, run your opponent into your teammates or his teammates. You can screen effectively away from the ball while being played closely because your guard usually concentrates on you so completely that he abandons team defensive principles—for example, he may neglect the switch, or he may neglect to drop off from the weak side to help teammates.

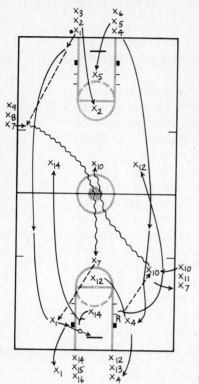

DIAGRAM 5–12

Diagram 5–12. Both-Ends Three-Two Drill.

This is fairly complicated, but it is such a complete-action, rapidly moving drill, any team—especially one that wishes to incorporate the fast break in its offense—should use it as soon as the players can learn it. Players X_1 to X_{16} are placed at six spots around the court: at one end of the court at each foul lane extended; at the hash mark to the right of the first spots, at the far end of the court at both foul lanes extended; and at the hash mark to the right of those foul lanes. X_1, with the ball, X_7, to his right, and X_4, the other under man, step on the court, ready to attack in a three-on-two situation. X_{12} and X_{14} are defenders in tandem position front and back at the far end of the court. X_1 initiates the drill by passing to X_7. X_7 dribbles to the middle as X_1 and X_4 fill the fast-break lanes. X_7 penetrates and attempts to make a scoring pass to X_1 or X_4. Only one shot is allowed. X_1, X_7, and X_4 do not rebound. X_{12} and X_{14} attempt to break up the fast three-on-two break coming at them. If they cannot, they rebound the shot. X_{10}, at their right at the hash mark, steps inbounds. If X_{12} has rebounded, he immediately turns to his outside and pitches to X_{10}, who assumes the middle man's role. If X_{10} observes the rebound going to the opposite side of the court to X_{14}, he must move cross-court, calling for the ball, and get in outlet position to receive a pass from X_{14}. X_{10} takes the ball to the middle with rebounders X_{12} and X_{14} filling the wing lanes. The two defenders waiting are X_2 and X_5, who have stepped onto the court in front and back tandem position to attempt to stop the fast break. X_{10} penetrates. X_{14} and X_{12} run their lanes looking for good position to get a shot. X_2 and X_5 rebound, and X_8, at the right hash mark, steps inbounds to become the middle man. X_{15} and X_{13}, at the far end, have now stepped on the court to defend against this break, with X_8 as a middle man and X_2 and X_5 as the wing men.

This extremely good continuous-motion drill contains all the fundamentals of three-two fast-break basketball. Coaches should not run this drill for more than ten minutes at a stretch. However, it is especially effective during the last three minutes, when the players become a little tired as they would late in a game. As this drill is used periodically in the daily practices during the preseason and season, the players will be able to sustain themselves longer and longer.

Preferably, the middle men in the fast break should be at the hash mark position so that they handle the middle on the break most frequently in this drill. However, at times coaches can place the middle men underneath so that they have experience playing defense against a three-on-two break. For a change of pace, coaches can sometimes allow one of their big men who fancies himself a ball handler to assume the outlet position and handle the ball coming up the middle. This shows players that certain players make better middle men than others. _____

Diagram 5–13. One-Two-Three Drill. This drill starts at the far end of the court. The coach is in the free-throw circle. X_1 and X_2, the rebounders, and X_3, the middle man, are in the classic triangle rebound position. The coach shoots. X_1 or X_2 rebounds, turns to the outside, and looks for X_3, who must move to the proper side for the outlet pass. When X_3 obtains the ball, he dribbles hard to the middle, with X_1 and X_2 as wing men in the classic three-on-two break. X_4 and X_5 defend against them at the other end as they come downcourt and attempt to score. Only one shot is allowed. X_4 and X_5 rebound. X_6, who is at the right-side mid-court area, moves onto the court, near the center circle. X_4 and X_5 move up the court with the ball, attempting to score against X_6 in a two-on-one posture. After a shot, X_6, X_4, and X_5 stay at that end, returning the ball to the coach. X_4 and X_5 become rebounders, and X_6 becomes the middle man, setting up the rebound triangle. X_9 and X_{12} step on court at the other end to act as defenders. The coach again initiates the three-on-two phase of the drill by shooting.

Next to our both-ends three-two fast-break drill, this is our favorite continuous-action drill. Practicing it frequently is extremely beneficial because it gives big men experience in the two-on-one attacking postures. _____

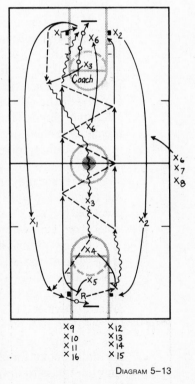

DIAGRAM 5–13

When playing against a team that jump switches, the passer-off should cut directly to the basket as soon as he hands off. The receiver should anticipate the jump switch and stop immediately on receiving the ball, remaining alive, alert for possible double-team situations, and in a position to return the ball immediately to the teammate who passed it to him if he's free on his cut to the basket. If the receiver cannot pass back to his teammate, he should reverse pivot when the jump switch is used and dribble away from the jump switch toward his original direction.

When playing against a defensive opponent who uses floating or sagging tactics, dropping back to the basket at all opportunities, look for medium-range shots that are in a high-percentage area. Try to divert his attention from the focal point, and look for lateral screens from teammates away from the ball. If the defender is a long way off, walk into him toward the screener. If he doesn't move, use a change of direction or pace as you approach him and cut tight off the screen to open yourself near the ball. If he retreats, continue to take him in closer. If there is no screen, a quick fake toward the basket and a quick step back will open you for a short or medium shot.

If your team is using a pivot offense and the pivot player is being fronted, teammates should clear the weak side. This action increases the possibility and effectiveness of a lob pass by taking a possible floating defender away from the area of defensive help. If the closest defender insists on staying in the double-team area to prevent the effectiveness of a lob pass to a pivot, the weak-side offensive player clearing should go immediately to the best intermediate shooting area. He'll get an easy shot, or he can pass in to the fronted pivot player if his defender leaves the pivot area and moves toward the ball.

All pivot players must be able to use evasive tactics in moving toward the ball, and the passer-in should be able to tell the pivot player the location of his guard by passing to the hand farthest from this defender.

Every offensive pattern used against man-to-man defense must spread the offense to spread the defense. Such spreading can be affected (1) by use of screens, (2) by movement away from the ball, and (3) by good passing and ball handling. The passer must always see the guard of the man he passes to, see options for the man he's passing to, and know the limitations of the man he's passing to. If the potential receiver is a good shooter who normally looks for shots when he receives the ball, the passer shouldn't pass to him unless there is a good shooting opportunity. If the player is a poor ball handler on low passes, the passer shouldn't bounce pass to him. If he's a poor dribbler and must dribble more than one bounce in order to obtain a favorable offensive position, the ball handler should hold the pass.

PLAY SITUATIONS AND SET PATTERNS FROM MAN-TO-MAN OFFENSIVE SYSTEMS

We will discuss play situations and set patterns from the following six types of offensive systems:

1. *Single-pivot offense.* The first such offense uses two guards out front (normally the ball handlers), two forwards, and a strong, big pivot man who takes care of the pivot area. In a second single-pivot offense, the pivot man is used as a screener. A third uses a basic screening figure-eight movement between the three inside players, who are fairly agile, big men, not one of whom has more outstanding pivotability than the others. This offense keeps the three big men in close to the basket and allows a good offensive rebounding potential.

2. *Double-pivot offense.* In a one-three-one structure, one pivot player (the better ball handler) is always in the high position or middle position, while the less agile pivot or the better rebounder is the low man under the basket. In a three-two structure, a continuity pattern is used, with the two pivot men starting from a medium-post position.

3. *Basic free-lance offense.* In a three-two structure, three men are out front and two are wide underneath. In a two-one-two structure, two guards are out front ball handling, two agile forwards are in the corners, and an agile pivot man moves from low to medium to high position at random. The passing game is a more structured version of free-lance offense that is now in popular use.

4. *Overload.* Four players on the same side of the court use a continuity-movement, or shuffle.

5. *Basic stack offense.* Four offensive players are placed within ten feet of the basket, two along each of the foul lanes, facing each other. This is an excellent offense for cutting down the number of bad passes, in keeping with the margin-of-error theory.

6. *Continuity offenses.* There are a number of patterns that allow all players to attack from each defensive position without resetting the alignment. Rapid call movement and cutting from one side to the other are employed.

Following are basic rules for running plays from all offensive formations.

1. Fake the first pass to check and hold the defense.
2. Pass toward the receiver's outside shoulder, away from his defender. The man receiving the pass should meet and protect the ball.
3. Cut to the basket sharply, leaving no daylight if using a screen.
4. Unless the coach gives orders to the contrary, set the screen facing the basket whenever possible.
5. Proper timing in running plays is the key to successful execution.
6. When making the pass or using a screen and receiving the ball, always keep yourself alive by maintaining your dribble.
7. The men not involved directly in the play should continue movement (for example, exchange positions to discourage floating by defense).
8. If defense overplays the switches, be prepared to exercise play options immediately.
9. Use a change of pace whenever cutting.

Single-Pivot Attack

A single-pivot attack may use one player in a two-three offense as the pivot man primarily. This player should be a tall, strong, mobile player who can get good pivot position. He must move in an area from the basket to sixteen feet away, constantly maneuvering for advantageous position, breaking from a low or away position to meet the ball.

If a pivot man is to be interchangeable with the forwards, normally he will be used to screen away from the ball, rebounding, and cutting off a low screen set by a fellow forward. The evasive moves of the player in the single-pivot position are of prime importance. He must be able to pivot away when closely guarded, reach the designated position at the correct time, break away from the ball position and cut back, keep the defender on his back as the ball changes from one side to the other, turn the defenders away from the position of the ball by using all possible evasive tactics, and have a variety of shots from the inside position. The pivot player must realize that it's very difficult to get the ball in to him when he's in a low pivot position, but if he can get the ball he must score himself, since it is hard to cut off a low pivot player toward the basket. Cuts from away from the ball are good moves when the ball is in this position.

The pivot player must be able to protect the ball, keeping the basket area clear and staying on the side away from the ball initially so that cutting players can take advantage of the middle.

He should never dribble more than one or two bounces, unless he is forced to dribble out away from the basket in a protective position. He must always be in good offensive rebound position, being able to roll off opponents, spin, slide, or exert pressure, without letting the opponent feel his position. He is used as a screen frequently, and he is always the key rebounder offensively.

The possible plays in single-pivot, two-three alignment, will each have a number. The key ball handler initiates a play by calling the number or by making a finger signal.

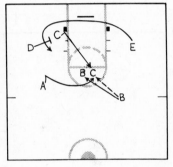

DIAGRAM 5–14

Diagram 5–14. Single-Pivot, Two-Three Alignment, Play Number 1. A and B, the guards, have brought the ball into attack position at approximately even with the hash marks on the side of the court and just to the outside of the foul lanes. D and E, the forwards, are even with the second foul-lane marker (the first lane marker after the buffer zone), a little wider than the guards. The center, C, started in a low-pivot position, opposite the ball position. As C, the pivot man, moves up to the high pivot, B passes to him and follows his pass, setting a double-screen at the foul line with C at the side to which he passed. A fakes a movement down the left sideline and cuts sharply behind the double screen set on the foul line by B and C. As B makes the pass, E, the forward on the same side, clears to the opposite side, opening the whole right corner of the court. C has the option of giving the ball to A for an eighteen-foot jump shot over the double screen set by C and B or passing it to A on a tight cut to the basket. D, the weak-side forward, sets a screen on that side for E. A has the option of taking the shot or continuing on to the basket with the ball. If A takes a jump shot, the rebounding will be done by D on the left, C on the right, and E in the middle, with A the intermediate rebounder. If A continues to the basket, the rebounders will be D on the strong side, C in the middle, and A on the right side. E, the intermediate rebounder, will move back toward B, the deep defender, as soon as A shoots or goes by. _____

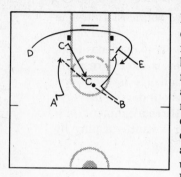

DIAGRAM 5–15

Diagram 5–15. Play Number 2. This play is a direct follow-up to Play Number 1. The play starts in basically the same fashion with B passing the ball into C, who has moved up after a preliminary fake. A makes the same basic move, faking away and then heading towards C's position. D, the corner man, opposite the original ball position, clears. A fakes a movement toward C and changes direction toward the basket, receiving a pass. B, after faking toward C, moves to his right and sets up a double screen with E along the right foul lane. D circles behind the double screen. The rebounding will be done by A on the left, C in the middle, E on the right, and D in the intermediate position. B will fall back quickly for defensive protection if A shoots or if D shoots over the double screen if C passes to him.

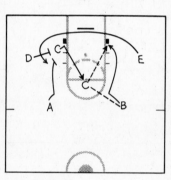

Diagram 5–16. Play Number 3. B passes into C, coming high. E clears the right side. B fakes toward C and reverses toward the basket to receive a pass from C. A, after faking in, sets a double screen on the left side of the foul lane with D. E circles behind this double screen. Rebounders will be D on the left, C in the middle, B on the right, and E in intermediate position. After a shot, A retreats quickly to a safety position.

DIAGRAM 5–16

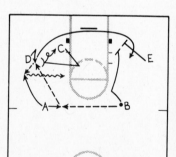

DIAGRAM 5–17

Diagram 5–17. Play Number 4. With all players in their basic starting positions, B passes to A. A moves to meet the pass. D fakes to the baseline and moves out to get the pass. A passes to D. C starts towards the foul-line area and reverses direction toward the ball. A cuts behind D for a return pass. After D returns the pass, he clears to the baseline under the basket. C sets a rear screen for A. A dribbles off the rear screen toward the center. C uses an offensive roll into the basket from the left side. A has the option of driving into the basket, stopping for a medium jump shot, passing to C on his offensive roll, or passing to D, who has circled under the basket and come behind a double screen set by E and B on the right foul lane. If any shot is taken, C will rebound the left side, E will rebound the right side, D will rebound the middle, A will be the intermediate rebounder, and B will retreat into a safety position.

Diagram 5–18. Alternative Play Number 4.
(An option of Play 4 in Diagram 5–17.) A receives
the pass from B and passes to D after D's fake. A
clears through, indicating to D that he will be
able to use C's screen. C sets a rear screen for D.
D dribbles off and has the same options as A in
the previous play. C rolls to the basket. A goes
behind the double screen set on the right foul lane
by E and B. C again rebounds the left, E rebounds
the right, D rebounds the middle, B is the intermediate rebounder, and A retreats for defensive
purposes. _____

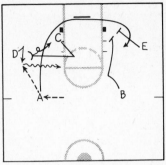

DIAGRAM 5–18

Diagram 5–19. Play Number 40 or 41. Guard
B has the ball before the preliminary movement.
On observing the defensive posture of the man
guarding E, B has two options. After a pass to E,
he may cut to E's inside between E and his defender to receive an inside hand-off, or he may
cut outside E and receive an outside hand-off. (40
is outside, 41 is inside.) He can then dribble into
the basket for a shot. The rebounders will be C
in the middle, D on the left, E, the intermediate
position, and B on the right. If B's shot is not a
driving lay-up, E will rebound the right, B will
be the intermediate rebounder, and A will move
back on defense. _____

DIAGRAM 5–19

Diagram 5–20. Play Number 5. B passes to E
and fakes to the center. C starts up from the low
side opposite the ball and reverses direction to a
medium pivot. E passes to C, follows his pass, and
sets a screen just above the foul line on the right
side of the circle. B reverses, cuts off the screens
set by E and C, and receives a pass from C. B may
take a short jump shot or drive into the basket.
D and A decoy their men away from the point of
attack. D rebounds the left side, C the center, and
B the right. E is the intermediate rebounder, and
A falls back. _____

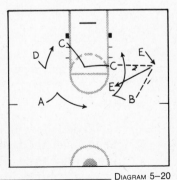

DIAGRAM 5–20

DIAGRAM 5-21

Diagram 5–21. Play Number 6. B passes to C moving into the high-pivot position. B moves as though to set a foul-line double screen. E clears. A fakes and deploys to his right. C has the option of turning and taking a jump shot or turning to the open side and driving into the basket with his man guarding him one-on-one. D moves in, and he and B set a double screen on the left side for E, who is circling around. If C's movement toward the basket is stopped, he has the option of passing to E. For rebounding, C is on the right side, D on the left side, E in the middle, and B in the intermediate position. A moves back on defense.

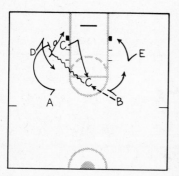

DIAGRAM 5-22

Diagram 5–22. Play Number 7. C moves up into high-pivot position and receives a pass from B. B fakes toward C and deploys to his right. E fakes and deploys to the baseline, keeping his man occupied. A fakes toward the ball and moves in to a low screening position. C fakes and dribbles to the offensive left, setting up a double screen for D on that side. D fakes toward the baseline and comes back off the double screen. C, after his screen, makes an offensive roll to the basket from the left side. D has the option of shooting, driving, or passing to C. C rebounds the left side, E the right side, and D the middle. A is the intermediate rebounder, and B falls back on defense.

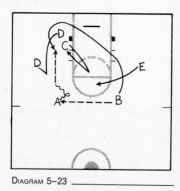

DIAGRAM 5-23

Diagram 5–23. Play Number 8. B passes to A. A starts as though to dribble into the middle, then changes direction to the left. B cuts through. C starts from the low position, opposite, toward the high pivot and reverses. D fakes, and C and D set a low double screen for B. A passes to B behind the double screen. B has the option of a drive or jump shot. E moves into the middle to decoy his man and to be open if his man sags toward the ball. A drops back on defense. D rebounds the left, C rebounds on the right, E rebounds the middle, and B is the intermediate rebounder.

The following series of plays involves a figure-eight movement under the basket from a two-three alignment. No name or number has to be called to initiate a play in this series. Each play is predetermined by the offensive team, and it is initiated by the movement of the guard with the ball (B in these diagrams).

Diagram 5–24. Basic Pattern. B passes to E, the forward. E should fake to the basket and come back to receive the pass. B cuts outside E. C sets a rear screen away from the ball for D. D fakes to the baseline and cuts off C's screen. E has the option of passing to D on the cut, passing to C if there is a switch, passing back to B in the corner, or passing to A, moving across, out front.

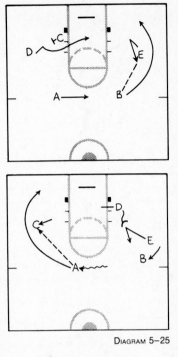

DIAGRAM 5–24

Diagram 5–25 (Continuation of movement in Diagram 5–24). E passes to A, who dribbles the ball toward C, the original low-pivot man. C has moved out to receive a pass after screening for D. A passes to C and cuts to the outside into the corner. D sets a rear screen away from the ball for E. E may cut to the ball. In this diagram, E has run into the screen, and as the men have fallen off he has dropped back. C may pass across the court to E. In Diagrams 5–24 and 5–25, C, D, and E are the rebound triangle under the basket, taking the position nearest their placement on the court. The guard in the corner is the intermediate rebounder, and the back guard is the safety man.

DIAGRAM 5–25

Diagram 5–26. B passes to E, then sets an inside screen. E dribbles off B's screen, and B rolls to the basket. E has the option of driving to the basket; shooting a medium jump shot; passing to B on the roll; passing to D, who has cut off C's position; or passing back out to A.

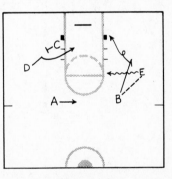

DIAGRAM 5–26

Diagram 5–27. B passes to E and signals the initiation of the offense by moving into the outer half of the free-throw circle. C moves from his low position, opposite, to a medium pivot on the ball side. E passes to C. A cuts off a screen set by B and follows E to the outside as E cuts over the ball position to the inside. D decoys his man away from the point of attack. The rebounding will be done by D on the left side, E, in the middle, C in the intermediate position, and A (if he's the shooter) on the right. B falls back on defense.

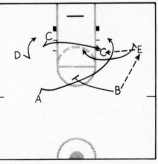

DIAGRAM 5–27

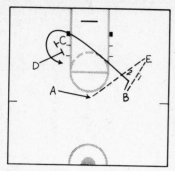

DIAGRAM 5–28

Diagram 5–28. B passes to E, takes one step toward the pass, and cuts diagonally across the court, his movement signalling the play. A moves to the head of the key. C and D set a double screen away from the ball, and B cuts around it. E passes to A at the head of the key. A looks for B coming around the double screen. If there is a switch, D can roll to the basket. Rebounding positions are C on the left, E on the right, and D in the middle, with B the intermediate rebounder. A plays defense.

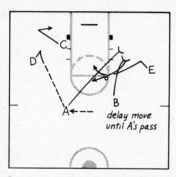

DIAGRAM 5–29

Diagram 5–29. B passes to A and holds position. Holding position is the signal for the play. A passes to D, then moves diagonally to the opposite foul-lane area. B moves as A moves to set a double screen for E. E cuts off the double screen, and C decoys his man away from the foul-lane area. D may pass to E or to B, who has rolled back toward the ball into the foul-line area. A retreats as a defensive safety factor. B, C, D, and E rebound the offensive board, with B in the intermediate position.

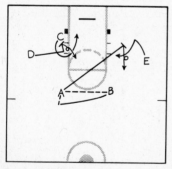

DIAGRAM 5–30

Diagram 5–30. B passes to A and cuts behind A to receive a return pass. As A returns the pass, D moves in and sets a screen for C. C rolls around the screen to the basket. A cuts diagonally and sets a screen for E, who fakes away and then cuts back over the screen. The timing is such that B's first option is to pass to C or (if C is not open) to pass to D on his roll to the ball. B's second option is to pass to E or (if E is not open) to pass to A on his roll back. B will retreat for defensive purposes while A, C, D, and E rebound with A as the intermediate rebounder.

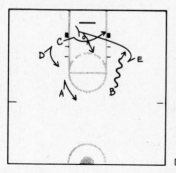

DIAGRAM 5–31

Diagram 5–31. B dribbles in toward E's position as the signal for initiating the offense. E fakes and reverses. If E is open, B may pass to him. If E is not open, he continues his movement, screening for C. C cuts off the screen to the basket. E may roll back toward the ball after C's cut. A and D decoy their men away from the point of attack. D, C, and E rebound inside, B is the intermediate rebounder, and A moves back on defense.

Diagram 5–32. B starts to dribble toward A, then passes to A as the keying maneuver. A dribbles off the inside screen set by B. E fakes to the ball and reverses. If he cuts clear into the basket, he may receive A's pass. If not, he V's out to the ball and receives a pass from A. A and B set a double screen along the left lane for D. D fakes toward the basket and cuts off the double screen to receive a pass from E. C decoys his man away from the point of attack and then moves into rebounding position. C rebounds left, E right, and D in the middle, and B moves back into safety position. A is the intermediate rebounder in this shot.

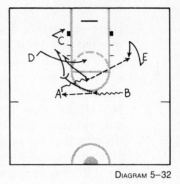

DIAGRAM 5–32

Diagram 5–33. B passes to A and sets an inside screen for E. D sets a screen for C, who is in a pivot position. C cuts back to the ball. D sets up in pivot position. E cuts to the basket. A has the options of passing (1) to E as he cuts off B's screen; (2) to B as he rolls back to the ball after screening; and (3) to C as he moves back off D's screen. If C receives the ball, he may pass into D in the pivot position, and A and C may scissor off D's position. B moves back into defensive position in this case. If E, B, or C takes the shot, A moves back while the others rebound, B being the intermediate rebounder.

DIAGRAM 5–33

Double-Pivot Offense

A double-pivot offense is excellent for a team with two taller players and three smaller, more agile players. Normally, players A, B, and C can be interchangeable in this offense. Good jump-shooting and set-shooting opportunities for these players appear frequently. The double-pivot offense is usually a tandem pivot, with one pivot man in a high position and one in a low position. D and E may exchange positions if they are fairly equal in ability. However, if one is less agile than the other and not as good a ball handler, he should be placed low, away from the ball, in position E. There he can be used as a screener for a cut to the ball, and he is in good rebound position. Screens off E may result in a mismatch that will allow him to receive the ball for an easy shot. The more mobile pivot player can play on the foul line because he will have more latitude than the slower player and will be able to move into the basket for rebounds with more agility. If the two pivot players are of equal ability, it is possible to play a three-out with a double medium-pivot system, with the players playing side by side and interchanging frequently.

A double-pivot offense lends itself very well to a disciplined style. It is easy to teach, and it has good balance, excellent continuity, and good ball-control potential. It puts personnel in their best offensive positions, and it is very adaptable as a zone offense, without much adjustment. It has good inside and outside offensive threats, it puts pressure on the defense (since they must play two pivot men), and it gets good high-percentage shots. It is excellent for taking advantage of one-on-one situations or two-on-two freelance basketball. There are good scissoring opportunities off either pivot player. It is hard for defensive players to sag effectively against this offense, as it gives good, quick intermediate shots when ball movement is reversed. When defensive players overplay wing men, good back-door and screening opportunities result.

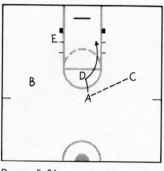

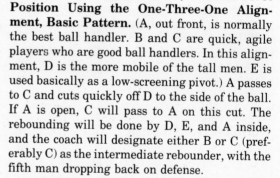

DIAGRAM 5–34

Diagram 5–34. Double Pivot, Tandem Pivot Position Using the One-Three-One Alignment, Basic Pattern. (A, out front, is normally the best ball handler. B and C are quick, agile players who are good ball handlers. In this alignment, D is the more mobile of the tall men. E is used basically as a low-screening pivot.) A passes to C and cuts quickly off D to the side of the ball. If A is open, C will pass to A on this cut. The rebounding will be done by D, E, and A inside, and the coach will designate either B or C (preferably C) as the intermediate rebounder, with the fifth man dropping back on defense.

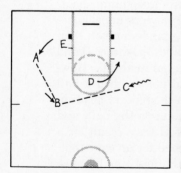

DIAGRAM 5–35

Diagram 5–35 (Continuation of movement in Diagram 5–34). If A cannot receive the pass on the cut, C will dribble toward the head of the key, and B will adjust up from his wing position. C will pass to B, and A will circle underneath and cut back out to the ball, using E as a stationary screen. B will pass into A if A is open, with D deploying to the right. If there is a switch between the defenders of E and A, A may pass into E immediately, as E will have the smaller defender guarding him.

The double-pivot is an excellent offense when one tall player is uncoordinated or slow or is not a good ball handler. He can be placed to advantage (see E in Diagram 5–34) without affecting the offensive maneuvering to any great extent. The double-pivot is also a good offense to use when trying to slow down the tempo of the game. It can be used very effectively against zone and combination defenses.

Diagram 5–36. Cut, Screen, and Roll Play. A passes to C and cuts off D. If A does not receive a return pass, he screens low for E. E cuts off the screen toward the ball. A makes an offensive roll into the under-basket area. C can pass to E or A. In this diagram E, D, and A will rebound under, C will be the intermediate rebounder, and B will go back on defense.

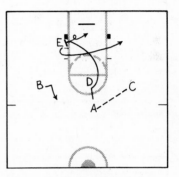

DIAGRAM 5–36

Diagram 5–37. Double Pivot, One-Three-One, Double Screen. A dribbles toward Wing Man B, passes to B, and moves inside toward the left corner. B dribbles off A. This signals a double screen on the low right side, with D moving in with C to set the double screen. E moves around behind the double screen. This keeps the big men, D and E, in low position for good rebounding balance. If E has the shot, he will take it after a pass from B.

DIAGRAM 5–37

Diagram 5–38. Double Pivot from One-Three-One Tandem Alignment, Screen Away. A passes to C, starts toward D, and cuts away, setting a screen away from the ball for B. B cuts off the screen into the foul-line area. D fakes toward the ball and cuts away, setting a screen for E. E cuts off the screen. C may pass to B or E after the cuts. A will come back for defense; E, D, and B will be the three inside rebounders; and C will be the intermediate rebounder. This positioning also gives good one-on-one opportunities to C against a weaker defender.

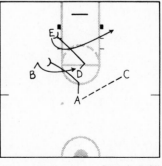

DIAGRAM 5–38

Diagrams 5–39 through 5–43 show three play situations from the one-three-one tandem alignment that are keyed to the movement of Guard A with the ball.

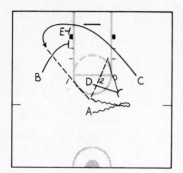

DIAGRAM 5–39

Diagram 5–39. Double Screen. A's dribble to the right signals the play. As A dribbles, C, the right wing, reverse cuts toward the basket. If he is open, he may receive a pass quickly from A. If he is not open, B and E set a double screen low on the left side. D, the high pivot, moves out to the right at the head of the key to set a block for A, who pivot dribbles off this block. As A dribbles back, A may (1) pass to C, if he is open behind the double screen, or (2) pass to D, who has used an offensive roll off the screen toward the basket.

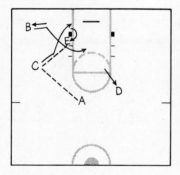

DIAGRAM 5–40

Diagram 5–40 (Following Diagram 5–39). Scissor after Double Screen. A passes to C, who does not have the shot. B moves into the left offensive corner. E turns into pivot position from his double screen position. C passes into E, and C and B scissor cut off E's position. D has moved out after not receiving a pass on his offensive roll in Diagram 5–39. B, C, and E will rebound in close to the basket, D will be the intermediate rebounder, and A will drop back on defense.

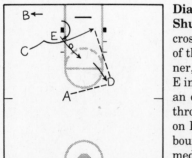

DIAGRAM 5–41

Diagram 5–41 (Alternative to Diagram 5–40). Shuffle Cut. If A cannot pass to C, he passes cross-court to D, who has moved out to the head of the key at the right. B moves into the left corner, E rolls into medium-pivot position, C cuts off E in a shuffle cut toward the basket, and E makes an offensive roll into the lower half of the free-throw circle. D may pass to C on his cut or to E on E's offensive roll. Again, B, C, and E will rebound in close to the basket, D will be the intermediate rebounder, and A will go back on defense.

Diagram 5–42. Double Pivot, One-Three-One, Triple Screen. A bounce passes to B, the left wing. On the bounce pass, E, D, and A form a triple screen along the right foul lane. C may cut to either side of this screen, hoping for a shot. If one doesn't materialize, B and C may play two-on-two on the left side, with A rolling back toward the ball. The signal is the bounce pass to the wing on the left.

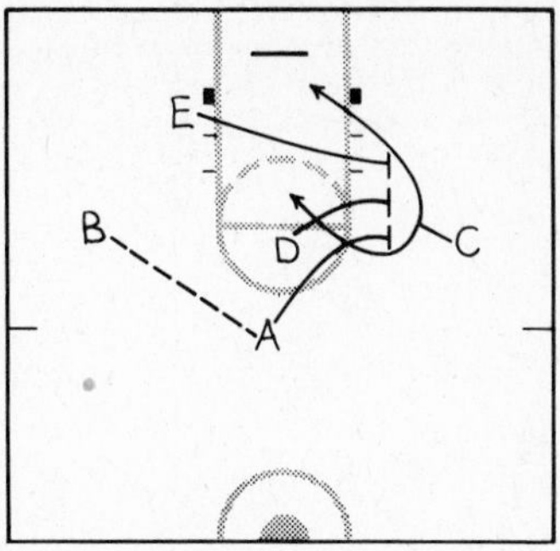

DIAGRAM 5–42

Diagram 5–43. Double Pivot, One-Three-One, High-Low Exchange. A dribbles and waves toward the basket to signal the play. On the hand wave, D and E exchange positions. E comes up strong from his low-pivot position, receives a high pass from A, and pivots toward the basket. At the same time, B moves in and screens low for D. D circles around behind B's screen. C moves into a low position on the right as D and E are exchanging. A sets a screen for C, and C rolls back. The timing is such that D will be open for a pass first and C second. If neither pass is possible, C should roll through the pivot area, going to the left. A, who has moved to the right corner after his screen, will receive the pass from E for a one-on-one move toward the basket.

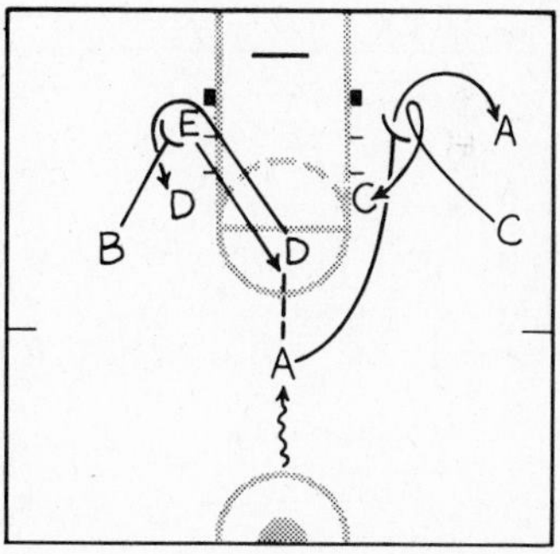

DIAGRAM 5–43

Diagrams 5–44 through 5–48 illustrate a double pivot, three-two continuity. All players keep moving, and each has several shooting opportunities as he goes through the continuity movement.

Diagram 5–44. A initiates the play movement by dribbling to his left. As he dribbles, E moves out of his medium-pivot position and sets a rear screen for C, who cuts to the outside toward the basket. D makes the same movement on the right side, and B cuts off D toward the basket. If C is open, A can pass to him. C and B continue their movement, cutting off each other on their right side, C moving out to the right side, B continuing to the left side. A may pass to B.

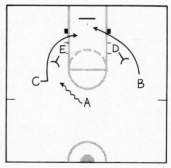

DIAGRAM 5–44

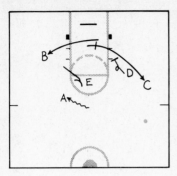

Diagram 5–45. After B cuts by D, D rolls and sets a block for C, coming out. C should be in good medium-range shooting territory after this second block. E rolls to the left end of the foul line to set a block for A, who may reverse his dribble off E's block for a jump shot from the foul-line area. A may also pass to B in this movement, for a one-on-one move, if B is open.

DIAGRAM 5–45

Diagram 5–46. A passes to B. E moves back toward his original position, and D rolls and cuts to the basket after screening for C.

DIAGRAM 5–46

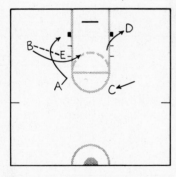

Diagram 5–47. B passes into E in the medium-pivot position on the left, and B and A scissor off the E pivot position. C moves back toward the middle as an outlet man or as a defensive safety man. D rolls toward the right side, low, in good rebound position.

DIAGRAM 5–47

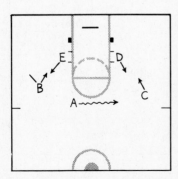

Diagram 5–48. If the play in Diagram 5–47 is not available, B will pass back to A, who will dribble toward the right. B and C are now back in the wing positions on opposite sides of the court from their original positions, D and E move back into their medium-pivot positions, and as A moves to the right, the continuity continues to the right side.

DIAGRAM 5–48

Free-lance Offense

Free-lance offenses use the play patterns outlined in Chapter 4. If players are not completely familiar with all of the movements of these play patterns and with their teammates' habits and movements with or without the ball, they should not use a free-lance offense. However, if players know each other's movements well and are good ball handlers, they can derive much satisfaction from such an offense, since it allows latitude for intuitive and instinctive movement. Of course, all players must be aware of the basic principles of team free-lance movement.

Basic Type. The first movement that is used frequently in free-lance offense is a weave, or figure-eight movement. This is basic ball movement in weave fashion, cutting to the basket, using inside screens to delay or impede opponents defensively so that receivers can cut free, using give-and-go plays, and cutting off the ball whenever the ball is between your defender and the basket. Give-and-go requires excellent fundamentals by all five offensive players—smooth ball handling with continuous movement, excellent screening and use of screens, and good movement without the ball. In using a freelance offense, all players must be aware of audible and visual signals that their teammates may use; for example, hand claps, peculiar vocal sounds such as "beep-beep," head and eye signals, and finger pointing.

The weave is used for circulation and for preliminary movement before a free-lance play. Set-pattern teams, as well as free-lance teams, make good use of the weave movement. Receivers cut close to, and outside, the ball. The passer usually uses a short, one- or two-hand underhand pass with good fingertip control. He follows his pass, and the receiver moves toward it. The passer may inside screen or outside screen (usually the latter).

If players move too close together in a weave, the man with the ball should skip a man, and the man who did not receive the ball should cut for the basket. Players must move.

Weaving is very effective against close guarding, but it is ineffectual if the players are cutting toward the sidelines habitually and if the defenders are playing zone. It may be used by three, four, or five men. The circulation may be deep from the basket (as in a four- or five-man weave movement) or it may be flat, parallel to the mid-court line (as in a three-man weave).

An essential of weaving is excellent ball handling, with the passer always crossing in front of the receiver. If there is no pass, the man with the ball may stop and pivot in front of his teammate, who may cut off the ball, or run around the ball, to the basket, cutting tight off the player screening with the ball. The middle in a five- or four-man weave must be kept open at all times. When the weave is used with a three-two free-lance offense, the player who passes off cuts down the middle toward the basket, expecting a return pass. If he does not receive a pass, he cuts to the corner on the same side he passed to. Constant effective weaving can make defenders retreat toward their basket so that the offense can obtain easy medium jump-shooting opportunities.

In a three-two free-lance pattern, the middle man out front with the ball should be an excellent quarterback, dribbler, and ball handler. The wing men should be good ball handlers and outside shooters. The corner men must be mobile, good ball handlers who are able to move in and out of the pivot in a flash pivot maneuver.

In a five-man pattern, all the offensive players are in constant movement. (In practice, this helps the defensive unit because each player is defending against opponents in all postures— near the basket, in the medium areas, in the corners, and out front.) Regardless of the deployment used in a free-lance offense— whether it's a two-one-two or a three-two—the floor must be kept balanced, the player with the ball must determine the play, and all players must compound the defensive problems as much as possible.

The following rules should be enforced in the free-lance movement. The player with the ball always determines the play. He should be facing the basket at all times, he should be alive, and he should be in triple-threat position where he can pass, shoot, or dribble. For best results, he should see all offensive and defensive positionings.

The passer off, on cutting toward the basket, should set an inside screen for the player he passes to, if possible.

The offensive players must be well spaced. If they are too close, a player moving toward a teammate who has the ball should reverse direction toward the basket.

Players should dribble minimally, and only as a protective reaction against a good defensive move by an opponent, for good shooting position on driving to the basket, or for offensive balance when the team position is poor.

Initial probing passes should be used; however, a penetrating pass should be made immediately, if possible. When players are bringing the ball upcourt on the side, they should pass into the corner man immediately and work a two-on-two play on that side, rather than pass the ball back to the middle and have two or three initial probing passes before the offense moves into a penetrating position.

It's possible to work the ball in close for shots. Therefore, long shots against man-to-man are not needed unless the defense is in a complete floating or sagging posture.

Players should not hold the ball. If they do not have a play, they should pass it to another player and continue the movement.

In playing without the ball, offensive players should use deceptive moves and fakes. First, they should determine where the player with the ball wants them to position themselves. Second, they should screen weak-side away, using inside screening and roll techniques. Third, they should cut to the basket, using either a back-door or inside cut to the ball or a weak-side cut off the screen, tight, toward the ball. A cutter should always stop if he is the second cutter and is not open. If he is the second cutter and is open, he should make an audible sound to alert the man with the ball that he is open away from the point of attack.

Players receiving a pass should V away and come back to the ball. In reversing direction to the basket, they should make a V toward the ball and then push off toward the basket.

Players using a free-lance offense should never shoot a hurried shot or a forced shot under pressure.

In using two- and three-man plays as described in Chapter 4, all players should know their teammates' moves. The man with the ball has five options. First, he may pass and not move, telling the receiver and the three other teammates he is relinquishing the pattern selection to the receiver. Second, he may pass and screen away, with teammates moving the ball to the best area for open passing lanes to the cutter. Third, he may pass and screen toward the ball, with the receiver driving off the screen toward the side the screen came from. Fourth, he may pass and go behind the receiver, indicating that he expects the receiver to return the pass, move away, and screen. Fifth, if the passer wants the ball back on an inside hand-off (for example, a wing man passing to a corner man), he should nod his head as he passes to signal the hand-off, then cut between the man with the ball and his defender so that he may get the hand-off and drive to the basket.

The position replacements should always be from the weak side, out front, away from the ball. Players should never go to the area near the ball too quickly. In a three-out–two-in offense, a corner man should never cross both foul lanes when moving toward the ball. He may move and cross both foul lanes when screening away from the ball.

If a primary receiver cannot get open for the pass, he should reverse and go to the basket. If a cutter off the ball is open for a pass, he should cut off the ball toward the basket quickly. Cutting off the ball puts an extra pair of defensive hands near the ball, so it puts the ball in a very dangerous position if the movement is not quick, fast, and toward the basket. Movements must be balanced, deceptive, quick, and varied. Footwork and feints must be used to put the defender at a disadvantage that should be readily discernible and understandable to the teammate with the ball.

When a cutter is using an inside screen and the defenders switch, the cutter should stop and screen for the screener after cutting off him. This generally will open the cutting screener for a shot. If both defenders follow the first cutter, the screener will be open for a medium shot himself.

Passing Game. The seventies saw a proliferation of free-lance offensive attacks against man-to-man defenses that became known collectively as passing-game offenses. Technically, any offense, whether zone or man-to-man, qualifies as a passing-game offense if it (1) does not feature dribbling as a planned part of the continuity and (2) permits both free-lance and patterned movements within the continuity. However, while strictly patterned man-to-man continuity offenses like the shuffle and the wheel rely on automatics[1] to continue movement when the basic pattern is stopped, and strictly free-lance offenses may not follow any pattern at all, passing-game offenses draw from both styles indiscriminately.

Passing-game movements are based on rules governing individual-player movement, angles of attack, court balance, and so forth. Generally, the movements include cuts and screens away from the ball, rapid ball and player movement and rotation, and one-on-one and two-on-two confrontations arising out of the cuts, screens, and ball movement and rotation.

The concept underlying the use of passing-game offenses represents the offensive ideal of most basketball coaches today; namely, that players operate best under conditions in which they are allowed to free-lance within a controlled system of play. Controlled free-lancing is the heart and soul of modern-day offensive basketball: the passing game structures the players' free-lance movements, and free-lancing reduces the defenders' ability to defeat the offense by playing the pattern rather than the players.

However, not all teams can or should use passing-game patterns. Skilled, experienced players are needed to take full of-

---

[1] Automatic and prearranged offensive movements designed to permit the offensive team to continue a pattern or attack the defense when it shuts off the primary attack. For example, when a perimeter passing lane in a continuity pattern is shut off by defensive overplaying, someone—either the ball handler or one or more of his teammates—will automatically move to a position that will enable the pattern to be continued or reset.

fensive advantage of one-on-one, two-on-two, or three-on-three situations, particularly as they arise within the team's movement structure. Generally, ball handling along the perimeter is divided among at least three offensive players in most passing-game systems, and many systems (e.g., the triple-cut sequence described later) require all five offensive players to handle the ball periodically along the perimeter. Players who do not play well without the ball do not normally excel in passing-game offenses, nor do players who are overly pattern-oriented or free-lance–oriented.

The key to success in using passing-game techniques lies in moderation and restraint. Players should maintain continuity through court balance and ball rotation until one or more defenders or areas of the court become vulnerable to attack. Only then should the offensive players break the continuity to shoot, pass inside, or take the ball to the basket. When used judiciously in this manner, the passing game provides a necessary balance between using a controlled offensive attack and permitting players to use their individual talents to the fullest in free-lancing; thus it is superior to either mode of play used exclusively.

Passing-Game Rules. Rules governing passing-game movements are both general and specific. General rules apply to all passing-game movements (and to all free-lance movements as well). Specific rules apply to movements, alignments, court positions, etc., within a particular style of passing-game attack. In addition to the rules previously discussed, we offer the following general passing-game rules:

Cut away from the ball (or the basket) to receive perimeter passes.

Pass and cut. Always move after passing the ball. Cut either toward the basket (preferably back-door) or away from the ball. Do not cut toward the man you passed to.

Look for opportunities to screen for teammates away from the ball. (Passing-game offenses seldom feature screens for the ball handler, for three reasons: first, he will have to dribble around the screen, which tends to change the offensive emphasis from passing to free-lancing; second, the likelihood of trapping the ball handler increases drastically; and third, moving away from the ball tends to isolate the ball handler for one-on-one confrontations.)

Begin your movement—either shooting, passing or starting a move toward the basket—within half a second after receiving the pass. Delaying the move for even a full second is likely to give the defense time to react and increase its coverage.

Keep the offense balanced, as shown in Diagram 5–49.

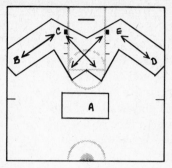

DIAGRAM 5-49

Diagram 5–49. Balancing the Offense. The three areas within a passing-game pattern are the point of attack (which may also have a secondary point of attack); the rotation area, or area where the ball is rotated to the other side of the court; and the weak side, or area of the court away from the point of attack. Balancing the offense refers to keeping players in each of these three areas, but moving them and the ball constantly from one area to another as a means of shifting the point of attack.

The easiest way to make a team defend honestly against the passing-game cuts and movements is for players to work the ball inside whenever opportunities arise. When defenders begin to play the pattern and anticipate the cuts and passes, the ball handler should break the sequence and take the ball to the basket

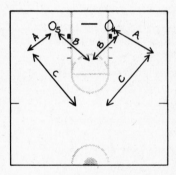

Diagram 5–50. Diagonal Cutting Routes in Passing-Game Offenses. Cutting Route A occurs most often in stack or screening situations, when an offensive player at low post cuts outside toward the wing to free himself to receive a pass, or an offensive player at the wing moves inside to screen for a teammate at low post who is cutting outside. Route B depicts cuts into and across the lane. Route C shows the diagonal cutting routes along the perimeter of the defense.

DIAGRAM 5-50

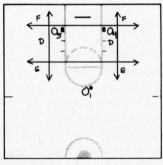

DIAGRAM 5-51

Diagram 5–51. Straight Cutting Routes in Passing-Game Offenses. Compare the following: the ball handler is at the top of the circle in Diagrams 5–50 and 5–51. An offensive player (either O_5 or O_4) is at low post in both situations. He wants to cut outside to receive the ball. It should be fairly obvious that Route A in Diagram 5–50 is less time-consuming than Route DE in Diagram 5–51, and the angle of the cutting routes also makes the pass from the point to the wing easier to catch in the first instance. However, when the cuts are not screened, Player O_5 or O_4's cut to the wing from high post in Route DE is much more difficult to overguard than the diagonal cut of Route A.

Diagram 5–52. Comparing Diagonal and Straight Cutting Routes. An excellent way of comparing diagonal and straight cutting routes is afforded by the cutting and passing options shown in Diagram 5–52. Route 1, the diagonal route, is more difficult to defense, since a pass along that route travels a shorter distance and can be completed more quickly. Too, the pass is easier to catch, since the receiver's body is not turned away from the passer as much as it would be in Route 2.

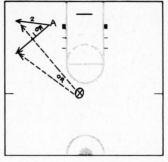

DIAGRAM 5–52

or attempt to go one-on-one with his man. (Of course, we aren't talking about forcing the ball to the basket or taking the first shot that arises simply for the sake of shooting.)

Diagonal cuts (Diagram 5–50) are normally more effective than straight cuts (Diagram 5–51) in passing-game sequences. Diagonal cuts generally spread the defense more than straight cuts, and they usually take less time to complete. Exceptions exist, of course, particularly in starting a passing-game sequence without using screens to free an offensive player, but diagonal cuts are usually more effective in maintaining continuity.

Straight cuts are desirable on occasion, if for no other reason than to vary the look of one's passing game, but diagonal cuts are generally superior for spreading the defense and permitting the offensive players to make a series of quick, short passes. (The straight cut designated Route F in Diagram 5–51 is often useful in establishing ball rotation in passing-game patterns and in providing a safe passing outlet when the regular cutting routes are overplayed or cut off.)

Establishing a Passing-Game Attack from Stack Alignment. Although a passing-game offense may be effected from any offensive alignment, we have chosen the stack alignment to illustrate the versatility of both the passing game and the stack alignment (Diagram 5–53). We could as easily have used a 1-2-2 alignment with B and D at the wings and C and E at the low-post positions (Diagram 5–55).

Single-, Double-, and Triple-Cut Passing-Game Attacks. In their elementary form, passing-game offenses feature players making single cuts or screens, with inside players screening for each other inside, and with outside players either cutting along the perimeter routes or screening down for inside players on their sides. Other forms of passing-game offenses may call for players to make two movements (e.g., setting a screen for a cutting teammate and then moving to set a second screen, or setting a screen and then cutting around a screening teammate) to receive the ball. To perform these movements, called double cuts, all the players involved must have a measure of court awareness. They must also be able to operate effectively along the perimeters as well as inside. Finally, in triple-cut offenses, players may be required to make three consecutive movements to afford continuity to the attack from one side of the court to the other.

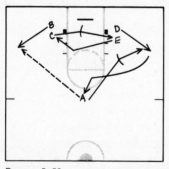

DIAGRAM 5–53

Diagram 5–53. Setting Up a Single-Cut Passing-Game Attack. D and B cut outside as A maneuvers with the ball. A passes to B. C will screen for E, who cuts to the ball-side low post. C clears the lane to the weak side. After passing to B, A will cut to the weak side and screen D's man. D will cut around the screen to high post and then step out to the point to become the point guard. B and E represent the point of attack. (If A and D continue to cut and screen for each other, their defenders may be kept so busy cutting off the passing lanes to the point that B and C can perform any number of two-on-two maneuvers on their half of the court.)

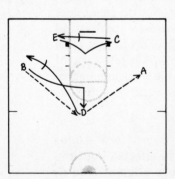

DIAGRAM 5–54

Diagram 5–54. Ball and Player Rotation (Continuation of movement in Diagram 5–53). If B does not work his man one-on-one or pass inside, he will pass to D at the point to begin ball rotation and shift the point of attack to the other side of the court. Ball and player rotation involve D relaying the ball to A and cutting weak side to screen for B, with C again moving into the lane to screen for E cutting to the ball-side low post. C will set up at the weak-side low post, and D will set up at the weak-side wing.

A variation of the elementary single-cut inside movement often seen with teams who prefer to keep their big men inside is the high-low post interchange. This type of movement is particularly valuable when only one of the big men is an authentic offensive threat, although it can be altered to provide equal scoring opportunities for both players.

Diagram 5–55. High-Low Post Interchange, Passing-Game Offense. E's first movement with A's pass to D involves what is known as balancing the posts. After moving up to high post, E cuts into the lane and sets a screen on C's man. C cuts around the screen and moves to either high or low post. (The high-post move, involving a diagonal cut away from the basket, is more difficult to defense properly.) If A's pass had been to B, C's and E's movements would have been reversed, with C cutting to high post to set up the high-low screen and cut.

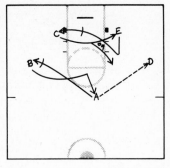

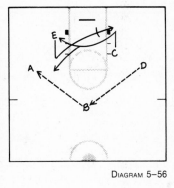

DIAGRAM 5–55

Diagram 5–56. High-Low Post Interchange with Ball Rotation. In the version shown, E and C will move to high and low post, respectively, to balance the posts, and E will be the screener and C the cutter/pass receiver on both sides of the court. If the coach wanted his post men to share screening and cutting responsibilities, he would have C and E reverse themselves across the lane instead of moving up and down the lane. Thus, when the ball was reversed from D to B to A as shown, C would cut across the lane to ball-side high post, and E would cut across the lane to weak-side low post. C would then move into the lane to screen for E cutting to ball-side high post.

DIAGRAM 5–56

Strengths of the single-cut passing game are the following:

1. It is easily learned, even by inexperienced and unskilled players.
2. Big men can be kept inside, with the ball in possession of the team's best ball handlers almost exclusively.
3. Because the basic pattern is so easily learned, players may be less likely to become so engrossed in running the pattern that they forget to take advantage of scoring opportunities or one-on-one or two-on-two confrontations.
4. Offensive rebounding is strengthened by the players' constantly balancing the offense on either side of the court. (This holds true for double- and triple-cut passing-game patterns as well.) In the previous example (Diagram 5–55), if wings B and D move inside to screen for C and E, all they have done essentially is switch positions. One player cuts, another player fills. The only time this is not true is when a player clears his area to permit the ball handler to go one-on-one with his man.

Weaknesses of the single-cut passing game are:

1. Since it is easy to learn and simple to run, it can be easy to defense, particularly with inexperienced, pattern-oriented players who have difficulty taking advantage of offensive opportunities gained when the defenders overplay the pattern.

2. When the opponents' big men are superior, it may be to the offensive team's advantage to use more motion and outside cuts than are found in the single-cut style to draw the big men away from the basket. This is particularly true when the opponents have only one big man and use semi-zone techniques to keep him inside.

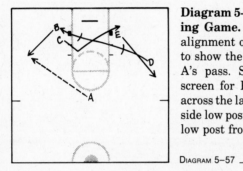

Diagram 5–57. Setting Up a Double-Cut Passing Game. In this diagram we've used a stack alignment on only one side of the court in order to show the double cut. B cuts outside to receive A's pass. Simultaneously, D moves inside to screen for E cutting outside. D then continues across the lane to screen for C cutting to the weak-side low post—unless C has received a pass at the low post from B at the wing.

DIAGRAM 5–57 _____

A strength of the pattern as thus far conceived is that only D is moving toward the ball. While the defenders must honor all ball-side thrusts such as D's, the offense is setting up possible mismatches on the weak side. Rapid ball rotation can take advantage of offensive mismatches as well as spread the defense to its limits when one-on-one confrontations occur.

The main weakness of this style of passing-game attack is that A, the point guard, must remain at, or near, the point, since

Diagram 5–58. Rotating the Ball and Players, Double-Cut Passing Game. B passes to A and moves inside to screen for D cutting outside. A relays the ball to E. C screens for B and clears to weak-side low post. B cuts around the screen and works for offensive position inside. (Of course, A could as easily pass to D, in which case B would screen for C instead of C screening for B as shown.)

DIAGRAM 5–58 _____

Diagram 5–59. Attack Areas When the Defense Overplays to Deny the Rotation Pass to the Point Guard. B has the ball. If he decides to break the pattern and attack the defense, he may go one-on-one on X_3, or he may attempt to force a double-team from X_2 or X_5 and in the process free D or C for a shot.

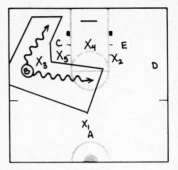

DIAGRAM 5–59

the wings will be continuously occupied. As a result, the defense will almost certainly have one player move outside to deny the rotation pass from the wing to the point guard. When he does, coaches may back-door against the overplay or pull their point guard out as far as necessary toward mid-court to spread the defense, as in Diagram 5–59.

Following are some other alternatives for the offensive team when the defense overplays.

1. C moves outside to screen for B.
2. C sets a screen on X_4 for E cutting across the lane.
3. A interchanges with D to see if the defense will still overplay the pass to the point.

Such alternatives exist with almost every pass in passing-game offenses. For a team to use passing-game concepts to best advantage, the players must understand their options and alternatives from each court position, and they must be willing to accept the responsibility for both individual- and team-oriented movements as the need arises.

Diagram 5–60. Triple-Cut Passing-Game Movement. In starting the triple-cut sequence, D starts moving inside to screen for E cutting outside as B passes to A at the point. D continues across the lane to screen for C cutting to low post. D clears the lane and sets up at high post. At this point, A may pass to E to set up a C-E point of attack on that side of the court, or D can cut outside behind B's screen to set up a B-D point of attack.

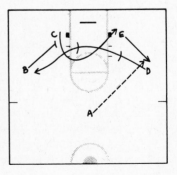

DIAGRAM 5–60

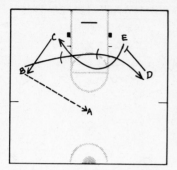

Diagram 5–61. Triple-Cut Passing-Game Sequence, Alternate Method. In Diagram 5–60, D made the three cuts in the triple-cut sequence. The same movement may also be effected by having B set two screens and cut around a teammate's screen. B passes to A and moves inside to pick for C cutting outside, then moves into the lane to screen for E cutting across to low post, and then cuts behind D's screen. A may pass to either C or B.

DIAGRAM 5–61

A movement associated with this pattern can increase the effectiveness of the one-on-one game and inside movements when the defense overplays the pattern. (See Diagram 5–62.)

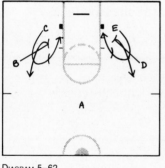

Diagram 5–62. Reverse Cutting against Defensive Overplay in Passing-Game Offense. D and B have moved inside to screen for E and C cutting outside. When the men guarding E and C move out with them to cut off those passing lanes, E and C should reverse and move back inside to screen for D and B cutting outside, and then post up low. If the defenders on D, B, E, and C are working especially hard at cutting off the passing lanes at the wings as well as inside, they will be too preoccupied to provide any kind of effective help for A's defender if A decides to go one-on-one with his man at the center of the court.

DIAGRAM 5–62

Modifying the Basic Passing-Game Movements to Set Up an Inside Attack. Passing-game movements are not randomly selected; that is, they are not free-lance movements made by offensive players to set up other free-lance movements. Although a player may have several options available in deciding where he will go and what he will do at any given point (e.g., cut outside to receive a pass, cut away from the ball to clear an area for a teammate to go one-on-one with his man, move inside to screen for a teammate), his movements will be structured insofar as court balance, ball rotation, and the other passing-game rules are concerned.

Probably the most difficult aspect of defensing a passing-game attack is keeping the ball away from the post positions on either side of the court when the offensive players are rotating the ball rapidly and constantly screening and interchanging inside. The easiest way for the inside defenders to effect such coverage is to switch automatically on inside screens. If they do not switch, the cutter will very likely be free under the basket for an easy score. If the defenders switch against inside screens, however, the offense may force the defenders to overguard on one side of the court, as shown in Diagram 5–63, then rotate the ball quickly to the other side of the court and take advantage of the overplaying to work the ball inside. (The high post/low post alignment is ideal for this sort of attack. If defenders are switching against inside screens and overplaying the post men to deny inside passes, the offensive coach might consider using this type of movement to take advantage of the defensive overplaying.)

Diagram 5–63. Overguarding the Inside Interchange, Passing Game. The offense is balanced in a 1-2-2 alignment. As A passes to B, X_5 moves into an overguarding stance on C at low post. A interchanges with D to provide motion along the perimeter. C, who has been maneuvering around the post in an attempt to free himself for B's pass, moves into the lane and sets a screen for E cutting to ball side, then clears to weak-side low post. However, the inside defenders switch, and X_5 immediately overguards E. If the ball is rotated to A at weak-side wing, X_4 will have ample time to move into position to deny C the ball. If C repeats his cut away from the ball and screens for E, the defenders will merely switch back to their original defensive assignments and maintain their overguarding positions at ballside low post.

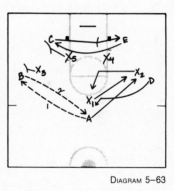

DIAGRAM 5–63

Any alignment may be used to run a passing-game offense. Because passing-game movements seldom involve all five players at one time, players should receive extensive practice and drill in the kind of one-on-one, two-on-two, three-on-three, and four-on-four techniques described earlier in this chapter, in addition to learning the specific techniques and routes of the particular passing game being employed.

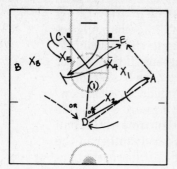

DIAGRAM 5–54

Diagram 5–64. Counteracting Defensive Overguarding Inside, Passing Game. As in Diagram 5–63, the offense is in a balanced 1-2-2 alignment, with inside defenders X_4 and X_5 overplaying at the ball-side post positions to deny passes inside and C trying to position himself to receive a pass from B. In this case, however, E does not screen for C at all, but rather cuts into the lane and continues to ball-side high post, creating a high-low post arrangement with A's pass to B. A interchanges with D (as shown in Diagram 5–63). X_2 will cover D's cut toward the ball. When B passes to D at the top of the circle, the stage is set for C to take advantage of X_5's overplaying: simultaneously with B's pass to the point, C will cut into the lane, keeping X_5 behind him. No other defenders are available to help out if D passes to C. (X_4 had to overguard E toward the ball side to deny the pass to high post, and X_1, who may have dropped away from A slightly when A cut to weak-side wing, is still out of position to provide more than token assistance if the pass is made to C in the lane.) If D cannot make the pass, he quickly relays the ball to A at the wing and cuts weak side to interchange with B. C clears the lane and maintains position to receive a pass from A. C's movement is simple. Defensing it by having X_5 overguard C on both sides of the court is incredibly difficult, particularly if C moves well and maintains a wide stance to keep X_5 away from him as he maneuvers into position to receive a pass from D or A.

Overload Offense

This offense overbalances on one side of the court at the inception of each play, then moves to the other side. Players use rear-screen cuts away from the ball, scissor moves off the ball and off the post, and several secondary screens to exploit switching or sagging tactics. All types of shots will appear from this type of offense.

Diagram 5–65. Overload Offense, Guard Through. In basic positions, A, a guard, is on the left side of the court, with B, the second guard, at the head of the key. The forward, C, is close to the sideline, below the medium pivot, D. E is in low-pivot position opposite. A initiates the play by passing to C and cutting off D to the basket. C has the following options: (1) He may pass to A if he appears free after his cut off D. (2) He may drive to the baseline. (3) He may drive over a screen set by D and take a jump shot, or drive into the basket if the lane is open. (4) He may pass to D on D's offensive roll to the basket.

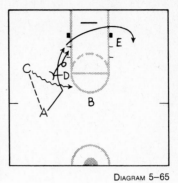

DIAGRAM 5–65

Diagram 5–66. Overload Offense, Double Screen (Continuation of movement in Diagram 5–65). C passes to B. E has moved up the right foul lane. D and C have moved across the foul lane, setting a double screen for A. B may drive into the basket if he is open, or he may pull to the left and look for A's cut either to the low side or into the middle off the double screen set by D and C.

DIAGRAM 5–66

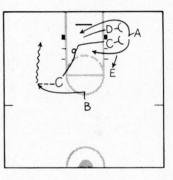

Diagram 5–67. Overload Offense, Scissor. This play starts from the alignment shown in Diagram 5–65. If A does not cut after pass in to C (1), C may pass to D (2). C and A may scissor cut off D.

DIAGRAM 5–67

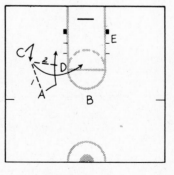

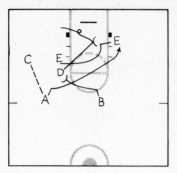

DIAGRAM 5–68

Diagram 5–68. Overload Offense with a High-Low Exchange by the Pivot Men. As A passes to C, D moves toward E's position and screens. E moves off the screen into D's former position in medium pivot on the ball side. D rolls off his screen, low on the ball side. After the exchange of high-low pivot, B screens for A. A cuts. The options: (1) C may pass to E as E moves into the medium pivot for a pivot shot. (2) C may pass to D in the low pivot. (3) C, D, or E may pass to A, opposite, after his cut off B, for a quick shot or a one-on-one move. This play for A will appear on the weak side, as the defense is concentrating on the overloaded side of the court.

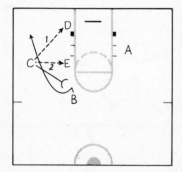

DIAGRAM 5–69

Diagram 5–69. Overload Offense, High-Low Exchange (Continuation of movement in Diagram 5–68). C has passed to D (1) or E (2) and screens for B, who can cut left into good medium shooting area. After the pass in to D or E, the opportunities for an open shot after a screen are magnified, because the defense concentrates in the pivot areas.

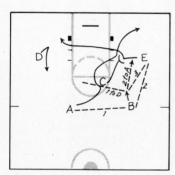

DIAGRAM 5–70

Diagram 5–70. Overload Offense, to the Right. A and B are the guards. A is a little off center at the head of the key, B is to his right between him and the sideline, C is in a high pivot, and D and E are in forward positions. This play frees A, the tall guard, along the baseline where he can rebound offensively and, after the play movement, go one-on-one. A passes to B (1) and cuts off C's screen on the high pivot. B passes to E (2). E may pass to A if A is open; he may reverse the ball by passing back to B; or he may pass to C, who has rolled into the medium pivot after A's cut and the pass to E. If E passes back to B (3), B has two options. (1) He may pass to D for a pass to E, who is cutting off C's medium-pivot position. (2) He may pass into the corner to A for a one-on-one move by A from the corner. A may pass to C, now in the medium pivot, then scissor cut off him with B or fake toward C and make a back-door cut to the basket.

The Stack Offense

Our basic offense, the stack offense, has many advantages in modern basketball. Primarily, it cuts down the margin of error, because the best ball handler (A) generally handles the ball most of the time and brings it into scoring position. It is more difficult for teams using pressure-type defense (especially from the man-to-man posture) to pressure one outstanding dribbler and ball handler into offensive mistakes.

After the ball is in the offensive set position, the only person who is required to dribble the ball is A, whose dribbling movement keys the offense. By observing the defenders, he can determine which play to use in a given situation. Against man-to-man defense, he can call the plays by name or he can let his teammates determine the correct play by watching the defensive deployment. After one or two short passes, a team should get a good shot at the basket from this offense—either a high-percentage medium-jump shot or a shot from the low-pivot area. Other advantages of the stack offense are as follows:

1. The stack should neutralize any defense, forcing it to play man-to-man and match players man-to-man.
2. Setting up double teams against one opposing star is difficult. If the defense doubles up on one player, an open man is usually in position close to the basket for an easy shot.
3. The coach can easily arrange mismatches by altering the starting position of the men.
4. The stack can take advantage of any individual defensive weakness.
5. Setting a defense against the stack is difficult. The offense can go left or right quickly from the starting position, and all players interchange positions, with the possible exception of the A man.
6. The stack is excellent with big men. Once a shot is taken, all of the big men jam the offensive boards for a second and third effort at the basket.
7. The stack is not tiring, and its simple patterns are easy to understand.
8. Players can easily work away from the opposition's defensive strength.
9. Options show up immediately, which forces defensive players to stay honest if they try to realign for better protection.
10. It's impossible to keep this offense from getting a good shot if it is properly timed and executed.

11. The one-man front is the hardest type of offense to press man-to-man.

12. When two big men are not adaptable to a forward position, you can use this offense effectively, keeping them in their best rebounding positions and shooting positions with a minimum of movement.

13. Most teams practice defense against the normal set systems; for example, a three-two offense, a two-three offense or a one-three-one offense. The use of the stack presents added defensive difficulties.

14. There is no defense against a good reverse movement.

The stack offense also has the following disadvantages.

1. If the ball is stolen from the outside man or the team cannot control the offensive board consistently, the stack is susceptible to a fast-break team.

2. It is not as effective when used as the only offense for the entire game. However, all teams should have a secondary offense. (We try to use our fast-break offense at all times, penetrating against the defense whenever possible, even if the defense has three men back against our three men. Our primary set offense is the stack, and our secondary set offense is either a two-one-two free-lance type or a two-three single-pivot type.)

3. If the entire team does not move together on the outside man's keys, the offense will fail. Timing and surprise are essential in this type of offense.

Basic Qualifications. A is the quarterback, the best dribbler, the best ball handler, the play-maker who has speed and is a threat from the outside. He should be able to take defensive pressure, and he must always be able to get back on defense quickly.

B should be a big, strong, tough offensive player, probably the best scorer among the big men. He should have a good hook shot and move well from the low pivot, with his back to the basket. Whenever he gets the ball in the low-pivot position, he should be good for a basket or, if he is double-teamed, a pass-off to E on the weak side if E's man leaves him to help double team. He should be a good one-on-one man in this low position, with excellent moves close to the basket.

C is the best shooter facing the hoop. He should be an excellent short- to medium-jump shooter and a very good feeder from the side or corner into the pivot. He should be capable of playing two-on-two basketball with B, and he should be able to move one-on-one from his side position. C's position is good for a left-handed shooter.

D is usually a smaller man than C. He should be an excellent jump shooter from the medium shooting area. D's position is good for a right-handed jump shooter or for the second guard if there is a good shooting forward to play in the C position.

E, usually the second big man, should be a strong rebounder who can block out well. He must be alert for all movement when he is away from the ball because he will open frequently, since his defender is often called in to help a teammate toward the ball.

A will always be back as the defensive safety in all plays except those in which he moves to the basket. On those plays, either C or D (depending on the movements) will assume A's defensive position. B, D, and E, the best rebounders, are normally in a triangle arrangement moving to the board whenever a shot is taken, with C the intermediate rebounder in most situations. After the initial movement to the left or right, A, the best ball handler, is in position to pass to B, C, D, or E from either side off his dribble, depending on the defensive alignment and position.

Starting Positions. The starting positions as outlined are planned to operate mainly to the right side. The positions would be reversed if you were working to the left. A is at the top of the key in possession of the ball. All inside men in the stack (see Diagram 5–71) place their feet close to the foul lane, and each side faces the other. C and D are approximately four feet from the basket, just outside the buffer zone. C's left foot should be behind B's right foot. D's right foot should be behind E's left foot.

The distance of the inside men from the baseline will be determined by B's position. He will pivot counterclockwise on his right foot after initial movement to his side to assume a low-pivot position with his back to the basket. Once he has found a low-pivot position he prefers, he will always set up where he can make his pivot into that position, and everyone else will set up accordingly. It is possible to be closer to the foul line than the original positions indicate or anywhere from one to four feet farther back from the foul lanes if the offense works better from that alignment. The position varies slightly, but normally B's left foot will be about even with the broken line of the lower half of the free-throw circle.

Keys to the Offense. The big men, B and E, must get into position on the lanes as quickly as possible. If they can't set up on the lane, they should set up as close to the lane as they can. The timing and execution are important. All players must move together as A makes a definite penetrating move to the right or to the left after bringing the ball up to the head of the circle. Quick passing is important, particularly hitting the open man as soon as he is free.

Basic Stack Offense. Everything described will be on the right movement. (Reverse procedures for left movement.) As A dribbles to the right, the following moves are made simultaneously: C pops out from ten to fourteen feet, continuing to face the hoop, moving toward the ball at a forty-five-degree angle from the basket, adjusting position depending on the way his defender plays him. B pivots on his right foot into a low-pivot position. D moves behind E to the foul-line area, adjusting position for best advantage. E adjusts position depending on the defense, usually maneuvering toward the basket.

Basic Options. A may hit C for a medium to short jumper as soon as C opens. A may hit D coming around E's screen to the foul line. A may hit B in his low-pivot position if his defender is behind him. A may pass to E across the court if E's defender is in front, lobbing the ball to him or possibly bounce passing through the opening that may appear after defensive deployment. A may go one-on-one for himself, taking a medium or outside shot if the defense sags to jam the middle or cut off the pass.

C may shoot a medium or short jump shot. C may pass into B for a pivot shot or one-on-one movement in the low pivot. B may hand off to C, cutting off his pivot position from the outside. B and C may use any number of two-on-two moves as outlined in Chapter 4. C may pass to D after he has come around E's screen. C may play one-on-one against the weak defender. D may take a shot from the foul-line area. D may make a quick pass in to B or E if their defensive men try to help out against D.

There are many alternate options on special calls by A. C may cut behind a double screen set opposite by D and E to receive a pass from A and make a short jump shot. If C is not free, A and B may work two-on-two on the open side of the floor. This is particularly effective if the defense is setting itself to play C to drop out to the right initially as the ball goes in toward the right side.

At a special call by A, C and D can pop out simultaneously while B and E crisscross to low pivot on opposite sides of the foul lane from their original position. A may pass to B or E, depending on the defensive switching. This play allows a two-on-two possibility for either C and E on one side or B and D on the other, depending on the side that A passes to.

All coaches can find many other variations. For example:

1. If B is being double-teamed, he may exchange positions with C. This should leave a man alone underneath.

2. If C has a small opponent, he may exchange movements with B and work on his opponent in the low pivot as B moves out for the initial pass.

3. If B has a big man who can't move, he may change positions with C to take the big man outside for one-on-one moves facing the basket.

4. If the defense is keying on B, placing him in C's position and running the plays to the left will allow the best shooter to get the ball at the foul line at the top of the key, where the defense will have more trouble defending against him.

The following diagrams will help explain many of the moves available and the basic alignments.

Diagram 5–71. Stack Offense, Team Alignment. A is outside with the ball. B and C are along the right foul lane with C's left foot behind B's right foot. D and E are along the left foul lane with D's right foot behind E's left foot. The pairs are facing each other along the foul lanes (Figure 5–11). These positions are adjustable out toward the foul line or back away from the foul lane, depending upon defensive alignments.

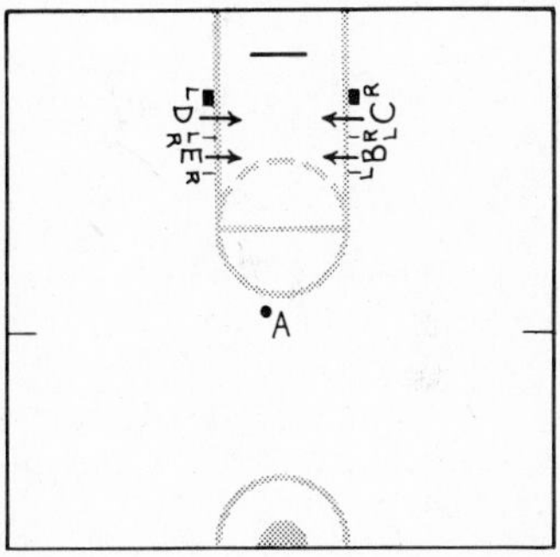

DIAGRAM 5–71

Figure 5–11. Stack offense team alignment.

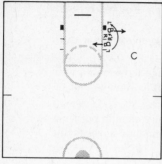

DIAGRAM 5–72

Diagram 5–72. Stack Offense, Strong-Side Pivot Movement by B as C Moves Out for the Ball. C has moved out to receive a pass. B pivots on his right foot, counterclockwise, and ends up with his back to the basket. In his original position B faces across the lane; in his final position he faces C and the right sideline. B's position is adjustable toward the foul line if he wishes to obtain a higher pivot position. C, D, and E will adjust with B's position.

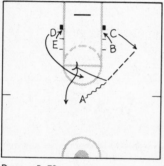

DIAGRAM 5–73

Diagram 5–73. Stack Offense, Basic Movement. The play is keyed by A's penetrating dribble to his right. C moves out at a forty-five-degree angle and receives a pass. B pivots on his right foot to the low position on ball side. D has moved around E's screen. If C's reception of the pass is without great defensive pressure, A slides back toward D, setting a secondary screen at the foul line for D and then rotating back into defensive position or into position as the safety outlet if the ball is tied up. E's position is adjustable along the left foul lane. C's options after receiving A's pass: (1) shoot if open; (2) pass to B in the low pivot; (3) pass to D in the outer half of the foul circle after a screen.

Figure 5–12. Stack offense: "One." Point man calls "One" and dribbles left while E screens.

Diagram 5–74. Stack Offense, "One." A calls "One" and dribbles to the right (Figure 5–12). C fakes toward the ball and then cuts across the foul lane behind D and E. B moves up to set a screen at approximately the foul line extended. A dribbles off his screen. B makes an offensive roll to the basket after A cuts off his screen. D makes his normal move to the foul line and is the back man defensively if a shot is taken. E adjusts along the left foul lane. A may also pass into B and use B as a screen, cutting off him for a return pass.

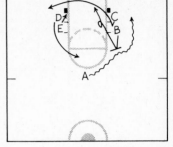

DIAGRAM 5–74

Diagram 5–75. Stack Offense, "Clear for A." On the clearing movement, C taps B and both C and B clear baseline to the opposite side, leaving the whole right side open for an offensive move by A. D makes his normal move to the foul line, and E adjusts along the left lane. C will fall back into defensive safety position.

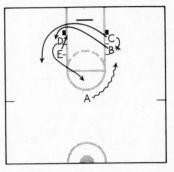

DIAGRAM 5–75

Diagram 5–76. Stack Offense, "Cut." If C's position or A's position is being overplayed, a cut off a stationary pivot is possible. A dribbles as though to start the offense, and C cuts out at a sharper angle and deeper than usual. B sets a stationary screen at the right end of the foul line. A cuts to the inside off this screen to receive a return pass from C. D and E make their normal basic maneuvers.

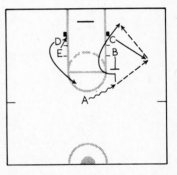

DIAGRAM 5–76

Diagram 5–77. Stack Offense, "Get Two for D." A starts his dribble to the right and then quickly reverses to the left, setting up a double screen along the left foul lane for D. D cuts tightly behind the double screen of E and A and receives a back pass from A for a quick, short jump shot. C's move is similar to the move of D in the basic pattern, with B moving into rebounding position. If the shot is taken, C's move starts him back into good defensive position.

DIAGRAM 5–77

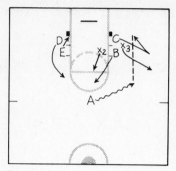

DIAGRAM 5–78

Diagram 5–78. Stack Offense, "Back Door."
X_3 has played between B and C, trying to over-play C's move out to the ball to prevent the pass. On observing this, A calls "Back Door" and dribbles over normally. B immediately comes up to the high-pivot position on the ball side, bringing his defender, X_2, with him. C comes out into his normal position, being overplayed by X_3, and D and E make their normal moves. If C opens, the normal pass on this play would be for A to make the pass directly to C on his reverse move. The options: (1) A may pass to B, who may pass to C. (2) After C's cut, if the reverse doesn't show, A may pass to B and go back door. (3) D may hold his position, and C may continue to cut around D and E for a double screen.

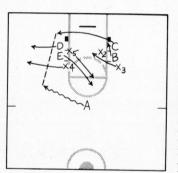

DIAGRAM 5–79

Diagram 5–79. Stack Offense, "Split." Some defenses will attempt to play a defender in front of B to guard C and in front of E to guard D. To counteract this defense, A calls "Split" and dribbles opposite C, the man he wants to pass to. (See Figure 5–13.) Here, X_3 is guarding C, and X_4 is guarding D. E breaks to the foul line, taking his defender, X_5, with him. D breaks to the left side, his defender, X_4, moving with him. On this movement, C fakes and cuts left on the low side, opposite, under the basket. A dribbles left and passes, timing C's cut. X_3, C's defender, cannot effectively guard C. If X_2 picks up C, A can make a quick lob pass to B, who will have X_3 on his back as he moves into the basket area. X_3 is normally a smaller defender, giving B the height advantage in the in-close area.

Figure 5–13. Stack offense: "Split." Defender playing outside D (24). A calls "Split" and dribbles right.

Diagram 5–80. Stack Offense, "Overplay."
Many defenses will attempt to put X_2, the defender guarding B, high, between B and the ball. When A observes this while dribbling, he calls "Overplay." C, instead of coming out at a forty-five-degree angle, uses a more direct path toward the sidelines, paralleling the baseline. A passes to C. B, instead of pivoting counterclockwise on his right foot, will step into the pivot lane with his left foot, pivoting in a clockwise fashion so that he will be facing the basket with X_2 on his back. C simply has to pass the ball to the front of B for B to receive an easy shot, defeating the defensive alignment of X_2.

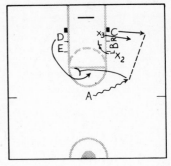

DIAGRAM 5–80

Diagram 5–81. Stack Offense, "Double." A starts his dribble to the right and changes direction on the call. C fakes a move out to the ball on the right side, then goes behind the natural double screen set by D and E on the left side. As C comes behind the double screen, A passes to him. If C is not open for the pass, A and B have an excellent two-on-two opportunity on the right side.

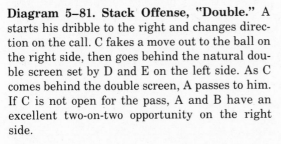

DIAGRAM 5–81

Diagram 5–82. Stack Offense, "Help C." The offense moves as originally planned, C coming out to the ball and receiving the pass after A's penetrating dribble toward his right. B then sets a rear screen for C. C dribbles off the screen, and B offensively rolls to the basket. C may shoot, drive into the basket, pass back to B on his offensive roll, or pass to D, who is making his normal movement off the stack alignment.

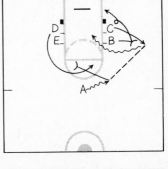

DIAGRAM 5–82

Diagram 5–83. Stack Offense, "Leave C Alone." A dribbles, and C moves out to receive the ball. B clears to the opposite side, allowing C one-on-one opportunity on the open side. D and E make their normal movements, D cutting off E's screen and taking advantage of A's screen in the outer half of the foul circle. (The plays in this diagram and in Diagram 5–82 can also be used with B popping out to receive the ball.)

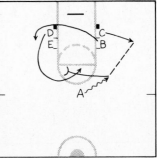

DIAGRAM 5–83

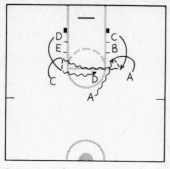

DIAGRAM 5–84

Diagram 5–84. Stack Offense, "Weave." From the stack alignment, it is possible to have a tight weave using A, C, and D. On the weave call, A dribbles in. C comes around B and behind A, receives a hand-off or flip pass from A, and dribbles across the foul line. D, timing his movement with that of A and C, comes around E and behind C, receiving the hand-off from C. A and C both buttonhook back to continue the weave if a good shooting opportunity has not appeared. B and E will normally move into the basket for offensive rebound position.

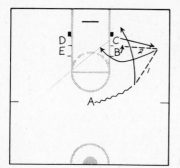

Diagram 5–85. Stack Offense, "Scissor." A passes to C (1). B pivots for best position. C passes to B (2). C cuts first, A second, in a scissor move off B's pivot position.

DIAGRAM 5–85

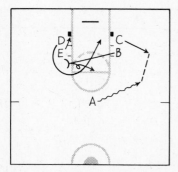

Diagram 5–86. Stack Offense, "Opposite." A passes to C. B moves across the lane next to E. D cuts around the double screen set by E and B opposite the ball and drives into the basket. B makes an offensive roll into the lower half of the free-throw circle to be open on his roll back toward the ball if there is a switch. C passes to D, if open, or to B rolling back if defense switches.

DIAGRAM 5–86

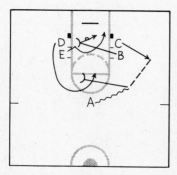

Diagram 5–87. Stack Offense, "Pick Low." A dribbles to the right, passing to C. B moves as though to set up the opposite play but screens low for E. E cuts off B's screen to the basket, and B rolls back toward the ball to be in position to receive a pass if a switch is made. C may pass to E on the first cut, to B on his roll back to the ball, or to D coming over E and A's screen.

DIAGRAM 5–87

Figure 5–14. Stack offense. Pivot defender fronts B with ball in right corner (C). The pass back to A opens B.

Diagram 5–88. Stack Offense, "Float." Many times the defenders on the weak side, guarding D and E, will attempt to float toward the strong side as A moves. This play counteracts a float toward the B and C side and anticipation of D's movement around E's screen. As C pops out to position with A's dribbling movement to the offensive right, D starts around the screen that E would normally set. Simultaneously, E moves to the foul line. A quickly passes to E (1). D reverses and is usually open for an easy shot on a pass in from E (2).

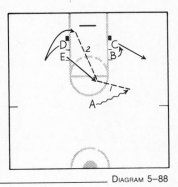

DIAGRAM 5–88

Diagram 5–89. Stack Offense, "Quick." Observing that D's defender assumes the usual cut around E in the basic stack movement, A calls "Quick." As A starts his dribble, D cuts quickly between E and his defender into the area just below the foul line as the other players make their normal offensive moves. Usually, D's defender will be anticipating normal movement (around E), and a quick pass from A to D will give D a short jump shot.

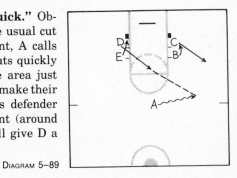

DIAGRAM 5–89

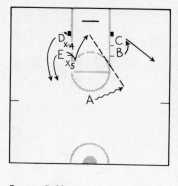

DIAGRAM 5–90

Diagram 5–90. Stack Offense, "Lob Left." E is being played in front by X_5, either for position or to help defensively from the weak side. The play starts toward the right, as usual, with players making their normal moves. E, however, takes a step as though to come to the foul line, forcing X_5 high. As X_5 steps toward the foul line, E quickly reverses and A makes a lob pass over X_5 into the basket. It is essential that D make his normal move, staying a little wider than usual, however, to deploy X_4 with him, and that B and C make their normal offensive moves on the right side.

Stack Offense Drills. Players work on all phases of the stack offense, drilling from three skeleton positions. A coach should be with each group.

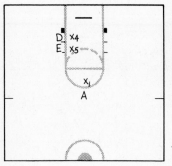

Diagram 5–91. Left. D and E are in their stack positions at the left of the foul lane, and the point man, A, is in position. From this stack and point position, they work all the plays that have been outlined in this chapter on stack offense. This is a fundamental drill that we work on daily in the preseason practice.

DIAGRAM 5–91

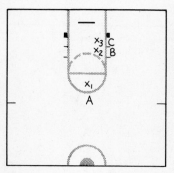

Diagram 5–92. Right. B and C are on the right, and A is at the point. All phases of the stack offense are worked from these three positions. The play should be called by the point man or coach, and the players should react. Normally these drills are used only in early preseason practice.

DIAGRAM 5–92

Continuity Patterns—The Shuffle and Wheel Offenses

In broadest terms, continuity offenses are offensive patterns in which the players do not have to reset themselves or return to their basic positions in order to repeat the pattern once they have run through it. Most zone offenses, for example, involve continuity techniques such as maintaining court balance, rotating the ball rapidly from one side of the court to the other, and filling the perimeter passing lanes as cutters penetrate into or through the zone. Such continuity is necessary for several reasons, chief of which is that failure to provide side-to-side continuity limits the offense to effective use of only one side of the court and permits the zone defense to overplay toward the ball side.

For man-to-man offenses, continuity patterns may be either free-lance or tightly structured. Passing-game offenses, for example, involve loosely structured free-lance patterns or movements based on rules such as balancing the posts or cutting away from the ball after passing. These patterns may use continuity in the process of setting up matchups in certain areas of the court, but continuity is always a secondary concern to the goal of breaking the pattern to go one-on-one or two-on-two.

For a shuffle or wheel offense, on the other hand, the continuity pattern is tightly structured. The pattern itself is designed to spring players free for lay-ups or short jumpers, and if no such openings arise immediately, the team will merely repeat the pattern until the defenders either overcommit themselves or make a mistake. Players break the pattern in only three instances: when a shot or move to the basket is immediately available, when the player with the ball decides to go one-on-one against his man, or when the defense overplays the rotation passes.

The shuffle and wheel patterns provide ball-handling and shooting opportunities for all five players, which may be either a strength or a weakness of these offenses, depending upon the players' ball-handling and shooting skills. Players who cannot make the open shot, take the ball to the basket when opportunities arise, or hit the open man with a quick pass tend to severely limit the effectiveness of the basic shuffle and wheel patterns, although variations such as three-man shuffle and four-man wheel are sometimes used to hide players with such deficiencies.

Continuity in any offensive pattern breaks down when a player decides to shoot or go one-on-one with his man. And because coaches who use shuffle or wheel patterns tend to prefer tightly structured offenses, most coaches who use these offenses tend to play down their free-lance aspects. After all, if all they wanted was to set up free-lance situations, they'd have selected patterns where continuity and "running the play" were less important. They will, of course, tell their players to break the pattern whenever openings arise, but the bulk of their practice time is usually spent teaching the basic pattern and its options, rather than teaching the players how to set up and attack one-on-one confrontations. If the players run their shuffle cuts correctly, for example, they're supposed to get lay-ups or short jumpers without having to go one-on-one.

A good example of the difference between free-lance and tightly structured patterns may be seen in the offensive teams' reaction to overplaying. In free-lancing, the offensive team is likely to go one-on-one or two-on-two when a defender overplays a perimeter passing lane. In more highly structured patterns, however, the offensive team normally reverts to automatics, or predetermined movements designed to restore the pattern's continuity, when the basic pattern breaks down because of defenders' overplaying the passing lanes.

The shuffle offense enjoyed great popularity during the early sixties, and is still seen in various forms in many parts of the country. The term *shuffle cut* has become part of the language of basketball, describing any offensive player's cut around a high post or weak-side screen, whether or not the team is running a shuffle pattern.

The shuffle is basically an overload offense away from the ball, with players constantly passing, cutting along predetermined routes, and screening for teammates. Some shuffle variations feature double screens away from the ball, but this technique is more widely associated with the wheel offense than with the shuffle.

Major advantages of the shuffle include the following:

Since shooting options exist for all five players, no one is excluded from the offense.

Scoring is usually well-balanced, which means that opponents cannot focus their coverage on one or two offensive players.

It is an excellent ball-control offense, particularly for small teams who do not have an effective post man or effective offensive rebounders and therefore must rely on play execution and shot selection.

It forces the defenders to work constantly on defense.

It is a good offense for teams with no outstanding personnel.

Since the areas from which shots are taken remain fairly constant, players are more likely to benefit from spot shooting drills for the shuffle than for most other man-to-man offenses.

As has been pointed out, however, the basic shuffle pattern requires all five players to handle the ball. Defenders are likely to disrupt the pattern by pressuring weak ball handlers and cutting off the passing lanes. And if the coach isn't careful, his team can become so pattern-conscious that the players overlook opportunities to shoot or drive.

There is, of course, far more to the shuffle than is given in this brief analysis. Interested readers may wish to refer to full texts on this offense listed in the Bibliography.

Diagram 5–93. Basic Shuffle Alignment and First Movements. C passes to B and cuts around E's screen at high post. (All cuts around screens in the shuffle may be either back-door or between the screening player and the ball.) B quickly relays the ball to A, who V'd outside to get open. B screens for E and continues low. A can pass to C in the lane, to E cutting into the lane, or to D, who cuts behind B's low pick and into the lane. (Or A can drive, although C's cut to low post and D's cut to high post invite double-teaming.)

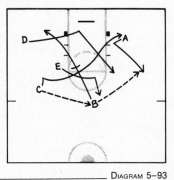

DIAGRAM 5–93

Diagram 5–94. Shuffle Continuity: Ball and Player Rotation. If the previous cuts do not produce a high-percentage scoring opportunity, the offensive players will rotate the ball to the other side of the court and initiate another series of cuts and screens to that side, as follows: A passes to E and cuts through the lane to low post. E relays the ball to B cutting outside. E screens for D and continues to weak-side low post. C scissors behind A and continues to high post. B can pass to A (generally unproductive), to C cutting behind A, or to D at high post. If D doesn't receive B's pass immediately, he slides outside to relay the ball to the other side in rotation.

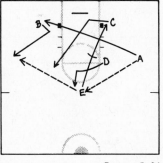

DIAGRAM 5–94

Diagram 5–95. Shuffle Automatic When the Relay Pass to B Is Overplayed. C has the ball but cannot pass to B to begin the shuffle pass-and-cut sequence as X is overplaying B. D cuts outside to receive C's pass. B cuts behind his man to ball-side low post. C passes to D, then cuts away from the ball to weak side. A uses C's pick to free himself from his man and receive D's pass at the top of the circle. With D's pass to A, the alignment is reset. When C cuts to the wing to receive A's pass, the shuffle sequence will begin again.

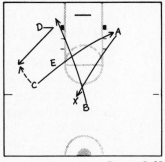

DIAGRAM 5–95

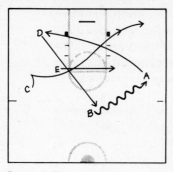

DIAGRAM 5-96

Diagram 5–96. Shuffle Automatic When the Pass from B to A Is Overplayed. A second automatic is likely to be necessary in running the shuffle if a defender overplays A to stop the pass along the perimeter. In such cases, A will cut to the basket behind his man and clear to weak side. C has already cut and posted low after passing to B. E could step out from his position at high post to receive B's pass, but the easiest way to maintain continuity is for B to dribble to the right wing position. D moves out to fill the point position. When C sees B dribbling, he cuts to the corner.

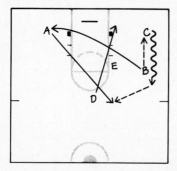

DIAGRAM 5-97

Diagram 5–97 (Continuation of movement in Diagram 5–96). B passes to C and cuts through the lane to the weak side. E moves across the lane, and A fills the point position as D cuts to low post and C dribbles out of the corner. C passes to A.

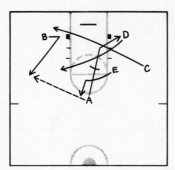

DIAGRAM 5-98

Diagram 5–98 (Continuation of movement in Diagram 5–97). When C passes to A, B cuts outside to receive A's pass, C cuts to ball-side low post, and the shuffle continuity is restored.

The wheel man-to-man offense features constant movement, cuts toward and away from the ball by all five players, and double screens away from the ball. Like the shuffle, the wheel is an excellent ball-control offense, particularly for small teams, teams with balanced scoring or rebounding, and players who do not excel at one-on-one and free-lance play. Like the shuffle, the wheel is not a good offense for teams with weak overall ball-handling skills or teams that rely heavily on the scoring or rebounding skills of one person.

Unlike the shuffle, the wheel can be run from any of several alignments and can be started as easily to the left side as to the right without altering the positions of any of the players. The two-one-two alignment shown in Diagram 5–99 is highly productive because it features *two* double screens.

Diagram 5–99. Basic Wheel Alignment and Movements. B passes to A cutting outside. (On the other side of the court, C would pass to cutter D.) B and C split the post around E, with B cutting first and C using E's screen and B's pick to brush his man off. If the defenders do not switch, C is likely to have an open lay-up if A can get the ball to him. Assuming that C is not clear, however, B will continue low to screen for D, C will set up at low post, and E will slide from high post to low post. D will cut around B's screen to the vicinity of the free-throw line, and if he doesn't receive the ball in that area, he will cut beyond the top of the circle to receive A's pass and start ball rotation.

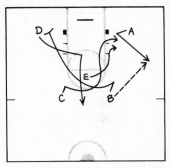

DIAGRAM 5–99

Diagram 5–100. Wheel Continuity, Ball and Player Rotation (To Left). A passes to D and cuts behind (or in front of) the double screen set by C and E. D passes to B cutting outside and moves into the lane to set a momentary screen for C, who cuts around D and E and moves to ball-side low post. D clears to weak side. E cuts behind C into the lane. If E doesn't receive the ball, he cuts to the point to receive the rotation pass from B.

DIAGRAM 5–100

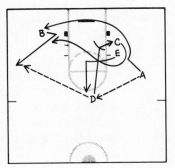

Diagram 5–101. Wheel Continuity, Ball and Player Rotation (To Right). The pattern shown in Diagram 5–100 continues on the other side. The pattern may, of course, be repeated as many times as necessary until the desired shot or scoring opportunity arises.

DIAGRAM 5–101

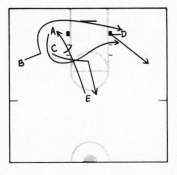

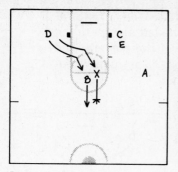

DIAGRAM 5–102

Diagrams 5–102 and 5–103. Wheel Automatic When B Is Overplayed. The most commonly encountered technique used in defensing the wheel is to overplay the pass to the point that rotates the ball to weak side. When this occurs, C cuts to the corner, A passes to C and cuts through the lane to the weak side, E cuts to the wing to receive C's pass, B moves inside to low post, and D cuts outside to B's position at the point.

The pattern is now reset. E will pass to D. C will return to low post, and E will cut behind the double screen set by B and C. A will slide outside to receive the rotation pass from D, etc.

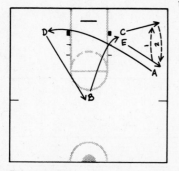

DIAGRAM 5–103

We might note that the automatics in the previous and following illustrations may have to be called by the ball handler, since the other offensive players may not be in position to see defenders overguarding the players cutting outside. A single code word is normally sufficient to set the automatic in motion.

Diagram 5–104. Rotation Pass to the Wing Is Overplayed. A passes to D and cuts behind the double screen to low post. B cuts outside, but his man overplays him to deny the pass.

DIAGRAM 5–104

Diagram 5–105. Wheel Automatic When Rotation Pass to Wing Is Overplayed (Continuation of movement in Diagram 5–104). When D calls the automatic, E will cut across to low post, and C will cut outside to receive D's pass. B will move inside and around the double screen set by A and E. D passes to C and screens inside, and continuity is restored.

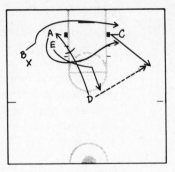

_____ DIAGRAM 5–105

ZONE OFFENSE

In determining what type of a zone offense to use, the coach should consider, first, his personnel and, second, the man-to-man offense he has designed. The closer the two offenses are in principle and in movement, the better the zone offense will be. He next should consider why the opponents are using a zone defense. Normally, they are doing so because their personnel is best suited for a zone. Other reasons include the following:

1. To institute an aggressive offense
2. To disrupt a team that has a good set pattern against a man-to-man defense
3. To protect players who are in foul trouble
4. To protect a lead
5. To change the tempo of a game
6. To protect defensive players incapable of good man-to-man defense

Since the reason for using the zone defense is negative rather than positive, the offense should attack it from that point of view. If the opponents are protecting players in foul trouble, the zone offense should move at those players if possible, using fakes and feints with the ball to force them to commit another foul.

There are two important factors in attacking a zone defense: (1) the players must be patient, and (2) they must get a good shot every time they have possession. The basic facts to remember about a zone defense are that the zone moves with the ball, leaving areas away from the ball position open, and that the defensive rebounders are not in good blockout positions because of their slides. Offensive players must take advantage of this situation. First, the offensive players should get the ball in good shooting position. (Any shot within sixteen feet of the basket should be a good-percentage shot if it is not under pressure.) Second, they should move away from the ball position. All men must be in their most advantageous position. They should never be near a defensive man, and they should split defenders. Third, all players should know what they are going to do with the ball before they receive it.

Fundamentals

In zone offensive play the following fundamentals must be adhered to.

Dribbling. Dribble with caution against a zone because dribbling generally tends to stabilize the defense. Never dribble between men unless they are very widely spread or overextended. There are only two times when a player should dribble: (1) when he is driving with a lane to the basket either along the baseline or at a forty-five-degree angle or (2) when he is moving back toward mid-court for protection in order to keep the ball in play.

Cutting. When cutting against the zone, split defensive men. No more than two cutters should go in the same direction at one time. Attack a zone with player movements that counter defensive moves, cutting parallel to the path of the ball and constantly using a directional pattern toward the uncovered zone areas. Purposeful movement of men and the ball is essential. Cutting into the zone from behind the back men is effective. Fake without the ball while cutting in order to split men better.

Passing. Pass into the zone. Return the pass to the teammate you received it from. He will be open, because the zone moves with the ball. Never use routine or stereotyped passes or passing lanes. Because any zone focuses attention primarily on the ball, accurate, quick, precise ball movement is essential in spreading the zone. Good ball movement increases the zone's vulnerability. Passes should be short, if possible, and bounce passes are extremely effective. Passes should be against the flow of the zone at all possible times.

Screening. It is possible to screen against a zone. You may screen inside or outside the perimeter of a zone, preventing an opponent from sliding defensively and permitting your teammate to shoot over your screen. Screens should normally be toward the sideline and baseline, screening the defensive man in from his outside, taking advantage of his defensive position. Screens require quick reversing actions in the flow of the ball.

Rebounding. Offensive rebounding against a zone is of paramount importance. The players must aggressively move into rebounding position. As the zone defense slides, it sometimes takes the defenders away from the offensive players, so a quick, aggressive offense should be able to get good rebounding position inside opponents. Slap or deflect the ball if possible.

Ball Control. Good ball handling is extremely important against a zone defense. Only good shots should be taken. Any hurried, deflected, or poor-percentage shots hinder the zone offense's effectiveness. Players should take only high-percentage shots without defensive pressure. Players should not expect to get a high-percentage shot immediately against a good zone, but they must take it as soon as it appears. Primarily, a team must score from outside the periphery of the zone in order to penetrate it. If outside shooting is successful, the zone must extend away from the basket, opening the center of the zone for quick cuts, passes, or drives into this area. When the ball can be passed into the crucial middle-zone area effectively, the defense must collapse toward the ball, opening the intermediate shooting areas on the side of the pass-in and perhaps freeing cutters in the area away from the pass-in.

Danger Areas. Two areas are dangerous for offensive men playing against a zone defense—the corners and the pivot area. If a player is in the corner, defenders can double-team him. In addition, he has only two passing lanes: back out or into the middle of the zone. Therefore, a player who receives the ball in the corner should pass it out immediately unless he is an exceptionally good ball handler. In any case, the ball should never be held in the corner for more than the count of two. Corner men, unless they have a baseline move to the basket, should never dribble the ball.

The pivot area is dangerous because the zone collapses back toward the ball. Therefore, before he receives the ball, the pivot man should know what he will do with it. He should know where the shooters are and consider passing to a wing man. If the pivot man's back is to the basket, the passer must tell him if he has a shot himself. He should never dribble the ball under any circumstances.

Overloading. Overloading the zone aids team maneuverability. Overloading can be from the stationary position at the outset or it can be from a moving posture after the ball has been passed one or two times.

Defensive Balance. All zone offenses must have built-in safety factors. One man must always be moving back into a defensive position during movement of the ball against a zone defense to prevent an easy basket by the opponents from a turnover or a fast break.

Attacking Principles

The following attacking principles should be incorporated into all offensive planning against zone defense.

Use the fast break immediately upon getting possession of the ball in order to get back before the defense can set up its zone. Even if the fast-break opportunity is not present, look for a high-percentage shot before starting the offensive pattern, before the zone has time to set up.

Spread the zone as much as possible, attempting to overextend it, and then pass behind the overextended players for penetration. Attack the weak spots in the zone, using probing passes to determine who the weak players are and working through them.

Offensive players, except for a pivot man, should never have their backs to the basket when attacking a zone. If they do, teammates should seldom pass to them. A man inside the zone forces the defense to guard him, thereby controlling the structure of the zone. With the ball in the pivot, opportune baseline cuts and weak-side cuts are possible. It is important that the zone offense shift with passes. Zone offense must be simple, but flexible. It must have a team offensive continuity with quick, coordinated team movement. Players should shuffle or rotate to outposition the zone, using an overload principle. Cutting through the zone is important in the zone offense.

An excellent maneuver is to use a good passer as the pivot man, regardless of his size. A small man (possibly a guard) in the center of a zone will be quicker and more agile in his deploying movements than a bigger man. He will be able to find the openings between men and keep the pass low.

Fake from the back of the zone to the open areas when the ball is passed into the pivot area. With every pass, reposition yourself in relation to the adjusting defense, except for the defensive safety man. If a zone adjusts to cover up for an overextended defensive player, the offensive team should fake toward this shift and penetrate into the newly opened areas away from the shift. Cut into a zone to an open area or to the baseline, looking for openings in the defense as you cut. A cutter may delay momentarily to take advantage of a defensive slide and then move between the defenders.

Regardless of the original alignment of the zone, all zones tend to flex into similar postures after basic ball and offensive player movement: for example, one defensive player must be at the ball position; one defensive player must be close to a pivot man; and one defensive player must be under the basket defending against lay-ups or weak-side movement. Therefore, in all zones, at least three men are actually immobilized, and it is easy to determine their positions.

Against an attack defense, it is best to get the ball inside the front line. There is usually an opening between the front and back line, because the front line is attacking defensively and the back line is generally thinking about protecting the basket; therefore, good intermediate shots are possible. The floor should be balanced at all times.

Players should know and see the passing lanes. They should not make routine passes. It is best to move a zone from the inside with a quick fake rather than from the outside.

A player can pass to a man inside the perimeter of the zone with his back to the basket if he is not under defensive pressure. If the receiver has a shot, the passer-in must call "Two" or some such signal to alert the receiver to his shooting opportunity. If a player passes in without a call, the receiver knows he does not have a shot, and he should pass to teammates with good shooting opportunities as the defenders move toward him.

Offensive teams should be alert for changing defenses. If you are ahead, and the opponents are playing a zone, do not slow down the game; try to move the front line of the zone out so that you can get good shots in the medium area. If the back line moves out, the weak side behind the back line is generally susceptible to cutting movements.

Zone Offense from a Three-Out–Two-In Attack Formation. When a three-two man-to-man offense is used, the offensive team should incorporate zone attack patterns from this alignment. These patterns should have a continuity and be adaptable for use against any zone defense.

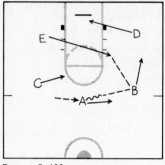

DIAGRAM 5–106

Diagram 5–106. Zone Offense, Three-Two Alignment. A dribbles to the right, indicating the direction of the movement against the zone. After one or two preliminary dribbles, he passes to B. As A starts his dribble, E moves from his low-left position into a medium-pivot position on the ball side. B passes into E, if possible, and moves parallel to the sideline toward the baseline. D parallels E's movement, cutting quickly under the basket. E may pass to D, cutting under; to B, moving along the sideline; or to C, moving into the outer half of the free-throw circle.

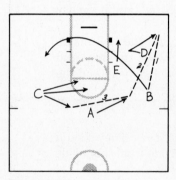

DIAGRAM 5–107

Diagram 5–107 (An alternative to Diagram 5–106). If B cannot pass into E, D will V out toward the corner, and B will pass into D (1). B then cuts immediately toward the basket. If he opens, he will receive a give-and-go return pass from D. After B's cut, E will slide from his medium-pivot position down to a low-pivot position on the ball side. A moves right as an outlet for the pass. C may move into the foul-line area or into the outer half of the free-throw circle in good shooting position for a possible quick pass from D. If D cannot pass to B, E, or C, he will pass back to A (2), and A will pass to C (3), who will move to the head of the circle. B circles out to the left side to an open medium-range shooting area.

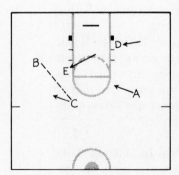

DIAGRAM 5–108

Diagram 5–108 (Continuation of movement in Diagram 5–107). C should pass quickly to B because the opponents may have shifted to the offensive right, allowing B a good intermediate jump-shot opportunity. E will move up from his low position into a medium-pivot position on the ball side. C moves toward B's side. D moves in under the basket, low, opposite the ball. A moves into the outer half of the free-throw circle, as he may be open because of the quick shift the opponents must make back to the offensive left.

Diagram 5–109. Zone Offense, Three-Two Alignment, Screening a Zone. A passes to C (1), who moves to meet the pass. E moves up into high-pivot position. B moves toward the head of the key, getting a quick return pass from C (2). During this movement, D waits and times his positioning until the zone has slid to the offensive left. He screens the outside low man, farthest from the ball position. This player normally will be moving in to protect the area under the basket. D holds the screen. A, after his pass to C, cuts down the middle and hooks behind D's screen. B passes in to A (3).

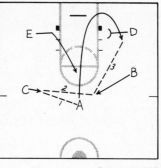

DIAGRAM 5–109

Diagram 5–110. Zone Offense, Three-Two Alignment, Move against a Two-Back Zone. Teams using a three-two or one-two-two zone defense may be attacked as follows: A passes to B (1). At the same instant, D moves up into medium-pivot position from the right corner, and E, the opposite corner man, moves over into the position vacated by D and receives a pass from B (2). C is moving into the outer half of the free-throw circle. B may pass to D or C if either appears open.

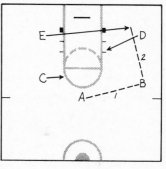

DIAGRAM 5–110

Zone Offense, Two-Three Alignment

The two-three zone offense continuity is our secondary zone offense. We have also used this offense as a diversionary man-to-man offense attack and against match-up defenses. In this offense A is the best ball handler, the quarterback, who should have a good outside shot. He looks for openings in the front line of the zone near the key and for good outside shooting position. As he rarely penetrates in this offense, he is usually back as the defensive safety factor.

B is normally the other guard. He should be a good outside and medium jump shooter, tall enough to rebound, because he occasionally cuts through the zone. He should be able to pass into the pivot man, feed a wing man on a give-and-go movement, or pass out to A over pressure in the corner. C and D are usually the forwards, who move in a rocking motion from left side to right side and back. Normally, they are looking for plays inside. They are always primary rebounders with E in this zone offense continuity.

E is the center. He generally moves up and down along the foul lanes and across the lanes looking for good openings in the zone structure as he comes to the ball. If he receives it, he looks quickly for medium shots for B, C, or D or for shots for A in the outer half of the free-throw circle.

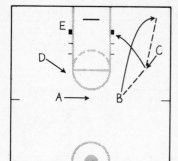

Diagram 5–111. Zone Offense, Two-Three Continuity. B passes to C as C moves up from his forward position at approximately the foul line extended. B cuts into the right corner. C returns the pass to B and cuts through the middle looking for a return pass from B. A and D adjust their positions toward the ball, A moving over to replace B. D moves up looking for good shooting position at the left side of the foul lane.

DIAGRAM 5–111

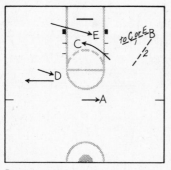

DIAGRAM 5–112

Diagram 5–112 (Continuation of movement in Diagram 5–111). B has two options with the ball in the corner. (1) He may execute a give-and-go pass to C, who is cutting through, or pass to E, who times his movement with C. As C is going away from the ball, E moves across the lane into low-pivot position, looking for seams in the zone. B may pass to E as he moves into this position. (2) If B does not find E or C open, he will pass back out to A. D has adjusted over toward the end of the foul line. If he does not get a quick pass from A, he will move back into a position on the foul line extended, closer to the left sideline.

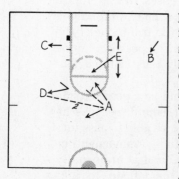

DIAGRAM 5–113

Diagram 5–113 (Continuation of movement in Diagram 5–112). Because D did not have the good shooting position (1), he has moved back to position to receive the pass (2). As D moves back, C moves into the left corner. E may adjust his position into medium-pivot position on the weak side, going into the lower half of the free-throw circle if it appears open, because the zone must slide to the offensive left. B moves back up toward his original position. A will adjust to the left with the ball movement. He may also break into the outer half of the free-throw circle for a quick return pass from D if the area is open.

Diagram 5–114 (Continuation of movement in Diagram 5–113). D, having passed the ball to C in the left corner, moves toward the ball and then cuts sharply across the middle. He may receive a return pass from C if he appears open. E comes across the lane, going on either side of D, looking for the open position inside the zone. Sometimes this position will appear higher than D's movement. As the zone drops back, the back line will drop back toward the basket to cover D's movement through. A adjusts to the offensive left. B moves out into his original position. B may move into the outer half of the free-throw circle if the opening appears for a quick pass from C to A to B.

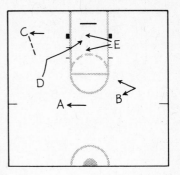

DIAGRAM 5–114

Diagram 5–115 (Continuation of movement in Diagram 5–114). C could not make the pass to D or E. He returns the ball out to A. B, who could not get the pass into the outer half of the free-throw circle in the previous diagram, moves back into his normal position. E is now in his original position along the foul lane. C moves up to the position that D had at the beginning. D moves out to C's initial position. The ball may now be passed back from A to B and the offense started again.

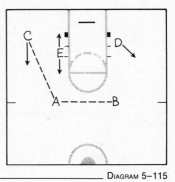

DIAGRAM 5–115

Options from these plays follow.

Diagram 5–116. Zone Offense, Two-Three. This is an alternative to the play in Diagram 5–114. D has the ball on the left side. A cuts through to the weak side, and B comes back into original position. D fakes the pass to C as A calls the cut through, then D passes back to B at the head of the key. E moves down the right pivot lane. A will appear open in the right corner as a quick reversal of the ball back to the head of the key breaks normal continuity. This is a good maneuver for two reasons: (1) it breaks away from the routine stereotyped passing lanes that the defense may get used to, and (2) it gives A a chance to cut through, a move he does not normally make in this offense. Because the zone is sliding from right to left quickly, this move will give A an open shot in a short-jump-shot area along the baseline.

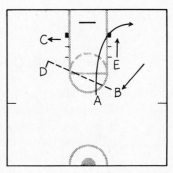

DIAGRAM 5–116

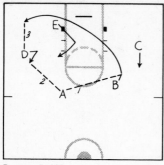

DIAGRAM 5–117

Diagram 5–117. Zone Offense from a Two-Three Alignment. Instead of passing into C in Diagram 5–111, B passes back to A (1) and cuts through diagonally. D fakes to the middle and comes back. A passes to D (2). E fakes as though he is going across and comes up into a medium position on the ball side. D passes to B (3) in the left corner after B's diagonal cut. B, D, and E form a good offensive triangle in an overload situation, as do D, E, and A.

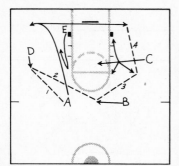

DIAGRAM 5–118

Diagram 5–118. Zone Offense, Two-Three. This is a free-lance variation of movement in Diagram 5–117. A passes to D (1), who is moving up from his forward position. A follows through into the corner on the strong side. As D moves up, E moves up to a point approximating the left end of the foul line. B moves to the head of the key, and C moves into the right-foul-lane area. C's position is adjustable up or down the foul lane or into either half of the free-throw circle if a shooting opportunity appears. D may pass to A. If A is covered by a back man, E may appear open within the zone perimeter in a pivot position. If neither A nor E appears open, and it is not possible to pass into C, D may pass to B (2), who may pass quickly to A running along the baseline. As the ball moves back from D to B, C should move out into good pass reception territory (3), looking for a quick pass along the baseline to A (4).

Zone Offense, One-Three-One Alignment

One of the most popular zone offensive attack patterns, the one-three-one, is used as a basic pattern against man-to-man and zone. It is a formidable offensive attack system because it also has excellent potential against a match-up-type defense. A, at the head of the key, should be the best passer and a good outside shooter, and he must be able to diagnose holes as they appear in the zone. He should be interchangeable with B or C if he moves through the pattern. B and C—the side, or wing men—should be good jump shooters and good drivers, as many times they will have an opportunity to drive at a forty-five-degree angle into the basket. They should not expect to drive all the way in this situation, but should be ready to stop short for quick medium jump shots or a pass-off to the weak side of the back side of the zone (if the back line of the zone overshifts its position). D, on the foul line, is a pivot player who has good hands. He should be a fairly mobile person. E, the baseline player, should be more mobile, and a better outside shooter, than D. If D and E have similar abilities, their positions are interchangeable.

Diagram 5–119. Zone Offense, One-Three-One Continuity. A passes to B. E breaks out to the corner. E's position is adjustable; he may be on the ball side or the weak side initially. Normally, the offense will start to the side on which E positions himself. B passes to E, who is moving out toward the corner. E's movement should be determined by the defensive alignment. He should only move out as far as he has to to receive the ball. Against some types of zone defenses (for example, a two-three), a wing man may move up to play B, which will allow E to stay fairly close in under the basket. E should be facing the basket when he receives the ball, ready to shoot if the opening occurs. B cuts through the zone looking for a return give-and-go pass from E. A has moved to the ball side. D, on the pivot, has turned toward the ball into a position where he may break down the right lane on the ball side as B clears through. C must take a step toward the basket as B cuts, because if E returns the ball to B, C should break for the baseline on the left side near the buffer zone marker. He will be open, because the zone will have to slide to stop B's shot. B knows that if he gets a return pass, C will be in this general area as a passing option. If the ball is not passed to B, he cuts through, away from the ball.

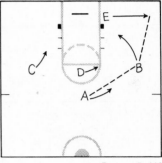

DIAGRAM 5–119

Diagram 5–120 (Continuation of movement in Diagram 5–119). E received the ball in the corner, but could not pass to B or D or shoot. He has to pass back out to A, who has moved from the head of the key into position as the outlet receiver. D has moved along the right foul lane into low-pivot position. C's position is now adjustable. He should look for an opening in the outer half of the free-throw circle for a quick shooting opportunity on a snap pass from A.

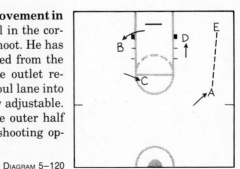

DIAGRAM 5–120

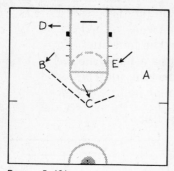

DIAGRAM 5–121

Diagram 5–121 (Continuation of movement in Diagram 5–120). None of the previous options have materialized. Therefore, C moves out to the head of the key and receives a pass from A. D now moves opposite to the left corner, anticipating movement of the offense to the left. E has moved from the corner position up into the foul-line high-pivot area. C passes to B, who has moved into the left wing spot, and since D is moving out, the continuity offense is now ready to move through from the left. The positions of A, C, and B are interchangeable, as are the positions of D and E.

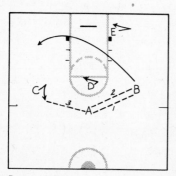

DIAGRAM 5–122

Diagram 5–122. Zone Offense, One-Three-One Alignment, "Opposite." This works from the same basic formation as the preceding plays, with A passing to B (1) and E and D moving as in Diagram 5–119. However, in this play, B passes back to A (2) and cuts through to the opposite corner away from E, the underneath man. E and D anticipate this move as they V back toward the ball. C has faked his baseline move and has dropped back to get a pass (3). All the possibilities mentioned for Diagram 5–119 are available. Normally, B will cut through for a good quick shot, or C and B will find themselves in a two-on-one situation against the defense.

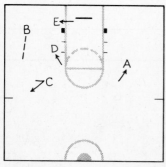

DIAGRAM 5–123

Diagram 5–123 (Continuation of movement in Diagram 5–122). Many times when defending against a reverse movement, the defense overadjusts back toward the ball. B has received the ball from C. C now adjusts his position on the ball side. E has moved into low position, and D has moved into medium-pivot position, focusing the attention of the zone to the left offensive side. A may sneak down the right side to receive a pass over the zone from B or C for an open shot. While this play will not work often against a zone, and the pass is dangerous, if it works once it will help subsequent "opposite" moves, as the zone will be expecting the over-pass to A on the weak side and will not shift as readily.

Free-lance Zone Movement (Wheel), Hitting the Post Man

In this zone offensive movement, four men are outside the zone perimeter with one man inside. If the four men who are outside are of comparable size and ability, and the inside player is a mobile, good-sized pivot man, this pattern is an excellent zone offense to use when players have good intuitive basketball sense and understand the precepts of good zone offensive attack. There are no prescribed patterns or passing lanes; therefore, all players are able to move freely within the framework of the rules of the basic high-post pattern, making it extremely difficult for the defense to analyze offensive movement. This is a balanced offensive movement, with all five players moving according to a set plan, all five having preknowledge of the movement of their teammates, and all five being able to pass the ball sharply and quickly.

We will describe the pattern from the one-three-one alignment that we use most frequently. Four men form the perimeter of the wheel, rotating to the right or to the left, with the pivot man, D, as the hub. The passing lanes into and out of the pivot are the spokes. The pivot must constantly adjust position toward the ball as the players rotate left or right. Since he is inside the zone, he is the focal point of the offensive attack. If the ball can reach him and he can make a quick move, he should be able to score.

Point Guard A may pass to either wing, B or C, who should dribble toward the basket, and shoot if open. If he is not open, he may dribble protectively as his teammates rotate toward or away from the ball. The offensive player at low post on ball side moves along the baseline and behind the zone coverage, stopping in good shooting position. Pivot Man D rolls to the ball side in medium pivot, forming an offensive triangle with the ball handler and the man along the baseline. The weak-side wing man will move down the foul lane toward the basket. A must delay at the outset to be sure that C, the ball handler, has an outlet if he is in trouble. If the ball moves to E along the baseline, or to D in the medium-pivot area, A will move in the same direction as B, looking for openings in the zone. C will shoot if he's open. If not, he looks to E at the baseline. E will shoot if open. If not, since the defense is sagging toward the ball, he may pass to D in the pivot; to B at weak-side wing; to C, who originally passed the ball to him; or to A at the point. If D receives the ball in the pivot area, he should shoot if open. If he is unable to shoot, he may pass back out to C at the wing; to B moving inside from weak-side wing; or to A, who has rotated away from the point into the medium shooting

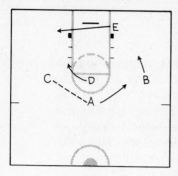

Diagram 5–124. Zone Offense, One-Three-One Free-lance Movement (Wheel), Hitting the Post Man. A passes to the left wing, C. A hesitates slightly to be sure that C is moving well with the ball, then moves away to the right. B also adjusts to his right. E moves over on the baseline side, close to the foul lane, behind the back line of the zone defense. D rotates to the medium-pivot position on the ball side.

DIAGRAM 5–124

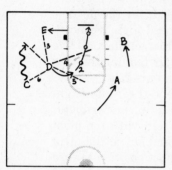

DIAGRAM 5–125

Diagram 5–125. One-Three-One Free-lance Movement (Wheel), Rotating around the Post Man. C dribbles, probingly, parallel to the left sideline, as he did not have a good shooting opportunity in Diagram 5–124. E moves out of the under-basket area, since C could not pass to him. C makes a quick pass (1) into D in the pivot. D now has five options with the ball: he may turn and shoot (C calls "Two" for D) (2); he may pass to E as the zone moves toward D (3); he may pass across the lane to B (4); he may pass to A, who is at the right end of the foul line (5); or he may pass back to C (6).

area at the opposite end of the foul line or in the outer half of the free-throw circle.

The movement may be started to either side, and it may rotate to the left or to the right. The offense must remain spread to be effective. The baseline man (E in Diagrams 5–124 and 5–125, although it could as easily be any of the four outside men) and the pivot man must know that their time with the ball is limited when the ball penetrates the zone; therefore, they must make their moves immediately upon reception. They should know what their moves are going to be before the ball reaches them. All outside players should be alert for openings in the defense for quick movements into shooting position. If they do not receive the ball immediately, however, they should continue with their normal rotation. All players along the perimeter should be able to maneuver from any one of the four outside positions. To be in good safety outlet position to protect possession, they must be alert for defensive maneuvers that may tie up the ball.

Overload Offense

The movements involved in setting up overloads and rotating the ball and players vary considerably among the diverse overload patterns. The pattern described here uses the entire halfcourt to spread and attack the defense. Basic movements against zone defense are similar to those in man-to-man offenses, omitting the inside screening and offensive-roll techniques, which are negated by the zone defense positions, since no switching is necessary.

Diagram 5–126. Overload Offense, Preliminary Movements. B passes to A. E cuts to high post, and C slides to the corner. A will pass to E in the post area if possible; if not, A passes to C in the corner, and E slides to low post, attempting to get position on his man inside. If C passes inside, he will pass to the side of E away from his defender.

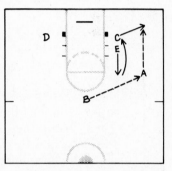

DIAGRAM 5–126

Diagram 5–127. Ball and Player Rotation, Overload Offense. If no scoring opportunities arise, C passes to A, A passes to B, and B passes to D cutting outside. C cuts to the corner to receive D's pass. E cuts across to the opposite low post if C doesn't shoot. After passing to C, D cuts to the basket and through the lane, looking for a return pass.

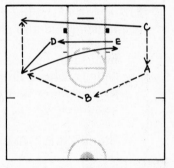

DIAGRAM 5–127

Diagram 5–128. A's Cut to Reestablish Ball Rotation. After D passes and cuts, A cuts from wing to wing. C passes to A and cuts to the opposite corner. E moves across the lane as before. A passes to B. D cuts outside to receive B's pass, relays the ball to C in the corner, and cuts to the basket and through the lane (not shown).

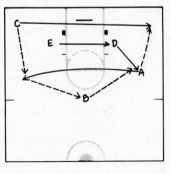

DIAGRAM 5–128

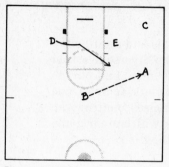

DIAGRAM 5–129

Diagram 5–129. Varying the Overload. One of the most likely defensive adjustments to offensive overloading is for the defense to match up with the players in the overload. In such cases, the offensive team can foil the matchups by switching to a four-man overload, particularly when the defense has been lulled into shifting automatically with ball rotation. If the defensive team uses a guard to cover high post once the overload is established, D's cut to high post may create an offensive mismatch that can be disastrous to the defense.

The offensive team may rotate the overload to the other side of the court to coincide with ball rotation, or players may flash into the high post area as opportunities arise.

An often-used variation of A's movement from wing to wing is for B to cut to the wing and for A to fill the point position. Then, in rotation, A returns to the wing position on his side of the court and B returns to the point.

The movements shown in this pattern are ideally suited to gearing the zone offense to specific personnel. If A brings the ball down the sideline to start the pattern, A is the team's best ball handler and also a proficient outside shooter. C should be a good baseline shooter. The E position is excellent for the team's big man inside. D should be able to rebound effectively from weak side; it helps if he's a good wing shooter, too. B should be a good point shooter, but does not have to be a particularly good ball handler.

Stack Zone Offense

We use stack offense as the primary attack weapon against all types of zone defenses. In using this offense against a zone, quickness of movement and timing are essential, as all moves must be made simultaneously when the defense is at its weakest posture. Basically, the positions are the same as in the stack man-to-man offense. The moves are also basically the same. In a zone, however, the point man, A, will dribble into a wing man in an odd-front defensive alignment, and he will dribble at a front-line man against an even alignment. (A must be ready to reverse quickly on the dribble so that he will not be trapped by the even-front defense.)

Another adjustment against the zone occurs if the point is dribbling to the right. Instead of going behind E to the foul-line area, D, the off-side man, cuts in front of E in a straight-line cut to the foul-line area. In offensive zone movement, the strong-side pivot (B on the right and E on the left) must adjust his position between the defensive men in the zone structure. The man who pops out quickly (C to the right and D to the left) must pick the most advantageous position as he moves out. This again is determined by the type of zone.

Most teams resort to some type of man-to-man defense against the stack, because this offense quickly finds openings in most zone alignments.

Diagram 5–130. Stack Zone Offense against a Two-Three Zone. A dribbles hard at X_2. If X_2 retreats, A looks quickly for C. If X_4 moves with C and X_2 has retreated slightly, a passing lane opens immediately to B. If X_2 attacks A, A quickly passes to D, coming up the lane. Many times A will find that if X_4 has moved with C, X_5 has moved up to position on B, and X_3 has adjusted slightly toward D's position, it allows a quick, immediate lob opposite into E as E moves down the left lane.

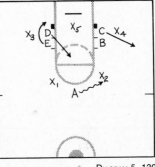

DIAGRAM 5–130

Diagram 5–131. Stack Offense against Two-One-Two Zone. A dribbles at the front man, X_2, again ready to change direction. Against the two-man front, A gets a lot of quick jump shots from the head of the key, especially if he is moving right and is a left-handed shooter or vice versa. C pops out normally, X_4 moving out with him. X_3 generally will overcompensate toward B to cut off the pivot position. If X_3 moves quickly and X_4 moves out with C, the lob will show over X_3 into B along the right lane. D adjusts slightly, compensating for X_3's movement, positioning near the left end of the foul line. As X_3 expects X_1 to drop back, X_3 may move to the ball side. Sometimes, however, X_3 will not shift, opening the lane into B.

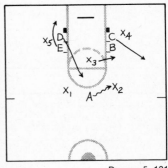

DIAGRAM 5–131

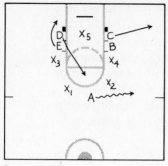

DIAGRAM 5–132

Diagram 5–132. Stack Offense against Two-Two-One Zone. A will try to dribble a little to the outside of X_2 if possible, because C will pop into the right corner, which is a good shooting area since X_4 is fronting B. A will look for a quick pass-in to C. If X_4 moves in that direction, A can pass into the pivot man, B, who should be adjusting up. B can shoot himself, pass back to A, pass to C in the corner, pass to D on the foul line, or pass to E, who has moved under the basket opposite.

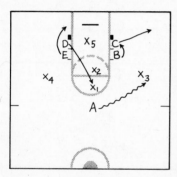

Diagram 5–133. Stack Offense against One-Three-One Zone. A dribbles right at the wing man, X_3. C moves into the right corner. B can move low, waiting for defensive adjustment until he sees how C will be covered. Normally, C will be wide open. In this defense, X_2 will sometimes move over to front B, leaving C open. If X_3 falls back to cover C, and X_1 shifts toward A, D will be open high on the foul line.

DIAGRAM 5–133

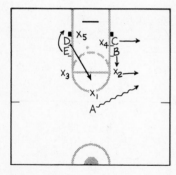

Diagram 5–134. Stack Offense against One-Two-Two Zone. A dribbles quickly toward the wing man, X_2. C pops out parallel to the baseline. B will adjust up slightly, giving X_4 the problem of covering B or C. Normally, C will be open for a shot from the right sideline, or B, in the pivot area, may receive a quick pass-in. Sometimes X_5 adjusts quickly across the lane, leaving E free on the weak-side under.

DIAGRAM 5–134

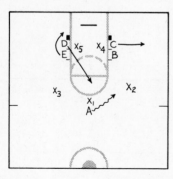

Diagram 5–135. Stack Offense against Three-Two Zone. A dribbles between the front men, X_1 and X_2, at X_2. C pops out and generally is open unless X_2 falls back. This gives A a good medium shot. B is in front of X_4 for a quick pass-in, or D will be open quickly near the foul line.

DIAGRAM 5–135

Diagram 5–136. "Red." X_1 and X_2 are attacking A. "Red" has been called. B moves up and receives a quick pass-in from A. B immediately turns to face the basket, taking a sixteen-foot shot if he is open. C moves into the right corner, D moves slightly to the left sideline in good shooting position, and E moves in directly to the basket. If the ball gets by X_1 and X_2, and B's pivot move is quick, one of the three players inside will have an easy, high-percentage shot.

_____ DIAGRAM 5–136

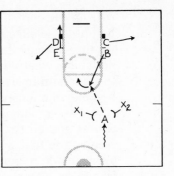

DIAGRAM 5–136

Many teams using a zone defense against the stack will attempt to double-team the point man as he moves into offensive position. To eliminate any risk and to attack aggressively, all players must be looking at the ball to see an attack movement by X_1 and X_2 as A dribbles into position. On this movement, a player (usually A) calls "Red." On the call, either B or E—generally the man on the side of the ball—moves up as high as he must to receive a high pass from A. The others deploy as shown in Diagram 5–136.

ATTACKING MATCH-UP DEFENSES

A match-up defense—zone or man-to-man—attempts to force the pattern team out of its set patterns, getting the offense to stand still. Teams playing against a match-up defense should not congest areas away from the ball where one defender may guard two offensive players. Attackers should also omit inside screens, which are usually ineffective against this defense.

The offense used against a match-up defense must be a well-executed, properly timed, intelligent moving offense that utilizes pre-knowledge of the defense's principles. Good ball handling and ball control are essential. We recommend the stack offense, which takes teams out of a match-up defense and forces them into a straight man-to-man or zone set-up, since it's impossible to match up the men when they are in a close-to-the-basket position.

The offensive team must determine the type of match-up defense being used and attack it. Primarily, the offense should beat it back to the set position by fast breaking and taking good high-percentage shots quickly before the defense has a chance to align itself. Diagonal cuts make trading of men—essential in a match-up defense—difficult, and they confuse the defense. Long cuts on the same side as the ball and diagonal cuts opposite the ball are also effective. Cuts paralleling the path of the ball make trading difficult and force a small defender to make a difficult decision—whether to stay with the man paralleling the ball or to trade him to someone else. This defensive indecisiveness must become an offensive asset.

Passers should be alert for defenders playing intercepting angles and cutting off passing lanes, and they must move and receive the ball with assurance. Offensive players should shoot over outside screens. With quick ball movement it is possible to isolate an offensive player for a one-on-one situation. Since the primary receiver is usually overplayed, passers should pass by him, using a safe passing lane. Moving in quickly without the ball behind a teammate's movement with or without the ball is a good trailing maneuver.

The offense should reverse the direction of the ball quickly against a match-up defense. Players should use back-door moves in the front line to combat overplaying outlets. Since defenders are normally overplaying to prevent a forward from getting the ball, a quick fake toward the ball and a reverse movement may open the offensive player. Simply reversing the ball movement may take advantage of two offensive players who are guarded by one man in a defensive area away from the ball. Smaller players should use bounce passes to penetrate past the big men who are kept inside by the match-up defensive deployment.

Two-Three and Three-Two Offenses

Good cutting opportunities such as long cuts on the ball side, diagonal cuts through the match-up defense, and back-doors should be incorporated into the two-three and three-two offenses against a match-up defense.

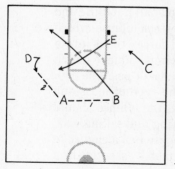

Diagram 5–137. Two-Three Offense against Match-up Defense. B passes to A (1). D, the left forward, fakes and comes back to receive a pass from A (2). B makes a diagonal cut paralleling the path of the ball. B's cut makes it difficult for B's defender to trade off, as he would normally do on a normal passing maneuver from B to A to D. Therefore, B should be open for a shot. E moves behind B's cut into medium-pivot position. C makes a parallel cut to the weak side.

DIAGRAM 5–137

Diagram 5–138 (Continuation of movement in Diagram 5–137). If B does not have a shot, he passes back out to D (1). D passes to A (2) moving away from the ball, and A passes to C (3), who has V'd back out. D makes a diagonal cut off E to the opposite corner. A trade is possible here, with the big man switching from D to E. E (now being guarded by a small man) makes an offensive roll to the ball for possession and a shot if possible. It's also possible that D may open. A continues moving toward the ball. B, after his pass, moves out of the corner as a safety man. _____

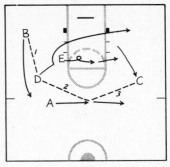

DIAGRAM 5–138

Diagram 5–139. Three-Two Offense against Match-up Defense. C passes to A (1) and parallels the pass with his cut (2), moving into the outer half of the free-throw circle. As A passes to B (3), C parallels this pass, cutting (4) to the right end of the foul line. D makes a V and moves out for a pass from B (5). C parallels this pass along the foul lane (6). E moves out of his position, alert for rebounding on the weak side if a shot is taken from the right and ready to move into good offensive position.

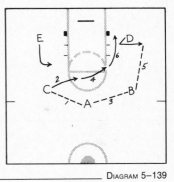

DIAGRAM 5–139

Diagram 5–140 (Continuation of movement in Diagram 5–139). Since D cannot pass into C's movement, B V's out and receives a return pass from D (1). E has moved into the high-pivot area. C moves across under the basket (2), paralleling B's pass to E (3). E passes out to A (4). C moves out from underneath (5), again paralleling the path of the pass. A good parallel path causes the defensive man to move through with the offensive player. Any player may make this paralleling cut. E, after passing back to A, moves down the middle in a give-and-go movement and cuts out to the left offensive corner to resume position to start the offense again. _____

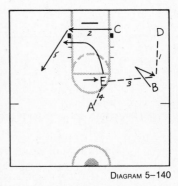

DIAGRAM 5–140

One-Three-One Offense

Along with the stack, the one-three-one presents the best opportunities against a match-up defense.

DIAGRAM 5–141

Diagram 5–141. One-Three-One Offense, Rocker Move against a Match-up Defense. C initiates the offense by passing to A. A passes to B, then moves to the right of the head of the key. B must be alert for C's cut, diagonally paralleling the path of the passes, to the right corner. B has three options: (1) he may pass to C if C cuts free on his movement; (2) he may pass to E in the low pivot on the ball side if there is a trade between C's man and E's man; and (3) he may pass back to A, who has adjusted position. (This rocker movement may be made in both directions. If B moved from right to left, E would adjust across the pivot lane as the passes were being made to allow B to cut off him.)

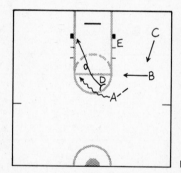

Diagram 5–142 (Continuation of movement in Diagram 5–141). As soon as D sees B pass back to A, he moves out and screens A's defender. A dribbles tightly off D's screen and has many good jump-shooting opportunities at the left end of the foul line. A may continue all the way to the basket if it is open. If a switch is made, D makes an offensive roll to the basket, moving along the left lane, away from the defensive congestion to the right.

DIAGRAM 5–142

OFFENSES AGAINST COMBINATION DEFENSES

Normally a stack offense negates the effectiveness of a combination defense against an outstanding player. If the player is put on the point, it is difficult to double-team him. The defense must play some type of a two-man front zone, which will allow the offense to penetrate and take advantage of the stack alignment.

If the man being played man-to-man is put inside in a stack of-fense, natural screens are set up. Since the zone defenders are concentrating on double-teaming this star, they will leave lanes open for easy shots from basic stack movement.

The defense does not want the outstanding player to get his normal share of points or to handle the ball. Therefore, the offense must concentrate on getting the ball to him. A big man may be inside in the stack, on the baseline, low on a one-three-one offense, or in pivot position. A small man should move according to plan.

The team should plan to cause defensive confusion, setting screens for the outstanding player and getting him open away from the zone for a one-on-one situation against his man-to-man guard. Teammates may pass directly to him when he cuts into the seam of a box or diamond zone.

Diagram 5–143. Combination Offense against a Zone-and-One. A, the outstanding player, has the ball but is bothered by his defender and is double-teamed. A passes in to C (1) in the corner and moves off D's screen. B has moved into re-ceiving position to the right side of the head of the key. C has these options: he may pass to A cutting off D's screen to the basket (2); he may pass to A behind D's screen for a shot (3); or he may pass back to B (4). He passes to B, who drib-bles in, pivots, and sets a post at the foul line. A reverses direction, cuts off D and B, receiving a hand-back or flip pass from B. A dribbles into the open area, left, for a one-on-one maneuver against the man playing him man-to-man.

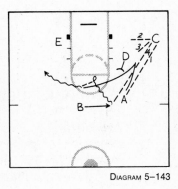

DIAGRAM 5–143

Diagram 5–144. Combination Offense Using One-Three-One against a Zone-and-One. A, the outstanding player, has the ball without being able to move on the right side. A passes to B (1). B passes to C, who has V'd out (2). D, at the pass from A to B, sets a screen. A runs his de-fender into the screen. E, low on the left side, moves up and sets another screen. A maneuvers his man into this screen. C moves out, receives the pass from B (2), and relays the ball to A (3) for an offensive move.

DIAGRAM 5–144

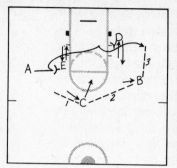

DIAGRAM 5–145

Diagram 5–145 (Continuation of movement in Diagram 5–144). If A does not have the shot, he passes back out to C (1). C and B have moved to the right in this offense, rotating away from the ball. E moves up from the low position on the left side and sets a screen. A maneuvers his defender into this screen. D sets a low screen on the right. The ball moves from C to B (2) to A (3), who cuts off the two screens trying to elude his defender. C steps into the outer half of the free-throw circle. If B can't get the ball to A, C may appear open for an easy shot. This is a rocker type of offense that can be moved from side to side, with B and C rotating opposite the flow of the ball and D and E switching from the foul line in a high-pivot position to the buffer zone in low pivot. D and E are always opposite each other, setting continual high-low screens for A to run off.

ATTACKING PRESSURE DEFENSES

A predominant part of current defensive planning in basketball defies the old theory of keeping a man defensively between his man and the basket. That is being discarded for an aggressive new theory. In man-to-man defense, men play between the ball and the men they are guarding, force reverses, force longer passes, and try to intercept the ball. When playing zone, they invite long passes and attempt to harry the offensive team into difficult situations by the threat of double-teaming and by using zone techniques full-court, three-quarter court, or half-court. This type of basketball defeats the old offensive tactic of passing to a man and screening away—first, the defenders won't allow the pass, and second, they will jump switch on the crosses.

Modern defensive maneuvers require intelligent offensive planning and coaching innovations. They require an aggressive offensive tactic of quick penetration.

One of the most important aspects in preparing for defensive pressure is the preplanning stage. The coach should be ready for the defense. He should have scouted the opponent, be abreast of modern trends, and know the principles of the defense he will be attacking. Preknowledge makes the attack much easier to put into effect.

There are several theories concerning playing against pressure defenses. The first one recommends having the nearest man pass the ball in quickly, as soon as it is out of bounds after a basket or foul shot. The speedy pass-in takes advantage of the fact that pressure defenses—especially zone—need time to set up. According to a second theory, however, hurrying may result in an intercepted ball if the wrong man takes the ball out of bounds.

The coach must prepare his team psychologically not to be upset by pressing tactics. He should tell the players that structurally and theoretically pressing defenses are the weakest defenses in basketball, because they overplay or double-team opponents. Overplaying leaves openings that an offensive team can attack and take advantage of if it plays with poise, confidence and preknowledge. If the ball can successfully escape the double-team, the attackers have a one-man advantage at the other end of the court when the ball is moved upcourt quickly. Man-to-man press and zone press attempt to do in a full-court area what it is difficult to do in the area within twenty-one feet of the basket—prevent the opposing team from scoring baskets. Teams must understand that with preparation and confidence, they can discourage this type of defense.

Players should get the ball in play quickly if the ball is out of bounds after a basket. They should look for quick penetration against a man-to-man press by using fakes and reverses or sideline screens. Intelligent aggressiveness should be a basic attack philosophy. Quick upcourt movement forces situations that might not have been there at the time of the change in possession. Aggressive attack may cause mistakes, but they will be counteracted by the opportunities opened.

In the attack philosophy, the middle man should know the position of offensive and defensive men before the ball is centered. He should know which men are breaking downcourt on his team and which opponents are moving into position to protect against them. If the outlets are cut off when the ball is rebounded defensively, it is possible to pass up the middle to a teammate who may then pass to the middle man. This strategy puts the middle man in front of the man who was overplaying him to the ball at the defensive end.

When the ball is moving upcourt quickly, it should be passed only to men moving toward the basket. Men who are cutting away from the basket toward the baseline or the sidelines are not usually in good penetrating offensive position and should not be given the ball upcourt unless they may easily take an unopposed good-percentage shot.

Team Offense against Man-to-Man Press

Against man-to-man press, work within the margin-of-error theory, allowing the best dribbler and ball handler to dribble the ball up. Most good dribblers have little difficulty alone in the back court dribbling upcourt against one opponent. If the best dribbler does have difficulty, the most mobile offensive player with a weaker defender—perhaps the other guard or a forward—can dribble the ball upcourt alone. Against man-to-man pressure, a good dribbler will use a controlled dribble, change of direction, and reverse dribble.

The good dribbler can beat most defenders one-on-one if he can control his defensive man until he gets to the front court. If he is double-teamed there, he should try to pass into the pivot. The pivot must protect the ball and pass it quickly, usually to a weak-side cutter or back to the man who passed it in.

Players must know the intent of the team playing man-to-man pressure defense full court in order to prepare to combat it. The usual reasons for playing this type of defense follow on page 264.

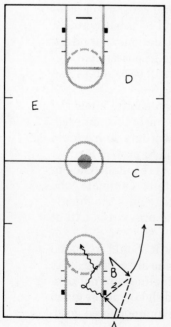

Diagram 5–146. Attacking Full-Court Man-to-Man Defensive Press, Best Dribbler Taking the Ball Up. C, D, and E are upcourt. A, the best dribbler, takes the ball from out-of-bounds, passing it inbounds to B (1). B immediately returns the pass to A (2). Both B and A use defensive fakes to decoy the defensive men away from their intended positions. A dribbles upcourt, using reverse dribbles and protecting the ball. B moves away from A. The positions of A and B may be reversed.

DIAGRAM 5–146

**Diagram 5–147. Allowing a Good, Big Drib-
bler to Bring the Ball Up Alone against a
Weak Defender.** B, the best ball handler, has
been double-teamed in the back court by X_1 and
X_2. A cannot pass the ball to B. E has the weakest
opponent in the man-to-man defensive structure.
D V's to the ball and moves away downcourt. C
fakes to the ball, then breaks to the middle as
though to receive a pass. A moves along the end
line so that the basket will not interfere with his
pass-in. E, who has a weak defender, deploys a
step up, then comes back to the ball, receiving A's
pass-in. All players now clear E so that he may
dribble up without being double-teamed. As soon
as it is safe, E will pass the ball back to Guard A
or Guard B in the front court.

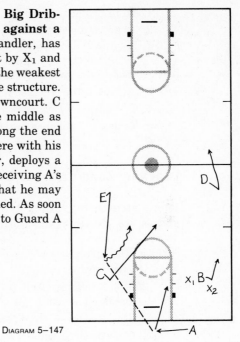

DIAGRAM 5–147

**Diagram 5–148. Backcourt Screen Play
against Full-Court Man-to-Man Pressure
with All Five Offensive Players in the Backcourt.** A has the ball out of bounds. D and E, near
mid-court, fake to the ball and pull their men upcourt. B moves across the foul lane, setting a
screen for C. C V's away, then comes back and
receives the pass-in from A (1). If there is a switch
on the play, A may pass to B (2) after B executes
an offensive roll moving upcourt. If a switch is
made, B will often have a slower defender on him,
as C's defender may be a forward. A full-court
three-on-two break is possible if B gets ahead of
the switching defender on his offensive roll. A
should be in protective position to get a return
pass from B or C.

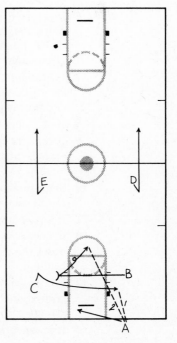

DIAGRAM 5–148

1. To intercept the pass by overplaying the men on the court
2. To prevent penetration by the good ball handler by double-teaming him and forcing the ball toward a weaker ball handler, playing intercepting angle to prevent the ball from being passed back to the good ball handler
3. To harass the receiver for a violation or a misplay
4. To invite the long pass for interception
5. To deter the offense in the back court for a ten-second violation

Attacking Zone-Pressure Defenses

Before structuring an offense against various types of zone presses, we should examine the uses of zone press.

1. The zone press is a psychological attempt to disrupt an offensive routine.
2. It is an offense itself, attacking to intercept passes and to fast-break on steals.
3. It is used when a team has good pressing personnel defensively.
4. It is used by smaller teams against bigger, less coordinated opponents.
5. It is used to upset the poise of the opponents, especially inexperienced teams.
6. It is used to upset a team offense, attempting to force opponents to use lob passes, cross-court passes, and long passes to get the ball upcourt with either more than one man moving the ball or one man trying to bring the ball upcourt alone.
7. It attempts to force the opponents into double-teaming situations that affect the peripheral vision of the man with the ball, delimit his passing lanes, and negate his dribbling ability.
8. It attempts to force misplays and violations.
9. It changes the offensive stratagem and patterns because it overplays and plays in the passing lanes, using intercepting angles.
10. Since it is usually well conceived and well coached, it requires a well conceived and well coached offensive attack to beat it.
11. It forces hurried, poor, low-percentage shots.
12. It forces turnovers, or loss of possession, and mistakes that upset the confidence of a team, especially when that team is leading.
13. It is an excellent late-game defense when the leading opponent is tired or the game is close, as it forces physical and mental errors.
14. It upsets and determines the tempo a game will be played at.
15. It takes calculated risks to force the opponents to hurry.

The following points should be incorporated into a team's zone-pressure offense. The team should attempt to keep the ball in the middle of the court at all times. Therefore, players should never pass to teammates moving into a corner, toward a sideline, or at a hash mark, except in desperate circumstances. A jump ball may be preferable. When players are double-teamed near a sideline, the sideline becomes in effect a third defender. Get the ball over mid-court safely and quickly. Once the ball is over mid-court, the guards should get over the mid-court line quickly to negate a back-court violation and to help the forwards and centers in the front court who haven't been able to penetrate to the basket.

If a dribbler is being double-teamed, he should never turn his back to his own basket in the back court. He should anticipate a double-team with the ball, see as much of the court as possible at all times, and know his primary outlets.

If he has dribbled by an opponent and the man is behind him, he should push the dribble far in front of him or change hands immediately on the dribble to prevent a rear flick by the defender. Players in possession of the ball should always expect pressure from behind and from the blind side when the ball has broken by the front line of a zone-press defense.

After a basket, a team should get the ball in play quickly, before the press can set up. The near man should retrieve the ball before it hits the floor after going through the basket, step out of bounds, and inbound it to his offensive advantage.

Players should go to the basket in attacking a zone pressure defense. A fast-break situation is always possible when a player is double-teamed, as the offensive team has a one-man advantage. Players should be able to sense a double-team moving toward them. They should practice defeating it every day. A teammate of a man being double-teamed should approach within his visual field, using a recognizable voice signal and spreading wide so that he is not close to another defensive player.

It is difficult to tell a man who is about to be double-teamed when he should pass. He should try to maintain control of the ball until he is attacked, but if the double-team trap can be sprung on him, he should pass early rather than too late.

Zone offenses against pressure need a series of release men. One man should always be behind the ball handler in the back-court, serving as a safety outlet. The ball should always be returned to the best ball handler quickly. If forwards or centers are handling the ball, they should know the good ball handlers, their position, and where to look for them. Conversely, the ball handlers should always be coming to the ball, in keeping with the margin-of-error theory. They are much less likely to make ball handling mistakes.

Players normally should go away from the pressure after they have passed off. All players should fill fast-break lanes when the ball has penetrated by the front line of the opponent's zone-press defense. Players with the ball should fake, then pass quickly, because a fake freezes most defenders momentarily.

The offense must organize well and set up quickly. It must be practiced daily. A team must know its offense and have confidence in it. Practicing against inferior defenders at first will instill this confidence. Teams should remember when they are moving the ball upcourt against a pressure-zone defense that ten seconds is a long time and they need not fear the ten-second rule unduly.

In practicing, players should first walk through their zone-press offense. Each position, its responsibilities, and its options should be delineated. Then they should move through the offense at half speed in skeleton form. Next they should play against stationary defenders, then against slow-moving defenders, then against a defensive team whose players are not allowed to use their hands. Finally, to perfect timing and coordination and to instill confidence, the players should use the offense against weak defenders. Drills should cover maintaining good vision, handling the ball while moving, and playing against outnumbered defenses. All players must recognize the defenses that they are practicing against and their positions and deployment, making their own moves counter to the defensive moves. After a team has mastered fundamentals of the zone offense and can move through its various maneuvers smoothly and with good timing, coaches may use extra defenders in practice sessions to give offensive players poise and confidence. It is also useful in practice to forbid dribbling when moving the ball upcourt against a zone-press defense. Practice time should also be given to using a controlled dribble—bouncing a dribble into a trap purposefully so as to get the defenders moving toward the ball—and then passing.

Coaches should seek questions. The players must be interested and intent. They must know the how, what, where, and why of their zone-pressure offense. Coaches should also question the players, especially those who are making mistakes, for mistakes in this offense always lead to an opponent's basket. Mistakes should be corrected immediately or the player should be replaced. A player should never make a cross-court pass unless he is 100 percent certain of success.

It is easy to double-team a man who has used his dribble; therefore, players should use the dribble effectively and purposefully. Good ball handlers should dribble if they are in the middle lane and the ball is by the front line. They may also dribble to avoid trouble, to drive to the basket, and to decoy a double-team.

Players must meet passes. They should make sure they have possession of the ball before they attempt to make a pass themselves. Some players try to catch and pass in the same motion to hurry the offense upcourt. This is disastrous. Deceptive deployment prior to meeting the pass is a must for all offensive players.

The zone-press offense must get by the front line and attack. It must attempt to distort the front line. A player should move up behind one of the front-line defenders and try to draw him away so as to get the ball by the front line quicker. Once the ball gets by, the guards must sprint upcourt to get it back in order to bring it quickly into position for the good high-percentage shot. A positive, aggressive attack is necessary against any zone press. The ball handler must dribble under control toward the trap with his head up. As the defenders approach, he makes his preassigned move to gain a one-man advantage as the ball moves upcourt. The dribbler can pass back in the backcourt. If a ball handler passes back, he must drop back as a safety outlet for the teammate he has passed to, or he can angle toward the ball to a position behind the defenders and in front of the teammate who has received his pass for a quick pass splitting defenders.

Players must be prepared for zone-pressure tactics at any time in a ball game, especially after a time-out or the insertion of substitutes with known speed and good defensive ability. They should also be prepared for zone pressure when they are ahead in a ball game.

The following three passes are available to players in a zone-pressure offense: (1) back to a trailer; (2) to a man in a predetermined position upcourt in the ball handler's field of vision; and (3) between a double-team to a teammate moving behind double teamers into a position to get the ball. A long diagonal pass is possible if all defenders are accountable and the possible receiver can get into good scoring position without defensive pressure. This means the passer must know the exact location of the five defensive players before making the pass. With extreme caution, a long two-hand lead pass may be made to a teammate moving downcourt away from the ball, the pass travelling over a defender. A lob pass should never be made.

Players should remember the following important factors. Coaches would rather have a jump ball in a pressure situation than have a player throw the ball away. A player may dribble when no double-team is coming at him, but his head must be up. He should never try to dribble unless he has room to dribble, and he shouldn't stop once he has started unless he has to. He should dribble when no good pass can be made, using it as a penetrating dribble. It's important to spread the defense as widely as possible in a full-court posture according to the preconceived offensive plan. Players should never leave the ball in the backcourt in the possession of a teammate by himself. Players should never cluster in one area; they must stay spread.

If a player is pressured on the end line, he may back up, run the end line, or pass to a teammate out of bounds. If he passes to a teammate along the end-line out of bounds, he should move toward the ball for a return pass, using decoying tactics so that he will be open.

To be successful against a zone-press attack, each player must break toward passes when he is the primary receiver, and he should not stop until he has received the ball. If he receives the ball with his back to the offensive basket, he should pivot immediately and look upcourt without dribbling. He should pass to an open man and cut quickly to his assigned area, being certain that there is good offensive floor balance.

The team should stay as close to the prescribed method of attack as possible. While players may sometimes use an extemporaneous move, it is best for all if the practiced method of sifting through a zone-press defense is used.

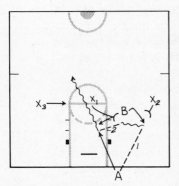

DIAGRAM 5–149

Diagram 5–149. Splitting a Possible Zone Defense Trap with a Dribble. A, the best ball handler, has passed the ball in bounds to B (1). B has V'd away and come back to the ball to receive A's pass. B uses a controlled dribble to draw the trap of X_1 and X_2. As X_1 and X_2 move into trapping position, B passes back to teammate A (2), who has timed his move from out-of-bounds so as to be as close to B as necessary without allowing X_1 an intercepting chance. A will drive hard at X_3's position through the attempted trap by X_1 and X_3 before X_1 can double-team. This is a good maneuver with a strong dribbler.

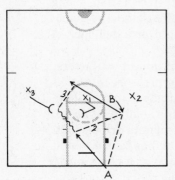

Diagram 5–150. Splitting through a Zone Defense after the Trap and Angling to the Ball. A passes into B (1). B passes back to A (2). A dribbles under control into X_1 and X_3's trap. B angles sharply to a position in front of A, behind X_1, so that he is in A's field of vision. A splits the trap with a quick pass (3). A should be the best ball handler.

DIAGRAM 5–150

Diagram 5–151. Splitting a Zone Defense Trap after Passing. A, the best ball handler, passes from out-of-bounds to B to the side (1). B returns the pass to A (2). A uses a controlled dribble into X_2 and X_1's trap. Just as X_2 makes his move for the trap, A passes quickly to B (3), who is moving up the right sideline, and breaks through the trap, receiving a return pass from B (4).

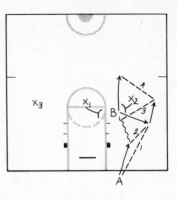

DIAGRAM 5–151

Diagram 5–152. One-One-Two-One Zone-Press Offense. A is out of bounds with the ball, whether the opposing front is odd or even. B is near the foul line or the foul line extended, usually starting behind X_1 for greater deception. C and D are near the mid-court line, with C having the responsibility of moving a front line defender (X_3 in this case) away from the front line so that the offense can control its initial pass-in for its advantage. Because A is to the right of the foul lane, X_4, the deep defensive player, will probably favor this side so as to be fronting the ball. Therefore, X_3 will have to move back to be certain that C cannot receive a pass beyond the front line. C must keep X_3 aware of his presence so that he will be more inclined to move back toward C than to attack the ball. B, the best ball handler, fakes and moves toward the ball. A passes the ball inbounds to B (1). As soon as A has passed to B, A moves into the court, away from the side that B is on. B uses a controlled one- or two-bounce dribble to lure the trap of X_1 and X_2 toward him and passes back to A (2) as quickly as feasible. A drives directly toward the position that X_3 is moving back into. As X_3 moves away from him, C comes back to receive a pass. A passes to C (3), because X_4 cannot cross the court to stop the pass. As soon as A passes, he breaks up the middle as an alternate receiver. Without dribbling, C passes to B (4), who has broken up the middle through the trap. C must be aware of X_4's coming across the court hard at him, but as C's pass is backward (B being behind C), it is usually a safe pass. Either A or B must have the ball for a drive down the middle to obtain a fast-break basket.

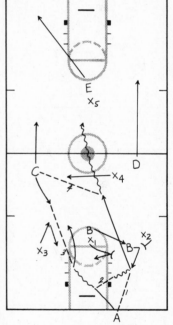

DIAGRAM 5–152

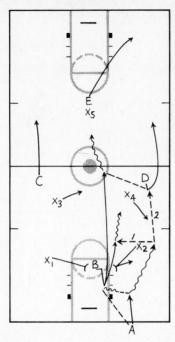

Diagram 5–153. One-One-Two-One Zone-Press Offense against an Even Defense Front. B is in the center. A passes to B, who takes a controlled dribble and passes back to A. A dribbles hard to the right, where the defense wants him to go. As X_4 and X_2 react to trap A, B will break up the middle of the court to receive a return pass from A (1). If X_2 overplays on the side of A so that A feels he can't get the pass to B, he may pass to D (2), who will take a step toward A to receive the pass as X_4 comes up quickly. B would continue upcourt and receive a pass from D.

DIAGRAM 5–153 _____

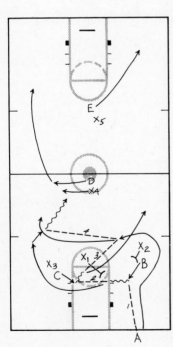

DIAGRAM 5–154

Diagram 5–154. Figure-Eight Zone-Press Offense from a One-Two-One-One Alignment. This is a little-used and hardly ever mentioned offense against zone pressure, yet it is one of the most practiced fundamental drills in the game of basketball and is an easy, effective method of moving the ball upcourt against any type of zone press. A player simply passes and goes behind the receiver, who passes to a third teammate. The first player looks for a pass from the third player as he cuts into the player's field of vision. D should always go opposite the first pass in this type of zone-press offense. A passes in to B (1) and cuts behind him. B takes a controlled dribble left to lure X_1 and X_2 to trap him. B passes to C (2). B cuts behind C. C knows that A, the first cutter in the figure-8, will be moving from right to left into his field of vision. C takes a controlled dribble, then makes the third pass to A, splitting X_1 and X_3. C cuts behind A. A now knows that B will be cutting into his vision left to right and may make a fourth pass to B. When either guard, A or B, has broken the front line of the zone press, he should be the middle man in a fast break.

SPECIAL DRILLS

We incorporate the following drills into our practice sessions with
excellent results.

**Diagram 5–155. Full-Court, Five-on-Five
Double Whistle Drill.** Whenever the coach sees
any obvious mistake on the court from which all
players in a full-court five-on-five situation can
profit, he double whistles. At that signal, all players must instantly freeze in position so that the
coach can point out and correct the mistake for
the benefit of all. We use this drill frequently with
excellent results. The diagramed play is an example of a situation calling for a double whistle.
Offensive players are O_1, O_2, O_3, O_4, and O_5; defensive players are X_1, X_2, X_3, X_4, and X_5. O_1
passes upcourt to O_3, who dribbles, stops, and
shoots, with X_3 in good defensive position. O_4 is
in the left corner. Once O_3 started to dribble we
would double whistle. As soon as he received the
ball, he should have passed to O_4. If O_4 had received the pass and dribbled toward the basket,
either he or O_5, coming in from the other side,
would get a lay-up.

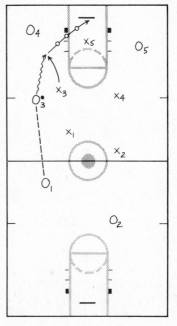

DIAGRAM 5–155

Full-Court, Five-on-Five No-Bounce Drill

This fun drill works to greatest advantage during the regular
season, although it may be used occasionally in preseason. No
player may put the ball on the floor, except to bounce pass, on
penalty of losing the ball. Dribbling is a violation, except in two
situations: when an unopposed player is within 15 feet of the
basket, one bounce is allowed for a lay-up. One bounce is also
permitted to clear a rebound if the rebounder is tied up.

This is a very interesting drill to use with players at any
level, especially young players. It is amazing how difficult it is
for players to advance the ball up the court without bouncing. At
first, they will stand in one place when they can't dribble.
Through this drill, players learn to pass the ball upcourt, and
players without the ball learn the importance of moving into receiving position.

part three

THE DEFENSE

Basic Defense

6

It's probably no great exaggeration to say that all great basketball teams are outstanding defensively. While even the best offenses in basketball go sour occasionally, defense is dependable, reliable: good defenders don't have off nights. Basic defense doesn't involve finely tuned neuromuscular skills and coordination; rather, it involves such traits as alertness, aggressiveness, desire, pride, and anticipation. The physical traits most necessary for defensive effectiveness are speed and quickness; still, even relatively slow players can largely make up for their physical shortcomings by outhustling and outthinking their opponents on defense. Players do not have to be highly skilled to play effective, hard-nosed defense. They need not be tall, nor must they be outstanding leapers or superbly gifted athletes. But they must be willing to work hard, both physically and mentally, and they must want to excel and take pride in their performance.

In Chapter 4 we discussed attributes of offensive basketball that make acquisition of offensive skills worthwhile and desirable. In like manner, we might point out the advantages of defensive basketball. First (and probably most important), anyone can, through hard work and attention to detail, learn to play good, solid defense—and he can learn the basic skills of defense far more quickly than he can learn to properly execute basic offensive skills. On defense, hustle, aggressiveness, and anticipation tend to make up for other deficiencies in a player's game. This is true because of the second advantage of the defense: The ball handler's aggressiveness is limited by the necessity of protecting the ball.

The defender, unhampered by any such problem, is free to attack the ball handler aggressively—if the defender is skilled enough not to be faked out of position.

The defender's basic position on the court is a third advantage of the defense in one-on-one confrontations. In most cases, the defender positions himself either between his man and the basket (particularly in guarding the ball handler) or partially or wholly between his man and the ball. Both positions can serve to reduce the action-reaction advantage favoring the offensive player, by forcing the offensive player to work harder than he normally would to get the ball or move into scoring position.

INDIVIDUAL PREREQUISITES

Defensive team plans are only as effective as the individual ability of each player. Attributes to be sought individually are speed, quickness, mental alertness, aggressiveness, desire, pride, anticipation, and adaptability.

1. Speed and Quickness. Sheer running speed enables a defensive player to move from one court position to another more rapidly than other players. It allows him to recover from defensive mistakes and assume a new defensive position with little overall team danger. Quickness, usually of feet, hands, and arms, enables a defensive player to keep the offense in a protective attitude by individual harassment. It effectively neutralizes an opponent's superior speed. Because the normal defensive distance from the basket is between eighteen and twenty-two feet or less, quickness of reaction and reflex may be more of an asset than speed; however, both are essential for good defensive posture.

2. Mental Alertness and Aggressiveness. The player who reacts immediately to a change from offense to defense will be in position to cover unguarded opponents, prevent the surprise offensive maneuver, and place the offense at a disadvantage. This mental alertness, coupled with aggressiveness (the ability to attack defensively) and defensive faking, can actually force an opponent into a defensive posture while he is in control of the ball.

3. Desire and Pride. Regardless of how fundamentally sound a player may be, he cannot play effective defense without desire and pride, because defense requires hard work and determination, while offering very little praise or recognition. Hustle springs from desire, which includes the determination to play defense well, to concentrate wholly on an assignment, and to work tirelessly. The extra effort expended when tired is the keynote to success.

Pride is the satisfaction a person feels when he knows that he did his part to the best of his ability while receiving little or no credit.

4. Anticipation and Adaptability. Anticipation is the ability to predetermine offensive patterns—to decide whether a pass can be intercepted or whether to exchange offensive men with a teammate before the situation presents itself. Adjusting to changes with the correct defensive action indicates adaptability. This ability is not entirely based on instinct but rather on the intelligent study of an opponent's individual and team offensive moves from the moment a game begins.

DEFENSIVE STANCE AND BALANCE

There are two basic defensive stances for playing the man with the ball. The first is the staggered, or stride, stance (boxer stance); the other is the squared stance (wrestler's stance).

Staggered Stance

For the staggered stance (Figure 6–1) the feet should be spread approximately the width of the shoulders, with either foot forward. Right-handed players seem more comfortable with the left foot forward; left-handed players prefer the right foot forward. The foot spread varies slightly with the player. A taller player may be more comfortable with a slightly wider foot spread than

Figure 6–1. Basic defensive stance—staggered.

a smaller player. However, there are dangers in having the feet too close together or too widely spread. The closer together the feet, the less balance the player has. The wider the base, the slower the initial movement. The body weight must be distributed evenly on the balls of the feet, never forward on the toes, with the heels touching the court. If body weight has to be shifted to maintain balance, it should be shifted back, never front. The knees must be flexed to facilitate movement. Hips and buttocks should be low to maintain a low center of gravity, with the trunk slightly forward, shoulders approximately above the knees, and head held high. Head, shoulders, and back are in a straight line and stationary. Any movement of head and shoulders will destroy body balance and give the offensive man with the ball an advantage.

The arms and hands should be carried in a comfortable position and moved or waved in direct proportion to how this action affects body balance. The hand above the front foot should be up and moving from side to side; the other hand should be at the side or reaching backwards. Over-extension of the hands and arms is a deterrent to basic defensive principles, since it shifts the player's balance and prevents mobility.

The amount of movement expended on defense varies greatly in different persons. Many players waste a great deal of energy and motion. Every defense move should be made with a specific purpose in mind.

Squared Stance

In the squared stance (Figure 6–2), the feet are side by side rather than staggered. Normally, they are spread wider than the shoulders and are perpendicular to the ball or the offensive player. Weight is evenly distributed over the hips, the knees are bent, hips and buttocks are low, the trunk is more erect than in the staggered stance, and hands and arms are held low. This stance is primarily used when aggressively attacking a player who has finished dribbling. Functionally, this is the position in which defenders find themselves when guarding a dribbler who is moving downcourt or when guarding a cutter who is away from the ball.

USE OF SIGHT, HEARING, AND SPEECH

Three important adjuncts to fundamental defense are sight, hearing, and speech. A player must see everything around him, either directly or with peripheral vision. He should never concentrate

Figure 6–2. Basic defensive
stance—squared.

solely on his opponent when the opponent does not have the ball unless the coach has instructed him to do so. Normally, while he should be primarily concerned with his man, he should still be aware of the position of the ball and any lateral screens that may be set.

The defensive player guarding the man with the ball should always be alert to teammates' vocal warnings. The voice must be used constantly on defense to warn teammates of the offensive screening possibilities, to signal an intention to switch, to encourage teammates, to upset and disconcert opponents, and to improve team morale and alertness.

FOOTWORK AND MOVEMENT

Four foot movements are essential to good individual defense. The first is running backward; the second is the defensive shuffle, or boxer's slide; the third is running and stopping full stride; and the fourth is the wheel-and-guard maneuver.

All defensive players should be able to run backward as easily and as effectively as they run forward. Running backward is an unnatural physical ability requiring constant practice and perfect body balance. The weight must be centered above the foot spread and slightly forward to counteract the backward momentum. If body weight shifts to the rear, the player will fall on his back.

The *defensive shuffle* is the basic footwork involved in maintaining proper position defensively. When an offensive player moves cross-court, the first defensive movement is a short step with the foot to that side. The other foot is quickly brought to within six to nine inches of the first. The player repeats the short, fast, sliding steps, maintaining balance and position on the man with the ball and forcing him to the sideline or towards a teammate. The feet never cross in the defensive shuffle. (See Figure 6–3.)

When defending a dribbler who is moving vertically toward the basket, the defender begins the shuffle with the foot on that side, forcing the man to the end line or toward a defensive teammate. However, if the offensive player gains an advantage, the defensive man must cross his legs and run full-stride to regain his defensive position. (See Figure 6–4.)

When a defensive player is running in full stride, he must stop by planting his lead foot hard and dropping his hips low to maintain a low center of gravity, regain his balance, and immediately assume the fundamental defensive position.

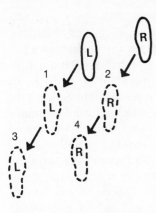

Figure 6–3. Shuffle.

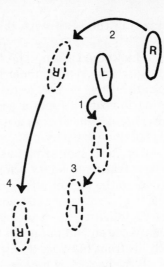

Figure 6–4. Stride.

A good defensive player must be conditioned mentally and physically to start quickly and change direction instantaneously. The start is initiated by a short step with the nearest foot in the direction the player wishes to go and a push off the far foot. Simultaneously, the rear arm and shoulder are swung in the same direction. The change of direction is begun by a balanced stop, without loss of time, and a reversal of the starting procedure.

The *wheel-and-guard* maneuver is the best way for a defender to pick up his opponent when the opponent dribbles by him after he has committed himself forward onto the right foot. When an opponent with the ball is driving opposite the defender's direction of commitment, the defender must make a 360-degree pivot turn by pushing off the overextended right foot, pivoting quickly on the rear foot, wheeling 180 degrees away from the dribbler, pushing off the left foot, pivoting on the right, and wheeling another 180 degrees to regain defensive position facing the dribbler. (The procedure is reversed if the defender's left foot is forward.)

INDIVIDUAL DEFENSIVE TECHNIQUES

All defenders must be well versed in their individual defensive techniques, as one poor defender greatly weakens the team defensive structure. Players must be proficient at defending opponents with or without the ball, regardless of their court position.

Guarding the Man with the Ball

Backcourt Man. The backcourt man, or guard, with the ball in scoring range (under thirty feet from the basket) is a potential shooter, passer, or dribbler. The advance scouting report should indicate if he is a good set or jump shooter; if he is an individualist who always dribbles when in possession, looking for his shot; if he is a play-maker who will be looking for a teammate to set up for a shot; if he has a favorite hand when dribbling; if he uses fakes and feints before shooting, passing or dribbling; if he cuts to the basket after passing, etc. If no report is available, the defensive player must adapt his defensive maneuvers to the guard's offensive tactics, assessing his opponent's potential quickly. He should maintain the fundamental defensive position with his front hand up and waving.

If the backcourt man is dribbling, the defensive player fakes with the hands, feints with the feet, and utilizes the sideline or a teammate to stop the dribbler and to force the dribbler away from his passing or shooting objective. The longer a player dribbles in a balanced offensive situation, the more help the guard's defensive teammates can give him.

A good dribbler with a strong hand should be overplayed one-half a man to the strong side to force him to his weaker side. Many left-handed players are completely one-handed and should be played a full-man to their left defensively. If the dribbler uses both hands well, he should always be forced to the middle, where the guard has more team help.

When the dribbler has gained an advantage, the defensive player must get in stride with him, maintaining good defensive balance, and harass him with an upward scooping motion of the near hand. The upward motion contributes to good balance and lessens the danger of fouling. The majority of fouls committed against dribblers are the result of the downward motion of the defender's hands and arms.

When the dribbler has been stopped, the defensive man should attack him aggressively with arms moving and maintain strong pressure on him until he releases the ball. He should be forced into a poor shooting position or into a passing situation where his only outlet is a ball-control pass to a teammate in a poor shooting area. The defender may touch or deflect a pass being made, but rarely intercepts it. Poor balance and reaction leaves the defender susceptible to a quick cut and a return pass inside (give-and-go).

After the ball is released, the defensive man should drop back quickly in the direction of the pass to defend against a cut

Figure 6–5. No. 25 passes to no. 5. No. 30 immediately retreats a step or two toward the direction of the pass.

by the passer, to maintain defensive position on his man in the eventuality of continued team movement, or to be in good defensive rebound position if a shot is taken. (See Figure 6–5.)

The most difficult situation for a defender guarding the dribbler is the one-on-one play near the basket. The lone defender must prevent the offensive player from getting past him for an unopposed basket. This opportunity arises most frequently after a pass interception, a long rebound, or recovery of a loose ball. The defender may be a guard, a forward, or a center. A retreating, delaying defense should be played, and the dribbler should be forced toward the sideline or baseline. When a man is dribbling, he must stop to shoot, except on a lay-in; therefore, the defender should stay away until he stops. A defender should never move in aggressively on a dribbler in this situation, as a change of direction will allow an unopposed lay-up.

When an offensive player in the backcourt fakes, the defender's initial move is a backward slide with the rear foot, with the front hand coming up quickly. (See Figure 6–6.) This movement deters an outside shot and keeps the defensive player in good position.

Caution must be used in approaching a backcourt man with the ball who has not dribbled. The defender should slide his front

a.   b.

Figure 6–6. Defending against a fake by a backcourt opponent: *a*, opponent fakes shot; *b*, defender's back foot slides back and his front hand comes up.

foot forward eight to twelve inches, keeping the body balance on the balls of both feet, and follow with a quick, short, forward slide of the rear foot, with the weight shifting to the rear foot. It is always better to be caught with the weight back rather than forward.

Any time an offensive man who has dribbled is strongly pressured defensively, all defensive men *must* cut off all outlets in order to intercept a desperate pass or to force a held ball.

Forward, or Corner Man. The forward, or corner man, with the ball is in a dangerous offensive position. He is in shooting range, can drive the baseline for a lay-up, and can feed the low or medium pivot effectively. The defensive man must be close enough to prevent a clear shot at the basket and should be half-a-man to the baseline side to prevent a move in that direction. The foot nearest the baseline should be forward. On a fake, the defender should drop his rear foot back and side step with the front foot to close the baseline drive. (See Figure 6–7.) His arms and hands should prevent an easy set shot or a pass to the pivot man. Any dribble by the corner man should be forced to the middle area, where teammates and congestion help the defensive player.

Figure 6–7. Guarding the baseline:
a, foot nearest baseline is forward; *b,* on
fake, rear foot slides back; *c,* step to
baseline closes it to drive.

Center, or Pivot Man. There are three pivot, or post, areas.
Low-pivot position is within nine feet of the basket; medium-pivot
position is between ten and fourteen feet from the basket; and
high-pivot position is fifteen feet or more from the basket. Normally, the low and medium positions are on the sides of the foul
lane area, and the high-pivot position is in the outer half of the
foul circle or higher, nearer the middle of the court. Each area
requires a different defensive technique.

Low Pivot. An offensive man receiving the ball in the low-
pivot area is primarily a scorer who will use quick, deceptive fakes
and then take the shot that presents itself. The man guarding
the low pivot must prevent the ball from reaching that position.
The initial defensive position is between the ball and the pivot

Figure 6–8. Defense against low pivot (defender may also be entirely in front).

man, three-quarters of the way in front, with the front hand outstretched and the rear hand lightly touching the offensive man. The defensive player's back is to the sideline, and his feet are to the outside of the low-pivot man. (See Figure 6–8.) When the ball is in the left corner, the left arm and foot are advanced; if it is in the right corner, the position is reversed.

The corner positions are the best areas from which to pass into the low pivot; if the ball cannot enter the low-pivot area from one corner, the offensive players will try to enter from the other corner. This necessitates a minimum of two passes to get the ball to the opposite corner. When these passes are being made, the low-pivot guard must keep between the ball and the pivot man, for if the defender goes behind the low pivot, the ball can easily be passed in from the backcourt area. With the ball reversing from right defensive to left corner, the defender maintains position, stepping forward with the baseline foot and fronting the low-pivot man to prevent him from moving up the free-throw lane. The defender feels the pivot with the left hand as the pivot crosses to his left, using the boxer's defensive glide to maintain his fronting position and dropping his right foot back to regain a three-quarter fronting position at the left low-pivot position. The right hand is pointing toward the ball during this movement.

If the defensive player is behind the pivot man when the pivot receives the ball in the low area, the defensive man should loosen his position slightly so that the pivot man cannot ascertain his exact location by pressure. The defender should give the pivot man the first fake or move, turn with him, and attempt to deflect or tip his shot. If the low pivot is a good hook-shot shooter, the defender must attempt to alter the hook-shot trajectory by forcing it higher, using the same hand the pivot is shooting with. Using this hand prevents fouling, and better rebound position results, since both men are turning with bodies parallel, and the defender is inside. If the other hand is used, it crosses the defender's body and may force him into the shooter. Another reason for using the near hand is that the defender can jump higher than he could if he used the far hand. The defender must maintain this inside position for rebounding. The defensive jump should be timed with the ball's release, and a deflection or bat at the height of a straight-up jump is a deterrent to further shots of this type.

When the low pivot out-positions his defender, the defender must alert his teammates with a loud vocal warning. Near teammates must immediately attack the ball in possession of a low-pivot opponent to help their outpositioned teammate and prevent an easy scoring opportunity by the low-pivot man. If the pivot man fakes, there is an excellent opportunity for an alert collapsing defender to force a held ball.

Medium Pivot. It is difficult to defend against the medium pivot, for he is in excellent position to fake and one-bounce drive, shoot, hand off to cutters, or return a pass quickly to a teammate for intermediate jump shots if defensive men attempt to help his guard. All defenders should recognize the dangerous potential of the ball's reaching the medium pivot and attempt to close passing lanes to him. The man guarding the pivot should play one-half a man to the ball side, with his front out to deflect or deter a pass and his feet straddling the foot of the pivot that is closest to the basket.

When the ball reverses direction outside and the pivot player crosses the foul line, the medium-pivot defender must slide behind his man to a new one-half-a-man defensive position. He is extremely vulnerable to a lob pass if he crosses in front. During this defensive transition, the defending teammates must prevent a direct pass-in to the pivot player.

If a pass-in to the medium pivot is successful, the defender should drop one foot behind the pivot, watching for cutters and forcing the pivot to the outside or to the sidelines if possible. If the guard is too close, the pivot can feel him and move accordingly. When attempting to block a shot by the pivot, the defender must stay on the floor until his opponent leaves the floor. If he jumps or moves with a fake, he allows the pivot an easy scoring opportunity.

High Pivot. The basic function of a high pivot is as a screener or feeder. The defensive man plays a high pivot two to three feet behind the pivot, between the man and the basket. Anticipating his opponent's probable maneuvers from the scouting report or the pattern of play, the guard should attempt to close passing lanes to the cutters and call out if he thinks the high pivot is going to be used as a screen. If the high pivot receives a pass and turns to face the basket, the defender must play him as a backcourt man would. He should allow the sixteen- to eighteen-foot shot, unless the pivot man has proven his ability to score from this range.

Guarding the Man without the Ball

When a defensive player is defending against a man without the ball, the distance the defender may drop off his opponent varies, depending on the position of the ball, his man's distance from the basket, the man's shooting range, and the offensive deployment in the basket area. No offensive player should be allowed to handle the ball within sixteen feet of the basket. If he does gain possession in this dangerous area, the defense must exert extreme pressure on the ball.

One Pass from the Ball. The ball is one pass away from the man being guarded when he may receive a pass from the man in possession without danger of interception.

Backcourt man. When a defender is guarding a backcourt man with the ball one pass away, in the other guard's possession, the defending team's man-to-man philosophy determines the defense. In a normal defense, the defender should drop off his man and open toward the ball, within the triangle formed by the man with the ball, the basket, and the man being guarded. Both the ball and the man being defended should be visible. The defensive man's stance should be a little higher than when he is playing an attacker with the ball, and he should be mentally aggressive and anticipatory. His hands should point in the direction of the ball and the man he is guarding. From this position, he must close passing lanes to the high post and anticipate a cut to the basket by his man. The cut to the basket usually occurs simultaneously with a pass by his man to the other guard (give-and-go). Interceptions generally are made by the defender of the man being passed to or by a third defender who is aware of the offensive passing lanes.

If the team's defensive pattern is an aggressive man-to-man technique, and the other guard has the ball, the defender positions himself between his man and the ball, inviting the cut behind and the return pass. Teammates behind the backcourt defenders must anticipate this move and float to the middle to minimize the opponents' opportunity to carry it out. If the guard cuts, his defender must open to the ball and retreat with the man, staying close to him, between him and the ball. The defender must challenge every pass aggressively, intercepting or deflecting it whenever possible. If the backcourt man is to receive a pass, he should be forced to move away from the basket.

When the near forward has the ball, the man defending against the near guard should drop back two steps, opening his stance toward the sideline so that he is standing in the triangle formed by the ball, the basket, and the man being guarded, with both the ball and his man in sight. He must be ready to defend against the forward drive to the middle area and to deflect or intercept a pass to a medium or high pivot. If the guard goes away from the ball, his defender must maintain the same relative position within the ball-basket-man triangle. The farther the guard goes from the ball, the greater the distance between him and his defender. Since any cut by the guard will be away from the ball, the defender should keep between the ball and the man, close enough to the man to prevent pass reception. He must anticipate a quick stop by his man that may afford him a good shooting opportunity, or a change of direction that will allow him easy pass reception.

If the guard cuts outside toward the corner, his defender should overplay slightly to the sideline to prevent him from working a two-on-two play with the corner man.

When the medium or high pivot has the ball, the backcourt guard should drop back and pressure the ball as far as his man's outside shooting ability will allow.

Forward, or corner man. When the ball is in the backcourt, the defender against the corner man on the same side may assume one of two basic positions. He may overplay with the right hand and foot forward on the defensive left side (and vice versa) to challenge or prevent a pass to this position. (See Figure 6–9.) Usually, reception in the mid-court area should be allowed, as it removes the corner man from his strongest offensive position and puts him in an unfamiliar position with the ball. However, some forwards are able to fake to the ball, then reverse direction. When

Figure 6–9. Overplay defense against corner man.

preliminary information indicates the offensive man has this ability to a high degree, the defender can assume the alternate defensive position, in which the left hand and foot are forward on the left defensive side. This second position makes possible a cut to the ball in front of the defender. As a corner man receiving the ball on this move is in excellent position to go toward the basket, the defender must take every precaution to prevent this reception. The corner man can now receive the ball more readily, so the defender should challenge each pass to move the man farther from his normal position.

If the forward has good shooting range, but is not a good ball handler or does not like to move without the ball, the first position is preferable. If the forward reverses well, and does not have a long range, the alternate stance should be used.

The defensive man, either from scouting information or from personally analyzing his man's moves, should anticipate cutting moves by legally moving into his man's path, thereby either preventing the cut or hindering it to the point where it becomes ineffectual.

When the defender loses his defensive advantage to a cutter behind him, he should turn quickly toward the basket and attempt to stay between the man and the ball. If possible, the turn should be to the inside, so he will not lose sight of the ball. After turning, he should keep active and low, ready to deflect a bounce pass, the usual pass in this situation.

If the cut is between the defender and the ball, the defender should turn in the direction of the cut and run hard to regain a legal defensive position as soon as possible. He should not attempt to use his hands or arms, as such movement will slow the recovery and result in fouls. The defender may receive help from a teammate in the area, who may switch assignments with him by picking up his man.

Pivot man. The defender of the high-pivot man should be to the ball side, with the near hand moving in front of the pivot to discourage a pass-in from the backcourt man. If the ball is passed cross-court, the defender goes behind the pivot and assumes the same position on the other side. When the ball is passed to the front court, the defender should step up with the near foot and play one-half a man to the ball side, the near hand waving actively to discourage a pivot roll and reception of the ball in the medium-pivot area.

When his opponent is in the medium-pivot area, the defender should position himself one-half a man on the ball side to prevent the pass-in, if possible. Since the medium-pivot man usually changes position frequently, using fakes, feints, sudden directional changes, and quick pivots, the defender must be alert for these moves, basing his movement and position on the actions of the man with the ball and on the ball's location. When a medium pivot moves away from the ball area and his guard is overplaying him to the ball, the danger of a lob pass should be compensated for by the alert positioning of the far defensive forward.

A pass to the low-pivot area usually comes from the corner position; therefore, the pivot's defender should play him three-quarters front or full in front. Since the low pivot is constantly looking for good shooting position, there is more body contact in this area than in any other on the court. The defender must never allow himself to be pushed or moved under the basket behind the pivot man, as that is a very poor position from which to prevent a pass-in or to rebound another's shot. If he is extremely alert, anticipatory, and mobile, the defender should be able to maintain a solid fronting position. When a team relies primarily on a pivot man as the focal point of its pattern or as its scorer, defending the pivot requires constant and complete concentration, and even then the defender may require help from his teammates. However, if the pivot position is defended properly, the defender can be responsible for stopping the opponent's team offense almost completely.

Two Passes from the Ball. The ball is two passes away from the man being guarded if it can be intercepted by any defender other than the guards of the passer and the receiver.

Guard, or backcourt man. When the ball position is two passes away from the backcourt man being defended against, usually in the possession of the far corner man or the low or medium pivot on the far side, the backcourt defender should open his stance toward the ball and back off from his man toward the middle of the court near the foul-line area to aid in team defense. He should watch both his man and the ball, preventing the man from cutting to the ball and taking any good opportunity to intercept a pass or cause a held-ball situation. Of course, he must always be ready to return quickly to his man if the situation warrants it.

Forward, or corner man. If defending against a corner man when the ball is held by the far guard, the defender should open toward the ball, seeing both his man and the ball, and move toward the foul-lane area, in line with his man (this line being parallel to the base line). He should point one hand at his man, the other toward the ball, and be ready to prevent his man from cutting between him and the ball. If the ball is passed cross-court, he should return to basic defensive position. If the pass goes to the far corner man, the defender retreats two steps into the foul-lane area, keeping alert for a lob pass to a low- or medium-pivot man and anticipating movement by his man toward the ball. When the defender is opposite a low pivot, he must realize that his forward may move to the foul-line area to receive a quick pass for a short jump shot. At all times he must look for interceptions, guards cutting without the ball, and held-ball opportunities.

Center, or pivot. Normally, the high-pivot man is never more than one pass from the ball. In the medium-pivot and low-pivot areas, the pivot man may be more than one pass away, but quick movement on his part and lack of anticipation or alertness by his defender can allow the pivot to obtain excellent position on the ball side. Any offensive player, regardless of size, can play the pivot, and if he receives the ball in the low area easily, he has a good scoring opportunity. Therefore, the best method of defending the pivot areas is to prevent the ball from getting in to the post man.

If prevention is not possible, the pivot man should be forced into reception in positions where a good shooting opportunity is difficult—on the base line, ten or more feet from the basket, or two or three steps from the foul lane, near the free-throw line. The defender must always challenge the pivot for position, anticipating his moves. By knowing the pivot's favorite areas, the defender can beat him to those spots.

The man guarding the pivot should only help teammates defensively when an unopposed scoring opportunity arises. When the man defending the low or medium post picks up an offensive man who has shaken his guard, that guard must sprint to an intercepting position between the free pivot man and the ball to prevent an easy return pass to the open pivot area. As this situation usually involves a big man switching to a small man, the big defender can try to block the shot. In attempting to block shots, the defender should never bring the blocking arm down or jump into the shooter, as fouls always result. He should try to deflect the shot or distract the shooter with arm movement. He should not leave the floor until the shooter has left the floor or the ball has been released.

If the defensive center helps out on a drive situation, the offside defenders can rotate in front of the offensive post man to keep him off the boards.

The man guarding the low- and medium-pivot areas is in excellent position to observe the opponent's offensive patterns, and he should shout instructions constantly to his teammates.

If the pivot moves away from the basket, he is not very dangerous. He usually moves away from the ball to clear the middle for a cutter or driver, or to screen for a teammate. The alert defender should remain in the pivot area to hinder the driver or cutter and should play the screening or clearing pivot man loose.

DEFENSIVE DRILLS

Defensive drills are worked one-on-one, two-on-two, three-on-three and in full team alignment. In all of the drills, the coach must insist on the following fundamentals. Players must maintain good body balance and good position, bothering the men they are guarding. Whenever possible, they must use peripheral vision to watch both the man and the ball, and they must always be alert to help teammates. They must keep pressure on the ball and on potential receivers, without being overly aggressive and causing fouls that hurt their team. The men must be able to recognize when an opponent is not in position to make a good offensive play.

BLOCKING OUT DEFENSIVELY

Defensive guards (except the man guarding a low or medium pivot) almost always have inside position on their men initially, and their first duty is to retain this advantage. Defenders must

Figure 6–10. Defensive box out.

assume that all shots will be missed, and then prevent their men from obtaining possession of the rebound by blocking them from the defensive boards or getting the ball themselves. (See Figure 6–10.) The best fast-break opportunity results from a defensive rebound possession (Figure 6–11) and the proper clearing out of the ball to an attack position.

When a shot is taken, the shooter is in the best position to judge the eventual area in which the rebound will fall; therefore, his guard must block off the path the shooter attempts to take to retrieve the ball.

Figure 6–11. Two-hand rebound.

Backcourt Man

If the shooter is in the backcourt, the defender remains face to face with him no more than one step away until he makes his first move after the shot. If this move is to the outside, the defender pivots on his outside foot so that he is facing the basket in the path of the shooter and maintains this position, using the defensive shuffle to move the shooter away from his intended path to the rebound area. (If the shooter moves to the inside, the defender pivots on his inside foot.) If the defender has a chance for recovery, he should go to the ball immediately from this blockout position. If the ball is rebounded by a defending teammate he must quickly go to an area clear of an opponent, toward the near sideline, to receive an outlet pass. If the offensive team regains possession, he must pick his man up quickly in good defensive position.

The man defending against the other guard drops back two or three steps after the shot is taken and remains facing his man. Normally, an offensive team never rebounds both men farthest from the basket; therefore, if the shooting backcourt man moves in to rebound, the remaining guard will start back to defend. If the second guard does not break toward his offensive backboard, his defender should count one thousand and one, one thousand and two after the shot is released (this count allows for the flight of the ball before striking the rim or backboard and rebounding), turn quickly to face the defensive basket, looking for the rebounding ball, and ascertain who will obtain possession of it or whether he has a chance to retrieve it himself. If he can rebound the ball he must get it immediately. If a teammate rebounds the ball, he should go to the near sideline to receive a clearing pass out. If offense rebounds the ball, he must immediately revert to a defensive stance on his man.

Corner Man

When the shot is taken by a corner man or a pivot man, the backcourt defenders, whose positions may be some distance from the shooter, should take one step back toward the basket, concentrating face to face on their men, count to two slowly, then proceed as described above. An alert backcourt defender, by reacting quickly on defensive rebounds recovered by a taller opponent, can often cause a held-ball by attacking him aggressively.

The defensive man guarding a shooting corner man, a dangerous offensive rebounder, must keep him from following up his shot. The defender should allow his opponent's first move to the basket, then pivot in front of him, moving with his movement (determined by feel) and keeping in front of him. The defender can maintain front position by bracing himself firmly, arms up, elbows at shoulder height, knees slightly flexed, ready to jump if necessary.

The distance may vary, but ideally, the blocker should turn and make his contact when the offensive rebounder is within an eight-foot radius from the basket. Anything out farther than this gives the offensive rebounder a better opportunity to defeat the block. Anything in closer may result in the blocker's being forced too far under the basket to get the rebound himself.

When defending a corner man in the corner opposite the shooter, the defender normally positions himself several steps away from his man. He moves one step toward him after the shot, allows him to make his initial move, then pivots in his path, anticipating a change of direction by him. If the man reverses direction, the defender steps in that direction (but toward the basket to minimize danger of a foul for illegal blocking out) and goes to the ball aggressively when slight contact takes place. He must take care that his man does not get inside him.

Pivot Man

Usually the high-pivot defender is his team's best rebounder. Guarding a high pivot, he is stationed fourteen to sixteen feet from the basket, between his man and the basket. If he waits for the offensive movement, he may be too late in getting to the ball. Therefore, unless he has been specifically instructed otherwise, he should turn with the shot and go to the rebounding ball as soon as he judges where it is likely to fall. He has a rebound advantage on his man, and after his turn, he is in good position to move in, hold, or move laterally to his left or right to get the ball, if his teammates have reacted to the shot with good defensive rebounding techniques. When a high pivot shoots, he will always follow his shot. Therefore, the man guarding him should vary the above technique slightly and turn into the path the shooter takes. He then rebounds as instructed above.

The man guarding a medium pivot is generally at a disadvantage in defensive rebounding, as he may be one-half a man to a full man in front of the pivot man when the shot is taken. If he is one-half a man in front of the medium pivot (ball-side) when the shot is taken, the defender should pivot on the rear foot and establish a strong position—feet spread, arms and hands up, elbows at shoulder height—and hold position momentarily before going to the ball. If the defender is between his man and the ball (the shot taken from the far side of the court from the medium pivot), he should use the boxer's shuffle to maintain his advantageous position between his man and the basket, hold position, and then go to the ball strongly.

When the pivot is low, the defender will almost always be in a disadvantageous rebound position ball-side, as the offensive man will usually be inside him. Therefore, he must work aggressively to neutralize his man's position advantage. The defender should turn to the middle area and attempt to move into a siding position, shoulder to shoulder with his man, to his inside if possible. If the defender finds himself directly behind the offensive pivot, he should crowd him, attempting to force him farther in under the basket so that he is too far in to rebound effectively. If this maneuver is not successful (the pivot may lean back with his back and shoulder to counteract the crowding tactic), the defender should attempt to slide around his man into better rebounding position.

When the low or medium pivot shoots, his defender must block him out of the rebounding area. Usually the defender attempts to block or deflect the shot with extreme pressure, and both men are off their feet. The defender's jump should be up but not into the man. If he jumps toward the pivot shooter or the ball, he will take himself out of the rebounding action and possibly commit a two-shot foul. Upon landing, the defender must quickly turn into the path of the shooter and maintain this position.

Defensive Rebounding

The primary function in rebounding is gaining possession of the ball. The defensive man (except for the pivot defender) is usually closer to the basket. For his team to have a chance to obtain possession, he must maintain this position advantage, blocking his man from the rebound. If the shooting team rebounds the ball, the defender is still in excellent position to guard his man. Should the ball be batted or lost by the players in the rebound area, the defender is in position to recover or to prevent his man from recovering. If a teammate recovers the ball, they should switch to offense immediately.

As more shots are missed than made, the defensive rebounder should assume that every shot will miss and be ready to rebound after each shot. He should also assume that his opponent will try to rebound and that every rebound will come into his area; therefore, he must block out his man while watching the ball's flight and be prepared to meet the ball aggressively. In moving toward the rebounding area, he should hold his hands

Figure 6–12. Defensive rebounder pulling ball down away from pressure.

high, with elbows spread in anticipation of the recovery. As he steps in, before his jump to gain possession, he should mentally note the relative positions of his teammates so that when he obtains possession, he knows the best area for a quick pass out. When teammates block out properly it allows another teammate to obtain possession. (Figure 6–12.)

After making his complete turn to the basket, the rebounder must establish a wide, braced base from which to operate. This wide base will prevent his man from easy access to the ball, and the bracing will allow the defender to be jostled or leaned on without losing balance. The feet should be spread as wide as comfort and balance will allow. The knees should be slightly bent; the hips lowered; the elbows wide, at shoulder level; and the upper arms parallel to the floor. The forearms and hands should be held high, parallel to the body, with fingers widespread and palms facing the basket. The body balance should be slightly forward, with the weight on the balls of the feet for quick movement to retrieve the ball.

Several physical factors affect every rebound—the force and distance of the shot, the angle of the shooter with respect to the basket, the spot the ball hits (the backboard, or rim, or roll around

Figure 6–13. Two defenders box out while third gets rebound.

the rim), the resiliency or deadness of backboard and rim, the impetus and arch of the shot, and the spin imparted to the ball by the shooter. These components vary with each shot attempted and have a direct effect on timing. Players must consider all these factors when judging the rebound, remembering also that most shots rebound to the side of the basket opposite the side from which the shot was taken.

Excellent timing is a greater attribute for a rebounder than jumping high. He must spring into the ball, attempting to secure it with both hands as he approaches maximum jumping height. His elbows and legs should be widespread, his buttocks slightly extended rearward for maximum protection. (See Figure 6–13.) While in the air he should turn the ball over slightly so that one hand is above, the other below, the ball, which should be held strongly for protection.

He should land with the feet and elbows wide, buttocks extended slightly rearward, and the weight balanced. As he comes down, he should turn his head slightly toward the nearer sideline to ascertain whether or not a teammate is in good outlet passing position. On alighting, he must protect the ball before the pass by bringing it strongly to chest height or higher in both hands. If pressured, he should use quick fakes, holding the ball strongly, and pivot or dribble, if necessary, to prevent a held ball. The passout is usually to the outside on the side on which the rebound is recovered. It should rarely go across the free-throw lane at the defensive end.

Tall rebounders, holding the ball firmly in two hands, must keep it above shoulder height and decide quickly whether to release it or protect it further. A small man obtaining possession of a rebound must bring the ball close to the floor, protecting it with body and elbows, and pass it out immediately, if possible, or dribble rapidly away from the congested area.

Coordinating Individual Defense Techniques Against the Offense

7

Each defender must be aware of his team responsibilities against every offensive thrust. Players must know when to retreat purposefully and when to counterattack expediently from the defensive structure. Successful team defense results from constant practice. Mental alertness, aggressiveness, hustle, and anticipation enhance the defensive posture.

DEFENSING AGAINST SCREENS

Several maneuvers are appropriate for all defenders in defensing against screening techniques of their opponents. If the screener has the ball and is in a dangerous scoring area, the following methods of defense are possible. The screener's guard may step back and allow through a defensive teammate guarding a cutter off the ball. This teammate may discourage a shot by waving his hands at the screener so that he will try to protect the ball. A second method is for the man guarding the screener to stay tight and direct his teammate behind him. A third maneuver is for the man guarding the cutter to fight between the screener and his man, applying hard pressure on the ball so that the man in possession must protect the ball. The cutter's guard can also overplay to the side of the screen to force the cutter away from the screen. The main determinant of which method to use depends on the scoring ability of the screener with the ball and the cutter. These are coaching decisions.

The most common method of neutralizing a possible offensive advantage obtained in screening or blocking is to exchange defensive responsibility (switching). Of course, assignments should never be exchanged unless absolutely necessary. It is the responsibility of the man guarding the screener to warn his teammates loudly of the potential screen ("Screen left," "Screen right," "Watch the pick," etc.). After his clear vocal warning, he should step back to allow his teammate to slide through the screen, directing him through by shouting "Slide, slide."

If an exchange of men is necessary, the man guarding the screener must call "Switch" and quickly exchange assigned men with the teammate.

After an exchange of men, each defender is responsible for the man exchanged to. However, if in switching there is a decided mismatch in the comparative height of the offensive and defensive men, a switch back must be made as quickly as possible. If it is not made, a taller offensive player will move into the low-pivot area with a shorter defender. A shorter offensive player will have a distinct maneuvering advantage from the side areas against a taller opponent. If the opportunity to switch back does not arise, however, it should not be forced, as many times this results in an offensive player's being left completely free. The switches should remain until the play is over or the defenders' team gets possession of the ball.

Any time a defender picks up a loose opponent, he should call out loudly the exchange in assignments; for example, "I have 22; take 15." This warns the man originally assigned to guard Number 22 that his man has been picked up by an alert teammate, and his assignment has switched to Opponent Number 15. On this type of exchange, the defender looking for the new assignment must sprint to a position six to eight feet in front of the basket and then look to the outside for his new man.

When defending in an area where screening maneuvers are probable, the defender should feel to the rear with one hand in the direction from which a potential screen may come, and he must listen for any vocal instructions from a teammate.

A defensive man should never let himself be screened when his man is two passes from the ball. He should have dropped off his man and be opened toward the ball so that he can see any potential screen without relying on a verbal warning.

Lateral, or Cross-court, Screen

In a lateral, or cross-court, screen, the defender being screened can see his man and the screener. When offensive guards cross with each other outside the top of the foul-line circle (twenty-one or more feet from the basket), the man guarding a screener always steps back to allow his teammate to pass through. If either guard has excellent shooting range (twenty-one to twenty-five feet) and is screened for with the ball, the defender must fight over the screen to stay with the dangerous scorer. The man guarding a screener without the ball should be high to the side of his man toward which the potentially dangerous shooter is moving with the ball. This defender's hand and arm movement and the possibility of a switch should discourage a shot. The man guarding the screener must be alert for a quick cut to the basket by his man. An alternative to the above maneuvers is to overplay the good long-range outside shooter one-half a man to the side of the lateral screener and force him away from the screen. In this case, the defender must watch for a reverse cut without the ball or a drive with the ball. Inside defensive teammates must be cognizant of these possibilities and be prepared to help out if necessary.

Inside, or Rear, Screen

The inside, or rear, screen, in which the man being screened cannot see both the screener and his man, is used in the following five positions.

1. A backcourt man can dribble or cut tightly off a screen set by the other guard (who has the ball) in or near the outer half of the free-throw circle. The man guarding the cutter must force him to the middle; the defender must never allow the cutter to go to the outside, as the offense usually clears that corner for this maneuver. The man guarding the screener must overplay to the open side, shouting instructions to his teammate, indicating that the left or right corner is cleared and telling him the location of the screen.

2. A backcourt man has the ball and dribbles off his strong-side corner man positioned near the end of the foul line or foul line extended. In this case, the dribbler's guard must receive loud voice warning from the screener's man and attempt to overplay the dribbler strongly on the outside, forcing him to the middle. If he cannot force his man to the middle, the defender must try to fight his way between the screener and the dribbler.

If an exchange of men must be made, the screener's guard calls "Switch" and forces the dribbler to the end line to stop his dribble. He then attacks aggressively, both hands held high, to prevent a pass to the forward moving toward the basket with a smaller defender guarding him. The smaller defender must get between the ball and the forward to prevent a bounce pass to the forward. The ball is being attacked in such a way as to prevent a high pass, and the smaller defender must be in position to stop the bounce pass.

If the screening action takes place beyond the twenty-foot area, the screener's defender should call for the guard to slide through between screener and defender.

3. The backcourt man passes to the corner man positioned near the end of the foul line or foul line extended and cuts off him toward the baseline or basket. When this screen occurs, the screener's man must alert the cutter's guard, who must force the cutter to the middle. The guard keeps between the cutter and the ball and does not allow a return pass.

4. A corner man has the ball, and the guard can cut off a high- or medium-pivot screen. The man guarding the screening pivot must loudly warn the guard's defender of the screen. The defender should open to the ball side and stay between the cutter and the ball all the way from the outside starting position of the cutter to the basket.

5. The pivot screens for the corner man in possession and alive fourteen to eighteen feet from the basket. The screener's defender must warn the corner defender so he can protect the baseline to prevent an easy dribble-in lay-up. The men guarding the backcourt offensive players must fall back in position to help out on a drive off the screen to the middle. The man guarding the screening pivot should drop off his man a step toward the middle, to also discourage a dribble in that direction. He has to make the forward believe he will remain in this position to stop the dribble or shot in the middle, and he must still cover the screener on a roll to the basket. The corner defender remains responsible for his man, unless the screener's defender calls "Switch." If "Switch" is called, the defending forward must get between the screener and the ball as the screener rolls to the basket. Defense of a lob pass from the corner man becomes the responsibility of the weak-side corner defender.

Double Cuts (Scissors)

There are two types of double cuts that must be defended against: (1) a double cut off a high pivot by the two guards (either passing to the pivot) and (2) a double cut off a medium pivot by the forward (who passes in to the pivot) and strong-side guard. Both of these offensive maneuvers are extremely effective, producing open cuts, double-screened jump shots, or drive-in lay-up opportunities for the forward and/or guards and hook shots, drive-in lay-ups, or short jump-shot scoring possibilities for the pivot.

Preventing Double Cut off High Pivot. The defense must first prevent the ball from reaching the high-pivot man. To discourage a pass, the defender of the guard with the ball must play him with the inside foot and hand forward, and the other guard's defender should drop off his man toward the high pivot. The second defender should be opened toward the ball, one hand pointing to the pivot to prevent the pass, the other toward his man. If the ball is passed cross-court, the defensive procedure is reversed.

If the pivot man receives the pass-in from either guard, their defenders can remain close to their men, one-half a man toward the middle of the court, discouraging the guards from crossing if possible and fighting over the pivot if the cut is successful. The defenders must try to force a wide cut from the guard position and must be alert for a change of direction by either guard. When a change occurs, the offensive corner man on the same side as the reversing guard will clear to the opposite corner. The defending corner man must warn his teammates loudly if this happens. When the first cutter screens for the other guard, the second cutter's defensive man should attempt to force his man high above both the screening guard and the high-pivot man. Neither defending guard must ever drop to a position behind the pivot man, as this affords the offensive guard an easy jump shot over a double screen of pivot man and other guard.

The alternative defense is for the defensive guards to drop back from their men and in toward the high pivot with the ball. They should try to exert defensive pressure on the ball so that the pivot man has to pass it back out quickly to prevent a loose-ball or a held-ball situation. If the offensive guards cut, they must be forced to go outside the defensive guards, never between guard and pivot man. If the defending guards must switch, the man guarding the first cutter or screener calls "Switch." The guards now must be alert for both cutters heading for the basket on the same side of the pivot. Anticipating this maneuver will help to counteract its effectiveness.

The man guarding the high pivot should overplay his man one-half a man to the ball side to prevent a pass-in from either guard. If the pass-in is successful, the pivot defender should step back one step and line up between his man and the basket. He must alert both guard defenders of potentially dangerous moves, and he must be aware of his own man's potentialities, as the pivot can turn for a fifteen-foot jumper or fake the shot and drive in. If either cutter is open, the pivot defender, calling "Switch," must quickly pick up the free man with the ball and prepare to block the cutter's lay-up shot or deter a return pass to the pivot man.

Preventing Double Cut off Medium Pivot. When the forward passes to a medium pivot, the strong-side guard and forward may double cut off the pivot. Again, preventing the pass-in to the pivot is the first line of defense. The defending guard on the side of the ball should drop off toward the baseline and ball, and the pivot should be played a strong one-half man on the ball side. If the pass-in is successful, the far-side defensive guard, who has dropped far off his man, should attempt to tie up the pivot man. Both the far-side defensive guard and the forward must float protectively toward the ball position.

The forward passing in, usually the first cutter, cuts to the middle. The guard cuts to the outside off the forward. Defenders guarding either cutter can attempt to tie up the ball or prevent the cuts by legally maintaining defensive position in the cutter's path. All defenders should be alert for a "Switch" call.

Double Screens

Individual defensive players must be alert for two types of stationary double screens used effectively by many offenses. The first type results when two offensive players set a screen side by side at the foul-line area or to the side away from the ball. The cutter comes from the outside, away from the ball, off the double screen toward the basket. Players defending against the screeners and the cutter should drop off their men toward the middle in the direction of the ball. If they do this simultaneously with ball movement, the screen should be ineffectual, and switching and congesting the cutting area will be relatively easy.

The most difficult stationary double screen to defend against is set along the foul lanes, and the cutter goes behind the screen on the baseline side, cutting out to the ball from the inside for a short jump shot. Usually, the cutter is moving in the same direction as the ball is being passed, and the man defending the cutter must play between his man and the ball. The defenders guarding the potential passers should be alerted to the double screen by shouted warnings of its position by the screeners' defenders. The passers must be played with extreme pressure so that a pass-in is difficult.

DEFENSING THE OFFENSIVE ADVANTAGE

Several times during a game, defenders retreating after losing the ball will find themselves outnumbered by the offense. The player who has made the physical error of losing the ball should not commit the mental error of following the ball when it has been intercepted by the intended receiver's defender. His best defensive move is to drop back quickly for defensive position. If he moves toward the ball, he will give his defender a clear, unopposed break to the basket. There is no defense for this one-on-none break except to hustle back for a rebound in the event of a missed shot.

The most common offensive advantages are the two-on-one, three-on-one, three-on-two, four-on-two, four-on-three, and five-on-four situations.

The primary defensive strategy when outnumbered is to slow down the advance of the ball until teammates can recover and help out and, if possible, to prevent the easy lay-up shot and the good percentage shot. Defenders should use realistic fakes to stop the dribbler, and they should feint and shout loudly to make the offense commit itself. When outnumbered with more than one defender back, defensive players should use practical zone defense principles to delay, to force the least-advantageous shooting opportunity, and to help position the defenders in the best possible rebounding position. A defensive player who intercepts the ball, deflects the pass to the cutter, delays the attack until help arrives, or forces a shot beyond the sixteen-foot range has done an outstanding job of defending.

Two-on-One

When one defensive player is retreating and must defend against two fast-breaking opponents with the ball, he must run backward to a position at the top of the free-throw circle, keeping the ball and both men in view. If the front man has the ball, the defender, while retreating, must delay him as far out as possible. When a cutter is ahead of the ball handler, the defender must open his stance toward the cutter (since he is the more dangerous man), keep the foul-line area covered, and attempt to stop the dribbler without allowing him to make an easy pass to the cutter or execute a stop-and-go or change-of-pace dribble.

Knowledge of the abilities of the two fast-breaking opponents is important. If the cutter is a tall man, he may not be as good a ball handler or passer as the dribbler. In that case, the defender should attempt to force a pass to the cutter, then attack him aggressively to cause a fumble, violation, or poor return pass. The shot will generally be taken by the player on the right side, and the better shooter will look for the shot himself. If the ball is being brought down either side, the defender should try to keep it on the side, as the sideline and baseline can be utilized in defense, and the influencing maneuver tells fast-retreating team-mates where to position themselves.

A defender should never try to take the ball away from the dribbler unless he makes a careless tactical error. If the ball is being passed back and forth between the attackers, the defender should retreat to the foul line and then fake at the man nearer the middle to force a hurried pass or a hesitancy in the passing continuity. He should never allow a lay-up shot, and he should challenge any good shot without giving away rebound position or a better shooting opportunity.

Three-on-One

In the three-on-one break, the defender must retreat to the foul line and determine by preknowledge or judgment where the pass will go. If the dribbler stops, the defender must retreat back to within eight feet of the basket, allowing the foul-line shot. He must attempt to influence the dribbler to his weak hand to prevent an easy lay-up or pass. If necessary, he should foul the dribbler for a one-shot opportunity rather than give an unopposed lay-up.

Three-on-Two

There are two methods of defending against a three-on-two offensive advantage. The first method is a front and back defensive alignment, with the front man in the outer half of the free-throw circle and the back man between the foul lanes, six to eight feet in front of the basket. The front man must stop the dribbler as far out as possible and force a pass. (The more passes the attackers make, the greater the chance for errors on their part.) The back man must react to the side of the pass, but he cannot start until the ball has left the passer's hands. Moving before the release commits the defender to that side, and a good fake will leave the third man free for an easy lay-up. After the pass, the front man opens toward the side of the pass and drops back to the side opposite the pass. The back man should attack aggressively after committing himself, trying to step in and draw an offensive charge or to prevent the cross-court pass. If the dribbler does not stop or pass, the front defender influences him to one side or the other to limit his passing opportunities. If he succeeds, the back man should favor the opposite side, and the front man must retreat on the same side he forced the dribbler toward. A third retreating defender should come back to the foul-line area and cover there.

The second method of playing a three-on-two break is for the defense to play side by side, parallel to each other. The only time this method is preferable is when the middle man is not a good ball handler or when the opponents are not a good fast-break team. The two defensive men should take positions near the ends of the foul line, approximately fourteen feet apart, and open toward their respective sidelines, keeping the ball and the cutter on their side in view. The distance between the defenders should not be so great that the offensive man can dribble between them for the lay-up shot. The man on the side of the dribbling hand must try to stop the dribbler, using defensive fakes and feints and shouting to disconcert him, while retreating. When the dribbler stops, each man should fall off toward the cutter on his side, waving his hands and yelling to discourage a pass-in and make the middle man take the shot. If a pass is made to a cutter, the defender on that side must move with the pass to get position between the cutter and the basket to prevent an easy shot. The other defensive man opens toward the pass and must be alert for a rebound or a pass attempt to the cutter on his side. The third defensive man catching up takes the middle man.

Four-on-Two

On a four-on-two disadvantage, the defenders should play parallel at the ends of the foul line and attempt to slow the offensive man with the ball until other defenders can retreat to help out. They must try to force an outside shot, if possible, or foul advantageously to prevent an easy basket.

Four-on-Three

Against the four-on-three and five-on-four offensive advantages, the same basic principles mentioned previously apply. The defenders should use basic zone defense techniques. The maneuvering area is lessened for the offense by the additional defensive man.

In the four-on-three defensive situation, a triangular zone should be formed, with a front man in the outer half of the foul circle and the two rear men six to eight feet in front of the basket with their inside feet on the foul lane on their side. The three defenders should have their arms outstretched and moving to cover as much area as possible and must face the ball until their teammates can get back in defensive positions. The front man should force the ball toward the side with the fewer attackers and follow the pass. The defender away from the pass turns with the pass and steps into the foul lane, facing the ball. He must protect against a cutter coming down the middle and a pass underneath the basket on his side. The back defender on the side to which the pass was made turns with the pass to a man moving into the strong-side pivot area. The three men should cover the good percentage shooting areas to prevent a good offensive thrust, trying to keep the offense passing the ball by maintaining a shifting triangular defense until defensive help arrives. When defensive balance is achieved, the defender should return to man-to-man cautiously, being certain that all offensive players are matched closely in size.

Five-on-Four

The five-on-four defensive principle is similar to the four-on-three, except that the zone used initially should be in the form of a diamond when the ball position is in center court: one man in the outer half of the foul circle, two side men stationed fifteen feet apart one step below the foul line, and the back man six feet in front of the basket in the foul lane. The zone shifts from a diamond to a box with ball movement left or right.

DEFENSING THE DEFENSIVE ADVANTAGE

Many times during a game an offensive man will start toward his basket after receiving a pass-out only to discover that he is far ahead of his offensive teammates, and there are two defenders back. In this situation, one defender should play the man to stop his dribble, and the second defender should attack aggressively from a blind side to force the offensive player into making a bad pass or into a held-ball situation. The defenders must be certain that no other offensive player is in scoring position.

When two offensive players attack three defensive players, the nearest defender stops the dribble and a second defender attacks aggressively. The third defender plays between the second offensive man and the ball.

DEFENSIVE "CHANCES"

Present-day basic defensive philosophy has changed the defensive player from the retreating, passive, stay-between-your-man-and-the-basket prototype into a daring, aggressive attacker. When a defensive team elects to challenge the offense at any point—full-court, three-quarters court or half-court—much of its defensive strategy is based upon methods that previously were considered to be extremely poor defense, such as over-guarding or deliberately playing out of line to the basket. Constant defensive pressure has a twofold purpose. It disrupts the offensive team's preferred style of play, and it incorporates this aggressive defense into its own offensive pattern.

Interceptions

When bringing the ball upcourt, many backcourt men pass routinely from one to the other before reaching the offensive attack position. An aggressive guard should be encouraged to try to intercept a pass during this advance. If this attempt fails, and the defender is in poor defensive position because of his effort, his backcourt teammate, who is open toward the ball, should switch quickly to the man with the ball, calling out the exchange in responsibility, and the player who is out of position should recover as rapidly as possible and run to the defensive foul-line area to pick up the attacker left open. At the same time, defenders near the basket should move into position to prevent an easy cut to the basket and a return pass.

Defensive fakes can be passive as well as aggressive. As an attacker approaches the offensive maneuvering position, he is intent on the pattern he wants to put into operation. A defender can lure an unaware dribbler into thinking he is retreating routinely, then make a quick thrusting move to the ball and slap it free for a clean steal. A defensive player who is quicker than his man can entice the offense by falling farther off his man to invite a pass and reacting to an intercepting position. A corner defender can overplay to allow a reverse cut and react quickly to the ball when the pass is made to the cutter. A pivot defender can seemingly play behind his man until the pass is on its way, then quickly step in and flick it away. The determining factor on taking such defensive chances should be whether help is possible; if it is, take any good opportunity. The closer the play is to the basket, the less team help can be expected.

Double-Teaming

Doubling up on opponents, especially on the sideline or baseline after a dribble, is very effective as a defensive chance maneuver. When a dribbler is forced to the sideline by an aggressive defender and stops, the defender should overplay strongly to the sideline side, necessitating a pivot toward the mid-court line by the dribbler to protect the ball. The other guard should anticipate this pivot and charge the man with the ball from his blind side to effect a held-ball, a violation, or a bad pass. The same tactic can be used when a good defensive forward seemingly allows a baseline drive, then quickly closes the baseline and attacks the driver on the baseline side, forcing a pivot toward the near sideline. The backcourt defender on that side can approach from the forward's blind side to force an offensive mistake.

Defenders who double up on one man must aggressively attack the ball without fouling, using quick hand movement and outthrust feet to prevent a damaging pass-out. A defender should not deliberately try to steal the ball in any double-up situation, as fouls usually result. Defenders must be aware of the status of the man with the ball on a defensive double-team. If he has not dribbled, the defense can be hurt.

On all ball-exchange crosses by offensive men, guard to guard or guard to forward, a quick switch (jump switch by the screener's defender) into the path of the man receiving the ball, plus a rear follow-up by the receiver's guard, can put the offensive man at a disadvantage. The purpose of these double pincer movements is a resultant offensive mistake—an off-line pass that can be intercepted, a held-ball, or a violation. Often, the next closest defender to the double-teaming jump-switch can help, since the man being double-teamed will instinctively attempt to pass immediately to the man left unguarded. Anticipating this pass, the next nearest defender should leave his man and try for the interception.

In many offensive screens, the man guarding the screener can jump-switch into the path of a dribbler driving hard off the screen and draw an offensive foul. The same technique can be used on hard-running cutters at the end of a fast break.

An aggressive defensive player will occasionally be beaten by a good dribbler, but with a quick recovery he can turn his defensive lapse into a possible ball-stealing situation by coming up fast behind the dribbler, getting in a stride with him, and (using a darting, flicking hand thrust) attempting to tip or deflect the dribble. The same play can be used in overplaying a dribbler's strong side to force a pivot in order to remain dribbling. After the turn, a hustling defender can tap the ball free by pivoting behind the dribbler and swinging the far hand and arm with a sickle-like movement from behind. With all other defenders within the defensive triangle of ball, their men, and basket, a clean steal can result.

OVERPLAYING STRONG SIDE OF
SCREENER (HEDGING)

The defender guarding a screener must constantly be alert to overplay (hedge) to the ball side when an opponent cuts off the man he is guarding. He must be prepared to defend against three situations: (1) when the opponent using the screen has the ball, (2) when the screener has the ball (usually a post, back to basket), and (3) when a third player (other than the screener or cutter) has the ball.

Opponent Using the Screen Has the Ball

When an opponent with the ball is using dribbling maneuvers to force his defender into a screen, the player guarding the screener must move up toward the dribbling opponent on the strong side, approximately beside the screener, giving loud vocal warnings. The defender guarding the screener should be aware of the offensive potential of the dribbler. He must first be prepared to stop a drive-in if the dribbler's guard is rubbed off by the screen. Second, he must be prepared to impede a shot if the dribbler stops and jump shoots. Third, he must be able to maintain a fronting position on the screener to prevent a pass to him if he rolls to the basket anticipating a defensive switch.

The overplay must force the dribbler to take a wider path, thus allowing his guard to go over the top of the screen and regain good defensive position without giving an offensive advantage. With good anticipation, the screener's defender may cause an offensive charge by the dribbler. If a switch is necessitated, the screener's defender (the back man) calls it. (This defensive team play requires constant practice.) Weak-side teammates must help in defending against a lob pass if the screener rolls to the basket.

The distance the screener is from the basket also affects the defense. Beyond eighteen feet of the basket, the guard playing the dribbler must force over the screen, while the screener's defender fakes a strong-side overplay to slow down or stop the dribbler without committing himself. Within twelve feet, the hedger must overplay so completely it is impossible for the dribbler to shoot or pass. Passing in this area becomes increasingly more difficult because of the limited passing lanes.

Screener Has the Ball

When the screener has the ball, his distance from the basket is the most important consideration for his defender in determining how to overplay to the strong side. If the screener is within his effective shooting range, his defender must play close to him, anticipating the cutter and feinting quickly at him, but not losing defensive position on the screener. If the cutter's strong side is outside, the screener's guard must concentrate his defensive attention on his man, as any overt reaction to the cutter would allow a post screener to pivot and dribble into the basket unimpeded. If the cut is to the inside, off the screen, the hedger can more effectively overplay to this side without giving the screener with the ball too great an offensive advantage.

The man guarding the cutter must always try to go over the top of the screen, slashing at the ball as he retreats to force the screener to protect the ball. If the cutter is not a good outside shooter, his defender should go behind the screener's guard, not in front of him, because if the screener's guard had to step back to allow him through, the screener could then shoot. If the screener is in a low- or medium-pivot area, his defender must concentrate on him exclusively until a pass-off is made and then react quickly to the cutter.

Third Player Has the Ball

When a third player has the ball, the screener's defender should overplay strongly to the ball side, denying the cutter a good path toward the ball and forcing him as far out from the basket as possible without giving an offensive opportunity to his own man (the screener). Good basic defensive position (balancing to the ball) by both defenders away from the ball should negate any offensive attempts by their opponents.

DEFENSING THE OUTLET PASS AGAINST THE FAST BREAK

The first line of defense in stopping the fast break is at the defenders' offensive end of the court. The team breaking must first rebound at its defensive end and make an outlet pass. If the breaking team relies on one or two key rebounders to initiate the break, pressure must be exerted aggressively to tie up the rebounder or make him dribble. If the key fast-break rebounder has inside position on a rebound, and he recovers the ball, the man behind him should try to prevent a high pass-out by positioning himself to the outside of the rebounder with his hands and arms held high and moving to effect a possible deflection and to cause the rebounder to be protective. A second man can be assigned to help in harassing the rebounder, but both should retreat immediately if the player passes out. If the rebounder must pivot to protect the ball, the original pressure man should stay and the other man retreat. If the key rebounder is guarding an offensive pivot, he will usually be outside the pivot man when a shot is taken. The pivot must aggressively maintain this inside rebounding position. He should not move to get the ball, but hold off the other team's key rebounder to prevent the fast break. He only rebounds if he is certain of possession. A delay of only a few seconds is enough to impair the effectiveness of the organized fast break.

Coupled with the attempt to diminish the rebounding potentiality should be an effort to stop the effective outlet pass. For their first outlet pass, teams look to the sideline area near midcourt on the side on which the rebound is recovered. A quick guard should play an intercepting angle on the outlet receiver, forcing him to adjust his position or come back toward the rebounder for safe reception, thus slowing the initial thrust of the fast break. Overplaying this outlet to force him deeper toward the mid-court area will reduce the rebounder-passer's passing range, as a two-hand over-hand pass or a quick hook pass cannot be thrown accurately for too long a distance.

If the outlet pass is made, the assigned backcourt defender should try to keep the receiver from dribbling the ball to the middle or passing it to a teammate cutting to the middle lane. He should concentrate on forcing the ball up on the outside lane if possible.

DEFENSE AGAINST THE PASSER-IN ON OUT-OF-BOUNDS PLAYS

There are two accepted methods in defending against the inbounding passer on out-of-bounds plays. The first is a challenging, aggressive approach, with each defending teammate playing between the ball position and his man, forcing him away from the pass-in area so that any pass-in must be to a man retreating from the basket area. The player guarding the man making the pass-in stands directly in front of him and waves his arms, kicks with his feet, and yells loudly to disconcert the passer and prevent an effective pass.

The second method in popular use is for the defender of the passer-in to play between his man and the basket, keeping this position after the pass-in. All other defenders drop off their men toward the ball and the basket and open their position to enable them to see both their men and the ball. The man guarding the passer-in does not play too close to the passer and tries to cut off any pass-in to a cutter coming into the foul-line area or a possible pass-in to a pivot player. When the passer comes inbounds, the defender should force him away from the basket area to prevent a pass-and-cut situation.

8

The most obvious objective of individual and team defense is to stop the offensive team from scoring. With vertical jumps of 30 inches or more and shooting percentages above .500 commonplace among basketball players nowadays, however, it is both simplistic and unrealistic to expect to completely shut off the scoring of the better offensive players. Far more practical and feasible is the notion of attempting to take opponents out of their regular offense by forcing the ball toward low-percentage shooters or scoring areas (or away from high-percentage shooters or scoring areas, which amounts to practically the same thing); by fronting or overplaying the opponents' high scorers; by getting back quickly on defense to reduce the opponents' fast-breaking potential; and, on an individual basis within the team context, by forcing shooters to alter the timing, ball position, release, or arc of their shots.

Thus, the primary purpose of a team's defense is to limit the opponents' scoring opportunities by preventing them from fast-breaking and by disrupting the continuity and efficiency of their predesigned offensive patterns. The coach selects the type of team defense to be used, basing his selection on several factors, the most important being the personnel available.

The correct defense is that which best limits the opponents' primary offensive thrusts and procedures. A good team defense incorporates the strong points of both zone defense and man-to-man defense. The primary focus in man-to-man defense is the man, and the secondary objective is the ball. But teams that use man-to-man as a primary defense also use such zone defensive techniques as playing loosely away from the ball, collapsing weak-side toward the basket to prevent penetration of the crucial area, and compacting the defense in the basket area and the middle. Conversely, zone defensive players, who play the ball first and the man second, must be able to defend against the opponent with the ball on a man-to-man basis. Zones today do not cover just certain areas; they flex with a man-to-man attitude at the focal point (the ball), attacking the man with the ball and preventing reception in the pivot area.

THE COACH'S DEFENSIVE PHILOSOPHY

A coach must insist that his players never allow the offensive team to advance the ball to their point of attack without strong defensive pressure. (The offensive point of attack is the point at which opponents wish to put their set offensive pattern into operation.) The coach cannot use a single defense in his overall team preparation. He must adopt whatever defensive style is best suited to counteract the opponent's offensive moves. It is important that he understand the type of defense he wishes to use and that he be able to teach it to his players.

All coaches work hard at improving the defensive posture of their teams. The defense must be sound, both individually and as a team; it must be flexible; and it must be simple enough for the players to learn, yet complex for the opponents. Defensive ability is based on hard work, determination, dedication, discipline, concentration, responsibility, cooperation, physical and mental coordination, speed and quickness, willingness, and pride.

By scouting, opponents preview each other's defenses. Showing multiple defenses allows a coach to employ a defense that will give his opponents difficulty. They are forced to use practice time to prepare themselves for each defense, playing against substitutes or freshmen who must be taught each defense in order to act as opponents. If there has been no previous scouting, the coach should prepare defenses for any defensive contingency and be able to adapt mentally during the progress of the game, using his time-outs strategically and making good use of his half-time discussion period. The coach should make adjustments quickly, as soon as weak points are discovered. For example, if a good player is in foul trouble, the coach can keep him on the court by changing from a man-to-man to a zone defense. It is easiest to defend against a team with one inflexible set style. If the players do not vary their offense, the defensive team may implement double-teaming tactics.

The coach should pressure teams holding the ball for the last shot at the end of a quarter, at the end of a half, or at the end of the game. They are concentrating on maintaining possession and generally are not looking at the basket; therefore, it might be easy to force them into a violation or cause an interception or a held ball. Teams that are ahead should not become relaxed or passive defensively; they should maintain pressure. All teams must be able to press to some degree, especially in the late stages of the game. Defensive aggressiveness will cause the opponents to move out of their normal pattern so that the defensive team has a chance to obtain a possession of the ball.

Defensively, a team should change game pace to its own advantage, concentrating on the opponents' strengths and covering up its own weaknesses. The players must surprise and confuse the opponents. Surprise was the deciding factor in an NCAA regional game that our team played. With 40 seconds to go, we changed from the basic tight man-to-man defense the team had played for 39½ minutes to a half-court zone-press defense. By double-teaming the ball handler of the opposition, our players were able to intercept the ball and make an easy basket, resulting in a one-point win in an important, closely played game.

Saving some practiced defensive variations for the second half that were not shown in the first half is another good surprise maneuver. A coach could also use a defensive variation in the last few minutes of the first half so that the opposing coach will use much of his valuable half-time period discussing methods of attacking a defense that will not be used again in the course of that game.

The winning team in basketball is frequently the team with the quickest transition from offense to defense; therefore, all teams must maintain defensive balance while attacking offensively. In case they lose possession of the ball, they must have offensive players in a defensive safety position so that they may hinder or stop the opponents from scoring an easy, unopposed basket. A team should have three offensive rebounders; one man who is half offensive and half defensive, going to the ball only if he is certain of possession; and one player who is back on defense. Efficient transition from offense to defense is the most important single factor in maintaining a good team defensive posture in the course of a ball game.

Defensive Preparation

Defensive preparation starts the first day of practice. Team defensive fundamentals are of prime importance in early season drills, and coaches should constantly review them during the season. (The coach should have a five-man offensive skeleton group run the patterns. During each play, he should point out the offensive players who should be moving back as safety men for defense or to fill outletting areas to relieve pressure at the ball position when the play situation does not result in a shot. After a basket is made, he should have the five men on offense break quickly back on defense.)

The coach must practice double-teaming opponents, working on the double-teaming aspects for man-to-man, zone, or zone press defensive alignments. He must teach baseline defensive techniques and how to play men who do not have possession of the ball. If he wants an aggressive defense, he will have his men overplay. If not, he will have them play loose or sag back when the man is one pass away. He must teach his players never to allow an opponent to cut in front of them to the ball, especially not a corner man who wants to cut to the keyhole area with the ball out front or on the opposite side.

He must teach players to force opponents away from their favorite shooting spots by forcing them off course or by stepping into their path. (This action is especially useful when defensing against a fast break.)

The most important technical function of the basketball coach is making his players understand the importance of team defense. Defense in basketball is a constant; offense is a variable. Therefore, the coach should motivate the players to work to acquire proper defensive techniques. Each player must be made to understand the necessity of giving his all defensively for the good of the team. This we might call the perfect approach or perfect factor. Also, the player should know he will not be allowed to play if he cannot contribute to the team defense. This we might call imperfect motivation or the imperfect factor.

Each squad member should be made to understand that the greatest burden to a team is a weak or indifferent defensive player, and that the coach would prefer an aggressive defender who is uncoordinated offensively to a good shooter with a blasé attitude.

In emphasizing the necessity for good defense, the coach must follow these eight guidelines:

1. Convince the squad of the necessity for a cohesive, positive defensive policy.
2. Insist on adherence to detail when implementing the defensive philosophy.
3. Break the defense into component fundamental techniques.

4. Practice group defensive techniques each practice session, and develop rules and guidelines for each phase of defense.

5. Allot as much daily practice time to defense as to offense.

6. Disperse defensive drills discriminately through daily practice (at the beginning of one practice session, halfway through another, at the end of a third) so as to obtain maximum results by simulating playing conditions effectively. The tiredness of a player varies in the course of a game, and this factor must be taken into consideration during defensive practice.

7. Never allow improper, careless, or slovenly defensive practices. Correct poor defensive procedure immediately.

8. Place a premium on good defensive play by praising individuals both privately and publicly for outstanding defensive accomplishment. The stability and reliability of a good team defense must often counteract the inconsistency of poor offensive accomplishment.

Team Characteristics

The following characteristics should be intrinsic in all teams when playing defense.

1. A Positive Mental Approach. Since defense must be played at least fifty percent of the time in every game, the team must be completely prepared mentally. A good mental approach is made up of confidence, poise, mental aggressiveness, anticipation, and pride.

Confidence. The coach must convince the players that a selected method is the best possible defense. Both coach and team must have complete confidence in the strategy.

Poise. Good defensive players must be poised. They must not get upset, rattled, or unduly concerned over opposition moves; they should be emotionally prepared to overcome them.

Mental aggressiveness. (We use the term mental aggressiveness because we do not wish players to get physically aggressive to a point where they overextend themselves or foul.) Players must play within their limitations and understand the overall team philosophy of defense so that they can always make the right play at the right time.

Anticipation. Intelligent anticipation and reaction to this anticipation are important factors in team defense. Players must understand the philosophy of the offense that they are defending against so that they can prevent the opponents from getting the position they want or making the type of play they wish to make.

Pride. Pride in individual accomplishment and, more important, pride in team accomplishment on defense is an important mental aspect in the team defense posture.

2. Adaptability. The team must be able to vary its defense, depending on the following five factors.

1. The team's capabilities
2. The coach's understanding of the defense and his ability to teach it to his players
3. The physical appurtenances of the home court
4. The type of opposition that will be played against in the course of the team schedule
5. The level of competition
   (The lower the level of competition the more difficult it is to inculcate all of the proper fundamentals and team techniques necessary in building a complete team defense. At lower levels of competition we strongly recommend the use of man-to-man team defense for the best interests of the players.)

3. Good Floor Position and Floor Balance. Since the team must protect the goal, defense must be built from the basket out. The focal point of all defenses must be the ball position and its distance from the basket. Also to be considered are the type of defense and the relation of the floor position of the man being guarded with respect to the ball position. A defender should consider the man in his area if the team is playing a zone defense.

4. Physical Activity. Offense must be balanced, with one offensive player moving into good defensive position during all offensive maneuverings. All players must be able to change quickly from offense to defense, getting back down the court so that they can play defense from the basket out. They must be able to stop the ball's progress once the basket area is defended and be able to prevent penetration after stopping the ball movement.

5. Flexibility. The defense taught must be able to meet all types of offensive challenges, and it must be able to move into action at all times of the game from any court position. The defense used depends on the type of opposition, the game situation (whether the team is ahead or behind, the time left in the game), and special situations (out-of-bounds plays, foul shots, and last-second situations).

Basic Team Types

When determining a team's defense, basic team types should be considered. These are usually categorized by the heights of the players. High school guards generally range from quite short up to six foot or six foot one, while in college they will range up to approximately six foot three. Forwards in high school will be between six foot one and six foot three; in college they will probably range from six foot three to six foot six. Centers, generally the tallest boys on the squads, will be six foot three or taller in high school and six foot six or taller in college.

Each squad will be one of the following six types with respect to the height of the team members:

1. Five tall men
2. Four tall men and one small man
3. Three tall men and two small men
4. Two tall men and three small men
5. One tall man and four small men
6. Five small men

We will discuss the six types of teams and the type of defense we feel is best suited to the personnel involved.

Five Tall Men. If the team is playing man-to-man, it should play a loose man-to-man. If the coach prefers a zone defense, a passive type of zone would be best, especially if the team has two tall boys who are extremely awkward. In this type of defense they can defend the goal area. If pressure is needed, a type of half-court pressure is best, with one fast, tall man forcing the ball up toward the ten-second (mid-court) line as quickly as possible and then exerting the pressure in the half-court area.

Four Tall Men and One Small Man. This team should play a loose man-to-man defense or a one-two-two zone in which the one small man is given latitude to move to anticipate and intercept. Half-court pressure should be used.

Three Tall Men and Two Small Men. We recommend regular man-to-man defense. The team could also use a two-one-two zone or a two-three zone, a combination defense, or a pressure defense that could be extended to full court (probably a two-two-one full-court pressure).

Two Tall Men and Three Small Men. This team can use any type of man-to-man defense the coach wishes. For a zone defense the coach should use a three-two zone, a one-two-two zone, or a one-three-one zone. In this case, a combination defense is also a possibility.

One Tall Man and Four Small Men. We recommend a switching man-to-man defense in which the four smaller players are allowed to switch men on every lateral cross or movement toward the basket, staying with their men only on diagonal cuts. The best zone would be a two-two-one or a one-three-one in which the big man is left in the basket area at all times. The pressure defense should be either a man-to-man pressure or a zone pressure using a one-two-one-one press with the big man as the back man.

Five Small Men. This team should use a tight man-to-man in half court, with the double and turn procedures, or a full-court man-to-man. A zone press defense could be used, with five men crashing the defensive boards, or an aggressive two-three zone defense in which pressure is put on the ball at all areas of the front court.

Team Principles

All good team defenses are based on the following six principles.

1. Reduce the Frequency of High-Percentage Shots. This may be done by maintaining a good team balance defensively and by harrying the opponents, forcing them to take off-balance shots. The defenders should also allow the ball to be passed to the less-accurate shooters, permitting them to take low-percentage shots, and frustrate the good shooters by denying them the ball or by harassing them when they have the ball.

2. Decrease the Number of Close-in Shots (the Shots under the Eighteen-Foot Area). The more shots a team gets from the close-in area, the weaker the team defense structure is.

3. Diminish Second-Shot Possibilities. Prevent the offense from position by using good rebounding and blocking-out techniques. Be alert, active, and aggressive near the defensive basket.

4. Eliminate Give-Away Baskets. Fight to maintain ball possession. All players must be aware of the importance of possession of the ball.

5. Attack the Ball with Controlled Aggressiveness. The defensive point of attack must be predetermined by the coach, depending on the type of team defense he feels is best for his players. The minimum defensive attack point is the twenty-one-foot area. The reference point for this distance from the basket is the head of the free-throw circle. If the team is to attack here, then the front man should attack the ball when his feet are on the outer rim of this circle. By maintaining good defensive balance from this position, the defenders will cause the opponents to shoot from twenty-four feet or more from the basket. This is the first area of attack, and usually a loose man-to-man defense is used.

The second attack point is the mid-court line. Attacking from here the defenders would use a half-court pressure defense, either man-to-man pickup or aggressive zone. This leaves openings closer to the basket that must be filled by the team in its defensive reaction. One movement on defense by one player should result in four immediate reactions by his defensive teammates.

The third point of attack for the ball could be three-fourths court or full-court, using pressure from a zone or man-to-man defensive alignment. The purpose of this defense is to cause the opponents to make mistakes in the backcourt while they are bringing the ball up. Although a three-quarter press spreads the five men to a point where penetration is possible in many areas, if the team functions as a cohesive unit, it should be able to cut down the number of shots, make enough interceptions, and cause enough violations to make the gamble worthwhile.

6. Discourage the Opponents from Penetrating the Defensive Perimeter. Defensive players should never allow a free opponent under or near the basket, and they must prevent easy reception of the ball in this area. It is incumbent on all defenders to close off the keyhole area initially, then work the team defensive structure from the basket out. The coach must decide whether each defense (except the full-court and half-court pressure defenses) is to be played aggressively or passively. His choice will be determined by the physical makeup of his team and by the game situation. If he wishes to play an aggressive defense, the team must attack the ball at all junctures in the front court while overplaying passing outlets. Complete team alertness is necessary for intelligent aggressiveness. Two players should double-team by forcing a turn-and-pivot movement or by trapping a man at the sideline, at the juncture of the front-court hash-mark, or near the mid-court division line. Two of the remaining teammates should play intercepting angles on the two near receivers, while the fifth man zones the two opponents farthest from the ball, concentrating on the more dangerous of the two.

A passive defense in the front court permits perimeter movement and allows perimeter pass reception outside the twenty-one-foot area. It closes passing lanes away from the ball and passing lanes into the pivot. It prevents the lob pass to the pivot over a fronting defender, and it attacks the ball from the front when the ball is in the possession of a low- or medium-pivot opponent.

TYPES OF TEAM DEFENSE

There are four types of team defense: man-to-man, zone, combination, and pressure.

Man-to-Man Defense

Man-to-man may be played in six ways: normally (about three feet from the man with the ball), tightly, loosely, as an aggressive defense in which the man with the ball is turned from the basket and double-teamed by the nearest defender, as a switching man-to-man, and as a run-and-jump defense. The coach determines how the team defense will be played, and the position of the ball determines each individual's position in the defense.

Normal. In normal man-to-man defense each defender has two duties—to guard the opponent assigned to him by the coach and to cooperate with teammates to prevent structural weaknesses. His first duty is his man, and normally, he should expect a minimum of help from his teammates, who have their own basic responsibilities.

The basic position for defending man-to-man is a stance with the weight back, body crouched low, and hands up and moving, pointing to the man and the ball (when the defender's man does not have it). Each defender is stationed within a triangle formed by his designated opponent, the ball, and the basket.

When guarding a man who is dribbling, the defender must never lunge; he must move the man away from the advantage he is seeking.

The back man or the man guarding the screener should call every switch, and the players should talk their way through the maneuver. Both players should be aggressive, staying with the men they have switched to without retreating. In case of a mismatch, where a smaller defender must cover a taller opponent, a defensive teammate should collapse in to help him. The small man should play in front of his man in a pivot position, knowing he will get weak-side help from alert, defensive teammates. The men should switch back to their original opponents as quickly as possible under safe conditions, again calling the switch.

Men away from the point of attack should be ready to collapse toward the screen to help. To coordinate his movements to those of the team, each player has the following responsibilities in a normal man-to-man defense.

1. Force the opposing dribbler in a predetermined direction. This is called influencing the offense and the dribbler. There are four directions in which a defender can turn the man who brings the ball up-court. Each coach should teach his team the strategy he believes is most effective. The player guarding the man with the ball can influence him to the sidelines. (See Figure 8–1.) Advocates of this maneuver feel that the sidelines are a help to the

Figure 8–1. Influencing the dribbler to the left side.

defender, since the dribbler has only one direction—back toward the middle—in which to make an outlet pass, unless he wishes to throw the ball toward the division line.

A second philosophy recommends forcing the player toward the defensive strength (usually, but not always, to the middle.) This strategy is essential in the baseline area, for the defensive player cannot allow his offensive opponent to go between him and the end line where there is no help.

The third method of influencing is to force a player to dribble the ball with his weak hand by overplaying on the strong side.

The fourth direction in which to influence the ball handler is away from the good shooter.

2. If possible, watch both the designated opponent and the ball when another opponent has possession. Although the defender should concentrate primarily on his man, he should open toward the ball so that he can see it with peripheral vision. If he must give up one, he should give up the ball position to maintain proper defensive alignment on his man.

3. Be prepared to pick up opponents who are free coming off a screen or after a reverse cut.

4. Collapse to the middle to prevent easy reception in the pivot area or under the basket when the ball is away from your designated area.

5. Be vocal. Encourage and warn teammates, and discourage opponents.

6. Get back on defense quickly after the ball is lost offensively. Defenders should play defense from the basket out, sprinting to a position within six or eight feet of the basket to determine if there are any opponents in that area, then picking up the first loose opponent if he is in a scoring position or attacking the ball to stop its penetration into the scoring area.

7. Be alert to double-team opponents, and move in to overplay the man left open when a teammate doubles up on the ball.

8. Be mentally and physically alert to avert any opponent's scoring opportunities. Defenders should get inside rebound position on every opponent's shot.

9. Help the pivot defender in the following three ways. First, do not allow a pass-in to the pivot area; second, float into this area to discourage the ball from being passed when your man is on the weak side; and third, try to tie up a good pivot player from the front by following the pass-in if the ball does get to him.

10. Improve team defensive strength by playing toward the vital penetrating areas, going as far from your man as his floor position with respect to the ball allows.

11. Know your man's strengths and weaknesses and play him accordingly. Know your other opponents' individual

strengths and weaknesses so that you can help teammates guarding these opponents.

12. Intercept or deflect if possible. The intercepter or deflector rarely guards the passer. The passer's defender forces bad passes.

Diagram 8–1. Normal Man-to-Man Defense against a Two-Three Offense. A, a guard, has possession of the ball. X_1, his defender, is playing him normal, close to him, in line between him and the basket. The corner defender, X_3, guarding C, is up a little bit toward the ball but still close to C. X_2, defending against B, has dropped off a step toward the ball and in line with B. Pivot Defender X_4 has taken a half-fronting position toward the ball in guarding D. X_5, defending against the far forward, E, has loosened normally and has moved up to prevent E from cutting up to the high-pivot area to get a pass. He is also in position to help defend against D if the ball should pass to the corner player, C.

DIAGRAM 8–1

Diagram 8–2 (Continuation of movement in Diagram 8–1). The ball has been passed from A to C, the corner man. X_3 is playing C to the baseline side to prevent a drive in that direction. X_1 has moved to a position where he is overplaying slightly toward the ball. X_2 has dropped off B considerably, into the foul-lane area. X_5 has dropped off E, the opposite forward, into the area between the foul lanes. X_4 is fronting D in a low-pivot position to prevent him from getting an easy pass into the pivot area.

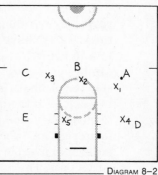

DIAGRAM 8–2

Diagram 8–3. Normal Man-to-Man Defense against a Three-Two Offensive Alignment. A has the ball and is guarded by X_1, who is in straightaway position between A and the basket. B is guarded by X_2, who has dropped off slightly and is playing a little bit toward the ball in line with the basket. X_3 has dropped off C. X_5 has dropped off E and is a little high on him so that he cannot get good pivot position at the outer half of the free-throw circle. X_4 has moved closer to D to prevent a direct pass-in or to pick him up if he cuts along the baseline without the ball.

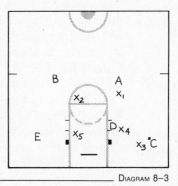

DIAGRAM 8–3

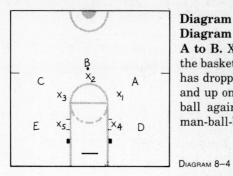

Diagram 8–4 (Continuation of movement in Diagram 8–3). The ball has been passed from A to B. X_2 is guarding B between the man and the basket. X_1 has dropped off slightly from A. X_4 has dropped off and up on D. X_5 has dropped off and up on E. X_3 has dropped off and toward the ball against C. Note: defenders are inside the man-ball-basket triangle.

DIAGRAM 8–4

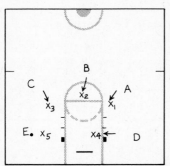

Diagram 8–5 (Continuation of movement in Diagram 8–4). The ball has been passed in to Corner Man E. X_5, guarding against E, must prevent a baseline drive. X_3 has dropped off C slightly toward the ball position. X_2 has dropped off a distance from B, as B is two passes from the ball. X_1 and X_4 have dropped off A and D, since A and D are far from the ball.

DIAGRAM 8–5

Tight Man-to-Man. In tight man-to-man defense players play closer to their men than normal, aggressively challenging them if they have the ball. The man playing the dribbler forces him to his weak side, not attempting to steal the ball but maintaining proximity to the man and faking and jabbing at him to stop the dribble. As soon as the dribbler stops, the defender moves in as close to the man as possible, waving his arms aggressively to block his vision, and attempts to overplay him without fouling, to prevent an easy pass. The two defenders nearest the ball handler should overplay their men to prevent their receiving an easy outlet pass. The other defenders should maintain position in their men's passing lanes to prevent them from receiving a pass. If the dribbler does pass off, his defender should immediately drop directly back toward the basket and in the direction that the pass was made, to prevent a reverse cut to the basket by the passer. This is basically a half-court defense, but it can be extended to full-court if the situation warrants.

The tight man-to-man is a good defense for a quick, small team. It would be used first to move the offensive point of attack farther out from its normal position, thus distracting and upsetting offensive movement. It is an excellent late-game defense when trailing. Tight man-to-man can be used effectively against

Diagram 8–6. Tight Man-to-Man Defense against a Two-Three Offense. A has possession of the ball and is dribbling. X_1, his defender, is closer to A than normal and forcing him toward the sideline to cut down on his passing lanes. All other players are guarding their men closely, except X_5, who is guarding E, the man farthest from the ball. X_5 has moved off to be in good intercepting position and to be able to help X_4, who has fronted D, in case of a long lob pass to the basket. X_3 has overplayed C to the ball side to prevent C from receiving the pass. X_2 has overplayed B to the ball side to prevent B from receiving a pass.

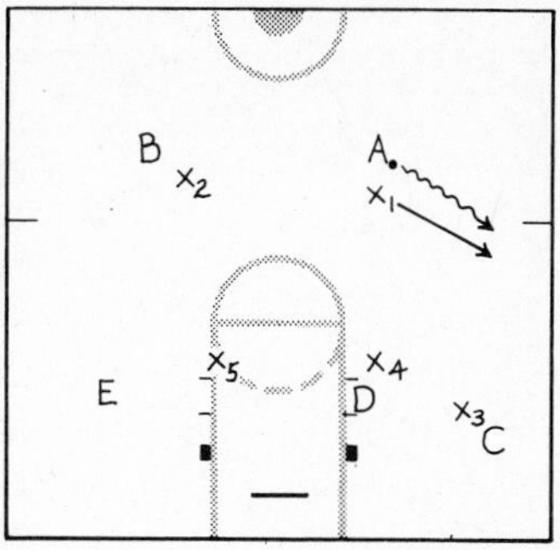

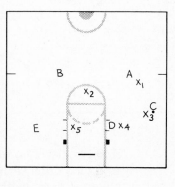

DIAGRAM 8–6

Diagram 8–7 (Continuation of movement in Diagram 8–6). C has come back up toward the ball and received a pass from A. X_3, his defender, has closed in on him aggressively. X_1 is overplaying A on the ball side. X_4 is still in a fronting position on D between D and the ball. X_5 has dropped down to stay between E and the ball, far enough off so as to help X_4 in the event of a lob pass to D over the head of X_4. X_2 has dropped off B, who is two passes from the ball, toward the position of the ball to prevent a cut by B, primarily, and to help X_1 if A should use a reverse cut to the basket. X_3 is in good position to intercept the pass.

DIAGRAM 8–7

a team that has poor ball handlers or against inexperienced teams.

Loose Man-to-Man. The loose man-to-man defense is played, as the name suggests, in a looser fashion than normal man-to-man, with the players collapsing, or sloughing, toward the penetrating area to prevent the ball from reaching that area. The normal pick-up point for any player in a loose man-to-man defense should be at the twenty-one-foot area (indicated by an imaginary semicircle on the court). (See Diagram 8–8.) The head of the key is twenty-one feet from the basket. The dead corners are twenty-five feet from the basket, and a player who is within or close to the twenty-one foot semicircle can effectively cover a player in those shooting areas.

The loose man-to-man is an excellent defense to use against poor outside-shooting opponents, a good cutting team, a team that

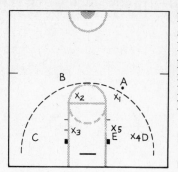

Diagram 8–8. Loose Man-to-Man Defense against a Two-Three Offense. A has the ball. X_1 is on the twenty-one-foot circle, playing A. X_4, playing the corner man, D, has floated off, allowing pass reception. X_5 is fronting the pivot man, E. X_2 has dropped back and is playing B loosely. X_3 is playing C loosely.

DIAGRAM 8–8

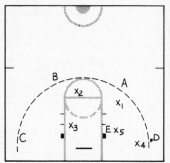

Diagram 8–9 (Continuation of movement in Diagram 8–8). D has received a pass from A. X_4 is playing close to the perimeter, on the baseline side of D. X_1 has dropped off A and is on the ball side, closer to the basket. X_2 has dropped farther off B and is in the foul-line area. X_3 has dropped off C and is in the foul lane. X_5 maintains a fronting position on E.

DIAGRAM 8–9

changes direction to the basket well, or a faster team. It is also good for a taller team that is playing man-to-man defense for good rebounding strength. It places a burden on the offensive team to score from the outside.

Turn-and-Double Man-to-Man Defense. The turn-and-double man-to-man defense is an aggressive double-teaming defense, used in the front court, in which the man guarding the dribbler influences him toward a sideline. As this influencing is taking place, the near defensive guard will cheat toward the dribbler between the man he is guarding and the ball. As soon as the dribbler stops his dribble, his guard forces him to pivot back toward the mid-court line. The guard who is cheating should sprint toward the man with the ball as he is pivoting and attempt to double-team him with the dribbler's defender.

Normally, a player who is double-teamed will attempt to pass in the direction the pressure comes from; therefore, the forward closest to the man who is leaving to make the double-team should move into an intercepting angle between the ball and the teammate's free offensive player. The near forward should play at an intercepting angle. The center should zone between the remaining two offensive opponents, staying closer to the more dangerous of the two.

If the ball is passed to a forward, the double-team would take place between the defensive forward and a guard. Normally, we expect that the two guards or a guard and a forward will be the double-team men, with the center in the middle area using zone defense principles to protect the area near the basket. Intercepting angles are played on offensive players who are one pass from the double team. A zone is played in the basket area by the fifth defender.

If the dribbler can get the ball to a teammate successfully, each defender must pick up the nearest man. The passer must be played by his original defender, and the double-teamer should sprint in toward the basket, because the loose opponent is usually the player farthest from the ball. To negate the offensive opportunities from the mismatch of a small man playing a big corner man, a switch may be necessary between the forward who has come out to pick up the man of the double-teaming guard and the guard who has picked up the far-corner offensive forward.

The best way to effect this switch is to allow the ball to be passed back to the original passer and have the men switch on the pass. This will not hurt the defense because these men are so far from the ball and the basket, and it will allow the defensive team to adjust to this situation and again attack in the turn-and-double posture. Rather than attacking this double-up defense, the offensive team is likely to bring the ball back into a defensive posture in front court. The hashmarks in the front court, the sidelines, and the mid-court line all act in favor of the defense, and forcing a five-second held-ball violation is a distinct possibility using this type of double-teaming. Good intercepting angles and intelligent play by either defensive player guarding the two offensive players closest to the ball result in many interceptions. If the ball reaches one of the men in the off-side area and they have a shot, the defenders should fake at them and allow the shot rather than give up an easy lay-up underneath.

The turn-and-double is an excellent surprise maneuver that is very effective against a taller team with poor ball handlers. It upsets the opponents' planned offensive system and increases the pace of the game. It is an excellent defense to use when behind in the late stages. While turn-and-double defense is a departure from man-to-man defense as it has been played in the past, we feel that it is an asset in certain situations, as it implements the best parts of an aggressive man-to-man defense with some of the thinking of zone defense.

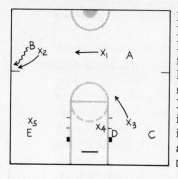

Diagram 8–10. Turn-and-Double Man-to-Man Defense against a Two-Three Offense. Player B has crossed the mid-court line, and his defender, X_2, forces him to dribble toward the sideline. X_1, guarding A, starts to cheat toward the same sideline. X_3 coordinates his movement with X_1 and starts to cheat up toward A's position. E is guarded by X_5 in an intercepting position. X_4 is guarding D, the pivot man opposite the ball, in an overplay position toward the ball.

DIAGRAM 8–10 ————————

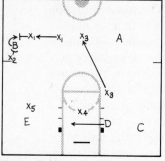

Diagram 8–11 (Continuation of movement in Diagram 8–10). B has stopped his dribble on being forced to the sideline by X_2. As B pivots back toward mid-court, X_1 charges from his mid-court position to double-team him with X_2. X_3 has moved up to an intercepting position between the ball and A. X_5 has overplayed E toward the ball. X_4 has moved to the center of the foul lane at the lower half of the free-throw circle to be in position to defend against D, who is moving across the foul lane, or C, who is the farthest player from the ball.

DIAGRAM 8–11 ————————————————

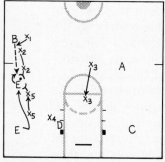

Diagram 8–12 (Continuation of movement in Diagram 8–11). B passes to E, who has faked or made a V into the basket and come back in order to relieve the pressure. Immediately upon this reception, X_5 plays E strongly on the baseline side to make E pivot, and X_2 leaves B, and attacks E from above to effect the double team. X_1 overplays B on the ball side, and X_4 overplays D, who is in the low pivot on the ball side. X_3 has fallen back from his position at an intercepting angle on A to the lower half of the foul circle to discourage a lob pass to D while still having an intercepting angle between A and C in case the ball is thrown cross-court.

DIAGRAM 8–12

Switching Man-To-Man. A switching man-to-man defense is one in which the defensive players switch on every offensive cross, except for a pivot defender. (They never switch on a diagonal cut or a reverse cut, since they would have to stay with the cutter.) If offensive guards are crossing laterally in the back court, a jump switch is very effective. The switching men are usually guards or forwards. If the center must switch while playing a pivot man against a two-three offense, he should call the switch, because his teammates will not be expecting it. If the opponents use an offense with three men out and two in, the defenders should switch on all crosses with all five players.

The switching man-to-man is an extremely effective defense against the weave or an offense using good guard-to-guard or guard-to-forward screens. It confuses the offense, as it looks like a zone defense. The weak-side men would be sagging toward the middle and playing their opponents loosely, with the ball on the weak side. The switching man-to-man is excellent for a team that has one big man and four smaller men. Since the smaller men are constantly exchanging opponents, they are not going to be hurt badly by any disparity in height.

Diagram 8–13. Switching Man-to-Man Defense against a Two-Three Offense. Offensive Guards A and B exchange the ball in the back court. X_1, guarding A, and X_2, guarding B, move together as A dribbles and hands off to B, who is cutting behind him. X_2 and X_1 automatically switch, with X_1 picking up B, who has begun a dribble, and X_2 picking up A. (There is also a good opportunity for X_1 to make a jump switch into the path of B.) X_3 is playing an intercepting angle on C, X_4 is defending D in the low pivot on the ball side, and X_5 has floated toward the center and a little higher, guarding the opposite corner. If B attempts to pass in this situation, there is a good opportunity at interception.

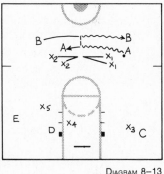

DIAGRAM 8–13

Diagram 8–14 (Continuation of movement in Diagram 8–13). A passes to C, who moves out to meet the ball. A cuts behind C. X_1 moves along the path that A is cutting. X_3 has moved out to guard against C. C starts to dribble, and as A and C cross, X_1 and X_3 automatically exchange guarding assignments, X_3 defending against A and X_1 picking up the dribbler.

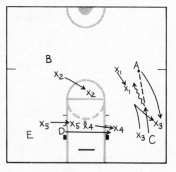

DIAGRAM 8–14

Advantages. The following are positive attributes of the man-to-man defense.

1. It fixes responsibility, issuing a challenge to each player.
2. It enables individual match-ups of opponents based on size, strength, speed, and height.

3. It can force the opposition when they are stalling or when you are behind.

4. It permits effective double-teaming.

5. It affords excellent defensive rebound position, since in most cases the defensive player is inside his offensive opponent.

6. It permits better preparation of each individual, since the coach can tell him the strong points and weaknesses of the single opponent he is to guard.

7. It makes good use of the fundamentals, providing they were taught properly.

8. It places high premium on good conditioning.

9. Pressure man-to-man defense allows for good fast-break opportunities.

10. It is adaptable to any opponent's offense, especially a delayed or wide-spread offensive system.

11. It can be used full-court to increase the game tempo.

12. It can be used in all situations during a game or during a season, changing only the team attitude (that is, tight, loose, half-court, full-court, etc.).

13. It makes it possible to recognize good individual defensive play, so the coach can credit the player publicly for his efforts.

Disadvantages. Before choosing man-to-man defense, the coach should assess the following negative characteristics in relation to his personnel.

1. It is much tougher on the individual physically, requiring excellent stamina and top condition.

2. Mismatches in size during switching maneuvers or an inability to match the opponents individually hurts the team.

3. It is ineffective against a good screening and cutting team.

4. It requires excellent fundamental ability and mental attitude on the part of each player.

5. Players are more prone to fouls using this defense.

6. It allows the opponents to exploit the poor defensive man by isolating him.

7. It requires flexibility in men who must switch during screening tactics.

8. In addition to their individual responsibilities, players must be aware of team responsibilities.

9. It requires extremely good knowledge of defensive fundamentals.

10. A normal or loose man-to-man defense may not be a good fast-break defense.

11. Overconcentration by a player hurts the team posture, as does a weak, overmatched man.

12. It requires a great deal of teaching time.

Run-And-Jump Defense. Possibly the most significant trend to develop in defensive basketball during the seventies was the emergence of a man-to-man style known as run-and-jump defense. Although radically different from most of the other forms of man-to-man defense presently in use, run-and-jump techniques have become an accepted part of basketball's ever-expanding body of knowledge.

Run-and-jump defense has been described as "trapping defense without trapping." Basically, run-and-jump defense is a kind of pressure man-to-man defense with automatic switching in which the dribbler is influenced toward a certain area of the court, then picked up by another defender who applies intense defensive pressure as the original defender completes the switch by covering his teammate's man.

Surprise is an important factor in the success of run-and-jump defense, and the technique requires skilled, experienced players. Still, two important aspects of the defense can serve to make it viable as a full-time defense rather than as a surprise tactic. First, a team can play its regular half-court man-to-man defense except against baseline drives, or it can use sideline-influence defensive techniques to set up the run-and-jump sequence. Second, even when the offensive team anticipates the run-and-jump, the ball handler still must find the open man, which can be difficult when the defense varies either the location of the run-and-jump or the player effecting the run-and-jump.

Sideline/baseline influence. As a rule, teams using run-and-jump defense use sideline-influence techniques in pressing full- or three-quarter-court, and they use baseline-influence techniques in their half-court defense. Although sideline-influence techniques could conceivably be used in a half-court run-and-jump context, most coaches prefer to play regular (i.e., sagging or pressure) man-to-man defense in their defensive half-court, using run-and-jump only when the opponents' ball handlers drive the baseline. Rather than influencing the dribbler away from the middle of the court and toward the sideline, and at the same time playing the passing lanes to deny reversals or passes that would enable the ball handler to avoid having to dribble toward the sideline, most run-and-jump teams will use one of the following two techniques: (1) they will play their normal man-to-man

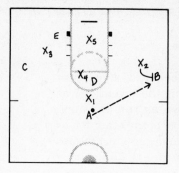

Diagram 8–15. Setting up the Baseline Drive, Run-and-Jump Defense. A has the ball beyond the point, guarded more or less loosely by X_1. X_4 is overguarding D at high post, and X_2 and X_3 are playing off B and C at the wings. The defenders are in control, if not actively controlling the offensive team, and they are looking for an opportunity to set up a run-and-jump situation. The opportunity arises when A passes to B.

DIAGRAM 8–15

defense until an offensive player attempts to drive the baseline, at which time they will automatically move into run-and-jump coverage, or (2) they will set up situations in which the dribbler or pass receiver is overplayed in such a manner that he thinks the baseline drive is open when in fact it is not.

In regular man-to-man coverage, X_3 and X_5 will sag away from their men, X_4 will continue to overguard D, X_1 will sag away from A and slightly toward the ball, and X_2 will move toward B, in a position directly between B and the basket. However, if the defenders are attempting to set up a run-and-jump situation when A passes to B, X_1 will move into the passing lane between A and B to deny B's return pass to A, and X_2 will move closer to B, but will position himself between B and the middle of the half-court. In this situation, B cannot risk a pass to any of his overplayed teammates, and his only open dribbling routes are toward the half-court line and the baseline. Since the former is unproductive for any reason except to reset the offense or continue a delay pattern, B is likely to accept X_2's invitation to drive the baseline.

If B's baseline move is slow and controlled, the run-and-jump will not occur, since it is both unnecessary and unlikely to catch the ball handler by surprise. Defenders should never switch if they do not have to: switching is, or should be, a reaction to loss or reduction of defensive control, and if the dribbler is not aggressively attacking the defensive team's apparent baseline weakness, his controlled movements may permit him to find the open man before the run-and-jump is completed. However, if B makes a strong move toward the baseline in reacting to X_2's overplaying, the stage is set for implementing the run-and-jump switch.

Diagram 8–16. Run-and-Jump Defense, Base-line. When B attempts the baseline drive, X_2 stays as close to him as possible, but without making any real effort to cut off his route to the basket. (He may, however, attempt to force B into a wide route before turning the corner toward the basket.) When X_5 sees B making his move toward the baseline, he will slide farther away from his man (E) and prepare to jump into position to stop B's drive (and perhaps draw a charging foul as well). If B is caught by surprise, he will pick up his dribble immediately, since as far as he knows he is being trapped by X_2 and X_5. X_5 will do everything in his power to deny B's pass from the baseline, particularly to E at weak-side low post. Meanwhile, X_2 continues across the lane to pick up E.

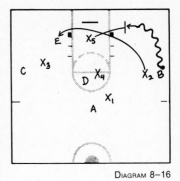

DIAGRAM 8–16

What does the defense hope to accomplish by the run-and-jump coverage? Turnovers, mostly. If B is moving at high speed when he picks up his dribble, he may commit a charging foul or traveling violation, or else he may throw the ball away. The only unguarded player in Diagram 8–16 is E, and B's pass must get by X_5, X_2, the rim and the net. Such a pass made at high speed is dangerous, to say the least, as the passing lane will not be open if X_2 and X_5 are trapping rather than switching. (If the defense is trapping, X_3 will drop low to cut off the baseline pass, X_1 will cut off passes along the ball-side perimeter, X_4 will continue to overguard D, and C will be the only offensive player left unguarded.) Thus, B has only a fraction of a second to determine whether the defense is switching (in which case he should pass to E at low post) or trapping (in which case he should pass to C). And if B has been forced wide before turning the corner, he will have to avoid committing a charging foul before he decides to whom he must pass. (If B is permitted to drive at a controlled speed, he will almost certainly be able to avoid the charge and find his open teammate.)

The defense can make the coverage even more effective by varying the player responsible for cutting off the dribbler—for example, by using a weak-side guard or forward, as shown in Diagram 8–17.

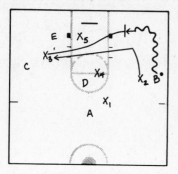

Diagram 8–17. Run-and-Jump Defense, Varying the Baseline Coverage. When B attempts to drive the baseline, X_2 tries to force him as wide as possible before he turns the corner and drives to the basket. Instead of X_5 coming across to effect the run-and-jump, however, weak-side wing defender X_3 moves across the lane and into B's path to the basket.

DIAGRAM 8–17 _____

Coaches may have any of several reasons for preferring X_3 to X_5 in making the run-and-jump switch: X_3 may be a better defensive player than X_5; B may not be able to find C as easily as he can find E along the baseline; or the coach may simply want to vary the coverage to give his defense a different look. Whatever the case, X_3—or any other weak-side defender covering an offen-

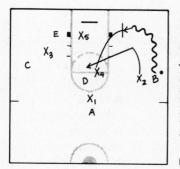

Diagram 8–18. High-Post Man Making the Run-and-Jump Movement. When the defense elects to have the high-post defender run-and-jump to stop the baseline drive, it had better be pretty sure of stopping the drive and the pass, since D, cutting to the basket from high post, is likely to have a tremendous size advantage over X_2 if B is able to dump the ball off before the run-and-jump is completed.

DIAGRAM 8–18 _____

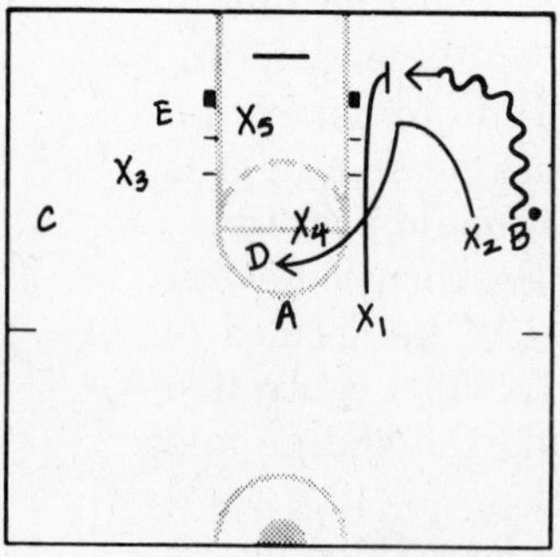

Diagram 8–19. Run-and-Jump with a Defensive Guard. Personally, we prefer the idea of having one of the guards run-and-jump. In our stack offense, we simplified our ball-handling responsibilities by having the point guard do most of the dribbling necessary to set the pattern in motion. In like manner, the defensive guard, X_1, is a primary candidate for the position of run-and-jumper: his movement to the basket begins at a point behind B as B faces the baseline in beginning his drive. Too, when X_1 steps into position to stop B's drive, B may have a hard time finding A before a held ball is called—and even if A fills B's wing position and B is able to pass back to A, the defense has given up nothing worse than the shot from the wing.

DIAGRAM 8–19

sive player along the perimeter—is a logical choice for making the run-and-jump switch, since the first player B will look for when a defender comes across to stop his drive is E under the basket.

Installing a run-and-jump defensive attack. At the risk of overstating the obvious, perhaps we should point out that the one-three-one offensive alignment shown in Diagrams 8–15 through 8–19 is used merely to illustrate the variations of run-and-jump defensive coverage available from that alignment. The actual court positions occupied by the offensive players may vary considerably from that shown in the diagrams. Still, most offensive systems require a degree of court balance—one or more players on strong side, one or more players away from the ball, one or more players in the mid-court area to rotate the ball to weak side and serve as a deterrent to the opponent's fast break when transition occurs, and possibly one or more players occupying the post areas—and the coach intending to implement run-and-jump coverage can use offensive court balance in deciding who to use in effecting the run-and-jump movement. Will he use the nearest weak-side defender inside (X_5 in the diagrams), or the defender at high post (X_4 in the diagrams)? They are the most obvious candidates, since they are closest to the play, but the resultant height mismatches may be a deterrent. Should he use a weak-side outside defender (X_3 in the diagrams) or the defender in the rotation-pass area (X_1 in the diagrams)? These players have a longer distance to run to position themselves to stop B's drive without fouling or surrendering the lay-up, but three factors may serve to make them even better candidates for the job than the inside defenders. First, the dribbler may not be able to see them among the other, taller players on both teams until it is too late for him to stop or avoid a charging foul. Second, even if he sees them in time to stop, he may not be able to find the open man and pass the ball away. And third, they may be the the most capable or experienced defenders on the team.

The last point merits closer attention. If a coach has a smart, hard-nosed player who doesn't mind the contact and really likes to draw charging fouls, he's a logical candidate to make the run-and-jump play any time an opponent drives, regardless of his court position. The coach doesn't even have to tell the team that he's using run-and-jump defense at any given time; he can just tell the player to run-and-jump whenever he feels that he can draw the charging foul. The player should use discretion, of course, but if he's a smart player he should be able to pick his spots without difficulty.

In installing a run-and-jump system, the coach must first decide where and when to set up the confrontation: Should it be near the half-court corner on the dribbler's right-hand side (so he'll have to reverse pivot to his right to pass the ball away) in full-court pressing defense? Or along the baseline on the right side in half-court defense—again, to force the dribbler to pivot to his left before attempting to pass the ball away? Once such guidelines have been set, the defenders will play their regular style of defense any time the ball handler is not being influenced toward the designated spot. This provides a measure of variability to the defense, in the same way that some teams use full-court pressure defense to surprise opponents, then abandon it until later in the game so the opponents won't grow accustomed to it.

In deciding who should be involved in the run-and-jump, coaches generally designate a specific player or a specific position. If one player excels in drawing charging fouls, he will always be the run-and-jumper. If not, the coach will designate a specific position (e.g., weak-side low post, weak-side wing) as the run-and-jump position, and whatever defender is occupying that position will make the play when the sideline/baseline drive occurs.

Perhaps the greatest strengths of the run-and-jump technique lie in its versatility. Run-and-jump defense is not a team's style of defense; rather, it is part of a team's overall style of defensive play. It can be as active or passive as the coach desires, actively setting up run-and-jump situations or merely reacting to offensive advantages as they arise. And if the run-and-jump coverage brings about two or three charging fouls or turnovers early in the game, opponents sometimes become reluctant to go hard to the basket even when the defense is not in position to run-and-jump.

Run-and-jump techniques are also used sometimes in full-court pressing defenses.

Zone Defense

The basic philosophy of zone defense is that every defensive player is responsible for a designated defensive floor area, primarily determined by the position of the ball. Each player faces the ball and moves in unison with each ball movement, adjusting position continuously as the ball position moves. Though the ball is of primary importance, position of offensive players must also be considered. A cut through the zone toward the ball, or an offensive player stationed in the low- or medium-pivot area inside the zone perimeter, would alter basic defensive movement.

Defensive movement depends on player reception of a pass. If the potential receiver is in a position to score, the nearest defender should prevent him from getting the ball, intercepting it, if possible. All players should position themselves where they will give the opponent the least advantage, defending from the basket area out. When the ball is passed to a position behind one of the front-line defensive players, he should move toward the basket until he can regain sight of the ball, at the same time concentrating on offensive player deployment in the immediate area. He should always permit the outside shot rather than allowing the ball to go to a player behind him in better shooting position.

The fundamental stance taken by a player in a zone defense is higher than the basic man-to-man boxer crouch, and the arms are widespread and windmilling to present an apparently impenetrable barrier to the attacking offensive player.

The zone defense lends itself to ideal placement of defenders according to physical and mental attributes. Taller, less agile players can be positioned near the basket to cut down their defensive movement, improve the defensive rebounding effort of the team, limit pivot playing by tall opponents, and negate the cutting opportunities of smaller opponents. The faster, usually smaller, players can be placed in the outside positions of a zone where they may have a wider defensive latitude in forcing the ball, attempting interception, and harassing the opponent more aggressively than they would if they were in a standard man-to-man defense.

The zone defense is easier to teach, and it can cover up weak man-to-man fundamentals in individuals that cannot be overcome because of lack of coordination or lack of speed. It allows room for intelligent, aggressive defensive imagination in the quicker players. Players in a zone defense are less afraid of mistakes, as they feel there is somebody behind them to help minimize the effects of a mistake. Each player has a chance to intercept the ball and gain an offensive advantage. All zone defenses have inherent weaknesses and vulnerable areas. It is incumbent on the defensive team to limit vulnerability to areas outside the zone perimeter and to influence the offense into the less vulnerable areas.

The penetration of the perimeter of a zone defense is the first sign of weakness in any zone. Because of the shifting essential to floor coverage, the zone loses its original shape after the first or second pass, and all types of zones tend to look alike. Thereafter, coordinated team movement is essential to maintain the restrictiveness of the zone. Zones contract and expand with ball and offensive player movement.

Zones have a tendency to overextend toward the ball in the corners and at forty-five-degree angles from the basket, allowing the offense to penetrate the back line by maneuvering from the side away from the ball or by cutting inside the zone paralleling the path of a pass. The back men must vocally warn overenthusiastic teammates when they overextend and distort the zone making it unnecessarily pregnable to these maneuvers by opponents.

Important Factors in the Use of a Zone Defense. The basic principle of protecting certain territories while shifting and concentrating on areas attacked is intrinsic in the zone defense. The zone allows much more liberty defensively. All players must move continuously, using their hands or feet to block passes that attempt to penetrate the zone. The player who is closest to the ball in good offensive territory must attack it aggressively, using good fundamental man-to-man principles and attempting to force a pass back to a protected area far from the basket or to hurry the shot. The change from defense to offense coordinates quickly, and a team can fast-break immediately from the basic defensive zone positions. The equally important change from offense to defense can also be effected quickly.

Players in a zone defense can play in front of, or to the side of, a player close to the basket on the ball side, as a defensive teammate is behind this opponent. Moving offensive players are guarded successively by various defenders as they sift through the zone. A player may leave his area open to protect a territory or uncovered offensive player close to the basket. Intelligent anticipation leads to interceptions. Offensive players moving away from the ball may seem to be weakening their position, while actually they are anticipating the ball's movement to the other side of the court. With good defensive anticipation alert defenders may intercept passes, creating good fast-break opportunities.

Zone defenses may be aggressive or passive. They should be used with caution when a team is behind in the score or when the team is playing against good long shooters or good ball handlers. If the zone is to be used when behind, it must be aggressive to force ball-handling mistakes and hurried shots.

Whether a zone defense is aggressive or passive is generally determined by the personnel, the opponents, the score, and the time remaining. A zone allows the most advantageous positioning of players, with the tall players under the basket and the quick players chasing in good position to inaugurate the fast break. The front line of a zone should be fast and aggressive; the back line taller with the better rebounders. A zone may send three, four, or five players to rebound at the defensive backboard. If five play-ers are sent, the zone is passive, or defensive.

If four defensive players move aggressively to the defensive backboard, maintaining position in front of offensive players and blocking them out, and the fifth defender sneaks toward the of-fensive end when the opponents shoot, at least one (normally two) offensive player will fall back defensively. Since only three op-ponents will be rebounding, the defenders will have an advantage. If the ball is rebounded by the defensive team and gets up the court fast, good penetration is possible at the offensive end.

Interceptions and steals by aggressive front-line players (who normally are the fastest) lead to quick baskets by the front-line players. Back-line defenders must stay close to an opponent near the ball. They should never let offensive opponents split them defensively near the ball. No player in a zone defense should ever guard an empty area or zone. It is important that the back men act as quarterbacks, directing the zone vocally to the strong or overloaded offensive side. All players defending in a zone should be aware of the imaginary semicircle twenty-one feet from the basket. Unless an aggressive zone is called for, defenders should stay within this semicircle or on its circumference with arms extended, either up or to the sides, to deter and upset op-ponents, because twenty-one feet is the limit of the high-per-centage shooting range for the majority of basketball players.

The floor markings pinpoint various areas of the court and help players determine their distance from the basket:

1. The head of the key is twenty-one feet from the basket.
2. A player taking one defensive slide and a step from either end of the foul line will be twenty-one feet from the basket.
3. A player taking three defensive slides and a step from the middle of foul-lane restraining lines will be twenty-one feet from the basket.
4. Both deep corners are twenty-five feet from the basket.

A disadvantage in a zone defense is that a moving, aggres-sive offensive rebounder can outmaneuver stationary defensive players for position. Often, defensive players in a zone back line turn in position and expect the rebound to come to them. If they do not look for a player on the offensive team to box out, the moving opponents will outposition them.

Types of Zone Defense. Zone defenses are classified by the alignment of the players from the front of the line in the area toward mid-court back toward the basket. The one-two-two zone, for example, has one player toward the center of the court, two players in the back line near the basket, and two players between the front line and the back line. The two types used today are those that have an odd front and those that have an even front.

The odd-front zones include the one-two-two zone, a one-three-one zone, and a three-two zone. The even zones are the two-one-two zone, the two-two-one zone, and the two-three zone.

One-two-two zone defense. The one-two-two zone defense has strength in the middle- and low-pivot areas. It is simple to use as the slides are basic and uncomplicated.

In Diagram 8–20, X_1, the quickest player, should be given latitude of movement within the zone setup. X_2 and X_3 should be agile and fairly tall. X_4 and X_5 should be the best rebounders, with X_5 the least coordinated of the two. X_1, X_2, or X_3 must maintain rebound position when the opponents shoot. There are good sneak-away opportunities for X_1 when the opponents shoot. The possibility of this maneuver will take one or two offensive players away from the backboard. X_4 or X_5 must guard the medium-pivot man in the opposite pivot area during ball movement. This leaves the one-two-two zone vulnerable from behind or from the weak side unless quick adjustments are made.

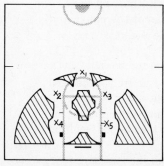

Diagram 8–20. One-Two-Two Zone Defense Alignment. Shaded areas indicate vulnerability. The initial positions are X_1 at the head of the key, X_2 and X_3 at the ends of the foul line on either side, and X_4 and X_5 straddling the foul lanes approximately six feet in front of the basket.

Diagram 8–20 _____

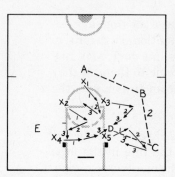

Diagram 8–21. One-Two-Two Zone Defense Movement. The slides made by each defender as the ball is passed from A to B (1) to C (2) to D (3) are numbered.

Diagram 8–21 _____

One-three-one zone defense. The one-three-one zone defense attempts to keep three defensive players in line between the ball and the basket by flexing with the passing movement of the ball. This zone is strong in all pivot areas, under the basket, and against medium jump shooters. It is weak against good outside-angle shooters and in the corners and is susceptible to baseline drives. Because of the positioning of the two big rebounders, there are rebounding difficulties in this zone.

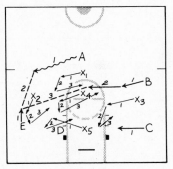

Diagram 8–22. One-Three-One Zone Defense Alignment. Shaded areas indicate vulnerability. X_1, the first guard, should be very quick and aggressive and should be given latitude for imaginative anticipation. He can sneak away when offense shoots. The wing men, X_2 and X_3, must be active. X_3 should be the second guard; X_2 the quickest forward; X_4 the slower, taller forward; and X_5 the center. X_5's position is good for big, uncoordinated players who are good rebounders.

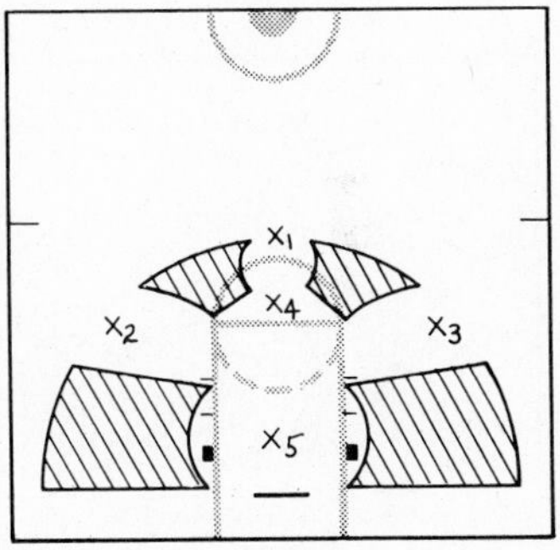

———————————————————— DIAGRAM 8–22

Diagram 8–23. One-Three-One Zone Defense Movement. Slides by defense are numbered as (1) A dribbles; (2) A passes to E; and (3) E passes to B. Each movement is indicated by an arrow with a number on the line. X_1, X_2, X_3, X_4, and X_5 are the defense; A, B, C, D, and E are the offense.

———————————————————— DIAGRAM 8–23

Three-two zone defense. The strength of the three-two zone defense lies in the mobility of its front line, which must attack opponents aggressively, attempting to cause misplays, violations, and bad passes. It is an excellent defense to fast break from. In Diagram 8–24, X_1, X_2, and X_3 should be the quickest players, because they are expected to make the most defensive movements and slides. X_1 is responsible for the foul-lane area. X_2 and X_3 are responsible for the weak-side medium and low areas near the basket when the ball is on the opposite side of the court. Against taller teams, X_1, X_2, and X_3 should play to the ball, doubling up when possible. This zone is weak in the medium-pivot areas and in the side areas when there is a pivot player. It needs rebound help from X_1, X_2, or X_3, and the back of the zone is vulnerable to quick movement from the corners. This zone is weak underneath, in the corners, and behind the front line if retreating movement by the front line isn't forthcoming. X_1 should be the quickest forward, as he has to drop into the middle foul-lane area frequently and he is the front-line player most likely to be in best rebound position. X_2 and X_3 should be the guards; X_4, the second forward; and X_5 the center.

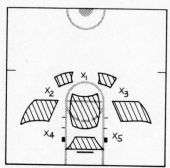

Diagram 8–24. Three-Two Zone Defense Alignment. Shaded areas indicate vulnerability.

DIAGRAM 8–24 _____

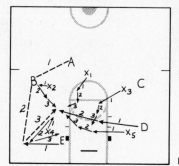

Diagram 8–25. Three-Two Zone Defense Movement. Slides by defense are numbered as ball is passed from (1) A to B, (2) B to E, and (3) E to D. The arrows indicate slides by the defensive players X_1 through X_5.

DIAGRAM 8–25 _____

Two-one-two zone defense. The two-one-two zone defense is strong underneath the basket, in the rebounding-triangle area, against good pivot men, and in the foul-line area. It is a good defense from which to fast break, as it allows one man, usually X_1, to break as soon as the offensive team shoots. It is vulnerable from the weak side along the baseline, from jump shooters on the side at forty-five-degree angles, from medium shooting areas, and from the top of the key.

Diagram 8–26. Two-One-Two Zone Defense Alignment. Shaded areas indicate vulnerability. X_1 and X_2 are fast, aggressive guards, X_3 is the center, X_4 is the best rebounding forward, and X_5 is the more mobile forward.

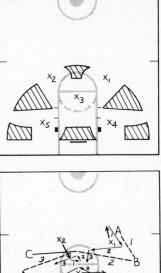

DIAGRAM 8–26

Diagram 8–27. Two-One-Two Zone Defense Movement. Slides by defense are numbered as the ball is passed. Initial adjustments by defensive players X_1 through X_5 are indicated by an unnumbered arrow. Arrows numbered 1, 2, and 3 indicate the slides they make during each pass. Movements by offensive players are also indicated by arrows. A, with the ball, has started at the offensive left-side area. The ball is passed (1) from A to B; (2) from B to C, who has moved into the high-pivot area; and (3) from C to E, who has moved up from the baseline-side offensive right corner.

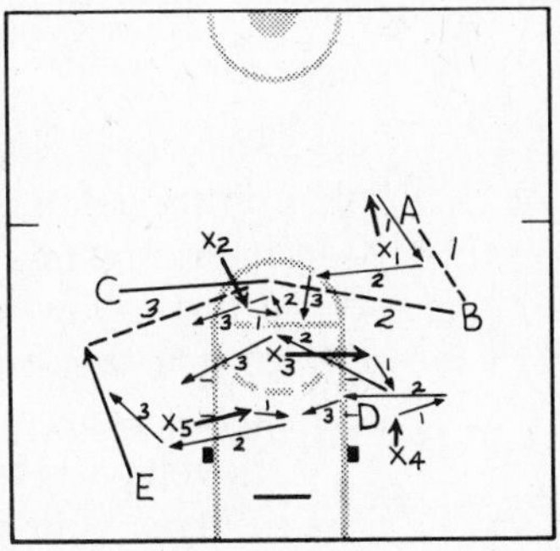

DIAGRAM 8–27

Two-two-one zone defense. The two-two-one zone defense is a very good basic defense from which to employ half-court trapping procedures.

There are excellent fast-break opportunities from this zone, and it is good against close shots and jumpers. It is weak at the top of the key, so the two front men must sag to prevent good shooting opportunities from this area. This is an aggressive defense that can be used well by a small, fast team with one big rebounder.

Diagram 8–28. Two-Two-One Zone Defense Alignment. Shaded areas indicate vulnerability. X_5 should be a big man and a good rebounder.

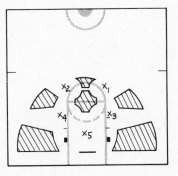

DIAGRAM 8–28

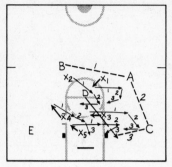

DIAGRAM 8–29

Diagram 8–29. Two-Two-One Zone Defense Movement. Arrows numbered 1, 2, and 3 indicate the defensive slides as the ball is passed (1) from B, backcourt at the offensive right side of the zone, to A; (2) from A to C; and (3) from C to D. D has moved from the foul line to a low-pivot area on the left offensive side. The unnumbered arrows originating at the defensive players indicate initial adjustment by the defense from their original positions to compensate for the ball's being on the offensive right-side backcourt.

Two-three zone defense. The two-three zone is an excellent rebounding defense with good sneak-away possibilities for X_1 or X_2. The zone lends itself to a fast-break type of offense. It is very strong in the low- and medium-pivot areas against a good pivot player. It is weak at the side, at the foul line, and in the high-pivot areas, especially against jump shooters at the top of the key.

Played passively by a team that is ahead or wishes to protect a key player who has four fouls, this defense prevents offensive penetration into good medium or close-in shooting position. Good outside shooting is the only offense that can beat it. It presents excellent double-teaming opportunities if the guards are aggressive enough.

Two-three-zone aggressive defense with traps. The two-three aggressive zone with traps requires determination, intelligent anticipation, and vigorous execution of the necessary slides. Players must be active and animated—their arms and hands held high, ready and probing, closing the passing lanes—and they must use vocal commands and warnings to teammates. The back line must direct the front-line players to the strong side of the offensive

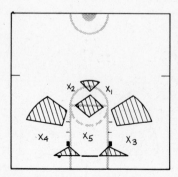

DIAGRAM 8–30

Diagram 8–30. Two-Three Zone Defense Alignment. Shaded areas indicate vulnerability. X_1 and X_2 are aggressive guards. X_3 and X_4 are the forwards, X_3 being the better rebounder. X_5 is the center.

Diagram 8–31. Two-Three Zone Defense Movement. Arrows numbered 1, 2, and 3 indicate slides by the defense as the ball passes (1) from B to C; (2) from C to D, and (3) from D to A. D has crossed from one side to the opposite side medium-pivot position. The unnumbered arrows leading from defenders indicate their initial adjustments to the offensive right necessitated by B's dribbling to his right before passing.

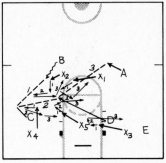

DIAGRAM 8–31

X_2's first sliding move is made at right angles, toward the baseline, to the pivot position, paralleling the foul lane before moving out toward C's position with the ball. If X_2 had taken a direct route to this position, he would have left a passing lane open into D, who moved quickly and assumed the pivot position. As X_2 moves, X_1 slides from his position on the far side at the top of the key to a cut-off position on D, thus negating the possibility of a pass into this area. X_2 and X_1 should move in when they are in a balanced position at the top of the key, because the greater danger emanates from the ball's penetrating the perimeter rather than from an outside shot from C, who is approximately twenty-one feet from the basket.

formation to prevent a high-pivot player from getting the ball. (In this type of zone the high pivot must be pinched from in front and in back.) The men in the front line have great latitude in forcing the ball. They can move out toward the center and influ-

Diagram 8–32. Two-Three-Zone Aggressive Defense Using Double-Teaming. Defenders are in their original positions, X_1 and X_2 at the head of the key area, X_5 just below the broken line of the lower half of the free-throw circle, and X_3 and X_4 in the low-wing positions. A has the ball out front at the top of the key. X_3 sees that there are four defensive players to his left and calls, "Strong side left." X_1 immediately shifts to the head of the key, and X_2 moves toward B. X_4 maintains his position. X_3 slides up toward the foul-lane area, and X_5 comes up to cover D. Arrows indicate this movement. X_1 should drop off from his position so that D is pinched from the front and the back.

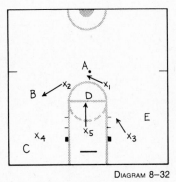

DIAGRAM 8–32

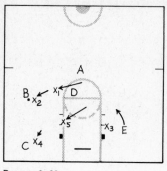

DIAGRAM 8–33

Diagram 8–33. Aggressive Two-Three Zone (Continued). A has passed to B. The arrows moving into the defensive positions indicate the sliding maneuvers of the zone to shift with the ball position. X_1 moves from the top of the key to front the pivot man, D, on the ball side. X_5 moves from the foul lane to the medium-pivot area. X_4 drops back as C drops back. X_2 moves toward B to challenge the ball. X_3 plays an intercepting angle on E. If D slides to medium- or low-pivot position, X_5 fronts him. X_4 is positioned to help X_2 at the ball location and to play C should he receive a pass.

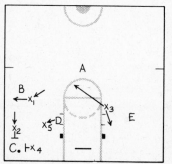

DIAGRAM 8–34

Diagram 8–34. Aggressive Two-Three Zone (Continued). B has passed to C. C's corner position indicates a good trapping situation. On C's reception X_4, the baseline trapper, and X_2, the side trapper, are in trapping position, X_2 having moved with the pass. X_1 moves from the free-throw-circle area to an overplaying position on B to deny him a pass. X_5 fronts D in the pivot area. X_3 should anticipate C's pass-out direction by observing his eye or arm movement. X_3 has good intercepting angle if he can anticipate a pass from C to A, but if he miscalculates, a pass to E will result in an easy basket. The trap will be effective if all five defenders coordinate their movements.

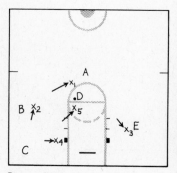

DIAGRAM 8–35

Diagram 8–35. Aggressive Two-Three Zone (Continued). C has made an outlet pass to D, who has moved from the medium-pivot area to the high-pivot area in the outer half of the free-throw circle. X_1 pressures the ball, moving from the position he had on B (in Diagram 8–34) to a high position on D. X_5 has slid up the foul lane to a low, aggressive, attacking position. X_4 must drop toward the foul lane to protect against movement in this area by D if he can get around X_5. X_2 and X_3 must be alert. X_2 has moved from the double-team on C to a position inside of B. X_3 must be aware of the weak-side potential of E and his under-the-basket possibilities.

ence the ball handler to the left or right side so that the initial pass will be made into a sideline area, allowing for double-teaming or trapping in these areas. When a trap is sprung in a corner, the far defensive player must anticipate a pass by observing the arm and head movements of the player in the trap with the ball. The back-line men must be constantly aware that this defense starts from the basket out and never allow anyone into the low basket area who is not covered by a defender.

Diagram 8–36. Aggressive Two-Three Zone (Continued). D passes to E at a weak-side outlet position. X_3 moves out cautiously on E. X_5 moves from the high-pivot position to a low, protective pivot position on the ball side. X_1 moves across the pivot lane, continuing to front D, the pivot player. X_5 must be conscious of the open low-pivot area. He is alerted by X_4, who calls that C has moved to the opposite low-pivot position. X_2 moves high toward the ball side. X_4, moving protectively into the center of the foul lane, low, must be aware of the possibility of B's cutting behind him to the basket or splitting the zone defenders by moving into the middle area to the medium pivot on the strong side. _____

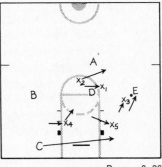

DIAGRAM 8–36

Diagram 8–37. Aggressive Two-Three Zone (Continued). E, on the left side offensively, has passed to C, who has moved from the low-pivot position to the corner. Normally, C would receive this pass moving toward the sideline with his back to the basket area and would have to pivot to make a move toward the basket. His corner position indicates a good trapping situation. X_3 moves to the baseline trap position with the pass. His responsibility is first to prevent the baseline drive and second to apply the baseline low trap. X_1 moves off the high pivot quickly to assume the sideline high-trap position. X_2 moves to cut off a passing lane to E. X_5 delays his move until X_3 reaches the baseline position then moves up on D, fronting him in this pivot position and cutting off a passing lane. X_4, at the weak-side foul lane, anticipates a long pass to A (by observing C's arm or eye movement) and may move to intercept it. Since he is the last line of defense, he must be ready to drop back if X_3 does not contain C. X_5 moves up to front D. _____

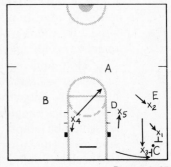

DIAGRAM 8–37

Help-and-Recover Defense. Most forms of zone defense are designed to provide defensive control of the basket area. With capable inside defenders, a team may be able to match up with opponents and single-guard low post. With small or inexperienced inside defenders, however, the low post may require double-teaming in certain ball positions, in which case the offensive team is likely to achieve an open perimeter shot by overloading one side of the court and then rotating the ball quickly to weak side.

When a team is forced, or decides, to double-team the low-post position, it obviously cannot also cover the ball, ball-side corner, high post, and weak side; thus, the coach must either decide which outside shot he is willing to give up or drill his players in help-and-recover defensive techniques to deny the open outside shot without surrendering defensive control inside.

Although help-and-recover defensive techniques can be used in either zone or man-to-man defense, they are generally considered to be more effective when applied to zone defense. Basically, help-and-recover defense is an extremely conservative style of zone coverage in which the defensive team attempts to deny the opponents ball entry into the low-post area and lane, while at the same time denying the opponents access to the perimeter shooting areas that so often make inside double-teaming impractical. There is nothing fancy about help-and-recover defense. Because it combines the best of two defenses—the increased inside coverage of zone defense with the pressure on the perimeter shooter found in man-to-man defense—help-and-recover defense can be a most formidable obstacle for opponents used to leisurely picking apart zone defenses with patient ball and player rotation.

Help-and-recover defense is relatively easy to learn and easy to operate—assuming, of course, that the players are willing to hustle. This defense is seen most often with teams composed of small, quick, aggressive players. While many styles of zone defense can be adapted to a certain extent to compensate for players who are either unwilling or unable to play defense aggressively, two styles of defense (trapping and help-and-recover) require aggressive players to be successful, since both styles feature double coverage that leaves one or more offensive players open at least momentarily.

While help-and-recover defense may be effected from any zone defensive alignment, the one-two-two, three-two, and two-one-two alignments are generally considered the most productive. Of these, the one-two-two is used more than the others, because it keeps four defenders within fifteen feet of the basket regardless of the location of the ball.

Teams using help-and-recover techniques will not double-team the low post in their original alignment. (If they did, a one-two-two zone would have only one player—the point guard—outside, with four players covering the low-post positions on either side.) Similarly, they will not double-team inside when the ball is at the wing, except when the opponents' big man is outstanding enough to require double-teaming anywhere he goes inside.

Diagram 8–38. Help-and-Recover Defense, Corner Coverage. When C passes to D in the corner, X_3 drops back toward low post, and X_4 moves near the edge of the lane to form a double-team on E. X_5 covers D along the baseline, playing him slightly toward the middle to force his drive toward the baseline, where he will be trapped by X_5 and X_4, with X_3 (or possibly X_2) picking up E if D drives. X_1, the point guard, is covering the ball-side high-post area. (If D drives the baseline, and X_2 moves across to pick up E, X_1 will cover B. This strategy will be worked out in advance by the coach.) X_2 is presently the only weak-side defender.

DIAGRAM 8–38

Diagram 8–39. Help-and-Recover Defense, Covering the Rotation Passes from the Corner. When D passes to C, X_3 moves out to guard C, and X_5 drops back to guard low post. C passes to A. X_1, covering the high-post position, cannot get to A in time to stop A's penetration unless he has help. This help will come from X_2, who takes a step or two toward A to stop his penetration and then moves quickly to his left to pick up B as X_1 arrives to cover A. On paper perhaps this may not appear to be a particularly effective defensive move, but without it X_4 would have to cover B in ball rotation. X_2 is a more likely candidate to cover B, since he has less distance to travel even after bluffing toward A. When A passes to B, X_2 will move into a close guarding position, and if B attempts to drive the baseline, X_4 will trap him with X_2.

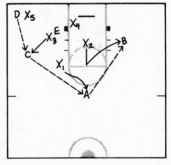

DIAGRAM 8–39

Sometimes X_2 may not have to help-and-recover for X_1. X_2 may merely cover A, with X_4 moving across the lane to cover (or help-and-recover) B. Still, without help-and-recover techniques as part of their defensive repertoire, the defenders are likely to find themselves giving up many open perimeter shots they'd prefer to deny.

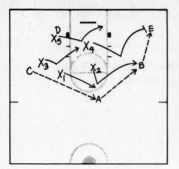

DIAGRAM 8-40

Diagram 8-40. Double Help-and-Recover Movement. C has the ball. When C passes to A, X_2 bluffs toward A, then slides to his left to pick up B. A passes to B, and X_4 bluffs toward B, then slides to his left to cover E in the corner. These two movements enable first X_1, and then X_2, to pick up their men before A or B can take advantage of the overload to penetrate or take the open shot.

When A passes to B, and when B passes to E, X_1, X_3, and X_5 will have already begun shifting their defense toward that side of the court. On the pass from A to B, X_1 will drop back to the free-throw line. (X_3 will have moved to the edge of the lane, and X_5 into the lane, with the pass from C to A.) When B passes to E, X_1 will move to cover high post, X_2 will drop back toward the basket, X_5 will move across (but not out of) the lane, and X_3 will move to the center of the lane. (X_1's movements after the help-and-recover with X_2 are not shown.)

Advantages of Zone Defense. Following are the positive attributes of zone defense.

1. It is effective against medium and close-in shots and against pass-and-cut moves.
2. Its compactness closes normal passing lanes and necessitates careful maneuvering and accurate passing; therefore it is effective against a pivot attack.
3. It develops aggressiveness in intercepting the ball.
4. It can conserve the energy of tired players.
5. It is an excellent defense from which to obtain good offensive fast-break opportunities.
6. It is an excellent defense against a poor ball-handling team and poor outside-shooting teams.
7. It is effective against teams using a set pattern, screening offense.
8. It is effective against teams using a free-lance offense.
9. It reduces the number of fouls.
10. It is a good defense if the court space is restricted.
11. It assures rebound position.
12. It is adaptable for tall, uncoordinated men who cannot play good man-to-man defense.
13. It is easier to teach from a team structure than man-to-man defense.
14. It protects players who are in foul trouble.

15. It is a good psychological defense against some opponents. They become cautious or take bad shots.
16. It hides weak defensive players.
17. Beating it requires a planned attack that must rely on accurate medium or outside shooting primarily.
18. It is an effective surprise maneuver, especially if the team can play different types of zones from the initial zone structure.
19. A passive zone protecting the keyhole area forces a trailing opponent to take outside or low-percentage shots.
20. It is easily adaptable to a well-schooled man-to-man defensive team as an auxiliary defense.
21. It is effective against a team with an outstanding driver, as it tends to immobilize the team and restrict the driver.

Disadvantages. The negative characteristics of a zone defense are as follows:

1. It is weak against side and long shots and in the areas behind the back men when opponents move in from the weak side away from the ball.
2. It loses its compactness if it is spread or if players do not coordinate their sliding movements.
3. Overshifting weakens the offside or backside of a zone.
4. It is weak in the foul-line area and the short-jump-shooting areas if the front line overextends or players don't coordinate their movement.
5. Sometimes players forget man-to-man principles when the team is behind and they must leave the zone posture to pressure the ball.
6. It tends to weaken individual responsibility, as no match-up of men according to height, speed, and ability takes place.
7. Normally it cannot increase the tempo of the opponents' attack.
8. It is not good at the end of a losing game, because it does not attack the ball as well as man-to-man or pressure defense.
9. It is ineffective at times against overloading one side of the zone defense, a strategy that tends to get good shots for the offensive team.
10. Smart ball handlers can probe the zone, shift it, tire the defenders, and fake them out of position to pass inside the perimeter for good short shooting opportunities.
11. It is ineffectual against a good fast-break team or a team that penetrates quickly before the zone can set up.
12. It can make a game dull for players and spectators.
13. Defenders may become listless or complacent.
14. In some zones, if the rebounders do not block out their opponents, they can be out-hustled under the boards.

Combination Defenses

Combination defenses utilize the strengths of both man-to-man and zone defenses.

Combination defenses fall into three categories. The first includes two types of match-up defenses in which both the man and the ball are focal points. In one type, the defense starts as a zone front then switches to a man-to-man pick-up strategy. In the second, the defenders guard the opponents man-to-man, determining match-ups according to the type of offense being used. After the first pass, they switch to zone techniques.

The second category includes combination defenses in which three of the men play one type of defense while the other two play another type. The back three men may play zone in a triangle while the front two men play man-to-man, or three men in front play man-to-man while the back two men play zone, either side by side or one in front of the other.

The third category includes defenses in which four men play zone while one plays man-to-man against the outstanding player on the opposing team. The zone men may position themselves so that together they form a box, a diamond, or a **T** (the back three play triangle, the fourth plays in front of the point man).

Match-up Defense. The match-up defense consolidates cogent features of man-to-man and zone into a defense that is sound, facile, and flexible and that stymies most basic offensive patterns. The match-up defense decreases the effectiveness of offensive screens and cuts, eliminating the necessity of switching and allowing floating from the weak side or from vacated offensive areas. It also permits cutting off passing lanes to the pivot areas.

The defense uses the following man-to-man tactics: pressure on the ball at all times, close defensive play on men adjacent to the ball, overplaying or forcing opponents out of position for pass reception when they are close to the ball, and fronting and closely guarding the men in under-the-basket areas. It diminishes the chances of being badly hurt by outside shooting as can happen in a zone, because defenders are close to, and aggressively playing, the man with the ball and other players in near pass-reception areas. The match-up can neutralize the advantage of a superior opponent and is an excellent surprise maneuver. The defense can force passes to weak ball handlers by closing the passing lane to a good ball handler, overplaying aggressively between him and the ball. The only place the defense allows the outstanding players to receive the ball is near mid-court, and then it double-teams him for a quick release of the ball.

The match-up defense keeps specific personnel in their most advantageous defensive areas while apparently changing team identity frequently. This defense gives the appearance of a zone primarily, making many offensive teams resort to the traditional zone attack of patient perimeter passing, probing on cuts, and, finally, taking poor-percentage shots.

Zone origin. The first match-up discussed is zone in origin and converts to man-to-man coverage after the first pass that goes

Diagram 8–41. Match-Up Defense, Zone Origin, Switching to Man-to-Man Coverage after the First Pass. A has the ball at the head of the key, approximately twenty-three feet from the basket. A passes to B. The arrows show the movement as the defense adjusts to man-to-man pickup coverage. The initial defensive alignment is X_1 and X_2 at the head of the key at the foul lanes extended, X_3 in the middle area a step below the foul lane, and X_4 and X_5 approximately five feet from the basket with their inside feet touching the foul lane. This zone structure is in effect until the ball goes past an imaginary line extended across the head of the key to the sidelines. The defense keys on allowing opponents to shoot long outside and preventing pivot penetration. If the ball reaches a high pivot, defenders must be alert for cutters.

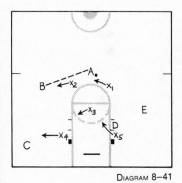

DIAGRAM 8–41

The personnel should be placed as follows: X_1 should be the quickest player on the team, with the best anticipation. After the offense's initial movement, he should have free-lance defensive latitude in the keyhole area. X_2 is usually the second guard. X_5, normally the best rebounder, plays on the right defensive side, because shots taken from the opposite side will rebound in his direction. X_4 and X_5, the slower men, must quarterback the flexing of the zone, using vocal warnings to keep teammates in position on the strong side. X_3, the quickest of the tall men, plays the pivot man on the strong side in all three pivot areas. He must box the pivot player on all shots, holding his block-out position and never moving for the ball. His lack of height may be a hindrance at times, but his quickness, agility, and aggressiveness should be able to neutralize the opponent's height advantage. _____

by the head of the key. It is described here from the two-one-two posture, although it could also start from a one-two-two zone or a two-two-one zone.

For several reasons, the front-line men should influence the ball to the side. This movement limits the offensive possibilities— the players may pass in through the defensive perimeter, they may pass to the corner or they may pass back outside the twenty-one-foot radius, at which point the defense will revert to the two-

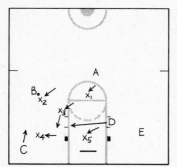

DIAGRAM 8-42

Diagram 8–42. Match-up Defense, Zone Origin (Continued). B has the ball, having received a pass from A. The arrows indicate the movement of the defensive players in assuming their man-to-man position. X_2 has moved to the left to pick up B, with the ball, man-to-man. X_4 has moved to pick up C, overplaying slightly to the ball side. X_3 has moved from the center of the foul lane into a medium-pivot protective position. X_1 has dropped off from his position on A into the upper half of the foul circle, and X_5, who has moved up to cover D, moves to the middle as D crosses the lane. X_5 must give an audible signal to X_3 that D is assuming this low-pivot position so that X_3 can front him. X_5 is responsible for D until X_3 picks him up. A pass from B to D would be difficult, so X_5 would not have to be extremely close to D. X_5 remains in position in the middle of the free-throw lane. He is primarily responsible for E, but E is on the weak side, far removed from the position of the ball.

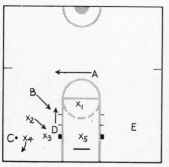

DIAGRAM 8-43

Diagram 8–43. Match-up Defense, Zone Origin (Continued). B has passed the ball into the corner to C. C is guarded by X_4, whose initial movement is toward the baseline to prevent a baseline drive. B is cutting through the pivot area. X_2 is playing an intercepting position between B and the ball, shutting off the passing lane until B enters the foul-lane area. B then remains strong-side. X_3 has fronted D in the pivot. X_1 has dropped just slightly below the foul line to be ready to double-team or pick up B if B V's out high with X_2 switching to A. X_5 has maintained his position in the center of the foul lane. The arrow indicates that D is moving up to a medium-pivot area.

Diagram 8–44. Match-up Defense, Zone Origin (Continued). C has passed the ball to D in the medium-pivot area. X_3 is playing D from behind. X_4 is overplaying C slightly toward the ball. X_2 has allowed B to cut through the foul-lane area, and B has moved out to A's original position. A has moved over to B's position. X_2 and X_1 are attacking D from the front to cause a tie-up or to prevent a good shooting or passing opportunity by D. X_5 is moving up with E to prevent a pass to E. If D were to pass the ball defensively back out to A or B, who are retreating into the back part of the front-court area, the zone alignment two-one-two would be reshaped. If the ball were passed from D to A, X_2 would play A man-to-man, and X_1 would play B.

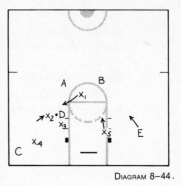

DIAGRAM 8–44.

one-two zone. Influencing the initial pass to the side allows the defense to match-up quickly in a man-to-man alignment, and it allows a defender to pick up the pivot man (if there is one) quickly. It also allows X_5 or X_4, the back men, to give audible signals from the weak side, directing the front men or X_3 into proper position.

The initial responsibility of the back-line men is to protect the baseline. They should influence to the middle, where they may obtain help from X_3. If they force the man fairly high, X_2 or X_1 must react to the ball and, together with X_3, may double-team.

Man-to-man origin. This match-up defense puts a defensive man in position on every offensive player regardless of the offensive pattern used. If the offense comes down in a three-two, the defense is in three-two man-to-man position on each player. The diagrams show the offense in a two-three alignment.

The defense should be playing zone when the offense is geared to man-to-man defense, and it should appear to be in man-to-man when the offense is expecting a zone. Disguising the defense will confuse the offense and perhaps get it into a zone offense pattern.

In man-to-man origin match-ups, the front line and back line influence the ball movement as they do in zone-origin match-ups. Defenders play men man-to-man in the area of the ball. When an opponent tries to cut through the defense to an area away from the ball, the defender guarding the cutter should allow him to go through, playing between him and the ball to a point where he cannot receive a pass. Trading men is an important factor in this defense. Each player is actually responsible for one man, but sometimes two offensive men will be close together in one area, making it possible for one defensive man to play both. However, the nearest defensive teammate must be prepared to pick up one of the men if he leaves the area. If one defender cannot play two, he must call to the nearest man for help.

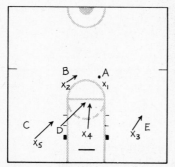

Diagram 8–45. Match-up Defense, Man-to-Man Origin, to Zone Coverage after the First Pass. A has the ball in the front of the offensive two-three alignment. D, in low pivot with X_4 playing off him to the ball side, moves up to a high-pivot position. X_4 follows him up to this position, guarding aggressively. X_5 adjusts toward the ball as though playing C in a normal man-to-man position. X_2 and X_3 move into intercepting angles on B and E, both one pass away from the ball.

DIAGRAM 8–45 ⎯⎯⎯⎯⎯⎯⎯⎯⎯⎯⎯⎯⎯

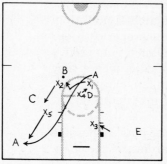

Diagram 8–46. Match-up Defense, Man-to-Man Origin (Continued). A has passed the ball to B. A makes a long diagonal cut through the defense to the opposite side. X_1 should follow A through the defense to a point where B cannot pass to A—usually to the foul line. X_1, X_2 and X_5 should trade responsibilities. X_1 should move to pick up B, X_2 should move to pick up C, and X_5 should pick up A. X_4 has overplayed D at the high pivot; and X_3 has moved into an intercepting position in the middle area, since his man, E, is far removed from the ball position.

DIAGRAM 8–46 ⎯⎯⎯⎯⎯⎯⎯⎯⎯⎯⎯⎯⎯

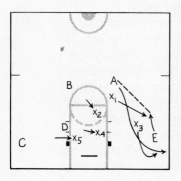

Diagram 8–47. Match-up Defense, Man-to-Man Origin (Continued). A passes to E and cuts through the defense on the ball side. X_1 follows A, positioning himself at a point where he can prevent a return pass to A. X_1 and X_3 trade responsibilities. D has moved to a low-pivot position opposite. X_2 has taken a long float off B. X_4 has moved long off D toward the ball position. X_5 has moved into the foul lane and can cover D. Now the defense appears to be in a zone structure.

DIAGRAM 8–47 ⎯⎯⎯⎯⎯⎯⎯⎯⎯⎯⎯⎯⎯

Diagram 8–48. Double-Team from Match-up Defense, Man-to-Man Origin (Continuation of movement in Diagram 8–47). E has passed the ball to A. A's position in the corner presents a good double-teaming situation. X_4 moves quickly from a low position in the foul lane guarding the basket to the corner to double-team on A. X_3 covers A on the baseline side. X_1 plays an intercepting angle on E as E moves away. X_5 adjusts to the middle of the foul-lane, five feet out from the basket. X_2 is in position to intercept a long pass across the court to C or out to B.

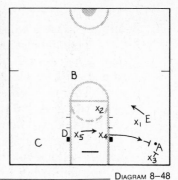

DIAGRAM 8–48

Diagram 8–49. Match-up Defense, Man-to-Man Origin (Alternative play). A passes to B, who has moved out for the ball. A cuts through away from the ball position. X_1 plays between A and the ball as A cuts down the lane. Just below the foul line X_1 realizes that a return pass to A would be intercepted by X_4 or X_5, therefore, X_1 can leave A. X_3 has fallen into the foul circle to assume a zone defensive position. X_5 moves to front D. X_4 is low enough to go to the basket to help if a lob pass is thrown from B to D. With A away from the ball it is possible for one man, X_4, to guard two, A and E. If an exchange had to be made, X_3 would drop down to pick up A. X_1 now has defensive latitude but must be alert to pick up a free opponent if warned verbally by a teammate.

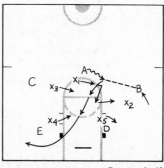

DIAGRAM 8–49

Triangle-and-Two Combination Defense. In this defense, two defenders play man-to-man against the two outstanding opponents while the three back-line men use a triangle zone defense near the basket against weaker or uncoordinated big men who are not basically good ball handlers. The zone players should permit outside shots but prevent close-in shots, preserving the defensive rebound triangle. The two men playing man-to-man should pressure and cut off all passing lanes. They can switch on crosses by the good offensive players, unless game plans indicate different defensive coverage. The triangle men should double-team the good offensive men when they are in the defensive zone. When pressure is applied man-to-man at half court, the three men in the zone should be close enough to opponents to cut off passing lanes to them without leaving the basket unguarded. If one of these opponents receives the ball, his defender should pressure him to cause a ball-handling error.

This defense is weak against good shooters, and opponents can penetrate the back line from the weak side. It is also weak if a good pivot player is one of the three being played zone.

This is a good basic defense against a weak-shooting team with two good ball handlers, and it presents good fast-break opportunities. It allows for defensive chances and aggressive play by the two men who are playing the man-to-man defense. Of course, defensive chances should be taken cautiously in close-to-the-basket areas. The unorthodox quality of this defense makes it an effective surprise maneuver, and it has the good team defensive elements of backboard control, ball pressure, and good defensive coverage near the basket and in the pivot area.

The alignment of this defense may vary: three men may play man-to-man in the front, with a two-man zone in back; or the front can play zone while the back line plays man-to-man. Coaches can improvise, using different combinations.

The initial zone alignment should have X_3 standing on the foul line and X_4 and X_5 standing with their inside foot on the foul lane, approximately six feet from the basket area. (X_1 and X_2 play man-to-man.)

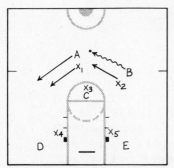

Diagram 8–50. Triangle-and-Two Combination Defense. B is dribbling the ball toward the head of the key. X_2 is moving in good man-to-man position on B. X_1 is guarding A man-to-man. X_3, X_4, and X_5 are in their original alignment in a triangle zone. X_3 is a little higher than in Diagram 8–49, blocking C from the ball.

DIAGRAM 8–50 _____

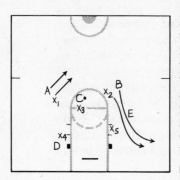

Diagram 8–51. Triangle-and-Two Combination Defense (Continued). C has moved higher for a pass from B. X_3 allows this reception. B cuts through to the corner, and X_2 guards him man-to-man. A moves out toward the head of the key, and X_1 guards him man-to-man. X_4 has played in front of D, who is low. X_5 is in position to stop any movement by E. If C takes a shot, which would be allowed, the triangle is in excellent rebound position.

DIAGRAM 8–51 _____

Box-and-One and Diamond-and-One Combination Defenses. The box-and-one and the diamond-and-one defenses will be discussed together, as they are basically the same defense after the initial movement of the zone formation once the offense has passed or dribbled. The box-and-one defense has one man playing man-to-man defense against an opponent and the other four players in a box arrangement; the diamond-and-one has one man playing man-to-man and the other four players in a diamond arrangement near the keyhole area.

The primary use of the two defenses is to limit the effectiveness of the high-scoring opponent. Cutting down greatly on the point production of any outstanding scorer hurts the opposing team in more ways than one; it can cause disharmony among them, with the star blaming the others for not getting the ball and the others perhaps blaming the star for taking bad shots.

The one free man (X_1) may be used in two ways. First he can be used to play man-to-man defense. Playing against a fast player who is an outside shooter and driver, the man-to-man defender should not let him get the ball. Playing against a good player who goes to the backboard strong offensively and is a good shooter, but is not a good driver, the defender would allow him to have the ball under pressure, boxing him at all times to keep him away from the rebound area.

The second method of using the fifth man is to allow him to move freely, especially if he is an aggressive defender with excellent stamina and good ball sense and anticipation.

The two front men (X_2 and X_3) in the box should be quick, with good reaction; they can be rovers on defense, covering the intermediate area and the high-pivot area. One must rebound at all times. The two back men (X_4 and X_5) should be the best rebounders; they are responsible for the pivot areas and the medium baseline area. Whenever the opponent who is being played man-to-man has the ball in a vulnerable area, all zone members must be prepared to double-team him. If the fifth defender is a floater or rover, not given man-to-man responsibilities, zone members should attempt to force the opponent's offensive patterns into movement than can be anticipated by the floater or by the rover. In the diamond-and-one alignment X_1, usually a guard, is assigned man-to-man. X_2 is normally the second guard. X_3 and X_4 are the forwards, with X_4 the better rebounder and X_3 perhaps the quicker. X_5 is the center.

If the fifth man is a floater or rover, he can sneak away. If he is assigned to play man-to-man, he cannot sneak away, as he must keep close check on the good opponent, harassing him as much as possible. In that case, we would recommend that the second guard, X_2, be used to sneak away. He will have good opportunity to do this, because the good offensive player will be intent on going to the boards to get the rebound offensively.

The sliding movement in this type of defense must be extremely quick, and the anticipation factor is essential. The single man and a zoner should double the star whenever possible, and two of the zoners may double-team the others. The four men in the zone posture must always be alert to shut off the weak areas—the foul-line area, the medium-side areas, and the pivot area. They also should be aware of the passing lanes into the difficult areas, closing them inside and opening them outside, laying off just enough for interception.

The four members playing zone should never overextend. They should give the outside shot when overextension is a factor. When playing a star with a box-and-one or a diamond-and-one defense, the four men in the zone alignment should use all available means and influencing tactics to deploy the ball away from the outstanding player.

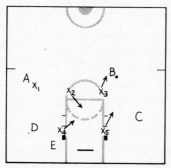

DIAGRAM 8–52

Diagram 8–52. Box-and-One Combination Defense, Initial Alignment. X_1 plays A, the opposing star, man-to-man. X_2 and X_3, the front men in the box position, are slightly above the foul line, straddling the circle area. X_4 and X_5, the back men, are rebounders, straddling the foul lane approximately six feet from the basket. B has the ball at the offensive left side. X_3 moves toward the ball, X_2 adjusts back in the lower half of the free-throw circle, X_4 adjusts slightly into the lane, and X_5 adjusts up outside the lane toward the ball position and C.

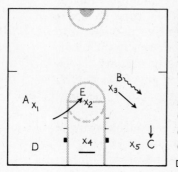

Diagram 8–53. Box-and-One Combination after Initial Slide. Diagram shows the flexing of the zone defense as B dribbles to his left and X_3 follows the ball. X_2 moves to the foul line as E comes up into a high-pivot position. X_5 moves toward the sideline, but not overextending, in the area of C as the ball moves into that vicinity and C moves into the corner. X_4 adjusts to the center of the foul lane, approximately three feet in front of the basket. X_1 stays man-to-man with A.

DIAGRAM 8–53

Diagram 8–54. Diamond-and-One Combination Defense, Initial Alignment. Again X_1 is playing A, the outstanding opponent, man-to-man. X_2, the point man in the diamond, is just below the outer circle at the head of the key. X_3 and X_4 are just below the foul line, straddling the foul lane. X_5 is in the center of the foul lane, approximately six feet in front of the basket. B has the ball. X_2 adjusts to the ball position. X_3 moves toward the middle of the lane. X_4 moves toward C. X_5 moves up in front of E, who is low.

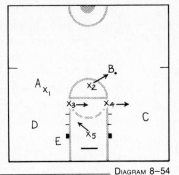

DIAGRAM 8–54

Diagram 8–55. Diamond-and-One Combination after the Initial Slide. B dribbles to the offensive left. X_2 is moving in position with him. E has moved up to the foul line again, and X_3 has adjusted his position up on the foul line. X_4 has moved to his right to be in position on the ball side with C in the vicinity of the ball. X_5 has dropped back to an under-the-basket position in the middle of the lane, about four feet in front of the basket. X_1 is guarding A man-to-man. There is a close similarity between Diagrams 8–53 and 8–55.

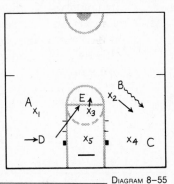

DIAGRAM 8–55

T-and-One Combination Defense. The **T**-and-One combination defense derives its name from the similarity between the letter **T** and the pattern formed by the four men playing zone-principle defense. X_1 plays the opposing star man-to-man. X_2, the more mobile forward, is in front. Since he is tall, the opponents will probably be unable to shoot over him effectively. X_3 is the quickest zone player with the best anticipation. He is used most to double-team and has the greatest range of movement of the four zoners. Usually he is the second guard. X_4 and X_5 are the remaining defensive players, X_5 being the better rebounder. X_2's initial position is in the outer half of the free-throw circle. X_3's initial position is in the inner half of the free-throw circle. X_4 and X_5 are approximately five feet in front of the basket, with their inside feet on the foul lanes.

This defense has good double-team potential. X_2 double-teams on A, the outstanding opponent, with X_1 in the front and side-front areas. X_3 double-teams on A with X_1 to the sides and at 45-degree-angle areas. X_4 and X_5 will double-team on A with

X_1 in the corner or pivot areas on their sides. The men playing this defense should be careful not to overextend.

The purposes of this combination alignment are to lessen the scoring efficiency of the outstanding opponent; to prevent close-in scoring opportunities for the other opponents; to encourage outside shooting opportunities by the other opponents, especially those beyond their range; and to get good rebounding position. X_2 will move closer to the basket after offensive movement and will be in good rebound position after a shot. Usually X_2 forms the rebounding triangle with X_4 and X_5, as X_3 shifts to the ball area. X_3 is the player who should break on a sneak-away attempt, as X_1 must remain in position on the outstanding opponent. Another reason to allow X_3 this sneak-away opportunity is as a bonus for his necessarily aggressive play. It is possible in this defense to interchange X_1 and X_3 if their defensive abilities are similar.

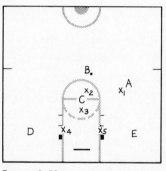

DIAGRAM 8–56

Diagram 8–56. T-and-One Combination Defense, Initial Alignment. A, the outstanding opponent, is to the offensive left, guarded man-to-man by X_1. B has the ball at the top of the key. X_2 is in position in the outer half of the free-throw circle. X_3 is in position in the lower half of the free-throw circle. X_4 and X_5 are straddling the lanes in position approximately five feet in front of the basket. After the flexing of the zone defense, X_2 is closer to rebound position than X_3, hence he should be the third rebounder with X_4 and X_5.

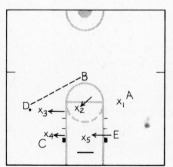

DIAGRAM 8–57

Diagram 8–57. T-and-One Combination Defense after the Initial Slide. B passes the ball to D. With the pass, the defensive alignment flexes toward the ball. X_3 moves directly toward the ball, challenging D. X_2 drops down into the lower half of the free-throw circle. X_4 overplays C. X_5 moves into the center of the foul-lane area. X_1 plays A man-to-man.

Diagram 8–58 (Continuation of movement in Diagram 8–57). D passes into the corner to C. X_4 has moved into position on C to prevent a baseline move. X_3 has dropped into this area. X_2 has moved to the side of the foul lane on the ball side. X_5 has remained in position. X_1 is still playing man-to-man at an intercepting angle on A.

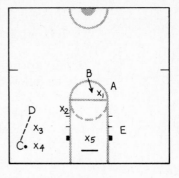

DIAGRAM 8–58

Diagram 8–59. T-and-One Combination Defense with a Double-Team on A (Continued). A has moved toward the ball and has received a pass. X_1 and X_3 are double-teaming him. X_4 is still overplaying in the corner on the side. X_5 is overplaying in the pivot. X_2 is in good position between B and E.

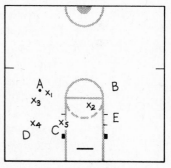

DIAGRAM 8–59

Advantages. Coaches should assess the following attributes of combination defense to determine whether such a defense is suitable for existing personnel to use against the teams to be played.

1. It is an extremely good defense by which to influence the ball away from an outstanding opposing scorer.
2. The defender guarding the outstanding player can overplay him to prevent his getting the ball, and the defender can be confident of help from his teammates.
3. It tends to confuse opponents, because combating it requires special offensive preparation.
4. It utilizes the best attributes of man-to-man and zone defenses.
5. It is a good double-teaming defense.
6. It is excellent against a good dribbler or a good dribbling team.
7. It is excellent against poor outside shooting.
8. It often prevents ball penetration to vulnerable areas.
9. It negates the effectiveness of a good screening and cutting opponent, as it eliminates the necessity of switching.
10. It places defensive personnel in their most effective areas.
11. It has good rebounding positions.

12. It permits good fast-break development.
13. It incorporates collapsing from the weak side.

Disadvantages. The negative factors in a combination defense are as follows:

1. It is vulnerable to good ball handlers.
2. It is vulnerable to diagonal cuts in the match-up structures, as it weakens or confuses defenders during the exchange of men.
3. It can be overloaded.
4. Overextension leaves combinations vulnerable to good short and medium shooting opportunities by opponents.
5. It is not effective against good outside shooting.
6. It leaves certain floor areas vulnerable to a deliberate probing team.
7. Teams must revert to a pressure defense if they are behind late in the game.
8. It requires specialized defensive abilities that not all teams or players may possess.
9. It requires time to set up, making it vulnerable to fast-break and quick-ball movement upcourt.
10. It requires a great deal of practice time.
11. It confuses individual defensive players at times, even when it is used as a primary defense.

Pressure Defenses

The best time for a coach to initiate a pressure defense is after a basket or a foul shot made by his team. There are two types of pressure defense—man-to-man and zone. Each type can be implemented in a full-court posture, at three-quarter court, or at half-court. Full-court pressure can begin with the man out-of-bounds or with the front defensive men at the backcourt foul line. Three-quarter pressure would be enforced at or behind the outer edge of the far keyhole area. Half-court pressure should be initiated one step before the division line at mid-court in the opponents' backcourt.

The term *pressure defense* implies use of advancing, attacking tactics by a forcing defense. Its purpose is to force misplays or bad passes by the opponents, taking advantage of the ten-second rule and overplay tactics. Successful execution of this defense requires fine conditioning and thorough knowledge of all the fundamentals.

Pressure defense should be used within the framework of the available personnel. Teams need good bench strength to sustain such a defense over an extended period of time during a game, plus much practice time on both man-to-man and zone presses. Full-court zone pressure in most instances is better than man-to-man pressure, as one good dribbler can defeat the man-to-man defense. A weak man-to-man player—usually the least mobile forward defender—can even be beaten by a dribbler who is only fair.

An all-out press is demanded when the situation requires forcing opponents in order to gain possession of the ball. Possession is essential when a team is one or two points behind with only seconds left to the game and the opponents are stalling. While shooting is improving (the shooting percentage today is the highest in the history of basketball), the quality of ball handling is decreasing. Therefore, pressure defense can counteract improved shooting (especially by jump shooters) by increasing the number of losses-of-possession by the offensive team.

Teaching Pressure Defensive Tactics. The coach should outline both man-to-man and zone pressure on paper and give each player a copy to be kept for reference. After the squad members have had time to study the outlines, the coach should present both defenses in a lecture, using a blackboard at the court, if possible, to diagram the tactics. He should cover each detail before moving on to actual demonstrations and insist that the assembled squad ask questions. After the diagraming, the coach should walk through the defensive movements on the court; then go through them in slow motion; and finally, use them at half speed against weak reserves, junior varsity players or freshmen.

The squad should practice the press every day, and the coach should try it out in a game situation where the team cannot be hurt by its use or as a last resort in a losing game when a surprise change in tactics is required. Normally, players master man-to-man press faster than zone press.

Man-to-Man Pressure Defense. Preseason practice drills and stressing of fundamentals are extremely important in the man-to-man pressure defense. It should be practiced one-on-one, two-on-two, three-on-three and full team, picking up at full-court. The coach should have a team of good man-to-man pressure defenders available for insertion in a game at the proper time.

Coaches may vary the pickup point of a man-to-man pressure defense. At full-court, the strategy is to cut off outlets, assuring that the pass will be received in the backcourt by a weaker offensive ball handler. The defender must harass the inbounder, distracting him, preventing him from passing to a good ball handler, and forcing him to hesitate so that he may incur a five-second violation.

An alternative strategy is for the man guarding the passer-in to fall off and double-team the best on-court dribbler with his defender, forcing the ball to a less-capable ball handler, then returning to pick up his out-of-bounds opponent.

If the press is applied at three-quarter court, at the head of the foul circle, the inbounder can pass the ball in. The three-quarter pickup allows the defense to assess the situation and take advantage of the opponent's necessity to bring the ball up-court over the mid-court line within ten seconds. This press is a good surprise tactic.

Picking up at half-court, one step into the opponent's backcourt, again takes advantage of the ten-second rule. It is effective because there is less area to cover than in the three-quarter or all-court man-to-man situation, and it can be used to force the opponents out of their positions for their set offensive attack. When the ball does go into the front court, the defensive team can use turn-and-double techniques.

In man-to-man pressure the defender should approach an alive opponent quickly, but under control, faking or feinting to make him start his dribble, then forcing him to his weak hand. It is possible to spring a surprise man-to-man press with two men pressuring at mid-court just as the opponents are bringing the ball over the division line. This tactic is used to force mistakes, loss of ball, or a backcourt violation; to trap opponents; and to pick up a loose opponent who may otherwise have eluded them. While two men are double-teaming on the ball, other teammates should play intercepting angles, watching both the ball and the men they are guarding. A corner defender should move up to play this intercepting angle so that a potential ball receiver will have to reverse, moving farther from the passer.

To make the long pass, the ball handler will have to draw back his arm, thus alerting the defenders. If an opponent gets out of his defender's sight by moving behind him, that defender should immediately go to the basket area, about a step inside the lower half of the foul circle, in the middle of the free-throw lane, and try to pick up his man by moving out from the basket area.

Defenders should jump-switch on all offensive team crosses. If a defender jump-switches into the path of a teammate's opponent, that teammate should switch immediately to defend against the jump-switcher's man. In some situations, the coach may decide to have the teammate stay to double-team with the jump-switcher. If the double-teaming fails, the teammate will then pick up the loose man. Guards should jump-switch at every opportunity.

When using man-to-man pressure defense full court, the near man should aggressively attack a rebounder to force him into a defense posture in the backcourt, slowing the movement of the ball upcourt so that all defensive teammates may pick up a man quickly before the ball penetrates. It is a good defensive tactic to turn the man with the ball, if possible, so that his back is to the basket. This maneuver causes him to lose sight of his teammates, allows his defender to move in on him, and makes double-teaming possible.

The man-to-man defender should force the dribbler to his weak hand, to the middle, or to the sidelines as instructed. If the dribbler gets even with or past his defender, the defender must turn and run in stride with the dribbler, forcing him toward the sidelines and striking up at the ball with his inside hand. He should use defensive fakes to attempt to stop the dribbler; he should not foul or try to steal the ball. If the dribbler stops, the defensive opponent should attack him aggressively to force a poor pass. If an offensive man dribbles by a defender some distance from the basket, that defender should quickly pivot behind him and attempt to deflect or bat the ball forward to a teammate, using a flicking motion from the rear. When a player who has stopped dribbling and has been aggressively attacked by his defender passes off, the defender must react instantly, dropping back toward the basket in the direction of the ball.

Players who are guarding teammates of a dribbler who has been stopped should play an intercepting angle on their opponents, being alert for a reverse movement. The defenders in a man-to-man pressure defense should attempt to force the ball to weaker offensive ball handlers by opening the door and allowing them to obtain possession of the ball. The center should overplay high on the opposing center to invite lob passes; however, as he is the back defender he must remember his primary responsibility of allowing no easy lay-ups. At times, opponents with the ball will sift through a man-to-man pressure defense and move in on this last defender in a two-on-one situation. If they do, he should zone the two, using delaying tactics to stall until a teammate can help him.

Run-and-Jump Full-Court Pressure Defense. As mentioned previously, the full-court version of run-and-jump defense involves influencing the dribbler toward the sideline by over-playing. Since most teams combat full-court man-to-man pressure by sending the other offensive players downcourt and isolating the dribbler to bring the ball down one-on-one, a measure of defensive control of the dribbler is necessary. If the dribbler is not moving downcourt at high speed to elude his defender, the run-and-jump movement may fail to take him by surprise, in which case the attacking advantage may shift dramatically to the offensive team.

The movements involved in setting up and springing the run-and-jump are identical to those used in trapping the dribbler, except that, instead of trapping A with X_2, X_1 will veer sharply away from A to cover B. This difference may appear slight, but it is vital to the success of the run-and-jump movement.

In trapping defense, either B or D on weak side would be open, but in run-and-jump defense neither man will be open. If the defense has played the run-and-jump to full advantage, A will

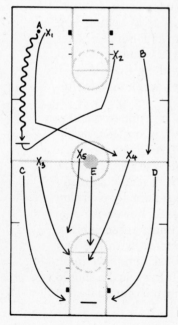

Diagram 8–60. Sideline-Influence Run-and-Jump Defense, Full-Court Press. X_1 begins in a close-guarding stance on A, playing him slightly toward the middle to influence his dribble toward the sideline. As A begins to dribble, X_1 attempts to guard him closely and force him toward the sideline to reduce his maneuvering room and vision of the court. Meanwhile, X_2 slides back downcourt, moving at an angle that gradually closes the distance between him and A. When A nears the mid-court area, X_2 sprints across the court and sets himself directly in A's path along the sideline. A, thinking that he is being trapped by X_1 and X_2, will normally pick up his dribble and pivot away from X_2 in his path. However, X_1 has abandoned A and is sprinting across to cover B on the other side of the court.

DIAGRAM 8–60

have no one to pass to, since all the defense has done is switch X_1 and X_2's defensive responsibilities. Having used up his dribble and being desperate to pass the ball away before a ten-second backcourt violation is called, A is likely to throw the ball away if the defenders away from the ball continue to cut off the passing lanes between their men and the ball. A's pass is made even more difficult by the fact that X_2 forced him to pivot away from him, and the resultant pass will have to be made left-handed. And even if A is able to pass to B, the offensive team still has not advanced the ball past the half-court line, and a ten-second violation is still a distinct possibility.

In trapping defense, the defenders attempt to pressure the ball handler into making a bad pass, aggressively double-teaming him and using the other three defenders to cut off the primary passing lanes. Pressure on the ball is increased, but defensive pressure away from the ball is necessarily reduced—if the ball handler is capable of finding the open man. In run-and-jump pressure, the ball handler encounters simular situations, but aggressive coverage away from the ball will reduce the ball handler's ability to pass the ball away. As a result, whereas trapping may be more likely to produce steals for the defense, run-and-jump defense is generally more effective in producing charging fouls, ten-second backcourt violations, or passes thrown out-of-bounds. Run-and-jump defense seldom gives up lay-ups, since no one is open downcourt when the switch occurs.

Although the run-and-jump can occur anywhere, and can be performed by any defender besides the one on the ball, it is best executed along the sideline by a player on the side of the court away from the ball—X_2 or X_4 in Diagram 8–60. Many teams have used the nearest defender on ball side (X_3 in Diagram 8–60) in making the run-and-jump switch; however, this movement is more commonly associated with zone pressure defense, since the dribbler can see X_3 coming up (or X_4 if the ball handler is dribbling along the other sideline), and only X_5 is in position to adequately cover the pass to C (or D) along the sideline.

The form of run-and-jump coverage shown in Diagram 8–61 is probably superior to the weak-side-guard technique shown in Diagram 8–60, since A is naturally inclined to look for the guard on the other side of the court when he pivots away from the defender who is performing the run-and-jump. In Diagram 8–61, however, B is still covered by X_2, and it is X_4 who is the switching defender.

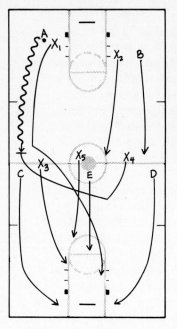

Diagram 8–61. Varying the Run-and-Jump, Full-Court Pressure Defense. X_2 covers B. X_3 is in position to cover passes to C or D. X_4 slides back and away from D as A begins his movement downcourt, then sprints into position to cut off A before he reaches the frontcourt. X_1 completes the switch by continuing down court to cover D. The pass from A to D (not shown in diagram) is extremely difficult to complete, particularly if X_4 succeeds in making A reverse-pivot toward the middle to protect the ball.

DIAGRAM 8–61 _____

Zone Pressure Defense. The zone-press defense uses basic zone principles in forcing opponents over full-court, three-quarter-court, or half-court areas in order to confuse and disrupt them.

Zone pressure defense is used (1) to surprise the opponents; (2) to upset their poise; (3) to make them cautious and protective of the ball; (4) to disrupt their basic patterns; (5) to lure them into trap or double-team situations; (6) to force misplays or mistakes; (7) to distort the opponents' patterns, and force bad shots; and (8) to speed up the pace of the game when the opponents wish to set a slower game tempo.

Defensive positioning and movement are based on offensive ball and player movement. Rather than sliding, the defensive players must in many instances sprint to their new positions, since a defender playing zone press covers a far greater area than the player in a normal zone defensive alignment.

Even if a team does not have occasion to use zone press often, two advantages accrue from perfecting it. First, by practicing the defense in actual game situations, the players learn to understand

Diagram 8–62. Defensive Reference Areas for Full-Court Zone Pressure. Zone 3 is from the endline to the backcourt hash mark, Zone 2 is from the backcourt hash mark to the frontcourt hash mark, and Zone 1 is from the frontcourt hash mark to the basket.

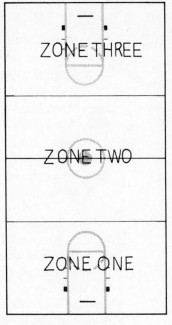

DIAGRAM 8–62

its principles so that they can attack an opponent's zone press defense effectively. Second, it is a good secondary defense that must be used as a primary defense under certain circumstances.

Other advantages include the following:

1. It compensates for a height disparity when the players on the defensive team are smaller than their opponents.
2. It is effective for a team with a speed advantage.
3. It is an excellent team conditioner.
4. It generates enthusiasm and a good team defensive attitude.
5. It forces the opponents into a running, pressure type of game.
6. It helps a fast-break offense by speeding up the game.
7. It simulates team defensive play by making players aware of its importance.
8. It discourages opponents if they misplay.
9. If used for a few minutes near the end of a half, it is an effective deceptive tactic. The opponents may use valuable intermission time postulating attack methods for a defense that may not be used again.

Zone press should be used at the following times:

1. When a team is behind
2. When big men on the opposition are defensive problems
3. When the opponents play a set pattern to force them out of the basic offense
4. When playing against a poor ball-handling team
5. When quick baskets are necessary
6. When a team has small, quick personnel
7. When aggressive pressure must be applied continuously
8. When opposing teams have a good pivot attack
9. When playing against slower, poorly conditioned teams

Coaches should not expect an immediate or quick return from zone-pressure tactics. Returns may be slow in coming, but they will accrue when the tactics become effective.

Teams should keep zone pressure on opponents after they make mistakes so that other mistakes will ensue. As setting up a zone pressure defense takes time, the defense should only be initiated at the following points in a game:

1. After a basket or successful free throw by your team
2. When the opponents have the ball out of bounds and are slow in getting into position to inbound it
3. After a time-out, especially if it has not been used before
4. At any time as a surprise maneuver
   (It is very effective at the begining of a game, at the quarter or at the half.)

Zone pressure defense, like normal zone defense, can be played from an odd front or an even front. The odd fronts possible at full-court, three-quarter court, or half-court position include a one-two-one-one zone press, a three-one-one, a three-two, and a one-two-two. The even presses are the two-two-one, two-one-two, and two-three zones. All zone presses will flex into similar structures after the ball has inbounded. We will outline an odd-front zone pressure defense, an even-front zone pressure defense, and a half-court odd-front zone pressure defense.

One-two-one-one three-quarter-court or full-court zone press, basic alignment. X_1, the middle man, is usually a guard. He should be a smaller player with good speed and quick hands for both defensive and offensive opportunities. He forces the opponents to move to the advantage of his team. The middle man is limited to double-team movements or lateral movements in the

Diagram 8–63. One-Two-One-One Zone Pressure, Full-Court or Three-Quarter-Court Basic Alignment. All players in a pressure defense should be identified by position as well as by number for easy reference. X_1, the middleman, positions himself initially in the front half of the near foul circle. X_2 and X_3, the wing men, are on opposite ends of the foul line extended, between the actual edge of the foul line and the sideline. X_4, called the four man, is at the front of the center circle, and X_5, the back man, is at the head of the far key.

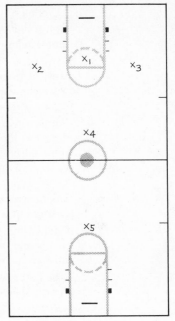

DIAGRAM 8–63

backcourt, and he must get back to the head of the key quickly whenever necessary.

The wing men, X_2 and X_3, are taller players, usually the forwards. The more maneuverable forward should be placed in the X_2 position, as the defensive team wishes to force the attack in his direction. X_2 or X_3, depending on the position of the ball, must go back to the defensive basket area frequently to protect underneath the basket from the weak side.

The four man, X_4, should be the quickest player on the team, with good court sense and anticipation. Whenever possible, he is the taller guard. He is given a great deal of latitude, as he has the greatest range of responsibility and must be overprotective of the middle area. The back man, X_5, is usually the center, the biggest man and best rebounder. The last line of defense protecting the basket, he is primarily responsible for preventing an easy shot by the opponents.

Following are play-by-play procedures for each player as the ball moves from the out-of-bounds position toward the basket.
Middleman, X_1

1. Direct the first pass-in, usually to defensive left. If necessary, move to your right to effect this pass-in.

2. Prevent a return pass to the inbounder by cutting off the passing lane to the foul-lane area.

3. Double-team with either wing, closing the backdoor trap.

4. If the wing man forces a dribble turn, attack the ball aggressively as the opponent turns, denying the dribbler the alley between the wing man and your own position.

5. If the ball is returned to the inbounder, use the same trapping techniques to the other side, trapping with the other wing. This trap will take longer to spring because of the distance the other wingman must travel back to initial position. Be patient.

6. When the ball passes over the front line, sprint to the defensive end, determining the most advantageous position by observing the offensive and defensive deployments and anticipating open passing lanes.

7. If the ball goes to the middle of the high-pivot area at the defensive end, attack it aggressively to force a pass back toward mid-court, a misplay, or a double-team situation.

8. If the ball goes to a frontcourt corner, protect the medium-pivot area on the ball side.

Wingmen, X_2 and X_3

1. If the pass-in is allowed to be made uncontested, it should be in front of X_2. X_3, if no opponent is in front of his initial position, drops back toward the nearest offensive player on his side or into the middle of the backcourt to prevent a pass over X_1 and the other wing.

2. Allow reception in your corner, standing back far enough to prevent a pass-in to the backcourt sideline area behind you. If the inbounder hesitates on his pass-in, delaying for a few seconds, attack the near-corner opponent aggressively to force a five-second violation or a long, hurried pass.

3. If reception is made on your side, approach the alive or dribbling opponent quickly, but under control, using good fundamental man-to-man defensive-approach techniques.

4. *Never* allow the dribbler to get between you and the sideline.

5. Attack aggressively if the dribbler stops, preventing a good upcourt pass opportunity along the sideline passing lane. Arms should be up to force a lob or deflection.

6. If the ball is inbounded opposite your position, drop back into the center of the floor in the opponent's backcourt, between mid-court and the foul circle. Anticipate and play intercepting position on the inbounder and any other opponent in the backcourt away from the trap area, decoying the ball handler into an apparently safe pass. Intercept cross-court or lob passes.

7. If the ball is passed back to the inbounder from the side opposite you, double-team with the middle man, being careful not to overextend your defensive position. Getting into position hurriedly may prevent an effective double-team. Be sure to protect your sideline against the dribbler.

8. If the first inbound receiver on your side passes up your sideline while you are double-teaming him, react immediately, following the pass along the sideline for a possible double-team with X_4.

9. Continue following the ball to the deep defensive corner if it is passed there. Double-team with X_5.

10. Cover the under-the-basket area as quickly as possible if the ball is in the opposite defensive corner. Cover in the middle of the foul lane if the ball is in the opposite sideline area near the hash mark or at the point of an imaginary extension of the foul line.

11. Anticipate and try to intercept a centering pass to the high pivot if the ball is just over mid-court at the opposite sideline. (Wing men can read the offensive zone pressure pattern after it is used a few times and make invaluable contributions through imagination and hustle.)

12. Sprint back under the basket if the ball breaks the front line of the press quickly on the opposite side.

13. If the ball is passed over the front line on your side, react immediately for possible double-teaming with X_4.

14. If you intercept, call "Ball" and look immediately for a guard, usually X_1. Give him the ball and break. Be aware of a ten-second violation possibility. Dribble only if you have a clear path to the basket.

Four Man, X_4

1. Know how the opponents position themselves to attack the zone press. Prevent a pass over the front line by playing an intercepting angle on an opponent near the mid-court area. The arm and body positions of the opponent's inbounder signal his intention. If he turns sideways, he may be preparing to make a long pass; if he is square to you with the ball in both hands, the pass normally will be a short one.

2. When the ball comes inbounds, move toward the sideline on the side it comes in on, approximately in line with the ball.

3. Be in intercepting position on a man in the mid-court area near that sideline, but be alert for cutters coming up in the middle and for cross-court lobs or short passes.

4. If there is a good double-team at the front line, anticipate the most likely passing areas and try to intercept or deflect the pass.

5. If a dribbler gets through on a sideline past your near wing, approach cautiously and anticipate a pass. If the pass is made, bother it or deflect it. If the dribbler continues, attack to stop him and double-team with the near wing man beyond the hash mark in the backcourt, as X_1 and the other wing man might become uncertain of floating responsibilities.

6. Attack the ball if it is passed to the middle from the mid-court side area on your side. This is a dangerous territory.

7. If the ball gets past your position on the far sideline, sprint to the pivot area ball-side and anticipate.

8. If the ball gets past your position on the near sideline, sprint to the pivot area on your side, observing the offensive opportunities as you move.

9. If the ball passes to a defensive corner, sprint to the lower medium-pivot position on that side and front an opponent in this area. Stay on the side of the ball in low position if there is no pivot. Be prepared to box anyone in the pivot area on a shot.

Back Man, X_5

1. Never allow a long pass to go over you to an opponent.

2. If there is no offensive player in frontcourt, move up to mid-court opposite the ball position. X_4 should be covering on that side to deny a pass over the front line into the mid-court area.

3. Double-team the ball in either frontcourt corner with a wing man.

4. Cover a pivot man to discourage a pass to him from the side mid-court area.

5. Protect the basket from quick, offensive penetration, never allowing a lay-up. Use good defensive delaying tactics when outnumbered two-on-one or three-on-one. Fake and feint, allow the outside shot, and rebound.

6. Intercept long passes with caution. If you mistime the pass or misjudge it, the opponents score.

7. Analyze ball movement, offensive player movement, and double-teaming by teammates to determine your most advantageous position. Go to passes in your area that you can intercept.

8. Play to the side of the foul lane as the ball crosses mid-court on that side, and anticipate a corner double-team if the ball goes there. Use swarming, aggressive tactics, but protect the baseline, as the ball handler is probably more agile than you.

9. Play a pass into the pivot aggressively, but be alert for free cutters to the side who can receive a dropdown pass for a lay-up. Use delaying zone tactics in this case, giving up the outside shot if necessary.

Diagram 8–64. One-Two-One-One Zone Press, Full Court, Movement after the Initial Pass. A, out of bounds, passes in to B. X_1 steps toward A, then moves left toward the ball position. X_2 approaches B cautiously as B dribbles with the ball, initiating a double-teaming movement by X_2 and X_1. X_3 adjusts position slightly toward A, then—after B makes his move—drops back into the middle as a floater. X_4 overplays C in intercepting position. X_5 adjusts slightly toward E.

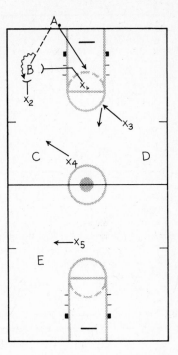

DIAGRAM 8–64

Diagram 8–65. One-Two-One-One Zone Press, Full-Court, Movement When B Passes up the Sideline to C. B passes from the trap position to C, near the backcourt hash mark. C has eluded X_4 or X_4 did not get in cutoff position quickly enough. X_4 approaches cautiously and sets the rear trap. X_2 follows the ball along the sideline and traps with X_4. X_1 becomes a floater in backcourt, guarding against a pass back to B or over to A. X_3 adjusts up in intercepting angle on D. As the ball reaches C, X_5 moves over so that he can cut off a pass to E, if necessary, without allowing a long pass over his position.

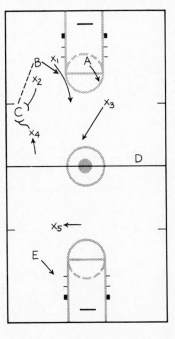

DIAGRAM 8–65

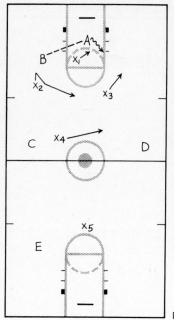

Diagram 8–66. One-Two-One-One Zone Press, Full-Court, Movement When Ball Is Passed Back to the Inbounder. This is a continuation of Diagram 8–64, an alternative to the offensive tactics shown in Diagram 8–65. B passes the ball back to A, who has come inbounds. X_1 adjusts from his position, staying on the side of A and forcing him, if possible, toward X_3 at the opposite sideline. X_3 adjusts back toward the sideline and up, cautiously, in an attempt to cut off A. X_1 and X_3 will double-team A. X_2, who had stepped up as B received the ball, retreats back toward the middle to become the floater as B passes back to A. X_4 quickly adjusts toward the opposite sideline in line with the ball. X_5 moves to the head of the key, still playing deep intercepting position on E.

DIAGRAM 8–66

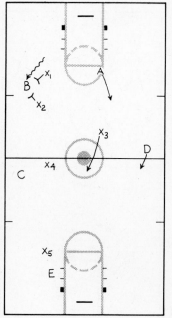

Diagram 8–67. One-Two-One-One Zone Press, Trap on B Near the Hash Mark Preliminary to a Pass along the Sideline to C. X_1 and X_2 have trapped on B after a return pass from A in Diagram 8–66. In this diagram the trap is higher than normal. X_1 and X_2 are trapping after the dribble, and X_4 has positioned on C. X_3 has adjusted back over half-court with the movement of D. If B passes back to A, X_3 can assume position on A to the outside, trapping with X_1. X_5 is low on E.

DIAGRAM 8–67

Diagram 8–68. One-Two-One-One Zone Press, Trap on C in the Frontcourt Near the Sideline. B has passed along the sideline to C. X_4 is the low trapper. X_2 is moving into position as the high trapper. D has moved toward the high-pivot position and is cut off by X_3. X_1 has come back inside the frontcourt area to cut off A, who has come over mid-court. E is cut off by X_5. It is impossible for C to pass back to B, who is in the backcourt, because it would be a violation.

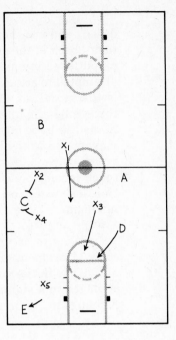

DIAGRAM 8–68

Diagram 8–69. One-Two-One-One Zone Press, Corner Trap on E. E has received a pass from C. X_2 continues his movement along his sideline to become the high trapper. X_5, the low trapper, must close off the baseline to E. X_4 has dropped from his trapping position to overplay D in the pivot area. X_1 is at the end of the foul line on the side of the ball, ready for any pass. X_3 is in the under-basket area, with the ball in the opposite corner.

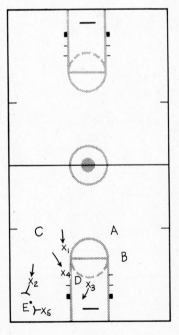

DIAGRAM 8–69

After a one-two-one-one zone press. If the one-two-one-one doesn't end in a shot or misplay, the defenders should be prepared to fall back in the predetermined defensive alignment. Normally, an outlet safety pass toward mid-court after the opponents have attempted to attack a full-court or three-quarter-court zone press is the signal for the defense to deploy into an aggressive two-three zone alignment with X_1 and X_4 as the front men, X_2 and X_3 as the back men, and X_5 in the middle. However, the coach may prefer that his men remain in the one-two-one-one zone press, using half-court principles. In making his decision, the coach considers factors such as personnel playing on both teams, time left, score, location of the game, and fouls on the players on his team.

Two-two-one zone press, full-court or three-quarter court. Placement of the players is shown in Diagram 8–70.
    If the initial pass-in can be influenced properly, this defense is played in a similar fashion to the one-two-one-one zone press. A change in alignment for defensive variations and change in the

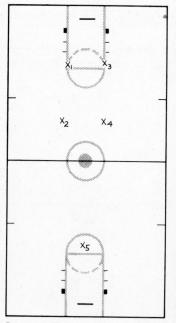

DIAGRAM 8–70

Diagram 8–70. Two-Two-One Zone Press, Full-Court or Three-Quarter Court, Basic Alignment. The front men, X_1 and X_3, position in front of the near foul line, with their feet straddling the lane, to influence the ball coming in to the sides and prevent the initial pass from going down the middle of the court. The left front, X_1, is usually a small, quick guard, with good speed and hands. His duties are similar to those of X_1 in the one-two-one-one zone press. The right front, X_3, is perhaps the taller of the forwards. His basic duties correspond to those of one of the wing men in the one-two-one-one press. He must get back extremely fast if the ball goes over the front line on the opposite side. X_2 and X_4 position themselves in backcourt between the hash mark and the mid-court line, approximately in line behind X_1 and X_3. X_2, the left trapper, is a fairly agile forward. X_4, the right trapper, is generally the second guard. As he has a lot of moving to do, he should be the quickest player, with good anticipation and speed and good stamina and range. X_5, the back man (positioned in the top half of the far free-throw circle), is the center. His primary responsibility is protecting the basket for he is the last line of defense.

structure of the zone offense is desirable at times. If the coach wishes, X_1 and X_3 can change sides, as can X_2 and X_4, and the influencing of the ball will be up the opposite side of the court, with the players maintaining the same basic responsibilities. X_4 always backs up X_3, and X_2 is always behind X_1.

If the area guarded by X_1 and X_3 is secure, X_3 may adjust position near an opponent on his side to direct the pass-in to the defensive left. If the initial pass comes into the defensive left, X_2 cheats up and moves to the ball. X_2 and X_4 may adjust their initial position, depending on the situation. They must never allow a pass up the middle. They must adjust slightly to prevent a long pass to either side that X_5 cannot prevent, since he must be back protecting against a baseline opponent. Either X_2 or X_4 may adjust to prevent a pass over X_3, as long as the adjustment doesn't permit a down-the-middle pass.

If the ball is influenced in to the defensive left, X_1 and X_2 trap as in the one-two-one-one press, and the other players also move as they do in the one-two-one-one. If the pass comes in to the defensive right, X_3 and X_4 are the trappers. X_1 assumes the duties held by X_2 in the one-two-one-one press, and X_2 assumes X_4's responsibilities. X_3 assumes the responsibilities of X_1 as the low trapper, and X_4 assumes the responsibilities of X_3 in the one-two-one-one press as the high trapper.

Diagram 8–71. Two-Two-One Zone Press, Full-Court, Movement after the Initial Pass. A, out of bounds, has passed in to B. B has started to dribble up the sideline. X_1 waits until B has moved by his position, then follows him. X_3 has taken an initial step toward the out-of-bounds area to prevent a quick return pass to A. When B starts his dribble, X_3 moves up-court to become a floater. X_2 moves from his initial position to become the high trap, stopping the dribble by B. X_1 closes the trap from the rear. X_4 has adjusted across court, taking an intercepting angle on C to prevent a pass. X_5 has adjusted to overplay E.

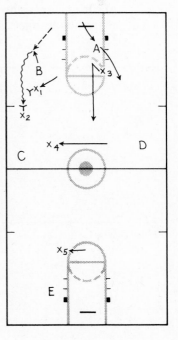

Diagram 8–71

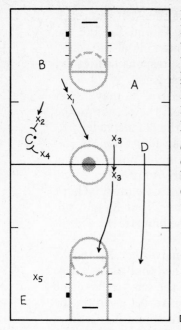

Diagram 8–72. Two-Two-One Zone Press, Full-Court (Continued). B has passed the ball to C, near the mid-court. X_4 becomes the high trap, and X_2 continues along the sideline, trapping from the rear. X_1 moves into the middle to become a floater between the ball position and A. X_5 has moved to overplay E in the deep corner. X_3 maintains an intercepting angle on D all the way to the basket, if necessary. As the trap is closed on C, D moves deep into the corner position or deep into frontcourt opposite E. X_3 must adjust back to the outer half of the free-throw circle to cut off a possible pass to D. On this movement, X_1 must adjust toward mid-court and be in position to overplay anyone that the ball is passed to in this area.

DIAGRAM 8–72

This exchange of duties weakens the structure of the two-two-one zone press somewhat, because of differences in basic abilities; therefore, defenders should influence toward the more-advantageous area whenever possible.

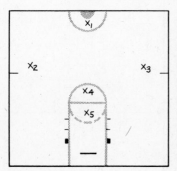

DIAGRAM 8–73

Diagram 8–73. One-Two-One-One Half-Court Zone Press, Basic Alignment. X_1 is in the front court, in the center circle, ready to step forward to influence the direction of the ball. X_2 and X_3, the wing men, are back near the hash marks on their respective sides. X_4 is at the top of the outer half of the free-throw circle, and X_5 is in the lower half of the free-throw circle. The basic alignment is almost one-three-one. If the ball gets by the front line on the strong side, X_2 and X_4 double-team. If it is returned cross-court and toward the center line, X_1 and X_3 double-team. The play continues as in the one-two-one-one full-court zone press until a shot is taken, an offensive mistake is made, or the coach decides to change the defensive structure when the ball is passed back toward the mid-court line.

Diagram 8–74. One-Two-One-One Half-Court Zone Press, Initial Movement. A, influenced by X_1 dribbles across mid-court line toward the defensive left. This causes X_4 to move, staying head-up on the dribbler. X_3 adjusts toward the center area. X_2 moves quickly and aggressively from his initial position as A is dribbling and traps him with X_1. (If the dribbler had been influenced to the right, X_3 would trap with X_1.) X_4 should now be in position to intercept if the ball is passed to C or E. X_3 is in position to intercept if the ball is passed to D or E. Since the most dangerous pass from A is into E in the pivot position, guarding the pivot area should be the first consideration of X_3 and X_4. X_5 is in position to guard the basket, yet close enough to discourage a pass in E.

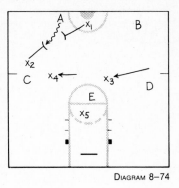

DIAGRAM 8–74

Diagram 8–75. One-Two-One-One Half-Court Zone Press (Continued). A passes cross-court to B. The arrows show the movement of the defensive players during the pass. X_1 and X_3 become the trap men at the ball position. X_4 adjusts back across court to play intercepting angle on D. X_2 reacts back to shut off E in the pivot. Again, the position of X_2 and X_4 are determined by their primary responsibility of keeping the ball out of the pivot. X_5 has adjusted slightly to the ball side behind E.

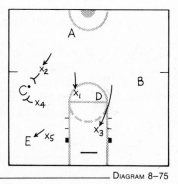

DIAGRAM 8–75

Diagram 8–76. One-Two-One-One Half-Court Zone Press (Alternative to movement in Diagram 8–75). From Diagram 8–74, A has passed to C. X_4 adjusts position to be the low trapper. X_2 follows the ball to become the high trapper. E has moved into a corner position. X_5 must move toward him, delaying slightly to check the positions of X_1 and X_3. X_1 drops from his trap position to cut off D in the high-pivot position. X_3 drops back under the basket, on the side away from the ball, to protect this area.

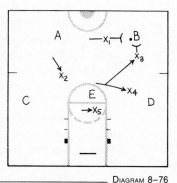

DIAGRAM 8–76

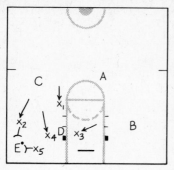

DIAGRAM 8–77

Diagram 8–77. One-Two-One-One Half-Court Zone Press (Continuation of movement in Diagram 8–76). C has passed to E. X_2 follows the movement to become the high trapper. X_5 is the low trapper, closing the baseline. D, has moved from the high pivot to a low-pivot area, so X_4 moves back to protect this area. X_1 adjusts toward the end of the foul line to be in position to intercept if the ball is passed back out. X_3 moves over to hamper D's movements from the rear if the ball should get to him and to be in rebound position under the basket should a shot be taken.

One-two-one-one half-court press. The basic responsibilities of the personnel and the names of the positions are the same as in the full-court one-two-one-one zone press, but the initial positions are different.

Tactics Requiring Special Drilling. To perfect the zone press, constant drill is essential in five areas of the defense.

1. All men must drill on quick alignment. Players must get into position quickly to implement the zone press with any degree of success.
2. All men must drill on cutoff positions for long initial passes so that they know the danger areas and are prepared to adjust their positions at a call from the back man, X_5, or from X_4. Teams should practice this initially in almost standstill position, with the coach realigning the offensive team indiscriminately to put players in positions where they may be able to make an initial long pass from out of bounds, over the front line, into Zone 2.
3. The big man should practice two-on-one and three-on-one situations while moving back toward the basket so that he may improve his delaying tactics and sharpen his ability to block a shot or give the outside shot.
4. Players in the front line should practice realigning when an offensive player passes out of bounds along the baseline.
5. Players should practice drop-back defense in situations in which their press has been broken.

Coaching Decisions. The coach is responsible for fundamental game strategy. Following are some of the decisions he must make concerning zone-press defense.

1. Whether to pressure the inbounder. If the coach decides to pressure, he must then decide whether to use a small man to distract

the inbounder or upset his poise or a big man to jump in front of him. In making this decision, the coach must remember that the ball may be passed or carried out of bounds behind the baseline after a basket or a foul shot. A big man will be slower in reacting.

2. Where to influence the direction of the pass-in. The decision depends primarily on the basic abilities of the defenders and secondarily on offensive-player alignment.

3. How to align the back two defenders if three men are up. Should they be side by side or one in front of the other? The offensive positioning generally determines this alignment.

4. Whether to apply pressure full-court, three-quarter-court or half-court. The coach must consider his team's personnel, their speed, their quickness, and their reaction time.

DRILLING

Daily drilling of the selected team defensive alignments is essential. It is strongly recommended that the coach incorporate frequent half-court team drills using (1) man-to-man defense with double-ups, (2) aggressive two-three zone with double-ups, and (3) one-two-one-one zone pressure. Full-court pressure defenses must also be practiced often so that the team will be prepared to use them at critical times, and so that team members can practice playing offense against them. Coaches should make up teams of specialists who can best get the ball when possession is essential.

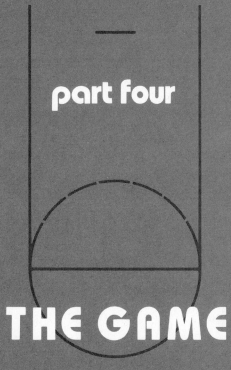

part four

THE GAME

Special Game Situations

9

The term *special situations* is used to denote those phases of the game of basketball that arise out of, or incidental to, the larger context of the game itself—free-throw situations, out-of-bounds plays (both under the basket and along the sideline), end-of-game situations, deliberate fouling when ahead or behind, stalling, and last-second situations. While special situations normally do not constitute a major portion of game time, the importance of preparing teams to deal with special situations may be seen in the fact that approximately four out of five basketball games go into the final four minutes with one team ahead by five points or less.

A coach should analyze and practice for all contingencies, even situations that may occur only once or twice during a season. If the coach waits to explain a situation until it occurs late in an actual game, the players will be ill-equipped mentally, emotionally, or physically to carry out the unfamiliar pattern efficiently. Winning a close game by virtue of a successful late-game stratagem has a powerful positive psychological impact on a team.

Drilling special game situations affords a change of pace during practice sessions, particularly in the preseason, but even more important, it is likely to provide the essential edge necessary to win close games. Preparing players to deal with special game situations is an attention to detail that no conscientious coach will overlook.

FREE-THROW SITUATIONS

When the opponent is shooting a free throw, we normally set up for our fast-break foul-line play (see Diagram 9–1).

When the ball is inbounded quickly after a successful free throw, it puts considerable pressure on the opponents. The free-throw shooter must be thinking of defense, as he has probably been alerted to defend against the foul-line fast-break play.

We work on the law of averages in planning this play. Game statistics over a period of years tell us that approximately seventy percent of all foul shots will be made and that over eighty percent of missed foul shots fall to the inside men. Therefore, less than five percent of all foul shots are normally retrieved by the shooting team. The fast-break foul-line play forces a defensive compensation that further lessens retrieval by the shooting team.

If one of the inside men retrieves a missed free throw, he turns to the outside and passes to the middle man, if possible. If he must pass to the second guard instead, the designated middle man should immediately break to the middle of the court to get the ball (see Diagram 9–2). The object is to get upcourt quickly in a three-on-two or three-on-three fast-break to capitalize on the three-on-two advantage, to obtain a good shot with minimal team

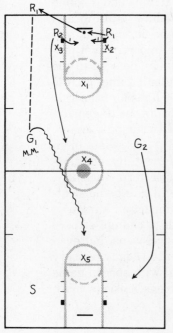

Diagram 9–1. Fast-Break Foul-Line Play. The two best rebounders are on the inside. They must step into the foul lane with the outside foot (the foot nearest the man in the second lane position) to block their opponents from the ball in case of a missed foul shot. The best rebounder-passer should be on the right lane, and if the shot is successful, he should catch the ball before it hits the floor, immediately step out of bounds to his left, and pass in quickly to the middle man, who is on the left side near mid-court. The two guards are in the mid-court area, near the sidelines. The best shooting forward is in the deep corner on the side of the middle man.

DIAGRAM 9–1

opposition (three-on-three), and to keep the biggest opponents from rebounding a missed shot.

When the opponent is free-throw shooting and the situation warrants it, other men should be put in defensive rebounding position. A coach might do this when a change in strategy is necessary near the end of a game to obtain or keep possession of the ball, or when a scouting report precludes using the fast break and recommends a controlled type of game.

In these situations, the best two rebounders will be inside, with the best rebounder on the same side as the opponent's best rebounder, as close to the restraining buffer zone as possible. He must box this man from the inside on a missed shot, stepping into the foul lane with the outside foot. The third and fourth best rebounders will be in the third lanes, as close to the restraining line as possible, crowding toward the best opposing rebounder to prevent his getting the ball. One of these rebounders must be designated to step in front of the shooter to prevent the ball from rebounding to him. The arms and hands of the rebounders must be up in ready position, primarily to try to get the rebound, but also to disconcert the foul shooter. The fifth man will be behind the shooter. After the shot, he will go to the corner on the side on which the ball is taken out of bounds or the rebound is retrieved to receive an outlet pass.

Diagram 9–2. Retrieving Missed Free Throw. R_1 retrieves missed free throw and passes to G_2. G_1 breaks to the middle of court to receive pass from G_1.

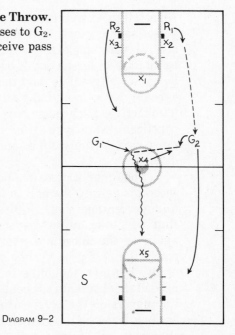

DIAGRAM 9–2

When a team is shooting a free-throw, the coach wants his two best rebounders in the second lane positions. They must step in with the inside foot (the one nearest the baseline), attempting to end up at the side of the opponents who have inside position on them. They should not let themselves be boxed out behind their opponents. Against an exceptionally strong rebounder, the player in the second lane position can fake to a middle siding position by making a jabbing step into the lane with his *outside* foot as though trying to get side position, pushing off that foot when the opponent steps in to box him, and swinging around the strong rebounder to his baseline side.

If a team is shooting a free-throw when playing against an exceptionally strong rebounder, the coach can sometimes station a teammate three feet behind the strong rebounder, toward the baseline. As soon as the ball hits the rim or the backboard, the player slides on the baseline side to the inside to pinch the rebounder from the front. When shooting a foul shot, the shooter and the other men who are back can expect a tip-out if the inside men are crowded but can get a slap at, or a hand on, the ball. If a tip-in is not possible, players may still control a tip of the ball back to the foul shooter or another man.

OFFENSIVE OUT-OF-BOUNDS PLAYS

All intelligent, well-coached teams should have a series of reliable out-of-bounds plays, from different areas of the court, that offensive players can execute quickly and without hesitation. The number of different out-of-bounds plays given to a team should be as few as possible, and they should be simple to learn and to execute. Every play must start from the same basic position to be effective. Each must have perfect timing, and coaches must practice constantly to attain this timing. All out-of-bounds plays must have a safety outlet and at least one player going back on defense.

The first objective in an out-of-bounds play is possession; the second is getting the ball to the best shooter with one pass for a high-percentage shot. Naturally, the coach should select plays that will take advantage of the available personnel. Working again on the margin-of-error theory, a designated player (normally the best passer) should always inbound the ball, and one or two big men should be in position near the basket in case a missed shot presents a rebounding situation. It is imperative that the players on the court set up in position as quickly as possible because from the time the official hands the ball to the inbounder, they have only five seconds in which to get the ball in play.

Another good tactic when a shooting opportunity does not appear is to return a pass to the inbounder if his defender is ignoring him to double-team or assist a teammate. The designated inbounder should call the play before taking the ball from the official, then take his time in getting to the spot where the ball is to be inbounded so that his teammates can get into their predetermined positions to execute the play.

The inbounder should be back far enough from the sidelines so that his arms do not extend over the plane of the boundary line. This position has a twofold purpose. First, it protects him from the defensive player guarding him, since that player cannot break the plane of the boundary line without committing a violation. Second, it gives the inbounder psychological security, as he does not feel defensive pressure being exerted on him.

The inbounder should initiate the play by a verbal signal, by slapping the ball, or by raising the ball over his head.

The player inbounding the ball should never inbound from directly under the basket and backboard (officials will not normally give the ball to a player in this position). He should stand to either side of the foul lane so that the backboard will not interfere with the pass-in.

If the offensive players use the basic alignments several times, they may lull the opponents into expecting those alignments. Then one of the offensive players may deviate his movements to get a quick basket. There are times also when one of the offensive players feels that he can fake and cut by his man for an easy basket. If a player plans to fake, he should inform his teammates at a time-out so that the play can be carried out. Players must be absolutely certain about this faking maneuver before they try it.

Many times teams do not get good results from their out-of-bounds plays because they have not spent enough time practicing them or because the play is not basically sound. Therefore, all players must practice every out-of-bounds play from every position so that they know the responsibilities of each spot. In preseason practice the coach should designate at least three inbounding players. If the first designated player is on the court, he will always inbound the ball for all out-of-bounds plays. If he is not on the court, the second designated player will inbound the ball. If neither the first nor the second man is on the court, the third man will inbound.

Several types of basic out-of-bounds plays may be used under the basket or at the side-court areas from the hash marks in. All these plays should be practiced from both the left and right sides of the court. The basic out-of-bounds plays close to the basket include screen-and-roll plays, cuts off a post, a box formation, one-on-one plays, a continuity play, and a double screen away from the pass-in area. Options in these plays depend on the positioning of the defensive players. Coaches should devise out-of-bounds plays that best suit their players' abilities.

Diagrams 9–3 through 9–11 describe the out-of-bounds plays that we have used successfully for years. On these plays, we work within our margin-of-error theory by cutting down the number of times the ball must be handled. The best shooter takes the shot, the big men stay in the best position to rebound, and men move into defensive position in case the pass is deflected or the shot is missed and the opponents rebound. Exact timing is extremely important. Normally, the best passer will inbound the ball in these plays, identifying the play by calling the number or by signalling with his fingers. He must call the play before accepting the ball from the official so that his teammates have time to get into position.

The movement of the defensive players will determine the play. In using any play, we are working within our margin-of-error theory because the best passer makes a single pass that results in a good jump shot for one of the best shooters.

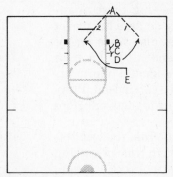

DIAGRAM 9–3

Diagram 9–3. Out-of-Bounds Play, Our Series, Under, Play One. A is the inbounder. B, C, and D set up as close to each other as they can in approximately the second and third foul lanes on the same side as the ball. E is approximately at the foul line extended and closer to the sideline (ball-side) than B, C, and D. When A slaps the ball to initiate the play, E cuts off D to decoy his defender away from the area of the play. D, the best shooter, then cuts quickly to the baseline ball-side, getting an inbound pass from A (1) for a short jump shot. As D initiates his movement, C steps back to administer a slight brush block to momentarily delay D's defender. If anyone tries to get between B and C, B immediately goes to the under-basket area. Many times E can cut off D to either side and be open for the shot (2).

An option of this play is to have D, the designated shooter, tap C, a good shooter. As E cuts off D, C pops out right to get the quick pass-in from A for the shot.

A second option is for E to cut to the corner on the same side as the ball to receive a pass. A will then cut as close to B, C, and D as he can, coming up the foul lane. He will receive a quick pass back from E and take a shot.

Diagram 9–4. Out-of-Bounds Play, Our Series, Under, Play Two. A, the best passer, inbounds the ball. B, C, D, and E line up shoulder to shoulder in the lane, approximately even with the second free-throw lanes, as close together as possible and facing the basket. As the play is initiated, E breaks quickly out to the ball-side corner to receive a pass-in from A. As soon as E receives the ball, B pops out, getting a pass from E for a short jump shot. C, leaning left, administers a slight brush block to impede the progress of B's defender. The option on this play is for B to tap C lightly on his buttocks as they line up to signal him to pop out. B and D will then pinch together to prevent C's defender from getting between the block. E again moves quickly to the side of the ball, receives a pass-in from A, and passes to C for a quick shot. ⎯⎯⎯⎯⎯

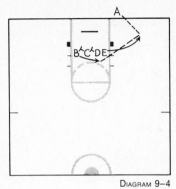

DIAGRAM 9–4

Diagram 9–5. Out-of-Bounds Play, Our Series, Under, Play Three. The alignment is the same as for Play Two. When A slaps the ball to initiate the play, B cuts behind C, D, and E to get the pass. C steps behind D and E as B receives the pass, ready for a pass from B and a quick, short jump shot. (See Figure 9–1.)

The option on this play is for B to pass to D popping back for the shot. (C will tap D to let him know he is expected to step back to receive B's pass.)

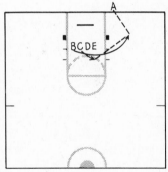

DIAGRAM 9–5

Figure 9–1. Three play from out of bounds. Only the pass receiver's legs are visible as he cuts. The man at right is about to step behind the screen for a pass and shot.

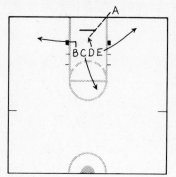

DIAGRAM 9–6

Diagram 9–6. Out-of-Bounds Play, Our Series, Under, Play Four. This is a one-on-one situation for the tall player, D, if his defender is shorter or less agile than he is. The alignment is the same as in Plays Two and Three. When A slaps the ball, E cuts quickly to the corner on the same side as the ball. B will fake and cut opposite, and C will drop back as though he is going to receive the ball as in Play Two. This clears the whole foul-lane area, except for D, who is near the basket with his defender. If the defender is face guarding, A should lob the ball to D, who will jump, catch the ball in the air, and shoot in the same motion. This dummy play is usually most effective against a smaller player. D could outmaneuver a less agile defender by faking and then going opposite or by faking away from the ball and then coming back to it.

DIAGRAM 9–7

Diagram 9–7. Out-of-Bounds Play, Our Series, Under, Play Five. This is a tight box formation that varies somewhat from the other plays, but all players are still in or near the foul lane. It is a pick-and-roll play. A is the designated inbounder. B and C, the two biggest men on the court, have their inside feet on the buffer zone at the foul lane. D and E are at the foul line extended, just outside the foul lane. At the signal, E moves across the foul lane to set a screen for D, and C moves across the lane to set a rear screen for B. D cuts off E's screen and toward the corner on the side from which the ball is being inbounded. E moves back in defensive position, and D becomes a safety outlet. B cuts off C's screen to the outside into the foul-lane area. C executes a screen-and-roll maneuver. A has the option of passing either to B, if no switch is made, or to C, if a switch is made putting C inside on the pick-and-roll maneuver.

Diagram 9–8. Out-of-Bounds Play, Our Series, Under, Play One, Diamond. Often, teams line up in different defensive formations from the ones expected. Any time a defender is outside our alignment (between one of our players and the side line in Play One alignment) we immediately call "Diamond." In this diagram, A is guarded by X_1, B is guarded by X_2, and C is guarded by X_3, who is between C and the sideline. D is guarded by X_4, and E is guarded by X_5. As soon as the inbounder calls "Diamond" and slaps the ball, the players move as follows: B moves to the corner on the same side as the ball, taking X_2 with him. E holds position. D moves back toward the foul line, taking X_4 with him. C now has an open move to the basket with X_3 on his back, and he can receive a pass-in from A for an easy shot.

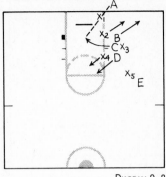

DIAGRAM 9–8

Diagram 9–9. Out-of-Bounds Play; Our Series; Under; Plays Two, Three, and Four; Diamond. A is guarded out-of-bounds by X_1. B is guarded by X_5, C by X_4, and E by X_2. D is guarded by X_3, who is behind D. As soon as A calls "Diamond" and slaps the ball, the players move as follows: E moves to the side on which the ball is to be inbounded, taking X_2 with him. B moves to the opposite corner, taking X_5 with him. C moves to an underneath position opposite the ball. If X_4 stays to guard D, C will be open. If X_4 goes with C, D steps directly toward the basket with X_3 on his back, receives an easy pass, and shoots.

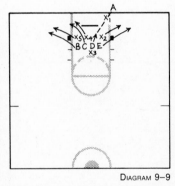

DIAGRAM 9–9

Diagram 9–10. Out-of-Bounds Play, Our Series, Side. B, C, D, and E line up along the foul line. A, the best passer, inbounds the ball. On A's signal, B, the best shooter, moves behind C, D and E's screen to receive the pass (1). If B's defender stays behind C, D, and E, B takes a high-percentage shot from the outer half of the free-throw circle. If B's defender comes with him to prevent the shot, B passes back to A (2) for a drive-in basket. (To receive the pass, A starts toward the ball, then reverses to the open corner on the side from which he inbounded the ball.)

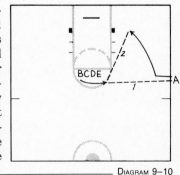

DIAGRAM 9–10

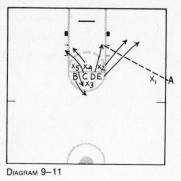

DIAGRAM 9–11

Diagram 9–11. Out-of-Bounds Play, Our Series, Side, Diamond. Because X_3 is behind D to negate B's movement to the ball, A calls "Diamond." On the initiation of the play, E cuts as quickly as possible to the corner, taking X_2 with him. B steps back as he normally would if he were going to get the ball, taking X_5 with him, and C moves down the opposite lane, taking X_4 with him. D then moves down the near foul lane toward the basket and receives a lead pass from A. D's left hand should be up as a target for A. If X_4 attempts to stay with D, he will leave C alone on the opposite side.

Many teams use a zone defense to protect against out-of-bounds plays.

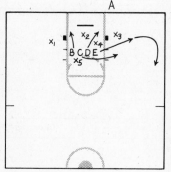

DIAGRAM 9–12

Diagram 9–12. Out-of-Bounds Play, Under, against a Two-Three Zone Defense. A, the best passer, takes the ball out. The other players assume their Play Two alignment across the foul lane just in front of the broken-line free-throw circle, with E, the best shooter, on the same side as the ball. E moves quickly to a position ballside, 16 feet from the basket along the baseline, perhaps taking X_3 with him. If X_3 does not cover E, E is in position to receive the pass and take the shot immediately. D and B are the big men. D steps into the right side of the lane in front of the ball, and B moves into the opposite lane position. Their movement puts extreme pressure on X_2, so he will need help from X_4. C, the second best shooter, cuts to the right, in line with the ball. If X_3 goes with E and X_4's attention is diverted by D, C is in excellent position to take a short, high-percentage jump shot. B's position inside X_1, underneath on the weak side, negates X_1's defensive position. E circles back in outlet position if the shot does not show for him immediately. B and D must be cautioned that they cannot remain in the three-second area if the safety outlet pass is made to E.

Diagram 9–13. Out-of-Bounds Play, Under, against a One-Three-One Zone Defense. E, the best shooter, breaks to the corner. If X_3 does not go with him, A passes to E for a quick jump shot from as close to the basket as possible. D steps straight in toward the ball, C steps straight toward the basket, and B, the second-best shooter, cuts behind C and D. C and D's movement will freeze X_2 and X_4, and B should be in front of X_5. If X_3 is guarding E, A may pass to B. If E cannot receive the pass-in, he should circle back to become a deep safety outlet in case the ball cannot be passed to a teammate who is in good shooting position. _____

DIAGRAM 9–13

DEFENSE AGAINST OUT-OF-BOUNDS PLAYS

When defending out-of-bounds plays under the basket, the man guarding the inbounder should position himself between that man and the basket, aggressively preventing him from passing in toward the basket. He should force the ball away from the basket or toward the corners, where the shots are more difficult to make. Other defenders should protect the underneath area primarily but remain alert for screening maneuvers that will set up a good outside shooter for a high-percentage shot. A man guarding a weaker shooter should step back into the middle of the foul-lane area in a man-to-man defense so that he can help out in double-teaming or in preventing a pass from coming into the close-in area, forcing the ball to be passed back out to the weak shooter he has left.

If scouting shows that the opponents have one man that they can one-on-one with or that they have a very good series of pick-and-roll plays, we may go to a zone defense to prevent those plays, giving up the outside shot rather than giving easy inside shooting position.

When defending against an out-of-bounds play on either sideline in frontcourt, players must force the pass to go toward the mid-court line; therefore, the man guarding the opponent inbounding the ball should be between his man and the basket. He should not allow passes into the inside penetrating area but rather should make the ball go back out toward mid-court. Players should maintain aggressive pressure on their men from the basket side, retreating if screens are set, to prevent inside shots.

OUT-OF-BOUNDS PLAYS FROM THE BACKCOURT

A team should not work an out-of-bounds play from the backcourt unless it was a last shot attempt and a time-out could not be taken. Normally, a team working from deep in the backcourt or from the far end line should try to get the ball in frontcourt quickly, using only one pass, and call a time-out. Then the players may pass the ball into scoring position using a frontcourt sideline play rather than one from the deep backcourt or far baseline. This procedure takes only a second or two. However, it must be practiced. If a play from the backcourt is necessary, it can be executed from two positions—either sideline or the far end line.

Two important aspects must be considered when determining whether to use a backcourt-to-basket play. The first factor is the type of defense the opponent is using, and the second is the length of time left to play. If the opponents are behind, they must press. If the score is tied or the opponents are ahead, they will not play tightly in the backcourt. If the ball is deep in the backcourt with no time-outs remaining (less than five seconds left), a backcourt-to-basket play should be used. Remember, it is possible to call a time-out to stop the clock when the ball goes through either basket after a floor shot. However, it is always best to work

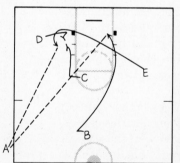

DIAGRAM 9–14

Diagram 9–14. Last-Shot Play, Mid-Court Sideline. Basically, this play presents itself from our single stack pattern. A, the best passer, inbounds the ball. D is in the corner on the same side as the ball, and C is on the same side in the outer half of the free-throw circle. B, the fastest player, fakes to the ball and cuts in a direct line to the basket, trying to outrun his opponent. D fakes to the basket and sets a screen. C steps to the ball and then sets a low double screen with D. E, the best jump shooter, starts as B fakes, cutting to the basket and around the double screen. B must time his movement so that he is cutting momentarily after E has made his initial movement. If B can outrun his man to the basket, A should pass directly to B for the shot. We cannot start from the original stack positions in this situation as it would place defensive men too close to the basket initially for B to cut clear. The other option is for E to receive a pass as he cuts behind the double screen, putting him in position to take the last shot in the ball game.

Diagram 9–15. Last-Shot Play, Far End Line.
After the opponents score a basket, the pass-in
may be made from anywhere along the end line,
and a pass may be made out of bounds along the
end line. B, C, D, and E line up opposite where
A has the ball. B fakes to the ball and steps out
of bounds. C and D cut toward the ball. E fakes
toward the ball, then cuts behind C and D to the
mid-court area in the backcourt on the same side
as A. If no time-out is left, A passes along the end
line to B. A, the fastest player, cuts diagonally
downcourt to receive a frontcourt pass from B.
The clock will not start until the ball touches A's
hand. If C, D, and E can decoy their defenders, A
may be able to outrun his man to the far end of
the court and get the last-second shot. However,
if a time-out is remaining, we would prefer to
have A pass to E at the mid-court area so that we
may call time-out, then use either last-second
play in Diagram 9–14 and Diagram 9–16.

DIAGRAM 9–15

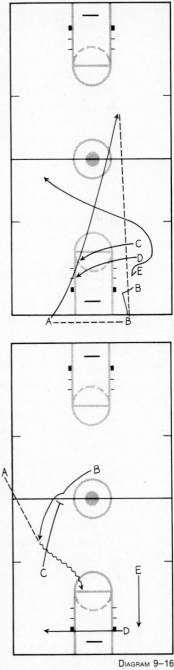

**Diagram 9–16. Last-Shot Play, Sideline,
Backcourt.** If the ball is on the sidelines in the
backcourt with three to five seconds remaining,
the offensive team may try to set up a fast-break,
a three-on-two situation, or a three-on-three situation at the offensive end. The best ball handler
should have the ball so that he can get it to the
good shooters. A, the second-best passer, has the
ball out of bounds on the sideline. D is a big man
who is underneath. B, the best ball handler and
designated middle man, is in backcourt as though
to receive a pass-in there. Normally he will be
closely guarded, as will C, a big forward near the
ball. C moves up as though to receive a pass but
sets a screen at about the mid-court line for B. B
cuts off this screen to either side, but preferably
between the sideline and the screen. A bigger,
less-agile opponent should switch to B. As soon
as B receives the ball, he dribbles into the outer
half of the free-throw circle, attempting to set up
a three-on-three situation and looking for a shot
for E, the best shooter. Many times, E's man will
be so intent on guarding him that B can drive all
the way to the basket. Even if this is a three-on-
three situation, there is time for a pass and a
screen to get a good shot off.

DIAGRAM 9–16

from a basic set pattern, as normally the defense will be alert for a backcourt-to-basket play in a late game situation.

If the ball is at a sideline position closer to frontcourt, and time is a factor, a team should go to its strength. It should go to its practiced pattern first, to its height second, and to its best shooter third. Normally, when a team goes to its pattern in this last-shot situation, the players should play to the defensive weakness of the other team, trying to get the best shooter in position to get a shot at the weak defensive position. They also may go to an opponent with four fouls, as despite the shortness of time remaining, he is psychologically aware that he is in foul trouble.

DEFENSING LAST-SECOND OUT-OF-BOUNDS PLAYS

When defensing out-of-bounds plays from the backcourt or at the far end line with the score tied or down a point or two in last-second situations, players should never allow an easy shot. They must keep pressure on the ball and be extremely aggressive, as officials are reluctant to make the foul call in this situation. They should try to make the passer-in make a short pass in the deep backcourt where they can attack the ball and double-team. A long pass to an open man precludes double-teaming and may lead to an easy basket.

The farthest man back should be cautioned that he must not let himself be decoyed away from the basket he is defending, because he must defend against any opponent cutting to the basket.

If the opponents are more than two points behind, players should not foul, which would allow a three-point play. Therefore, they should take good defensive position without getting too close to their men.

Coaches should practice all last-second situations during preseason practice and intermittently during the regular season so that all players on the team know their responsibilities and are acutely aware of the game situation.

END-OF-GAME SITUATION WHEN YOU ARE AHEAD OR BEHIND

The outcome of most close games that go into the late stages with less than five points separating the teams is determined by the ability of one team to control play as time is running out. Offensively, players can control the play by controlling the ball, using time-consuming tactics (such as a slowdown or a freeze) to protect the lead, and remaining alert for the unopposed high-percentage basket. Defensively, players may use a forcing, aggressive, pressure defense to harass, confuse, and upset the opponent into making mistakes when in possession of the ball.

Late in the game when the situation is tense and the men have played between thirty-five and thirty-eight minutes of extremely difficult basketball, the players will be physically mentally, and emotionally weary. The team that is in the best physical and mental condition will have a great advantage in this late-game situation.

Tactics When a Team Is Ahead

When a team is ahead in the late stages of a close basketball game, stalling tactics force opponents to come to the ball in an attempt to intercept or steal it, thus opening under-basket areas and affording good offensive opportunities for the team that is ahead. The defensive team is foul prone late in the game, and the teams are usually in a one-on-one foul-shooting situation. A team must never give up the ball except after a sure shot or a foul by the opponent. Giving up the ball should mean you scored two points.

As the team that is behind must defend aggressively, thereby becoming mistake prone, reverse or back-door movements are excellent offensive tactics. Defenders, when behind, are trying to steal the ball. As soon as a defender guarding an offensive player makes any movement in the direction of the ball, that player should immediately cut directly to the basket. The poised, prepared team can do well against this type of desperation pressure.

The best ball handlers must be in the game when a slowdown or complete freezing tactics are being used, and the stalling team must move continuously to present a constant offensive threat. The movement and positioning of players and the decoying of opponents must be adjusted constantly to prevent opponents from doubling up.

The most difficult thing for a coach to determine is exactly when his team should go into a stall. A team should go into a stall when there is not enough time left for the opponents to gain momentum to win the ball game. This point varies, depending on the type of opponent.

The team that is ahead when stalling tactics are put into effect must be prepared for pressure. This pressure may be full-court, three-quarter court or half-court, and it may be man-to-man or zone.

The team that is ahead must be constantly aware of several important factors. After an opponent's score, the ball may be in-bounded from any point along the end line. Therefore, players must practice passing the ball along the end line to a teammate who is also out of bounds to relieve pressure at the ball point or to take advantage of an open man who may be upcourt on the side opposite the ball.

When a team is ahead in a stalling game, the best passers and ball handlers should be in the game. Normally, they or the best dribblers should always have control of the ball.

The players must prevent opponents from double-teaming. Therefore, when a team is ahead and is stalling, teammates must never cross. When a pass is made, the passer should cut away from the man he has passed to. The players who are not involved in the ball handling, dribbling, or passing should move constantly to decoy their defenders away from the area of the ball, attracting their complete attention so that they cannot double-team the ball.

Player movements must be definite, sharp, and quick. Short, safe passes must be used, never lob passes or soft passes. A bounce pass is excellent as a lead pass on a reverse. It is better to have a held-ball situation than to make a bad or uncertain pass.

The receiver of a pass must meet the ball, never making any movements that will obscure his intent and confuse the passer. The passer must see both the man he is passing to and his de-fender. Players must keep the ball out of the corners and the sides of the court, especially near the hash marks or mid-court line, as double-teaming usually occurs in these areas. Players on offense should keep wide, spreading defenders, keeping them busy.

All offenses used in late game situations when ahead must be a constant threat, relying on extremely high-percentage shots that are good in-close shots. (Only take unopposed lay-ups if the coach desires.)

A player must dribble under control in late-game stall sit-uations, and he should expect to meet pressure. If he is forced to pivot during his dribble, he should expect double-teaming tactics. Therefore, he should not get himself into a position where double-teaming tactics can be costly. If a player is double-teamed while dribbling, he should know that the safety outlet is generally po-sitioned in the direction from which the double-team pressure was applied.

When a defender leaves his man near the basket to go double-team the ball, it may be impossible or impractical for the man with the ball to pass to the teammate who has been left undefended in the basket area. Therefore, the open teammate must vocally alert the man with the ball and go to an outlet area where the handler may pass to him safely. Trying to score at this time is not the most important consideration, possession and control of the ball are. It is the open teammate's responsibility to relieve pressure on the ball by getting himself into a safe position in the passer's visual field.

When receiving the ball in a slowdown or stall situation, the player must be aware of his court position before he uses his dribble. He should remain alive until he is sure what is in front of him.

Three types of stalls can be used: a five-man continuity, a dribble stall, and a pattern freeze. Using a five-man continuity, we prefer an open-middle three-two stall. After passing, the passer cuts away from the receiver toward the basket, clearing to the corner in the direction in which he has passed. This play should be a continuous motion, making use of all five players and looking primarily for a back-door or reverse cut if an opponent attempts to double-team.

Diagram 9–17. Basic Three-Two Stall. In this offense, the players are spread and the ball is long, which means it is out at least twenty-eight or thirty feet from the basket. A and E are wide in the corner positions. They should be decoying to keep their men occupied. B and D are in the front wing positions wide. C has the ball approximately thirty feet from the basket. He will pass to D. D should make a good fake away from the ball and come back to it to receive the pass, moving into the ball. C should not pass without making a preliminary fake and making sure that D is open as a receiver. After C passes, he cuts down the middle toward the basket and comes out on the right, the side the pass was made to. D dribbles the ball under control toward the opposite side, keeping it as long as possible from the basket. B makes a V fake to the basket, then comes to meet D's pass. D then cuts down the center. The ball is now in the approximate center of the court, still long from the basket. As C goes through and cuts right, he will relieve E, who will come out and take D's place. After D passes and goes down the middle, he will relieve A in the left corner, A will come out in B's place, and the process will continue.

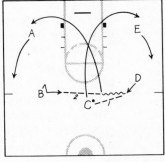

DIAGRAM 9–17

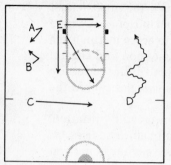

DIAGRAM 9–18

Diagram 9–18. Dribble Stall with Semi-Rotation. This is a stall that we have used successfully. A, B, and C are on the side of the court opposite the ball. The pivot man, E, is in a low position and has latitude in movement. He should remain opposite the ball. However, E breaks to the basket, under, any time his defender leaves him to double-team the dribbler. He can move up along the lane setting screens for A, B, or C as they approach the ball, or he can come high to the head of the key to relieve the pressure on D. D's job is to keep his man occupied while dribbling the ball on the right side of the court. He is going to drive to the basket in a one-on-one situation if possible, or he may pass to E in the pivot position in the outer half of the free-throw circle and cut to the basket using a back-door move. When D's dribble is stopped, C should use evasive tactics to get into position to take a safety outlet pass. C would continue dribbling, with D replacing C.

In a dribble stall, one, two, or three good dribblers will constantly handle the ball. A pivot man moves up and down along the foul lane away from the ball, coming as high as necessary to relieve the pressure in case a dribbler is double-teamed.

In a pattern freeze, three or four men will control the ball, screening away from it and then coming to it. The pivot man will be moving along the foul lane on the opposite side. Passing lanes must be kept open on the strong side so that if an opponent on this side does double-team the ball it is possible to make a lead pass to the free teammate if he has a break away or if he has reversed direction.

Generally, the coach should designate two or three players to dribble in this situation. Normally, the forwards (A and B) should not dribble in this type of stall. However, it is a good technique to allow a good dribbling forward to handle the ball if he is guarded by a less agile opponent.

Normally in a stall situation, the team is looking for the sure-shot quick basket that takes advantage of defensive mistakes (unopposed lay-ups after a good reverse or defenders leaving a man open underneath).

Good team technique dictates that a team does not gamble when it is in the lead, but the players must continue to penetrate with the ball so that they may take advantage of all good scoring opportunities in the late-game stages. These are usually better than the ones that presented themselves early in the game. Many coaches believe that a sound tactic when they are ahead in late-game situations is to press the opponents as soon as they begin pressing. Of course, coaches should not let the game become wild or unmanageable. Controlled aggressiveness is a positive team action that may force the opponents to make mistakes.

Tactics When a Team Is Behind

When a team is behind at the end of a game and the opponents are using stall tactics to control the tempo of the game, the team that is behind must force the ball upcourt fast. The players must pressure the ball, overplaying opponents meanwhile. It is best to apply pressure from a zone structure rather than man-to-man. In zone pressure someone will always be guarding the basket against an unopposed lay-up if defensive mistakes are made. It is a good tactic to allow opponents to pass to a weak ball handler and then exert extreme pressure on him.

Defenders must not allow lay-ups or easy shots. They should be aware that while they must be aggressive in pressing the ball, fouling will hurt the team, as normally a one-on-one foul-shooting situation exists. If an opponent is trapped or cornered, players should not try to steal the ball but harass the opponent so that he will make a bad or uncertain pass or be called for a violation or held ball. They should encourage outside shots, especially when the ball is in the hands of an opponent who likes to shoot or is a high scorer. To encourage a shot, players should yell "shoot, shoot." At the same time, they should harass the player by waving their arms wildly and faking at him.

It is important that all defenders in late-game situations understand and implement the predetermined team pattern. Any time opponents cross at or near the ball, a double-team of the ball should take place. The man with the ball should be harassed relentlessly in order to force mistakes. It is best to let the player with the ball start his dribble, then attempt to force him toward a teammate so as to get double-up pressure.

When the team that is behind obtains possession of the ball it is imperative that the players get good shots as quickly as possible, as the time factor is against them.

Practicing End-of-Game Situations

In preseason practice, the coach must practice both end-of-game situations—when the team is ahead and when the team is behind. These can be practiced together daily, using the clock and the scoreboard. The coach should allot a minimum of forty-five minutes of preseason practice time per week to this type of situation. He should put his players in special units, combining the best pressers on one team to be used when behind and combining the best ball handlers, passers, and dribblers on a team to be used when ahead. In early preseason practice these pressure-defense and ball-control units should be balanced to make the teams as equal in ability as possible so that coaches can find the players who react best to pressure situations.

The situation should simulate game conditions as much as possible. First, these conditions sustain player interest during practice; second and most important, they help players acquire the mental, emotional, and physical poise necessary in late-game situations; and third, they teach players what they will have to do and why in an actual game.

In practice, the coach should outline the game situations, breaking them down into five-, three-, two-, and one-minute situations and last-shot situations. For example:

1. Team A is six points ahead with five minutes remaining on the clock, and team B is in possession of the ball.
2. The score is tied with five minutes remaining, and the ball is in the possession of team B.

It is best to make the better group behind in the score, giving the ball to them when they are more than four points behind. It should be given to the weaker team when the score is closer. The clock and the scoreboard should be used for all strategic, simulated game conditions.

When simulating last-minute conditions, the coach should be certain that he uses his special-situation out-of-bounds plays. It is also imperative that late-game or last-minute situations be officiated. If regular officials are not available, managers or coaches should officiate. At times, the players should be allowed to handle these simulated situations themselves. The coaches then should observe who is making the recommendations, as this indicates a leader, and how well these recommendations are put into effect. They should also determine which players are calm and unemotional under stress, relying on their mental as well as their physical ability.

The coach should explain all of the alternatives before these simulated-game-condition pressure situations start. Notes should be taken during the play, and criticisms and observations should be given at the end of each session. As soon as a player makes a mistake, he should be told what he has done wrong, and he should be praised when he makes a good play.

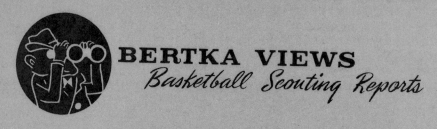

BERTKA VIEWS
Basketball Scouting Reports

Boston College
TEAM SCOUTED

BERTKA VIEWS
BASKETBALL SCOUTING REPORTS

WE'LL SCOUT 'EM — YOU PLAY 'EM — ANYWHERE IN THE U.S.A.

10

Scouting is unquestionably one of the most important aspects of coaching responsibility. When properly analyzed, objective data and subjective impressions obtained through scouting can help a team prepare for an upcoming game against the scouted opponent. Many coaches also have their own team scouted periodically to check their own strengths and weaknesses. The coach's ability to assimilate the information obtained from the scouting report and transmit it to his team is often a major factor in the team's success.

Perhaps the most important single value of scouting is that it helps to determine the immediate game plan. It also improves player confidence, preparing the team mentally for each game by giving members an accurate perspective on the opponent's strength.

Preferably, scouting should be done by a member of the coaching staff, and the coach who does the scouting should report to the team as simply as possible. If the scout is not a member of the coaching staff, his basic basketball philosophy and thinking should parallel that of the staff. He should know the makeup of the team's personnel—their capabilities, their strengths, and their weaknesses. As a final resort, if a member of the coaching staff or a person who knows the team cannot scout, a reliable, recommended scouting bureau can provide the report. However, since the scout from the bureau does not know the team, the report should not be very detailed. (Many scouting bureaus give complete analyses that are sometimes many pages long. While they are excellent scouting reports, the scout is giving an objective report rather than a subjective report, because he does not understand or does not know the personnel of the team he is scouting for.) Even though these reports are made by knowledgeable experts, they should be used with caution. An agreement with a scouting service should always be put in contract form. If a coach is planning to take a scouting report from an agency that he has not had personal contact with, he should preview the bureau's work before using it.

When an upcoming opponent is to be scouted, several factors should be taken into consideration in deciding which games to scout. First, it is best to scout the opponent against a team whose philosophy of play, both offensively and defensively, is similar to that of the scout's teams. The distance the scout has to travel should also be considered. If time permits, it is best to have the same person scout an opponent more than once. Opponents should always be scouted as close as possible to their game with the scout's team.

PREPARATIONS

Before leaving for a game, the scout should take care of several preliminary requirements. First, he should acquaint himself with the team that he is to scout. If there is a previous report on the team from the last season, he should go over it to recollect the salient points of the team's offense and defense. He should also look at any films of the team, paying special attention to the personnel who will be playing in the game he is about to scout. It is important that he review the philosophy of the opposing coach and the type of play that he presents. He should also go over any notes that may have been picked up through newspapers, from publicity brochures, or from statistical reports from sports information directors of the school that he is about to scout.

All material to be used on the scouting trip should be collected and put in one place, usually in a file folder or briefcase. Essential material includes a clipboard with a pad of paper (or a stenographer's notebook), several colored pencils and pens, and several mimeographed half-courts for diagraming play patterns. If more than one person is going, large shot charts should be included. They will be filled in by the second scout.

Well in advance of the trip, the scout should contact the home team of the game to be scouted to be certain that tickets are available. Travel arrangements should ensure that he will get to the game in plenty of time.

A scout should plan to arrive at the gym at least an hour and fifteen minutes to an hour and a half before the scheduled start of the game he is to scout. This allows time for any unexpected problems—a parking space a long way from the gym or a difficulty with the ticket arrangements—and avoidance of the rush before the start of the varsity game.

When a scout arrives in the gymnasium early, he should go immediately to the seat given to him by the home team. If no seat has been designated, he should sit as high above the court as possible, preferably at a corner. From that spot he can see the offensive and defensive patterns evolving, for he sees the full court at all times. (One of the worst seats to scout from is a seat directly at the court level, because you do not get a good picture of what is happening on the court.)

PREGAME TIME

For any scouting report to be effective, the maximum amount of accurate information must be obtained; therefore, the scout should analyze and summarize as much information as possible in the pregame period to supplement his understanding of the strategy during game time. He should pay close attention to a preliminary game, since all teams from one school will normally incorporate the same basketball philosophy into their pattern of play. Observing a junior varsity game allows the coach to diagram out-of-bounds plays and basic offensive and defensive sets.

The scout should check local newspapers for information concerning the team he is scouting. If he does not reveal his identity, he may also obtain valuable information by talking to spectators before the game. Normally the people who are at games early are very interested in the team that they are following, and they are very happy to discuss injuries, morale, team conflicts, basic characteristics of players, and other important items.

During the pregame time, the scout should observe the physical setup of the court that the game is being played on—the type of floor, the type of backboards, the type of supports on the backboard, the tightness or looseness of the rims, and the lighting. These notes are especially pertinent when the game with the scout's team is to be played on this court. The type of ball to be used should also be ascertained, as well as the proximity of the crowd to the court and the crowd reaction at certain times of play (for example, when players are shooting foul shots, when the ball is out of bounds). Scouts are often seated next to each other at games. Exchanging ideas and comparing notes with other scouts, some of whom may have already seen the team play, may help in early organization of notes. A perusal of a program that lists player's name, number, height, weight, and year in school is essential for the scouting report, and this information can be put down during the pregame observation.

When the team being scouted comes on the court, the scout should be especially observant of the type of warm-up followed—the type of shots the players take, their favorite shooting spots, their favorite shooting hands, their attitude.

GAME PROCEDURES

Game procedures are the most important part of the scouting report. All scouts should have a definite method for arranging and taking notes. The jump-ball alignment should be charted quickly. For the next four or five minutes, the scout should try to get a good picture of the game before starting to annotate and draw conclusions. Concentrated attention in the first minutes of the game is vital, because that is when the team is following the coach's basic instructions; free-lance patterns have not yet developed. If the players are going to run a pattern, that is when they are going to set it up. Once the scout has determined the pattern, he should note the personnel and place them in their respective positions, writing down who is handling the ball the most, who is inside, and who is outside. While many people believe that note-taking while the ball is in play is incorrect procedure, we feel that pertinent information should be written down immediately so that it won't be forgotten.

Scouts should take full advantage of any time the clock is stopped. It is usually stopped for a held ball, an out-of-bounds violation, or a time-out. A scout should record why time-outs are taken in the first half, and he should be alert for changes in offense or defense. Time-outs can be used to fill in personal summaries and to make a resumé of the game to that point. If the clock was stopped for a out-of-bounds violation, the scout should note the positions of personnel on the play.

Strategic changes often occur during time-out. A scout should watch for changes in personnel; he should note the times that substitutes enter, and for whom, and try to determine why the coach made the substitutions at that time. He should also observe whether a change in defense or offense takes place after a time-out. Such changes give an insight into a coach's philosophy. When defenses or offenses are changed, the scout should observe, if possible, how the changes are made. Sometimes they are made by arm signals or a sign held up from the bench; at other times a player on the court may institute this change in strategy. The best way to keep track of changes is to make slight symbolic notations as they occur and then elaborate on them at a time-out.

Many ideas should be incorporated in the game scouting report. The scout should note the team's physical and mental characteristics: Is it big? Is it fast? Is it aggressive? Is it in good condition? Are the members pulling together? Do they have great competitive spirit? A very important factor is the ability of the substitutes. If they are good, the coach of the scout's team may change the game strategy. If they are not good, he may use full-court pressure or some other type of defense that will attempt to tire out the opposing team.

Observing a Team's Offensive Characteristics

Some teams will use more than one type of attack. The scout should ascertain first the type of pattern that a team is going to use. Is it a one-three-one or three-two or two-three? Do they depend on a post man? Are they trying to get the ball into this post man? Do they rely on the outside men for a good deal of their scoring? Do they use plays going down the side of the court? Do they attempt to get the ball into the middle? Is the offense balanced?

The fast break, if it is used, should be analyzed. Do the players attempt a fast break after a field goal is made or after a successful free-throw try? Do they attempt the fast break and run all the time or just part of the time after a well-cleared rebound? Do they try to go full-court? Do they try to make an extremely long pass? Is it an organized break by which they go to an outlet man and fill the lanes properly? Do they leave the ball in the middle or do they pass it back and forth? How frequently does the ball go into the pivot man? Is the pivot man primarily a shooter or a feeder who is used to cut off when he has the ball? Where do the passes to the pivot man come from? Is the team a good ball-handling team? Is it a deliberate team or do they attempt to score fairly quickly after setting up a basic pattern? Are the cutters good? Do they move well when they don't have the ball? Do they pass and go using give-and-go plays? Do they look for screens of each other? Do they attempt to dummy the ball into the big man or lob it in? Which men shoot the most? Which men seem to take the bad shots? What type of shots do they take? Will they attempt to tap an offensive rebound back up or will they try to slap the ball out? Are the guards or the men who handle the ball prone to excessive dribbling? Are the patterns determined by the type of pass that is used to initiate the play, by a called name or a called number, or by fingers?

Observing a Team's Defensive Characteristics

The scout should determine the type of team defense used before he breaks down the individual abilities of the players. He should observe if the team uses any type of defense after it makes a successful foul shot or a basket. Some teams, without a signal, will press full-court man-to-man, or full-court zone, depending on the type of score that is made. That is a prearranged defense that should be noted.

Sometimes it is very difficult to ascertain a combination defense. Therefore, the scout should follow cutters on the team opposing the team he is scouting to see if men are chasing them through and how the men are setting up their defense—whether they are meeting the offensive team at half-court or three-quarter court. As soon as individual defensive mistakes are made, they should be jotted down.

The scout should observe the type of defense, (man-to-man, zone, or press), where the defense picks up, and whether it is an active defense. When the defense picks up, does it maintain pressure on the ball and on the outlet of the ball or is it a passive type of defense by which the ball is allowed to advance up to a certain point before the defensive posture is assumed? (Many teams will pick up strong defense at half-court, others at full-court, others at three-quarter court, some at the head of the offensive key of the team attacking.) Does the team react quickly on going from offense to defense?

It is important for the scout to know where the defense is being set up in order to determine the type of offense his own team will use against this team. The point of pickup determines how far the offensive team can penetrate before they meet the defense. Are the defenders working as a team to slide behind screens or to go over the top of screens? Do they switch well, allowing for a roll to the basket? How do they play the roll to the basket? Do they play between the man and the ball or the man and the basket when they switch men? Are they an extremely aggressive defensive team? Are they the type of team that is constantly trying to steal the ball defensively? Which men on the defensive team is it best to keep the ball away from if they are using any type of combination defense? Which type of men are most apt to be moving in on the ball? Is one side of the defense weaker than the other side? Does the team's defensive philosophy indicate that they want the pivot man completely fronted or played on the side, or do they play behind the pivot man?

The scout should know where the team's front line in a zone picks up and who plays the front line of the zone defense, who plays the back line near the basket, which men are the easiest to penetrate against, how they react getting back on defense, whether they are an easy team to run the fast break against or if they are fast getting back, and what type of pressure defense they use when they are behind in a ball game.

General Individual Characteristics

The individual characteristics of each player on a team that is being scouted should also be noted. These include height, weight, position, number, condition, reaction in a team posture, speed, and type of player. There are many offensive characteristics to look for. How well does the player react when he does not have the ball? Does he move well without the ball? Does he keep his defensive man occupied when other teammates have the ball? Basically, is he a good overall offensive player? (Normally, we think of a good overall offensive player as one who reacts well when he has the ball, but the work of a man without the ball is much more important, because if he is a cutter without the ball, then he must be covered at all times. When he does not move without the ball, then it is easier for the man guarding him.)

Is he a good dribbler? When he dribbles, does he penetrate toward the basket or is he more lateral in his movements, trying to keep the ball until he can move it to someone else? Is he a good passer? If the pass is not a good one does he handle the ball well or receive the ball well on the move? Is he looking for a teammate when he is cutting? When he cuts, does he go straight for the basket? Is he lazy offensively? Is he deceptive? Does he use a change of direction or a change of pace? Does he attempt to run the man guarding him into teammates or into opponents? Is he a good screener? Is he a good scorer? What position on the court does he generally take his shots from? Is he a good outside shooter? Does he shoot with both hands in close? Is he predominantly a one-handed ball player, mostly right or mostly left? Does he take good shots? Is he a good foul shooter? (This is an important item, because if the scout knows who the good foul shooters are, he'll know who must be fouled if his own team must get possession of the ball.) What is his posture on the offensive backboard? Does he attempt to gain control of the ball? Does he attempt to tap the ball back up on offense or does he attempt to tap the ball out offensively? Is the player an individualist? Does he only pass the ball when he has to and then pass it off-balance or to a teammate who has no idea the ball is coming to him?

Individual Characteristics by Position

The scout should find answers to all these questions: What type is the center? What is he doing when he is in the pivot? What type of shot does he take? Does he take hooks? Does he take turnaround shots? Does he fade away from the basket when he shoots? Which side does he prefer? Is he agile and active attempting to get position? When he is at the high post is he used as a screener or does he hand the ball off? How good a rebounder is he when he has to move from a position away from the basket, and how does he fight a good rebound position? Does he fight a boxer—is he passive or does he try to jump over the man who is boxing him?

What side of the court is each forward on? Does he step to the ball for pass reception or does he wait for the ball to come to him? Does he reverse well when he is overplayed? Is he a good driver? Does he look for position as soon as a shot is taken? Can he be boxed from the board?

Is the guard fast? What type of dribbler is he? Quick? Straight ahead? Does he use good change of direction? Does he dribble well with both hands? Do both guards bring the ball up or does the better ball handler bring it up? (If he does, the coach will naturally plan to have the other guard take it up.) Does the good ball-handling guard shoot well from the outside or is he reluctant to take a shot? Would he prefer to make the play than take the shot?

Defensively, the scout is looking for both positive and negative individual characteristics. Naturally, the first thing he looks for is the aggressiveness of a player on defense. Is he a good defensive player? Judgment is based more on his position and his defensive attitude than on anything else. Does he get back fast on defense? Does he react to fakes? Is he easy to move out of position? Does he turn his head in man-to-man defense to follow the path of the ball? Does he watch the ball when a shot is taken? Does he switch well? Does he talk when a switch is necessary? How does he react on defensive rebounds? When he rebounds does he protect the ball and make sure that a good outlet pass is possible? Does he box out well? Does he try to steal the ball? Does he stay on his feet until the man with the ball has jumped? Will he dive for loose balls? Does he protect the baseline if he is playing the forward? Does he work hard when he is screened off by an offensive man? Does he attempt to go through a screen? Does he stop when a screen is set? Does he fight over it or attempt to slide through? Does he double up well? Does he talk when he is being screened or when his man is screening someone?

Negative factors to be noted include the following: Does the person leave his feet when someone fakes? Does he foul unnecessarily? Is it easy to drive baseline against him? Does he box his man out after a shot is taken? Does he pay attention to his man when his man does not have the ball? When the ball is near him, does he lean toward it? Does he cross feet when he is moving or when he is shuffling on defense? Does he attempt to see the man and the ball at the same time? Does he talk on defense and point out to his teammates the man he is guarding? Does he leave as soon as an opponent shoots without waiting to ascertain possession?

HALF-TIME

At half-time, the good scout replays the first half mentally and records his impressions, diagraming the pertinent offensive and defensive alignments while they are fresh in his mind. He should review his notes and jot down doubtful items for checking in the second half. He should also get first-half statistics if they are available, and if someone else has kept a shot chart he should check it against his own. He should fill in as many individual personnel observations as he can at this time.

The scout should watch the players as they warm up for the second half, noting especially whether the players who did not perform well in the first half seem listless or dejected because of their play or whether they are enthusiastic and attempting to build up enthusiasm in their teammates. The attitude at half-time sometimes indicates the type of ball player a person is, and sometimes it indicates how he will perform during the second half.

SECOND HALF

In the second half, the scout again lists the starting lineups, making a point of observing which of the five players started in the first half. As the second half progresses, many changes may take place. One change might be the use of reserve players for starters. This may indicate a change in the coach's opinion of the player who has been replaced, and it may change the scout's thinking in regard to the game coming up with his team. As the game nears the end, he should note whether there is a slow down in the offensive if the team he is scouting is ahead, or the type of pressure that is exerted on the ball if the team is behind. In a stall game he should know exactly what time in the second half the players started to slow down the tempo of the game and what type of stall they are using. Is it a definite freeze or is it a semi-stall when they are still looking for a shot at the basket? Is it a team movement or does one man usually control the ball? The scout should determine if the players can be double-teamed while they are using this type of stall attack and at what time they can be expected to stall if they are ahead in the coming game with his own team.

The scout should follow the same procedures he followed in the first half, writing down impressions, making personal observations of the players, and noting the time that the substitutes enter. He should diagram all out-of-bounds plays as soon as possible, noting if they are organized and if they are progressive. (Does one play follow in the same setup as the one that has preceded it?) If the play is under the basket, does the same man take the ball out? Do they have a signal—do they slap the ball or call a name or a number to start the play? Are they looking for the same player—the big man or their best shooter? Do they have a safety outlet on their out-of-bounds plays if the man to whom they wish to pass is covered? What type of play is used from the sidelines? The scout should try to learn whether this play is going to the basket for the score or if the intention is to get the ball in play to start the regular offense. Do they have a systematic method of putting the ball in from the far end when the opponent is putting on a full-court press? Are they trying to penetrate or just maintain possession?

AFTER THE GAME

The scout should notice turning points in the game, the method by which a team was able to obtain the lead and gain control of the game, and the conditions that have changed the outcome. Immediately after the game, he should check his diagrams to make sure they are clear. Complete game statistics are usually available from the home team at the close of the game. At this time the scout should start to plan his post-game analysis and the procedures he will follow in writing his report.

To write his report, the scout should coordinate all of the information that he has. Statistics and play-by-play summaries may be available to help him in his final analysis of the game. He also should speak with any other scouts who were watching the same team so that they can compare notes. If the scout is driving home he should write as much as possible before he starts to travel. If he is going home by public transportation he can write his final draft during the trip.

The final draft should include, first, the individual characteristics of each starting player and each substitute who played—height, weight, relative speed, quickness, overall condition, team-playing ability, and individual ability. All positive factors and negative factors that were observed by the scout should be recorded. The report should reflect his own personal observations. Other scouts' comments and suggestions should be added in parentheses.

The report should be a brief account of the game as he has seen it—the way the game went, why the scouted team won or lost, what strategies were used, the type of offensive and defensive play used, and all special plays used. Primarily, the scout should report whether the team he is scouting can be played man-to-man and suggest defensive matchups for his team, giving reasons for his choices. He should also suggest specific offensive patterns for his team and maneuvers that he feels will be successful against the scouted team. He should include a summary of the statistics he has received and, if possible, clippings of local newspaper accounts of the game.

The scout should base all of his observations on fact, being positive and objective in the conclusions he comes to. However, he should state any intuitions that he may have had and any opinions that he may hold. The relative strength of the team opposing the scouted team should also be considered when writing the report.

COACH'S USE OF SCOUTING REPORT

The coaches review the scouting report and question the member of the staff who did the scouting. If the report was done by a scouting bureau, then important decisions regarding the individuals on the opposition should be made collectively by the coaching staff. The staff should analyze the offensive and defensive ability of each opponent and determine which players (both starters and reserves) on their own team will play him if using man-to-man defense.

Normal defensive strategy demands that the team (1) place as much pressure as possible on a good shooter at every opportunity and (2) play away from the strengths and to the weaknesses of each opponent. If one opponent is an outstanding shooter, the best defensive player will usually play him, and the coach will try to help that defender as much as possible by leaving weaker opponents unguarded momentarily to double up on the good shooter. If the opponent is a good outside shooter but not a good driver, he should be overplayed when he has the ball at all distances from the basket. Normally when a player is an outstanding shooter, it is wise to keep the ball from him for two reasons: (1) the offensive team will work harder to get shots for him, since the team depends on his scoring ability, and (2) when he does get the ball, he will be more apt to take a poor shot than he would if the pressure were not exerted on him.

A team must be told of the peculiarities in its opponents' offensive play, because the players should always play the percentages against opponents. For example, if an opposing team depends on getting the ball into the pivot area for its offense, stress should be placed on floating or dropping off the men who are designated to make the pass-ins to that area. This maneuver will cut off the passing lanes into the pivot area and will allow the passer-in to shoot. Normally, players do not take this opportunity if penetration to the post area is a fundamental in their offensive game strategy.

If an opponent is not a good shooter but a good driver, his guard should be told to stay off him to allow the outside shot and to take away his drive to the basket. If an opponent maneuvers well in only one direction, he should be overshifted so that his defender is playing to his strong side instead of directly in front of him. If he is a good shooter but must have the ball before he can make his offensive move, he should be played so that he does not receive the ball except in a disadvantageous position. He should be made to move as much as possible without the ball so that he has to work to obtain possession of the ball.

If a certain opponent must have the ball all the time, in a close ball game he will attempt to make the play himself. Therefore, when he has the ball in this situation, players near him should realize that they can double-team him.

When an opponent is a poor ball handler, more defensive chances can be taken against him. If an opponent lacks confidence—and this is especially true of a sub—it is best to try to force him to take shots in a position that is not to his advantage and to talk to him, yell at him, and fake rushing at him in an attempt to upset or confuse him. It is important to take advantage of all weaknesses observed by the scouts. However, when a coach finds an opponent who is an especially weak defensive player, he should not try to beat him all the time, as the opposing coach will replace him with a better defensive player if the situation is obvious. Therefore, in the normal course of events the coach should attempt all of the offensive patterns he feels will be to his advantage. If he does have one weak defensive opponent there may be a crucial time in the game when the coach must get a basket and he can get it against the weak player.

Naturally, the type of offense to be used against the opponent is based on the type of defense he plays. However, game strategy must always be within the framework of the fundamental offensive and defensive patterns that have been used during the year. No great change in basic procedure should be made, because any game plan that has any practical impact must be practiced, and there is not enough time to practice it in the day or two before a ball game.

Usually the best defensive players are matched against the best scorers on the opposing team, and size is a factor in match-ups of men who will be close to the basket. Normally, you play tall men against tall men; but a good strategy against a pivot man is to use a smaller, quicker defender who can outposition the good post opponent, especially if the post man is the type who shoots, or looks for his shot, when he gets the ball. Not allowing him to get the ball is the best defense.

Many idiosyncrasies appear in individual opponents' offensive maneuvers. Some good shooters must always fake after they receive the ball. Therefore, the defenders should be told not to move with the first fake. Other shooters must bounce the ball once after they get it in order to obtain body balance. Their defenders should be told to move in quickly as the players receive the ball to prevent them from putting the ball to the floor, thus making them take the shot in a posture that is not to their best advantage.

Players who are not playing one of the three strongest offensive opponents should know the latitude that they have in helping to double-team the better opponents. Many times, for example, when a pivot player gets the ball and he is to be double-teamed, the strong-side forward comes in to help the double-team. Often it is best for one of the guards to drop off to help double-team, especially if the pivot man has outmaneuvered his defender and his defender is behind him. Again, the relative outside shooting ability of the player guarding an opponent on the strong side must be considered. If the guard is the stronger outside shooter, then the defensive forward should drop back to double-team. If the forward is the better shooter, or is in a much closer position relative to the basket, then perhaps the guard should drop back.

In the pregame determination of strategy the scout must be as objective as possible in his appraisal of the opponent's strengths and weaknesses, because players sense whether they are being given accurate information, and it is imperative that they have complete confidence in the ability of the coaching staff.

Game Organization
and Team Strategy

11

After scouting a future opponent, the next step in preparing a team to play is to analyze the data and impressions drawn from the scouting report in order to determine how best to attack the opponent's weaknesses and play to one's own strengths. Every team should have an organized plan of attack covering every conceivable game situation for every opponent and every game, whether or not the coach has scouted that opponent. This predetermined plan, called a *game plan,* represents the coach's concept of how the upcoming game should be played. The game plan must be well organized and presented in its entirety to the assembled squad. Offensive and defensive adjustments must be explained in detail. The time has passed when players can simply be told to do something in a certain way. The coach must explain why and, like a good salesman, sell them on the merits of his game plan. The players must understand, and believe in, what they are doing if it is to succeed.

PLANNING FOR THE GAME

The coach must choose offensive patterns that are most likely to be successful against a particular opponent and explain why they will probably be successful. Defensive match-ups must be predetermined if man-to-man is to be used. The scouting reports, listing the individual tendencies of each starting opponent and each first-line substitute, must be discussed. Then every aspect of each pattern must be presented for the squad and the player concerned. The whole squad must understand the strategy, because conditions may necessitate another squad member's taking over the assignment at any time during the actual game. If a type of zone or combination will be used defensively, each man's responsibility must be outlined. Nothing must be left to chance. Within reason, every possible eventuality must be explored, taking human nature into consideration.

PRESENTING THE GAME PLAN TO THE TEAM

After making the individual defense assignments and determining the team's game strategy, the coach and his assistants should commit the basic game plan to paper. The plan should be presented to the players as follows: One assistant, using the basic game plan and a copy of the scouting report, should select personnel from the varsity or reserves whose physical attributes resemble closely those of the players on the opposing team. Then the assistant should acquaint those players with the personal characteristics of the players they are to imitate. Next he discusses the opponent's offensive and defensive play patterns. Finally, their out-of-bounds plays are discussed.

The presentation to the squad is made before the first practice session prior to the game. Usually, no more than two practice sessions can be devoted to the game plan report, since many teams will play a game in the middle of the week and a game on a weekend. If two consecutive games are to be played on a weekend, the scouting report for the first game only should be given before the first game is played (unless compelling factors dictate otherwise). If games are to be played on the coming Friday and Saturday, and there are no previous games that week, then the report for the Friday game will be given on the Monday and, if necessary, a partial report for the Saturday game will be given on the Tuesday. The partial report will cover only the essentials that require on-court practice. Practice time then must be allotted to both reports. However, because games are taken on a one-at-a-time basis, emphasis must be placed on the first game, and the players should never look beyond that to the second game. Normally, when games are to be played back-to-back, a full pregame skull session should be scheduled Saturday morning so that the scouting report for the Saturday night game can be evaluated when the team can concentrate on it.

Available movies of previous games played against the up-coming opponent should be shown to the squad when the scouting report and game plan are presented. If the opponent is still per-forming in a similar manner, the movies should be marked so that it is easy to get to the pertinent parts that will highlight what the scouting report shows. The person who scouted the game should give the report. He should have written up the individual characteristics so that the notes can be passed around and dis-cussed briefly by the coach. After that discussion, the scout should outline on a blackboard the pertinent offensive and defensive ma-neuvers and out-of-bounds plays, keeping the presentation as brief and inclusive as possible. The squad should then be asked if there are any questions. When all questions have been an-swered, the head coach should discuss the game plan with the assembled squad, while the assistant goes to the court to continue to work with the junior varsity or reserves who are going to be the opponents in the practice sessions.

When the squad reassembles on the court after going over the game plan, the coach who did the scouting and is handling the junior varsity–reserve group should present the opponents' individual characteristics and their offense and defense in skel-eton form. As each junior varsity opponent comes to the court, the assistant coach should list his capabilities as described in the scouting report. After the five players are on, the offensive pattern should be walked through, first without opposition and then with minimal pressure. The same procedure should be followed in out-lining the opponents' defense.

After the individual defensive strengths and weaknesses of the opponents have been discussed, the assistant coach goes over the team's defensive patterns. The team should be warned not to be too aggressive against the junior varsity group. The purpose of the practice game is to acquaint the players with the offensive and defensive structure and the individual strengths and weak-nesses of the upcoming opponents, not to stop the practice op-ponents. Therefore, minimal pressure should be used at first. After the reserve group is a little familiar with the offensive and defensive structure that they are using, stronger pressure can be applied. To reiterate, game strategy must always be within the framework of the team's offensive and defensive patterns, and great changes should never be made. The overall game plan must include second-half offensive and defensive stratagems. Defen-sively, a team may play the first half man-to-man, using man-to-man pressure on occasion. In the second half, perhaps after a score, a pre-practiced type of zone and zone pressure can be used.

TEAM STRATEGY

The most important factor in team strategy is to play your own game. Therefore, the opponent must be forced to play within the framework of your thinking. If an opposing team likes the fast break, it may be advantageous to you to be able to slow the ball down as a team, even though yours is a running team. You do not want the opponent to do what he wants to do, but rather what he does not want to do. It is important, therefore, that the team be prepared to meet any contingency on the court. All possible maneuvers must be completely discussed and practiced so that when the time comes to use a procedure, players will not have to attempt an entirely unfamiliar pattern.

A team should have one or two secondary defenses in addition to its primary defense, because a situation during a game may require a change from the primary defense. Normal strategy is to play a pressing or forcing defense against a bigger team, a slower team, or a mechanical team that uses many set patterns and wishes to control the ball. A team that is not in good condition should always be pressured and played aggressively. A team that dribbles frequently should also be pressured, because it is easy to double-team a player who is bouncing the ball frequently, and it is very difficult for the player to start passing the ball in the course of a game after he has been used to dribbling throughout the season. Any team that does not have good ball handlers should be forced aggressively at all times.

Offensively, screens should be used against any team that guards closely or uses a tight man-to-man defense. Not only is it easier to screen for a teammate if your opponent is guarding close, but it is also easier to rub a man off any screen set by a closely guarded teammate.

Any team that attempts to get the ball into a post area should be played with a floating defense to prevent the ball from getting in and to force the outside shot. The same tactic should be used against a driving team.

A change of strategy is normally advisable after a time-out. Certain plays should be saved to use when you have the ball following the time-out. Many teams also change their defense after certain maneuvers on the court. For example, after a successful basket or a free throw, many teams will change to some type of pressure defense or perhaps zone defense. As we said previously, against an excellent fast-breaking team or a team that is much bigger, it is normally best to play a slowed down, deliberate, ball-control game. The players should be conditioned to step in on the lane men as they come down on a fast break, because they are looking for the pass and are not anticipating this type of defensive maneuver.

The coach is responsible for getting a team prepared mentally for a game. Usually the players do not need a great deal of mental preparation for a game that is going to be extremely close or one in which their team is the underdog. A good scouting report and a good game strategy plan should be enough. However, for games they are expected to win, or should win, much mental preparation is necessary.

ORGANIZATION FOR THE GAME

The coach should arrive in the locker room approximately forty-five minutes before the start of the game, physically and mentally rested and thinking positively. He should check with the trainer and the team, indulging in basketball small talk to discover the team's frame of mind. Then he should confer ten or fifteen minutes with his staff to review the game strategy and to discuss the starters and the early substitutes. The game plan should include projected opponent reaction to proposed strategy so that countermeasures may be thought out in advance. If there is no trainer, the coach should take care of any training duties at this time, assisted by the manager.

At home, the managers should arrive at least an hour and a half before game time to supervise game arrangements. They should take care of the scorer's and timer's necessities and make certain that the game officials' room is in order. One manager should stay with the game officials before the game. At half time, and after the game, he should conduct officials to their room and open it for them. Other managers should make certain that statistical reports and programs are available for visitors or newspapermen, that the statistical recorders are placed, and that bench equipment is in order. One manager should check the home locker room to make sure that it is clean and has all the proper equipment. The manager assigned to the visiting team should check the cleanliness of their room and supply them with towels, blackboard, and chalk. He should let the visitors know that they may consult the home team's trainer when necessary if their own trainer did not come with them. For away-from-home games, the managers who are making the trip should arrive at the point of departure at least three quarters of an hour before the scheduled leaving to make certain that all trip arrangements have been taken care of.

The players should eat their pregame meal at least four hours before the start of the game. After the meal they should exercise and get a little rest. Players should arrive at the site of the game about an hour and a half to two hours before game time. They can spend some of this time watching a preliminary game if one is scheduled, but they should report to the locker room in time to have all preparations complete forty-five minutes before the scheduled starting time of their game. At this time, the trainer tapes the players and checks the emergency equipment he will be taking to the court.

The trainer renders great psychological support to the players before the squad assembles. It is his job to relax them and get them in the best frame of mind for the upcoming game.

The Pregame Warm-up

A pregame drill, about twenty minutes long, should be discussed and integrated into practice sessions before the first game. That eliminates confusion when the team goes out on the court and ensures efficient use of pregame practice time. Initially, players should use a dribble and passing lay-up drill to loosen up, then they should go into a three-line pass, cut, and shoot drill with all three men shooting and all three men rebounding. All players should practice shooting from their normal positions and take at least six practice shots from the foul line, with the starting team and the first line substitutes doubling this number. All must practice their foul shooting for rhythm.

We prefer to have a ball for every two men in the pregame warm-up (or, at most, a ball for every three players), which means six balls should be available for a twelve-man squad. The players should remove their warm-up pants and jackets as their body warmth increases.

Game Arrangements for the First Half

The coach and his assistants must exchange ideas frequently during the game. One assistant or a manager sitting next to the coach, must keep track of team and individual fouls on both teams, time-outs, opponent substitutions, and pertinent commentaries of the coach. Ideally, another assistant should be high above the court, in direct communication with the bench, for court level is one of the poorest locations from which to watch a game. This coach should check continually for any errors in the pregame plan and relay necessary adjustments immediately.

Seating should be arranged so that the first-line substitutes sit nearest the coaches, ready to enter the game. They should be close enough to listen to the coaches' comments as the game progresses. The bench should be constructively vocal, shouting encouragement and warning players on the court of any upcoming plays that they may see. They should participate in the game— concentrating on their part of the game in particular and the overall game in general—so that when they are called upon physically, they can enter the game without any loss of momentum for the team.

When considering substitution, the coach should take into consideration the fact that the substitute will be shooting cold. If a player on the court is taking and missing good shots and he is generally a good shooter, he should be encouraged before a substitute is sent in. If he is taking poor shots, he should be cautioned. Substitution should be made for team impetus if the team has a nonstarter who is an outstanding sixth man. The players on the court should be certain that the incoming replacement receives the ball immediately so that he feels he is a part of the game and loses the anxiety that all substitutes have.

During time-outs for psychological or strategic purposes, the team should remain standing or bent over slightly, hands on hips or knees or relaxed at the sides, grouped around the coach with the reserves behind the participants. *All* players and nonparticipants should concentrate on the advice of the coach.

Time-Outs

A coach should interject his thinking into all parts of the game strategy during the playing of the game. He determines when his team will call time-out and how it will handle substitutions. A team should have a general method for calling a time-out. Normally it should not call any time-outs (never more than one) in the first half, except for extreme emergencies—for example, to take care of a severe injury, to interrupt the momentum of an opponent who has scored several quick successive baskets, or to discuss what to do if the opponents have used a strategy the team has not been prepared to meet. In most circumstances, however, time-outs should be preserved so that a team has three or four going into the very last minutes of the ball game, when they can be used to advantage.

A time-out is a good strategic move when it is called to prevent loss of ball when a player is about to be tied up or cannot bring the ball upcourt late in a game. One can also be called in the late stages of a game when a player on the opposing team is about to shoot a crucial foul shot. The time-out will give him time to worry about the importance of making the shot. The coach can use a time-out late in the game to determine what the last play will be in a tie game when his team has the ball, and he can call another one within the last ten seconds to set up the play he wants the team to use. Both players and coaches should always be aware of the number of time-outs that each team has remaining. Remember, a time-out can be called when *you* score a basket.

Substitutions

A coach should substitute purposefully. Primarily, he takes men out for instruction, to rest, in case of an injury, or to prevent them from fouling out early. He should immediately substitute for any player who is hurting the team defensively.

The coach should always make essential defensive changes as soon as possible, either inserting substitutes or rearranging starters. Substitution during the game is one of the most important aspects of coaching strategy. A coach should insert substitutes frequently and early because they will hustle when they are in the game if they feel they have the coach's confidence. A time-out should never be used to rest a player. Fatigue normally is recognizable by slowness of a player—diminished reaction time, loafing on defense, and not hustling. If a player wishes to conserve his energy, he should do it on offense.

Taking themselves out of a game should be recommended to the players as a good team effort. Taking himself out to let a fresh player come in should be automatic to a player, and he should be commended for informing the coach that he is tired on the court. Normally it is the coach's responsibility to determine the condition of the players during the game.

Place of game is another factor in substitution. Some players play better at home; others are better away from home. The coach should be alert to a player's reaction to spectator response. If the player starts to get upset because he is the object of an away-from-home crowd's derision, then taking him out and talking to him is advisable.

The score is also an important factor when considering substitution. Normally, a coach shouldn't substitute when his team is ahead. If the team is falling behind, he can insert two or three substitutes for aggressiveness and hustle. The question now is whether the substitutes should be allowed to remain in the game after they obtain the lead or whether they should be replaced by the players that the coach thinks are the best players. We feel that you should have your five best players on the court whenever possible. Therefore, if the coach feels that the best players are rested and that their mental attitude is good, he should reinsert them. A coach who does not keep his five best players on the court at all times is second guessing himself. If the substitutes have gained the lead and the coach goes with them, he is telling the spectators that he made the mistake of not starting them as his five best players.

A coach should not lecture a substitute when putting him into the game. Anything he had to say to the player should have been said in his scouting and pregame strategy meeting. A long lecture will tend to confuse a sub. All the coach should do is pat him on the back and give him a few words of encouragement as he goes to report to the player he is replacing.

The coach should never talk to a player as soon as he comes out. The player should take the bench position of the teammate who replaced him, cover up to retain body warmth, towel himself dry, and rinse out his mouth. The coach should let him relax a bit and then go over the reasons he was replaced if they are not perfectly obvious to him. The coach does not owe an explanation to a replaced player, and one should not be demanded. However, we do feel that one should be given, and it makes its greatest impact when it is given immediately. After the coach or assistant has given him constructive advice, the replaced player should quickly get back in the game mentally.

A coach should protect a player from fouling out too early in the game. Normally he should allow his best players to have at least two fouls remaining at the start of the second half. If a key player has two fouls and there are only two or three minutes left to the half, it is a good idea to substitute for him in the time remaining so that he will start the second half with at least three fouls left and he will not lose any of his hustle or aggressiveness.

A coach should never let a starter with four fouls remain out of a ball game too long. Many coaches will replace a player who has only one foul left and then reinsert him at a time when the game is perhaps out of reach. If the team is behind in the second half and one of the best players has his fourth foul called, the coach should not replace him, especially if he is cautiously aggressive. However, the coach should substitute if the player is overcautious on defense and allows an opponent easy shots.

When substituting, the coach should always maintain team balance of size and speed, unless there is a compelling reason to alter this balance. The opponent's defensive tactics may be one reason. When a team is behind and is pressing, it must go with speed and aggressiveness. If the opponents have sprung a surprise zone defense on him, then the coach might go with a good shooter.

A coach should always be prepared to substitute for a special situation. For example, he should insert big men for a crucial foul shot recovery. He may substitute each time his team scores in order to slow down a good fast-break opponent.

A coach should never embarrass a player by putting him in for just a few seconds at the close of a game that is either completely lost or obviously a victory. If the coach wishes to elicit the plaudits of the crowd for a player who has played an outstanding game, he may replace him in the last few seconds, but if he does so, he should substitute a player who has previously been in the game.

A coach must always be cognizant of the number of fouls that each player on his own team has and, perhaps more important, the number of fouls that each player on an opposing team has. He should play at these men if they are key opponents. It is also a good idea to remind players which opponents have fouls so they can talk to the men who are in danger of fouling out to make them overcautious and then take advantage of their caution.

Half-Time Procedures

High school half time is ten minutes; in college it is fifteen minutes. Efficient use of this time is extremely important.

Players must go straight to the locker area at the half, use the lavatory if necessary, put on warm-up jackets, and relax, either lying or sitting. They should discuss the game quietly and constructively with the other players and nonparticipants until the coach is ready to discuss the first half happenings and the second half strategy with the assembled squad.

At this time the managers do not join in the discussion, but rather take care of the needs of the players and the coaches quietly and efficiently. They give the players sliced oranges (for saliva), bits of chocolate (for energy), and a prescribed drink (for a fluid reserve). They should have towels available and any training aids that are necessary. One manager should collate the available statistics for the coaches.

The trainer should administer any necessary first aid. He should check the physical condition of each player and rub him down slightly, concentrating on shoulders, arms, back, legs, and back of the neck.

The coaches should confer privately for about two or three minutes near the team's locker room. They should review the first half, perusing the score book and statistics and discussing alternative strategies. The first half strategy report (see Appendix D) should be used to assess the team game plan during the first half. When the managers and trainers have completed their ministrations, the coaches should discuss individual criticisms with the players concerned and make a group critique including suggested corrections and strategies. If a blackboard is available, the coaches should diagram maneuvers to be used in the second half, basing them on what has occurred in the first half. They should discuss the first half with the team, praising what has been done well and correcting mistakes. The discussion should be brief so that the players will have three to five minutes to warm up for the second half.

An inspirational pep talk has far more value at this time than before the game, for most of what is said pertains to what has taken place on the court in the first half. The coach must see that any momentum achieved in that half carries through to the second half. Victory often depends on the half-time instructions.

Offensive adjustments to the opponent's first-half defensive tactics must be made. The coach should be prepared for possible defensive changes by the opponent, as indicated on the scouting report. If the coach's out-of-bounds plays have been successful, perhaps an option will be a good strategy, as the opposing team similarly adjusts to his play in the first half.

The second-half offensive adjustments should include a discussion of who the team's best scorers have been and what type of offensive patterns have been successful, because the opponents are going to attempt to shut off the best scorers and the best offensive patterns in the second half. Therefore, though the coach should stay with his strength, he should be alert for possible defensive changes from the opponents. During half-time, he should discuss the possibility of using a good scorer as a decoy, waiting for a defensive adjustment, and then taking advantage of the adjustment.

Defensive adjustment to the play of the opponent in the first half must also be made. The coach should stress what patterns have worked best for them and discuss the various defensive techniques to counteract these moves. He should also name their best shooters and tell the team how to play them to cut down on their point production.

Second Half

The second-half arrangements on the bench should be similar to those used in the last half. The first-line substitutes should be placed close to the coach so that they can listen to his comments.

When the game outcome seems assured, the coach may substitute reserves to give them valuable game experience. As a morale factor, he should give playing time to as many players as possible. Generally, he should not take starters out as a group, and he should observe the performance of reserves with starters.

Time-outs become more strategic as the game progresses. A coach should call time-outs in the second half to change the defensive posture. For example, he might switch from man-to-man to a pressure zone to upset the opponents. That is especially effective after the opponents have called the time-out. He should be aware of key players who may be tiring and try to substitute for them as quickly as possible so that they may conserve energy and be at full strength in the final stretch. Also, he should be alert to insert key reserves with special ability. If the team is losing control of the backboards, he could insert a good rebounder. He should also call time-outs in the second half to implement prepracticed late game strategy. The coaches must keep track of the time-outs and fouls left for both teams. If a key opponent has four fouls, the team should try to foul him out if it is part of the overall strategy and the game situation warrants it.

Late-Game Strategy

Important strategies that must be preplanned and prepracticed for second-half implementation are the tactics for controlling the game if the coach's team is ahead. The coach will decide if or when the game should be slowed down and what type of offense should be used to slow it, depending on the second-half play and the time remaining in the game. The coach should also indicate when a complete freeze is to be used. If a team is behind, it is important that the players know who the weaker foul shooters on the opposing team are so that they can foul them to get the ball. Normally one does not foul the best ball handler and certainly not the best shooter, but they are usually the players who have the ball most in team offense. Therefore, it is important for the coach to stress which opponent he wants to take the foul shot and to discuss methods of forcing the ball toward him so that he may be fouled in a strategic situation.

If a team has not used the number of fouls allotted per half (six in college or four in high school) before the bonus situation, the players should know how to use strategic fouls, allowing the weak foul-shooting opponent to get the ball and then fouling him and taking a less-than-70-percent chance of his getting one point so that they may obtain the ball. (Normally, a team shoots no better than 70 percent from the foul line as a game percentage.)

Possession of the ball is approximately 0.9 points, based on an average shooting percentage of 45 percent, and is fast approaching one point per possession of ball.

Other tactics that should have been practiced and included in the pregame plan in case they have to be used in the second half are the last shot and the strategy when the opponent has the ball late in the game when the coach's team is ahead three or more points. The coach does not want any fouls with less than half a minute to go, and he wants strong but unaggressive pressure on the ball with all his defenders playing a defense that will force opponents away from the basket if they are to receive a pass. He wants five men boxing out for the defensive rebound. Never cause a three-point play.

If a team is behind three or more points with possession of the ball late in the game, the players must strive to have a good driver take the shot, looking for a three-point play.

If the team is more than three behind, naturally the players must bring the ball upcourt quickly and get it to a good shooter and have him take the best available shot while the other men crash the offensive boards.

If the team is one or two points behind and has the ball, then the coach is looking for a good shot from his basic pattern with his best shooters taking the shot if possible, and he must have strong offensive rebounding from at least four of his players.

If the team is one or two points ahead, and the opponents have the ball, the players must try to pressure the opponent with the ball, leaving no good openings for other opponents, and all five men must go strong to the defensive boards when a shot is taken. If the opponents penetrate the team's defense in this situation , all players must retreat immediately toward the defensive basket to help out, because if an opponent has penetrated, someone is going to have to pick him up, and an open man may be under the basket.

If the score is tied and the coach's team has possession of the ball, he wants the last shot so that he will finish the game with a victory or, at worst, with a tie game and an overtime period in which to win it. To make sure that the last shot is a good one, he should take a time-out with ten to twelve seconds left, if possible, to discuss what play is to be used and who is to take the shot.

A defense should be perfected for occasions when the score is tied and the opponents have the ball. Players should attempt to force a pass by the opponents' best ball handler, who normally will have possession of the ball, back toward mid-court to some other player, then keep the ball from getting back to the good ball handler, if possible. When the ball goes backwards they should attempt a double-team for a possible interception. If a team sits back and allows the other team to move the ball until the last ten or twelve seconds, it loses the possibility of ball possession, taking a chance of losing or at best ending the regulation game with no better than a tie score. The coach should not allow the long freeze for the last shot.

Psychologically, the coach should allow the opponents to go into a freeze, for when they are thinking in terms of freeze, they are not thinking of penetrating until a certain number of seconds are left on the clock. Normally, a team feeling pressure will try to pass back when it is freezing rather than passing into scoring area. By allowing the opponents to start the freeze, the coach lulls them into thinking he is going to allow the type of offensive that will give them the last shot. After they have been lulled, the team attacks in a surprise maneuver. Of course, the inside scoring area must be covered to prevent an easy shot.

When the team is behind ten or more points in the second half, a time-out must be taken to change strategy and personnel. A pressing, aggressive defense is called for, and the coach must make personnel changes for morale purposes and to change the course of the game. When a team is ahead ten or more points in the second half, the team must keep pressure on the opponents offensively because two or three quick baskets at that point will make it impossible for the opponents to catch up, and if they are discouraged, the game will change from a fairly close game into a game that will become an easy victory. It is psychologically important to keep a double digit lead on the score board.

Tactics for special situations (see Chapter 9) must be thoroughly inculcated for late-game use so that minimal explanations are necessary during the game.

After the Game

The coach has many post-game responsibilities. First, he should meet on the court briefly with the opposing coach to exchange gracious congratulations and condolences; then, he should go to the locker room with the team. He should be positive in any remarks he makes to the team, whether or not they have won the game.

The coach should see that either he or a staff member remains in the locker room vicinity immediately after every game. His presence prevents horseplay after a victory and wards off bitterness or vindictiveness after an extremely difficult loss. The coach should then meet privately with his assistants. This gives him time to recover from post-game exhilaration or depression. He should see the press as soon as his duties to the players are completed and he has control of his game feelings, always remembering the press's deadlines. He should be objective and positive in his comments, never criticizing players, opponents, the opposing coach, or officials.

POSTGAME REPORTS

All games played should be reviewed by the coaching staff and the team. A written report should include the coach's impressions of his own team's game (determined from the strategy reports) and his opinion of the effectiveness of the pregame scouting report on the opponent. It also covers how the game was played, whether or not the tactics conformed to the pregame strategy, where and why strategy was weak, where and why the strategy was effective, and any other pertinent comments. Game statistics and postgame notes, together with the scouting report, should emphasize positive and negative factors. Summarize the thinking of the players and assistant coaches after each game. The coach's own observations belong at the end of the summary. The coach should underscore what is especially pertinent and accurate; put question marks through anything that was erroneous; and revise the scouting reports in light of the game as it was played.

APPENDICES

Basketball Outline

1. Go over rules and regulations—look for any rule changes.
2. School work:
   a. Main reason for being here.
   b. Attendance and attention in class. Your attitude reflects on basketball program.
   c. Tutoring available for those who feel they need it—don't wait until it is too late.
   d. If you fall below average you are jeopardizing your chances of making the team.
3. Basketball practice rules:
   a. Be on time to all practices and meetings. The team will not wait for you.
   b. If you must miss a practice or be late, notify me as far in advance as possible.
   c. Stop all activity on whistle. Everyone give undivided attention. There's too much to be done in a short period to repeat for certain individuals.
   d. Anytime you come onto the floor, you are expected to give out 100% effort. We will get pleasure and enjoyment through accomplishment and hard work.
   e. Avoid all forms of horseplay. It is dangerous and it spoils the team morale.
   f. Profanity has no place in our practice—an educated man can express himself clearly without resorting to profanity.
   g. Don't be careless, slouchy, or vulgar in your actions or appearance.
4. Our aim: To prepare ourselves *mentally, physically,* and *technically* as individuals and as a team so we can play the game to the best of our capabilities, constantly, day after day.

a. Mental attitude:

> The mental attitude of each of us is the most important factor in the success of our team this year. It is always the most important single factor. Our mental attitudes are determined by how we react to our environment—our ability to get along with each other without conflict under stress and strains.

> It is not the things that happen to us that make or break us, it is our mental reaction to these influences that counts. Consequently, it is better to be logical and sensible than to be emotional and impractical.

Make wisdom your partner in all you think about and do. The normal, well-adjusted person is endowed with certain character traits:

1. He is emotionally mature. He thinks and behaves as a grownup should. He has a definite aim in life. He knows where he is going.
2. He accepts the hard knocks of life philosophically.
3. He keeps himself too busy to be unhappy.
4. He is able to get along with almost everyone, has a flexible personality, and is humanly understanding.
5. He goes about his life's business without too much complaining.
6. He does not act impulsively—he learns to control his emotions, exercises wise judgment, and is able to make intelligent decisions.
7. He is not a cynic, nor does he harbor neurotic prejudices.
8. He keeps his nose out of others' affairs.
9. He is tactful and not argumentative; tolerant and unselfish.
10. He is not oversensitive and is able to accept criticism.
11. He has a sense of humor and radiates self-confidence.
12. He has faith in mankind and possesses a healthy attitude toward people and the world around him.
13. He acquires wisdom through the experience of the past. He profits by his mistakes.
14. He has achieved a desirable way of life—one that makes living pleasant instead of a struggle and painful. He has acquired an ability to relax—*a capacity to enjoy life.*

The proper mental attitude is essential—a prerequisite to a successful basketball season:

1. *Emotions.* Your mental health is affected greatly by your control over your emotions. Recognize your own emotional status.

If you can recognize your problem then you may be able to do something about it. Then make up your mind to face it head on.

2. *Confidence.* A mental state that is necessary for success in any phase of life. We can't win games and establish a winning tradition unless we believe in ourselves, our teammates, our coaches, our system, etc. Confidence breeds confidence. If you believe in yourself, and act it, others will believe in you. Don't lose your confidence when you are criticized. Understand that constructive criticism is often a sign of interest by the coach. Coaches will seldom waste their time on a player they are not interested in. Don't see a dig or double meaning in every remark that is passed—don't be oversensitive.

3. *Victory Spirit.* To be a successful basketball player you must have a tremendous desire to win, coupled with a willingness to work hard and sacrifice for victory. You must be a great competitor, hustle constantly, and radiate confidence.

4. *Loyalty.* No basketball player will ever be great unless he has learned the importance of loyalty. It is more than giving all as far as physical effort goes. It involves a devotion to a cause.

5. *Respect.* The respect of a player for his coach, faculty, and teammates is invaluable. I cannot demand your respect. I will do all I can to earn it.

6. *Responsibility.* You are in the public eye—live up to your position, attend classes, make effort, be on your best behavior, respect others. Don't break training rules; it has a detrimental psychological effect and spoils team morale and confidence.

   A. Training program based on common sense:

   (1) Diet—Regular meals on athletic training table. Don't eat between meals. Fruit and fruit juices are all right.

   (2) Sleep—Offers the best and only means of recuperation.

   (a) Arise at a regular hour, regardless of early morning fatigue.

   (b) Stay awake all day.

   (c) Determine the number of hours sleep usually required to produce a feeling of absolute rest upon awakening. Calculate the hour of retirement accordingly; establish the habit of retiring regularly each night at this hour.

   (d) Avoid eating or drinking too much of anything before retiring.

   (3) Colds—One of our worst enemies.

   (a) Avoid undue exposure—dry thoroughly after taking shower.

   (b) Drink lots of fruit juices and water.

(4) Drinking—Cannot and will not be tolerated in any degree. Violation of this rule will result in immediate dismissal from the team.

(5) Smoking.

  (1) Doctors say smoking affects some of the physiological functions of the body.

  (2) Morally—The player who smokes is untrue to himself and his teammates and is doing something that wrecks his conscience because he is cheating and breaking a trust. Strong team morale cannot be built upon the willful violations of our training rules.

  (3) *Don't smoke!*

B. Physical training and conditioning:

When you report on the floor today, I assume you are prepared to make personal sacrifices and deny yourselves many of the social activities and pleasures that other students may have. You cannot function to your fullest potential unless you are in the best possible physical condition. Basketball is hard and strenuous, and condition counts more in this game than in any other. It cannot be forced upon you—you've got to get into the best possible shape because *you* want to. Don't deceive your teammates; don't let your school down; don't deceive your coach; and, mainly, don't deceive yourself by false condition, because in the final analysis you will find you have deceived yourself most of all.

C. Technical preparation:

The smart coach realizes the real answer to successful coaching does not lie in the development of some super-strategy or super-play or in brilliant direction from the bench during the game. The key to successful coaching lies in the effective teaching of fundamentals.

As players, you must realize that your natural ability can take you only to a certain level—whether or not you go beyond that level will depend on mastery of fundamentals. A player has learned a fundamental when it becomes so much habit that he will perform it instinctively, at the right time in the game.

If we practice the proper mechanics and techniques day after day, there will be an increase in the skill and efficiency of performance.

By practicing the proper fundamentals in the proper sequence and continually repeating them, we establish nervous patterns. The greater the number of times that impulses are sent over these nervous pathways, the more firmly established they become, until what has been practiced becomes habit and automatic.

This explains why proper execution is important. It also explains why bad habits, once formed, are hard to break. It is also true that the more a skill is practiced *properly*, the better you learn to use only the muscles involved in performing this particular skill. Thereby, you reduce the amount of energy necessary to perform a given amount of work. An increase in skill and efficiency will probably be the first change that occurs as a result of our practice sessions. "Practice makes perfect" is true only if the proper mechanics are being practiced. Bad habits can be practiced as well as good ones, so it is important that you begin building good habits from the start. Don't be careless.

Our practice sessions will be designed to give you the technical know-how of the game—to condition you physically, mentally, emotionally, and technically.

The final thought I leave with you is that if you give me 100 percent effort, I will return 150 percent to you. On the other hand, if you give less than your best, you won't find a place on our team.

Coach Bob Cousy

B

Pre-season Practice
First Week

Time: 1 hour and 30 minutes. (Have manager time each drill.)
30 minutes.—Chalk talk and drill explanation. First day—Rule
changes (explain). Coaches work each day 15 minutes prior to
practice with
(a) Big men—Kane, Adams, Vernon, Payne, Royer, and Carr.
(b) Small men—Shooting, passing, dribbling; individuals and
     pairs.

OBJECTIVES

1. Development of Basic Skills
   Offense:
      Passing
      Shooting
      Dribbling
      Rebounding and clear out
   Defense:
      Stance
      Movement
      Position
2. Development of Basic Team Concepts
   Offense:
      One-on-one—teach fakes
      Two-on-two—pick, roll, etc.
      Three-on-three
      Changes of direction—from stack alignment—from free-
         lance.

Defense:
  One-on-one
    Pressure
    Check advance
  Two-on-two
    Switch and slide
    Double up
    Check cutter—charge play—jump in
    Overplay pass receiver
  Three-on-three
    Overplay
  Two-on-one
    Double up
  Three-on-two
    Double up

Finish up with fast-break team drills.

C

Daily Practice Schedules

IN FIRST WEEK

Work before practice (15 minutes) on low stack moves. Williams, Payne, Adams, Kane, Doll

    a. Regular stack position with turn—Def.—fake left, go right

    b. Come across lane and meet ball—Def.

    c. Simulate overplay on B and E with reverse to basket and high lob pass (use Kunz and Evers)

    d. Cutting through middle—pass from side—trailer move

Drills

Explanation time for drills (20)*

    a. 5 Interval laps around court—3 backward laps and shuffle around court—captain lead (10)

    b. Lay-ups with bounce pass from middle (5)

    c. Stationary parallel passing lines—chest, bounce, overhead. Fake first, snap wrist, follow through—outside shoulder (5)

    d. 2-lane passing lanes—full court—side line to foul (5)

    e. Full-court dribble drill—down right, back left—side and front (5)

    f. Long pass drill—2 hands (10)

    g. Group shuffle drill—(Captain lead) very low, palms up (touch floor with palms), *growl* (2); shuffle completely around the court (1); group jump drill (2)

    h. Hands on belt "D" drill—both sides of court (match up positions) (5)

---

* ( ) indicate minutes per drill.

   i.   One-on-one—D overplays—off. Looks for backdoor—pass to outside, must return (side drill using coach as passer) (5)

   j.   Two-on-two—full court (5)

Foul Shooting

   k.   Shoot (5) at each basket—Total 40—manager record (10)

   l.   Drive in drill—side and front $\begin{cases} \text{side to side} \\ \text{Rocker fake—with "D" (10)} \\ \text{roll} \end{cases}$

   m.   21—jump shots stack positions A, C, D (small men)—Rebound and box-out drill with pivot and clear out positions (B and E) big men. (10)

   n.   Fast-break drill—3-on-2—full court—rotate (10)

   o.   Whistle sprints (5)

DAY BEFORE EARLY SEASON GAME

Before practice (varsity) (30)

   a.   Review films (last year's) emphasizing predetermined points on U. of F. offense

   b.   Go over U. of F. individual reports again

   c.   Go over U. of F. o.o.b. plays

   d.   Basic game plan review

On court (J.V.'s) (30)

   a.   Use J.V.'s as U. of F.

   b.   Have Frank go over individual reports with J.V.'s identified as U. of F. players

      1) Each J.V. knows what he's capable of—oral report

   c.   Slow motion (½ speed) skeleton U. of F. off. and def.

      1) ditto o.o.b.

Basic Game Plan Review

Preparation for U. of F.

   Defense—must step in.

Review movement on box-and-1 and 2-3 defense also; 3-1-1, demonstrate again position on defense and foul line step. Don't let ball in middle or low. If so, top men collapse and double team.

Rebounding

4 men in—must box out and go for ball. Don't start on break before we have ball.

(Review individual players on U. of F.)

Offense—Patience

1. Look for break each time, get ball downcourt quickly. However, don't force if play is not there.
2. Start with plays if its man—1R and 7 should work.
3. Review our Box-and-1 offense.
4. In shuffle work "Get one for Joe" if man overplays wing man.
5. If Bobb on Jones, put on post and send low off shuffle.
6. Set up offensive alignments.
7. Go over U. of F. out-of-bounds.
8. Pick up man-to-man and stay until play is finished.
9. Put ball on ground whenever possible.
10. Step in whenever opportunity arises.
11. Box out every time.
12. *Patience on offense.*

On Court Work

1. Work against 3-1-1—one-half court press. (5)
2. Work against box-and-1 with our alignment. (5)
3. Df. work with triangle-and-2—stressing boxing out and re-bounding, jabbing at man with ball. Don't commit too far. (5)
4. Df. work on using 3-1-1 press. (5)
5. Work on possible use of 2-3 zone. (5)
   N.B. This lineup should use plays on offense.
   Stress—stepping in; boxing out; patience on offense. Only good shots should be taken after everyone handles. (5)
6. Work 3-2 and shuffle using these principles. Everything on ground. (5)
7. Shooting (teams) and foul shots. (15)

Half-time
Strategy Report

1. Who controlled game tempo? If opponents, how did they do it? Diagram and annotate.

2. Are opponents switching defenses? If so, what are they keying on? What is their pickup point? Where is defense giving us most difficulty?

3. Is our man-to-man doing the job? If not, where or who is breaking down? Suggested changes? Is pressure high enough?

4. Is our zone press accomplishing our aim? If not, where or who is breaking down? What outlet are they going to on first penetrating pass? How high is he (or are they) coming? At what point in the pressure are we having most success?

5. What type of game (offensive) are opponents trying to play? Are we letting them play their game? If so, suggestions for shutting off key men—speeding up, slowing down, etc.

6. Offensive comments: Is our break working? Why not? Are we getting shot from stack? What options will work best against opponents' defense? What about 2-2-1 or 2-1-2?

7. Board control: Are we controlling "D" board? If not, what changes? Offensive boards—are we getting our share? Who should we box if necessary?

8. Individual comments:
    a. Def. matches re: speed, hgt., strength, etc. (suggest possible changes).

b. Are we stopping dribbler? Who isn't giving outlet pressure?
c. Is everyone getting back on "D"? Who is tiring?
d. Who isn't doing reb. job? Not boxing out if called for?
e. Williams and Kane—are they shooting properly? Going out too far on their men?
f. Are shooters getting good shot?
g. Are we overshooting, passing, and dribbling?
h. Too many long passes? Can we send men down sooner?
i. foul-line play—diagram the defensive coverage. Who is covering deep man, guard, or forward?

Selected and Annotated
BIBLIOGRAPHY

Abelsett, Bob. *Coaching Basketball's Combination Defenses*. West Nyack N.Y.; Parker Publishing Co., 1976.
   A usable coverage of defensive flexibility and aggressive tactics.

Allen, Forrest C. *Better Basketball*. New York: Whittlesey House, McGraw-Hill Book Co., 1937.
   A complete treatise on all phases of basketball by one of the game's most revered coaches. Still practical for the today's coach.

Allen, Forrest C. *My Basketball Bible*. 7th ed. Kansas City: Smith-Grieves Co., 1928.
   Covers material in all aspects of basketball incorporated in a later publication by the author. Excellent for reference.

Anderson, Forrest, and Albeck, Stan. *Coaching Better Basketball*. New York: Ronald Press Co., 1964.
   Text incorporates all aspects of basketball for the coach, especially from an organizational point of view. Meticulous in all areas covered.

Anderson, Forrest, and Tyler, Micoleau. *Basketball Techniques Illustrated*. New York: A. S. Barnes & Co., 1952.
   A short, well-illustrated book covering all individual fundamental techniques. Team defense and offense are presented in sketched outline form.

Angell, Lieut. E. D. *Basketball for Coach, Player, and Spectator*. New York: Thos. Wilson & Co., 1921.
   Interesting and valuable as a reference and for historical information. Book was written for the Wilson Athletic Library.

Antonacci, Robert J., and Barr, Jere. *Basketball for Young Champions*. New York: Whittlesey House, McGraw-Hill Book Co., 1960.
   A well-written short book focused on improving fundamental techniques in the beginning or younger basketball player.

Armstrong, Bill, with Cassidy, Fred. *How I Coach Championship High School Basketball*. West Nyack, N.Y.: Parker Publishing Co., 1973.
   A full-coverage treatise. All aspects of a successful system presented in detail.

The Athletic Institute—*Basketball Instructor's Guide*. Consultants: Dr. Forrest C. "Phog" Allen, Harold E. "Bud" Foster, Edward S. "Eddie" Hickey. Chicago: The Athletic Institute, 1958.
   A pictorial booklet dealing primarily with individual offensive techniques.

Athletic Journal. Evanston, Ill.: Athletic Journal Publishing Co.
   Monthly publication containing informative articles on current trends in all areas of basketball. Should be subscribed to by all coaches to keep abreast with modern thinking.

Auerbach, Arnold. *Basketball for the Player, the Fan, and the Coach*. New York: Pocket Books, 1957.
   For everyone interested in basketball. No diagrams. Contains excellent information on free-lance situations. Approaches the game from a practical, workable point of view. Invaluable material for all coaches.

Bachman, Carl C. *Basketball for High School Players and Coaches.* Dubuque, Iowa: Wm. C. Brown, Co., 1955.
Primarily designed for high school coaches and players, but common-sense approach is valuable at all levels of competition.

Baisi, Neal. *Coaching the Zone and Man-to-Man Pressing Defenses.* Englewood Cliffs, N.J.: Prentice-Hall, 1961.
Good material on coaching multiple defenses. Methods of attacking zone press tactics and drills should be useful to coaches.

Balch, J. W. *California Offense for Basketball.* Santa Barbara, Cal.: J. W. Balch, 1949.
Short book covers the author's version of California offensive theory.

Balch, J. W. *Theory for Basketball Offenses.* Santa Barbara, Cal.: J. W. Balch, 1949.
Small booklet covers basic offensive theory. Informative for coaches building their own offense.

Baratto, John, and Krajewski, Bob. *Coaching Junior-High Basketball.* East Chicago, Ind.: M R Studios, 1960.
A fine text on beginning basketball at lower levels of competition. Covers the "feeder" system for the high school expertly.

Barnes, Mildred J. *Women's Basketball.* 2d ed. Boston: Allyn and Bacon, 1980.
An excellent overview of the women's game by an excellent coach. The most definitive text of its type.

Barry, Justin M. *Basketball: Individual Play and Team Play.* Iowa City: Clio Press, 1926.
Good reference material, presented by an outstanding coach of the 1920s, provides insight into how the game was played at top college level in that era.

The Basketball Clinic's Treasury of Drills. West Nyack, N.Y.: Parker Publishing Co., 1977.
A compendium of drills covering offense, defense, fundamentals, and conditioning compiled from successful usage by 35 outstanding coaches.

Basketball Coaches Digest. Huntington, Ind.: Huntington Laboratories.
A free yearly publication for coaches, compiling excellent basketball articles from the previous season.

Bee, Clair. *Basketball.* New York: Townsend Publishing Company, 1939.
A short book on basketball as taught by the author at Long Island University.

Bee, Clair. *Basketball for Everyone.* New York: Ace Books, 1962.
An instructing pocketbook designed to appeal to spectator, player, and coach. Good individual techniques illustrated and explained.

Bee, Clair. *Make the Team in Basketball.* New York: Grosset & Dunlap, 1961.
Designed to help beginners improve their techniques. Illustrations use younger players in the development of these techniques.

Bee, Clair. *Winning Basketball Plays.* New York: Ronald Press Co., 1963.
A compilation of plays, including jump ball, out-of-bounds, and last-shot situation, contributed by eighty outstanding college coaches.

Bee, Clair, and Norton, Ken. *Basketball Fundamentals and Techniques.* New York: Ronald Press, 1959.
Describes all phases of basketball fundamentals. Game situations bring a competitive aspect to learning techniques. One of a series of five books.

Bee, Clair, and Norton, Ken. *Individual and Team Basketball Drills.* New York: Ronald Press, 1959.
Well illustrated. Wide range of drills outlined allows the coach to select those best suited to his team's needs. One of a series of five books.

Bee, Clair, and Norton, Ken. *Man-to-Man Defense and Attack.* New York: Ronald Press, 1959.
Explains man-to-man defense and the variations. Methods of attacking man-to-man defense outlined with copious diagrams. One of a series of five books.

Bee, Clair, and Norton, Ken. *The Science of Coaching.* New York: Ronald Press, 1959.
Discusses the role of the coach in basketball today. Excellent coverage of all strategic situations. One of a series of five books.

Bee, Clair, and Norton, Ken. *Zone Defense and Attack*. New York: Ronald Press, 1959.
Thorough treatment of all zone defense alignments and offensive systems of attacking zones. Recommends several offensive formations in combating the zone defense. One of a series of five books.

Best of Basketball from the Coaching Clinic. West Nyack, N.Y.: Parker Publishing Co., 1966.
Forty articles by many of the leading figures in basketball. Each article covers a different phase of the game. An excellent reference source for the young coach.

Bliss, James G. *Basketball*. Philadelphia: Lea & Febiger, 1929.
Written for coaches, players, recreation leaders, students, and teachers of physical education. Good historical reference covers all phases of basketball.

Bonder, James B. *How to Be a Successful Coach*. Englewood Cliffs, N.J.: Prentice-Hall, 1958.
Good practical information on dealing with the squad, public relations, and essential qualities and stepping stones in becoming a successful coach.

Bonham, Aubrey R. *Coaching the Flexible Man-to-Man Defense*. West Nyack, N.Y.: Parker Publishing Co., 1978.
A solid coaching manual for defense-oriented coaches at every level of play.

Brown, Glenn C. *Secrets of the Zone Press*. Danville, Ill.: School Aid Co., 1962.
Covers all phases of basketball with special emphasis on the zone-press defense. Good material for the coach wishing to install team pressing tactics.

Brown, Lyle. *Offensive and Defensive Drills for Winning Basketball*. Englewood Cliffs, N.J.: Prentice-Hall, 1965.
Contains 200 drills for all areas of team and individual basketball concepts. Diagraming easily understood and explicit.

Browning, W. *Basketball*. London: Sir Isaac Pittman & Sons, 1949.
Interesting publication by a founder of the Amateur Basketball Association of England and Wales. Change of pace reading for the basketball coach as it gives an insight into the game as played in England.

Buck, R., *Shuffle and Press Offense for Winning Basketball*. Englewood Cliffs, N.J.: Prentice-Hall, 1969.
Based on current offensive thinking on attacking modern pressure defenses.

Bunn, John W. *The Art of Basketball Officiating*. Springfield, Mass.: M. F. Stibbs, 1948.
Good supplementary material for coach to help him better understand problems and techniques of the basketball official.

Bunn, John W. *The Basketball Coach: Guides to Success*. Englewood Cliffs, N.J.: Prentice-Hall, 1961.
A theoretical yet practical approach to the science of coaching, written by one of basketball's better-known authors.

Bunn, John W. *Basketball Methods*. New York: Macmillan Co., 1939.
Complete text on all important general aspects and basic principles (especially good in the philosophy and methods sections).

Bunn, John. *Basketball Techniques and Team Play*. Englewood Cliffs, N.J.: Prentice-Hall, 1964.
The result of the author's forty years of coaching and his years as editor of the Basketball Rules Book. Advocates that the coach initiate and incorporate his own thinking and then test the validity of his theories.

Bunn, John W. *Scientific Principles of Coaching*. Englewood Cliffs, N.J.: Prentice-Hall, 1955.
A technical coverage of laws and principles of physics as applied to all sports areas. Interesting reading for coaches who wish to understand why certain techniques are more desirable than others in athletics.

Carlson, Henry Clifford. *Basketball: The American Game*. New York: Funk & Wagnalls Co., 1938.
Contains good background material on the use of the figure eight as expounded by its best-known advocate and innovator. Training, diet, and health references are applicable for today's coaches.

Carlson, Henry C. *You and Basketball*. Braddock, Pa.: Brown Publishing Co., 1929.

Good historical reference because of the author's association with the figure-eight five-man weave, discussed thoroughly in this book.

Carter, J. Ted. *Patterned Fast-Break Basketball.* West Nyack, N.Y.: Parker Publishing, Co., 1971.
A description of a total fast-break concept that is well organized. All aspects of the author's approach are predicated on attack.

Case, Everett N. *New Pressure Game in Basketball.* Raleigh, N.C.: Technical Press, 1948.
A short monograph dealing with pressure tactics in basketball. Coaches will find useful practical applications in this booklet.

Cathcart, Jim. *A Multiple-Continuous Offense for High School Basketball.* West Nyack, N.Y.: Parker Publishing Co., 1968.
A complete offensive continuity with options using a one-three-one pattern. Each position analyzed with personnel requirements.

Cella, George A. *The Young Sportsman's Guide to Basketball.* New York: Thomas Nelson & Sons, 1965.
Outlines the essential techniques for beginners. Good basic material for coaching younger players.

Ceravolo, Joseph J. *The Modern 1–4 Basketball Offense.* West Nyack, N.Y.: Parker Publishing Co., 1970.
A solid treatment of a multi-purpose offensive attack that is currently popular.

Chandler, Wm. A., and Miller, George F. *Basketball Technique.* (Publisher unknown) 1922.
Valuable as an historical reference.

Ciciora, Dale, and Sweet, Virgil. *Specific Drills for Basketball Fundamentals.* Valparaiso, Ind., 1966.
Fourth booklet in a series, the first three written by Virgil Sweet. Describes drills used by the authors in their successful coaching careers at Valparaiso Junior and Senior High School.

Cimbollek, Bob. *Basketball's Percentage Offense.* West Nyack, N.Y.: Parker Publishing Co., 1972.
A well-organized text explaining an offensive approach to breaking man-to-man pressure, controlling zones, beating zone presses. Offensive movement with options presented with clarity.

Coach and Athlete. 200 S. Hull Street, Montgomery, Ala. 36104.
A magazine containing many excellent articles. Published seven times a year.

The Coaching Clinic. Englewood Cliffs, N.J.: Prentice-Hall.
Monthly publication of articles by prominent coaches.

Colbeck, Arthur L. *Modern Basketball—A Fundamental Analysis of Skills and Tactics.* 3rd ed. Kaye and Ward, 1966.
A British version of current basketball techniques from a fundamental point of view. Of interest to students of basketball.

Coleman, Brian. *Basketball-Techniques, Teaching and Training.* 2d rev. ed. Cranbury, N.J.: A. S. Barnes and Co., 1978.
A basic text on individual skills and team play.

Converse Basketball Yearbook. Malden, Mass.: Converse Rubber Co.
A free yearly publication for coaches. Covers all levels of basketball with interesting technical articles by the year's most successful coaches. Published since 1922.

Cooke, David C. *Better Basketball for Boys.* New York: Dodd, Mead & Co., 1960.
Outlines proper techniques for the young beginner.

Cooper, John M., and Siedentop, Daryl. *The Theory and Science of Basketball.* 2d ed. Philadelphia: Lea and Febiger, 1975.
This book has two principal values: (1) as a check on fundamentals and (2) as a text for professional physical education classes.

Curran, Jack. *New York City High School Basketball.* West Nyack, N.Y.: Parker Publishing Co. 1972.
A well-written basketball book by one of the game's great teachers. It emphasizes successful techniques taught by New York's finest.

Davis, Bob. *Aggressive Basketball*. West Nyack, N.Y.: Parker Publishing, Co. 1969.
  The book focuses on an aggressive style of play on offense and defense. There is an excellent philosophy. The section on defense is especially well done.

Dean, Everett S. *Progressive Basketball*. Englewood Cliffs, N.J.: Prentice-Hall, 1950.
  Good coverage of the system used by the author. Contains worthwhile material on individual defense and individual offense.

Doane, Gene. *Basketball's Explosive Inside Power Game*. West Nyack, N.Y.: Parker Publishing Co., 1978.
  The concept of this author's offensive system is to provide maximum scoring opportunities inside fifteen feet. He develops his theory for all aspects of offense.

Dobbs, Wayne, and Pinholster, Garland. *Basketball's Stunting Defenses*. Englewood Cliffs, N.J.: Prentice-Hall, 1964.
  Outlines several varying defenses evolving from offensive efforts to combat them. Unique training devices illustrated in text.

Driesel, Lefty. *Secrets of Offensive Basketball*. Charlotte, N.C.: Meteor Publishing Co., 1966.
  Short booklet with material designed to develop or improve the offensive techniques of the team and the individual.

Dwyer, Bob. *How to Coach and Attack the Zone Defenses*. Englewood Cliffs, N.J.: Prentice-Hall, 1963.
  Good coverage of diversified systems designed to penetrate zone defenses.

Earle, Jimmy. *Coaching the Flip-Flop Basketball Offense*. West Nyack, N.Y.: Parker Publishing Co. 1969.
  A well-written, well-organized treatment of a successful offense.

Earle, Jimmy. *Complete Book of 1-3-1 Basketball*. West Nyack, N.Y.: Parker Publishing Co. 1976.
  A fine presentation of the 1-3-1 both offensively and defensively with variations and drills.

Eaves, Joel. *Basketball's Shuffle Offense*. Englewood Cliffs, N.J.: Prentice-Hall, 1960.
  A presentation of the shuffle offense used by the author. Clarity and continuity of diagrams and accompanying text make this treatment easy to assimilate.

Edmundson, Clarence (Hec), and Morris, Robert (Bobby). *Basketball for Players, Officials, and Spectators*. Seattle: Frayn Printing Company, 1931.
  Valuable as a historical reference.

Egli, John. *The Sliding Zone Defense for Winning Basketball*. West Nyack, N.Y.: Parker Publishing Co. 1969.
  An excellent breakdown of sliding zone defenses that depicts the Penn State 2-3 defense by the old master. Included in the text are various presses, a 2-1-2, and a combination man-zone defense.

Ellis, Cliff. *Complete Book of Fast Break Basketball*. West Nyack, N.Y.: Parker Publishing Co., 1979.
  This well-organized text expounds the theory that there is a fast-break opportunity every time a team obtains possession of the ball. Team and individual concepts are nicely handled.

Esposito, Michael. *Game Situation Strategy in Basketball*. Danville, Ill.: School Aid Co., 1966.
  Good coverage of all strategic game situations. Uses different text organization, placing diagram on right-hand page and explaining it on left page.

Esposito, Michael. *How to Coach Fast Break Basketball*. Englewood Cliffs, N.J.: Prentice-Hall, 1959.
  A thorough coverage of all aspects of the fast break from fundamental techniques and drills through complicated team patterns from all possible defensive postures.

Fengler, Hank. *Winning Basketball with the One Grand Offense*. West Nyack, N.Y.: Parker Publishing Co., 1977.

A simple offensive system that is a combination of patterned and free-lance styles using one guard.

Flack, Howard Watson. "Selected Basketball Systems Evaluated and Adapted for High School Coaching." Master's thesis, George Peabody College for Teachers, 1935.
Analyzes six methods of basketball theory by outstanding coach-authors. This is an outstanding research project that is not widely known. Second half of thesis discusses basketball as played in the early thirties. Extremely interesting material.

Ford, Duane. *The Area Key Offense.* West Nyack, N.Y.: Parker Publishing Co., 1975.
An offensive system that operates on predetermined keys relating to ball's position on court.

Fraley, Oscar. *Basketball in Action.* New York: A. A. Wyn, 1954.
Excellent photographic sequences of all areas of fundamental basketball techniques. Demonstrations and their analysis are beneficial to all coaches and players.

Fuller, Bob. *Basketball's Man-Zone Defense.* West Nyack, N.Y.: Parker Publishing Co., 1977.
The defenses used by Indiana's most successful high school coaches are described simply and thoroughly. A fine reference for defensive-oriented coaches.

Fuller, Bob. *Basketball's Wishbone Offense.* West Nyack, N.Y.: Parker Publishing Co., 1974.
A unique offensive approach that should be of interest to basketball coaches.

Gardner, Jack. *Championship Basketball with Jack Gardner.* Englewood Cliffs, N.J.: Prentice-Hall, 1961.
Covers all aspects of basketball as coached by the author. Sections on team offense and team defense adaptable to most systems of play.

Geyer, Dick. *Full Court Control Basketball.* West Nyack, N.Y.: Parker Publishing Co., 1977.
This book describes a flexible offense designed to attack the entire court exploiting any defense. A practical system approach that can be used by any personnel.

Gill, Amory T. (Slats). *Basic Basketball.* New York: Ronald Press Co., 1962.
Unique instructional guide presenting a sound and thorough approach to offensive and defensive play. Sequential checklists given for various phases of the game.

Gonzalez, Billy G. *Championship Basketball—Pre-Season To Post-Season.* Hollywood, Cal.: Creative Sports Books, 1970.
A valuable book that breaks down all team defenses. Well written with excellent diagrams.

Grawer, Richard. *Secrets of Winning Post Play Basketball.* West Nyack, N.Y.: Parker Publishing Co., 1980.
Describes a total developmental program for post players, including improving practice habits and evaluative techniques. Excellent for any inside player.

Gulick, Luther. *How to Play Basketball.* London: British Sports Publishing Co., 1907.
Reference material on the beginning era of the sport by one of the game's pioneers. One of the first books published on basketball.

Gullion, Blair. *Basketball Offensive Fundamentals.* Knoxville, Tenn.: The Author, 1936.
Contains primarily same material as author's Basketball Offensive Fundamentals Analyzed.

Gullion, Blair. *Basketball Offensive Fundamentals Analyzed.* St. Louis, Mo.: Universal Printing Co., 1954.
Contains a detailed analysis of all individual offensive fundamentals, well illustrated with sequence photographs demonstrating various steps for correct performance.

Gullion, Blair. *100 Drills for Teaching Basketball Fundamentals.* St. Louis, Mo.: Bardgett Printing & Publishing Co., 1953.

Deals with drills in all areas of basketball. Especially good selection in footwork, offensively and defensively. A practical book for coaches.

Gullion, Blair. *Techniques and Tactics of Basketball Defense.* St. Louis, Mo.: Bardgett Printing & Publishing Co., 1951.
Treats defensive techniques exclusively. Clear presentation makes this book an excellent source book for the coach.

Hager, Robert H. *Percentage Basketball.* Corvallis: Oregon State College, 1926.
Good historical reference covers systems of play and fundamentals in an earlier era of basketball.

Handbook of Basketball Drills from the Coaching Clinic. West Nyack, N.Y.: Parker Publishing Co., 1971.
A presentation of over 200 drills covering all aspects of the game.

Harkins, Harry L. *Coach's Guide to Basketball's 1-4 Offense.* West Nyack, N.Y.: Parker Publishing Co., 1980.
A comprehensive analysis of the popular 1-4 offense, including eight major varieties of offensive techniques against various defenses.

Harkins, Harry L. *Win with Pressure Game Basketball.* West Nyack, N.Y.: Parker Publishing Co., 1978.
A sound practical coverage of ways to apply individual and team pressure on offense or defense. Emphasis is on pressure with poised intensity.

Harkins, Harry L. *Seven Championship-Tested Basketball Offenses.* West Nyack, N.Y.: Parker Publishing Co., 1976.
A complete presentation of various successful team offenses.

Harkins, Mike. *Successful Team Techniques in Basketball.* West Nyack, N.Y.: Parker Publishing Co., 1967.
Develops team tactics to help the weaker team incorporate surprise patterns and spring the upset and to strengthen the team with a tendency to succumb to pressure in close games.

Harrell, Bill D. *Championship-Tested Offensive and Defensive Basketball Strategy.* West Nyack, N.Y.: Parker Publishing Co., 1967.
Offensive and defensive team strategies designed to keep a team in an attack position by confusing and upsetting the opposition.

Harris, Delmer, W. *Coaching Basketball Zone Offenses.* West Nyack, N.Y.: Parker Publishing Co., 1976.
An explicit coverage of usable zone-offense techniques with applicable drilling procedures.

Harris, Delmer, W. *Multiple Defenses for Winning Basketball.* West Nyack, N.Y.: Parker Publishing Co., 1971.
A superb presentation of multiple-defense theory. A good basic text with special situations and teaching drills well handled.

Harvey, Richard W. *Coaching Basketball's Multiple Set Zone Offense.* West Nyack, N.Y.: Parker Publishing Co., 1973.
Details multiple zone attack from five basic sets with strategies, options, adjustments, and drills.

Healey, William A. *Basketball's Rotation Offense.* Danville, Ill.: Interstate Printers & Publishers, 1964.
Describes in understandable terms the general theory outlining the basic positions, movements, and patterns of the rotation offensive.

Healey, William A. *High School Basketball: Coaching, Managing, Administering.* Danville, Ill.: Interstate Printers & Publishers, 1962.
A necessary reference for every high school basketball coach. Includes excellent material on coaching and is invaluable for basketball management and administration.

Healey, William A., and Hartley, Joseph W. *Basketball's Ten Greatest Defenses.* West Nyack, N.Y.: Parker Publishing Co., 1975.
The authors take the reader from basic man-to-man defense through every kind of pressure and zone defense. Diagrams and drills help illustrate and implement the techniques.

Healey, William A., and Hartley, Joseph W. *Ten Great Basketball Offenses.* West Nyack, N.Y.: Parker Publishing Co., 1970.

A fine reference source for the young coach and a solid review for the experienced coach. The authors pinpoint the best types of offenses.

Healey, William A., and Hartley, Joseph W. *The Winning Edge in Basketball: How to Coach Special Situation Plays.* West Nyack, N.Y.: Parker Publishing Co., 1973.
An outstanding text covering specific special situations that determine a game's outcome. Should be on every coach's shelf.

Hepbron, George T. *How to Play Basketball.* New York: American Sports Publishing Co., 1904.
Valuable historical reference for basketball researchers. Written by one of the founding fathers of the sport.

Hickey, Eddie. *Basketball Drills.* New York: Coaches Press, 1955.
Small booklet contains an excellent variety of fundamental, continuity, weave, and fun game drills.

Hobson, Howard A. *Basketball Illustrated.* New York: A. S. Barnes & Co., 1948.
Fine basic book on basketball fundamentals for beginners. Covers aspects of conditioning and self-evaluation thoroughly.

Hobson, Howard A. *Scientific Basketball.* Englewood Cliffs, N.J.: Prentice-Hall, 1949.
First part deals with scouting and statistics; second part is a check list covering individual and team techniques.

Hollander, Zander, ed. *The Modern Encyclopedia of Basketball.* Rev. ed. New York: Four Winds Press, 1973.
Excellent photo, statistical reference for the basketball aficionado.

Hollander, Zander, ed. *The Modern Encyclopedia of Basketball.* 3d ed. Garden City, N.Y.: Doubleday and Co., 1980.
A great library reference for the statistician and basketball lover.

Holman, Nat. *Scientific Basketball.* Incra Publishing Company, 1922.
Short booklet discusses professional influence during formative stages. Interesting historical reference written by one of basketball's best known figures.

Holman, Nathan. *Championship Basketball.* Chicago: Ziff-Davis Publishing Co., 1942.
Contains fine, useful material on individual techniques, especially man-to-man defense as performed and coached by one of basketball's legendary individuals.

Holman, Nathan. *Holman on Basketball.* New York: Crown Publishing, 1950.
Chronological treatment of author's years in basketball with reference to changes in the game from the early days of basketball to the modern era. Interesting for background material.

Holman, Nathan. *Winning Basketball.* New York: Charles Scribner's Sons, 1935.
Much of material outdated, but book has value for today's coaches in offensive and defensive systems.

Holzman, Red, and Lewin, Leonard. *Holzman's Basketball: Winning Strategy and Tactics.* New York: Macmillan Publishing Co., 1973.
One of the basketball immortals provides coaches with a clear, well-organized treatise on the right way to teach and simplify the game. This highly readable book explains the important fundamentals thoroughly. The diagrams are well done.

Hundley, "Hod-Rod." *Basketball—Individual Offense.* Delray Beach, Fla.: Gainsford Publishing, 1959.
Booklet covers the basic offensive fundamentals as illustrated by the author.

Hutton, Joe, and Hoffman, Vern B. *Basketball.* Mankato, Minn.: Creative Educational Society, 1966.
Designed to teach coordination and timing. Written for all stages of advancement—beginner to college. Appeals to player, spectator, and coach.

Hutton, Joseph W. *Learning How to Play Basketball.* Mankato, Minn.: Creative Educational Society, 1964.
Covers the learning process essential in acquiring and developing the important techniques of basketball.

Jagger, B. *Your Book of Basketball.* London: Faber & Faber, 1961.

Written for young players in England by the National Basketball Coach of England. Interesting treatment of fundamentals from a different point of view.

Jourdet, Lon W., and Hashagen, Kenneth A. *Modern Basketball.* Philadelphia: W. B. Saunders Co., 1939.
Good analysis of eastern philosophy and principles of offensive and defensive play as expounded and played in the 1930s.

Jucker, Ed. *Cincinnati Power Basketball.* Englewood Cliffs, N.J.: Prentice-Hall, 1962.
A description of the Cincinnati system of play that won two consecutive National Championships. Complete offensive and defensive techniques detailed.

Julian, Alvin F. *Bread and Butter Basketball.* Englewood Cliffs, N.J.: Prentice-Hall, 1960.
Covers team offense, with very useful material on free-lance aspect. Scouting hints and statistical information valuable.

Keller, Paul R. *Offense Efficiency Rating System.* Delaware, Ohio: The Author.
A widely used system designed to pinpoint causes of loss of possession. Remedial measures covered.

La Grand, Louis. *Coach's Complete Guide to Winning Basketball.* West Nyack, N.Y.: Parker Publishing Co., 1967.
A complete approach to basketball for the modern coach emphasizing a disciplined team attitude. Stresses psychological factors essential to team success.

Lai, William T. (Buck). *Winning Basketball: Individual and Team Strategy.* Englewood Cliffs, N.J.: Prentice-Hall, 1955.
An illustrated book explaining and diagraming fundamentals and techniques. Easy-to-read text makes the book more appealing. Discusses practical aspects in an interesting manner.

Lambert, Ward Lewis. *Practical Basketball.* Chicago: Athletic Journal Publishing Co., 1932.
An interesting, complete publication in an early era of basketball. Good reference material. Many suggestions applicable in today's approach to the game.

Lapchick, Joe. *50 Years of Basketball.* Englewood Cliffs, N.J.: Prentice-Hall, 1968.
Summary of author's fifty years as a player and coach. Interesting account of early days of the game. Contains complete details of a successful professional and college coach's approach to basketball.

Levitt, Bunny. *Basketball Handbook.* Neptune, N.J.: The Author, 1963.
A thirty-six-page pamphlet crammed with practical information for coach and player. Several pages diagramed with court outline only for inclusion of specific team patterns.

Levitt, Bunny. *Basketball Players Digest.* 707 Berkeley Lane, Neptune, N.J.: The Author, 1964.
Helpful training manual for coaches. All aspects of basketball are professionally treated.

Lewis, Dennis. *From Snake Pits to Field Houses.* Danville, Ill.: School Aid Co., 1977.
A paperback that contains coaching tips on a wide variety of subjects that are most helpful for the beginner coach.

Lindeburg, Franklin A. *How to Play and Teach Basketball.* New York: Association Press, 1963.
A complete textbook on the methods of teaching all phases of basketball. The section on selection and purchasing of equipment is very good. Has good variation in the offensive and defensive team aspects.

Loeffler, Ken. *Ken Loeffler on Basketball.* Englewood Cliffs, N.J.: Prentice-Hall, 1955.
Excellent instructional material, emphasizing man-to-man defense, is spiced liberally with bibliographical details and controversial opinions on rules, spectators, officials, etc.

McCracken, Branch. *Indiana Basketball.* Englewood Cliffs, N.J.: Prentice-Hall, 1955.
A thorough treatment of basketball as coached and played in the successful era of Indiana University. Well diagramed and illustrated.

McCreary, Jay. *Winning High School Basketball*. Englewood Cliffs, N.J.: Prentice-Hall, 1956.
> *Solid approach to high school coaching. Good technical coverage of all areas. Excellent for the young high school coach.*

McGuire, Frank. *Defensive Basketball*. Englewood Cliffs, N.J.: Prentice-Hall, 1959.
> *One of the better treatments of all phases of defensive basketball. Expertly handled, especially the individual phase.*

McGuire, Frank. *Offensive Basketball*. Englewood Cliffs, N.J.: Prentice-Hall, 1959.
> *A good development of offensive basketball's individual techniques.*

McGuire, Frank. *Team Basketball Offense and Defense*. Englewood Cliffs, N.J.: Prentice-Hall, 1967.
> *Coach McGuire divulges his coaching philosophy and includes a complete organizational check-off list as he discusses building a man-to-man and zone offense and defense.*

McLane, Hardin, ed. *Championship Basketball by 12 Great Coaches*. Englewood Cliffs, N.J.: Prentice-Hall, 1966.
> *Twelve outstanding coaches each develop a chapter covering one important aspect in basketball from either the individual or the team point of view.*

McLendon, John B. *Fast Break Basketball*. West Nyack, N.Y.: Parker Publishing Co., 1965.
> *Completely oriented to the fast break as taught by the author.*

Maravich, Press, and Steel, James C. *Basketball Scouting*. Author, 1949.
> *Pamphlet emphasizes the scouting chart.*

Martin, William L. *The Shifting Ball Defense in Basketball*. Author, 1929.
> *Deals exclusively with team defense from the zone aspect. Valuable as a historical reference only.*

Masin, Herman L., ed. *The Best of Basketball from Scholastic Coach*. Englewood Cliffs, N.J.: Prentice-Hall, 1962.
> *A compilation of twenty-four outstanding articles covering all aspects of basketball selected from over five hundred articles appearing in Scholastic Coach Magazine.*

Masin, Herman L. *How to Star in Basketball*. New York: Tab Books, 1958.
> *An elementary booklet on basketball designed primarily for players of pre-high school age.*

Mather, Edwin J., and Mitchell, Elmer D. *Basketball*. Ann Arbor, Mich.: Charles W. Graham, 1922.
> *Contains hints to the player of 1922. Historical reference only.*

Mather, Edwin J., and Mitchell, Elmer D. *Basketball: How to Coach the Game*. New York: A. S. Barnes and Co., 1925.
> *Outdated but has value historically.*

Meanwell, W. E. *Basketball for Men*. Madison, Wis.: Democrat Printing Co., 1922.
> *Book by one of the successful coaches of the era, has value as a historical reference. Discusses one-hand push shot.*

Meanwell, Walter E. *Science of Basketball for Men*. Madison, Wis.: H. D. Gath, 1924.
> *One of the outstanding early texts on basketball with fine fundamental treatment, especially in man-to-man defense. A good reference book for information on earlier-day techniques.*

Mears, Ray. *It's All in the State of Mind*. Springfield, Ohio: Mimeographed Notes, 1961.
> *Mimeographed booklet outlining coaching philosophy and principles of the author. Covers all aspects of basketball.*

Messer, G. N. *How to Play Basketball*. New York: American Sports Publishing, 1919.
> *Historical value. Booklet describes how to play various positions in basketball. Second section contains 1919 rules.*

Meyer, Ray. *Basketball as Coached by Ray Meyer*. Englewood Cliffs, N.J.: Prentice-Hall, 1967.

Coaching methods and offensive system of one of the country's best known and most successful coaches.

Meyer, Ray. *How to Play Winning Basketball.* Chicago: Wood Associates.
Designed to improve individual and team techniques.

Miller, William H. *Basketball of Tomorrow.* Tulsa, Okla.: Jordon Company, 1938.
Covers aspects of basketball from the amateur team post-college approach, the forerunner of our professional game today. Actual experiences of author described.

Moen, Aaron, M. *Basketball Performance Profiles.* Lansing, Mich.: Corner Brook Press, 1978.
A book for serious believers in basketball statistics. It converts statistics into ratios that help a coach utilize pertinent facts for improving team performance.

Mokray, Bill. *Averages.* Boston: Potter Printing Co., 1967.
Invaluable book for the statistician. Gives instant percentages for quick summaries of pertinent game data.

Mokray, William G. *Ronald Encyclopedia of Basketball.* New York: Ronald Press, 1963.
A complete presentation of basketball records and performances from the beginning of basketball to 1963. Excellent reference book.

Morley, Leroy; Ave, Harold C.; Beu, F. A.; and Newtson, Lawrence. *Fundamentals and Techniques for Winning Basketball.* Danville, Ill.: School Aid Company, 1951.
Basic fundamental play and individual techniques developed from the experiences of the four authors.

Morris, Don. *Kentucky High School Basketball.* West Nyack, N.Y.: Parker Publishing Co., 1969.
A well-written presentation of the collective thinking of Kentucky's best scholastic coaches. This solid compendium covers all the basics.

Mundell, Chuck. *Triple Threat Basketball.* West Nyack, N.Y.: Parker Publishing Co., 1968.
A complete diagnosis of current basketball team techniques both offensively and defensively. Outlines tactics designed to overpower the opposition.

Murphy, Charles C. *Basketball.* New York: A. S. Barnes & Co., 1939.
A short treatment of fundamentals with explicit illustrations. Question and answer section at the end of each chapter—a unique feature.

Naismith, James A. *Basketball: Its Origin and Development.* New York: Association Press, 1941.
Last basketball publication by the founder of the game. A treatise for all coaches for its content and for sentimental reasons.

Naismith, James A., and Gulick, Luther A. *Basketball.* New York: American Sports Publishing Co., 1896.
The first publication in basketball by the originator and his collaborator. First rules are included. Invaluable reference for all who love the game.

Newell, Pete, and Benington, John. *Basketball Methods.* New York: Ronald Press Co., 1962.
Combines best techniques of modern day team offense and defense with excellent suggestions for training and conditioning and morale incentives.

Newsom, Herbert. *Basketball for the High School Coach and the Physical Education Teacher.* Dubuque, Iowa: William C. Brown Co., 1952.
Covers all phases of individual and team offense and defense. Offers excellent material to the high school coach and teacher in areas of methodology and philosophy.

1980 Pro-Keds Coaches Digest. The Keds Corporation, 675 Massachusetts Avenue, Cambridge, Mass. 02139.
Sixteen excellent basketball articles by well-known coaches. Free to coaches.

Nisenson, Sam. *A Handy Illustrated Guide to Basketball.* New York: Permabooks, 1948.
Short book on fundamentals of basketball.

Nucatola, John. *Basketball Officiating.* Flushing, N.Y.: Republic Book Co., 1959.

Pamphlet deals with techniques of officiating and is meticulously presented. An excellent reference book for coaches.

Odle, Don J. *Basic Basketball*. Upland, Ind.: A. D. Freese & Son, 1950.
Compilation of ideas of author as a coach and player. Covers all aspects of the game.

Odle, Don J. *Basketball Around the World*. Berne, Ind.: Economy Printing Concern, 1961.
Basketball book with international flavor. Part I discusses basketball around the world. Part II covers all phases of the game.

Osborn, Chuck, with McClelland, Marshall K. *Basketball for Boys*. Chicago: Follett Publishing Co., 1960.
Booklet is based on individual fundamental techniques. Develops shooting and offensive areas very well.

Paye, Burrall. *Coaching the Full Court Man-To-Man Press*. West Nyack, N.Y.: Parker Publishing Co., 1978.
A complete guide to the man press, stopping the ball, stunting, and run-and-jump techniques. Many drills included.

Paye, Burrall. *Complete Coaching Guide to Basketball's Match Up Zone*. West Nyack, N.Y.: Parker Publishing Co., 1980.
Describes the match up zone defense (a zone with man-to-man principles using the best features of each), a difficult defense to run basic offenses against.

Paye, Burrall. *Secrets of the Passing-Dribbling Game Offense*. West Nyack, N.Y.: Parker Publishing Co. 1976.
A rule-oriented approach to offensive basketball from various patterns and formations.

Paye, Burrall. *The Winning Power of Pressure Defense in Basketball*. West Nyack, N.Y.: Parker Publishing Co., 1975.
A good coverage of defensive basics. Describes how to cover the cutter, control the ball, etc.

Peterman, Mark A. *Secrets of Winning Basketball*. Danville, Ill.: The Interstate, 1941.
Written from aspect of training players for a specific system of play.

Pinholster, Garland F. *Coach's Guide to Modern Basketball Defense*. Englewood Cliffs, N.J.: Prentice-Hall, 1962.
Completely covers defense for the individual and team, especially concealed and combination defenses.

Pinholster, Garland F. *Encyclopedia of Basketball Drills*. Englewood Cliffs, N.J.: Prentice-Hall, 1958.
The complete book on basketball drills. Should be one of the first books purchased by the new basketball coach.

Pinholster, Garland F. *Illustrated Basketball Coaching Techniques*. Englewood Cliffs, N.J.: Prentice-Hall, 1960.
Solid, fundamental approach to all aspects offensively and defensively. Well-illustrated. Chapter on coach as a teacher very well conceived.

Pinholster, Garland F. *Pinholster's Wheel Offense For Basketball*. Englewood Cliffs, N.J.: Prentice-Hall, 1966.
Describes a team offensive system designed to attack any defensive alignment without using a variety of team offensive patterns.

Porter, Archie. *Complete Book of Man for Man Defense*. West Nyack, N.Y.: Parker Publishing Co., 1976.
A fundamental text on basic defensive techniques. Simple, versatile, sound, and worthwhile.

Presley, Bud. *Pressure Defense—West Coast Style*. San Carlos, Cal.: D & G Sports Publications, 1962.
Covers defense from the pressure concept as played in West Coast basketball.

Ramsay, Jack. *Pressure Basketball*. Englewood Cliffs, N.J.: Prentice-Hall, 1963.
A detailed approach to basketball based on building the defense as an integral foundation for the offense. Coach Ramsay's aggressive pressure defense paves the way to many quick scores.

Raveling, George. *War on the Boards*. Mt. Pocono, Pa.: Athletic Technologists, 1973.
Devoted entirely to rebounding. Excellent reading and reference material.

Richards, Jack. *Attacking Zone Defenses in Basketball*. West Nyack, N.Y.: Parker Publishing Co., 1977.
This book catalogues every effective zone offense in use. Excellent reference for coaches.

Richards, Jack. *Scramble Attack for Winning Basketball*. Englewood Cliffs, N.J.: Prentice-Hall, 1968.
A presentation of offensive patterns designed to incorporate the offensive abilities of all players into a balanced scoring attack.

Richards, Jack, ed. *Treasury of Basketball Drills from Top Coaches*. West Nyack, N.Y.: Parker Publishing Co., 1971.
A compilation of 163 drills from top coaches covering all phases of basketball. A fine addition to any coach's shelf for ready reference.

Ridl, Charles. *How to Develop a Deliberate Basketball Offense*. Englewood Cliffs, N.J.: Prentice-Hall, 1966.
Author's version of developing a modern offense based on the deliberate style of play prevalent in many sections of the country today.

Riemcke, Cal. *The Guard Freedom Offense for Winning Basketball*. West Nyack, N.Y.: Parker Publishing Co., 1974.
A presentation of an offensive system keyed by guard movement.

Robertson, Oscar. *Play Better Basketball*. Cincinnati, Ohio: Oscar Robertson and Michael O'Daniel, 1964.
Individual techniques as used by one of the game's foremost exponents. Photographs of Robertson in action with descriptive text by the author.

Rosenburg, John M. *Basic Basketball*. Dobbs Ferry, N.Y.: Oceana Publications, 1962.
Aimed at high school level player and below, material is divided into individual skills, team play, and organization and development.

Rubin, Roy. *Attacking Basketball Pressure Defenses*. Englewood Cliffs, N.J.: Prentice-Hall, 1966.
Covers various methods of attacking pressure defenses with excellent results. Good pictorial development of methods.

Ruby, J. Craig. *How to Coach and Play Basketball*. Champaign, Ill.: Bailey & Himes, 1926.
Designed as a textbook and as an aid to coaches.

Ruby, James C. *Basketball Coaching*. Champaign, Ill.: Basketball Book Co., 1931.
Book has value for its insight into early style of play in midwestern section of country. Sound treatment of fundamentals.

Ruby, James C. *Team Play in Basketball*. Champaign, Ill.: Basketball Book Co., 1931.
Good treatment of team offensive and defensive play in midwestern college basketball.

Rupp, Adolph F. *Rupp's Basketball Guide Book*. New York: McGraw-Hill Book Co., 1967.
Designed for teaching fundamental techniques to young players by the game's most successful college coach.

Rupp, Adolph F. *Rupp's Championship Basketball*. 2d ed. Englewood Cliffs, N.J.: Prentice-Hall, 1957.
Covers all aspects of basketball as coached by the most successful college coach of all time. Seven cardinal principles of both offensive and defensive play are excellent.

Samaras, Bob. *Blitz Basketball*. West Nyack, N.Y.: Parker Publishing Co., 1966.
A complete description and discussion of Blitz basketball as coached successfully by the author.

Samaras, Bob (Dr.) *Cut-and-Slash Basketball*. West Nyack, N.Y.: Parker Publishing Co., 1974.
A well-presented offensive system with variations that many coaches will find interesting.

Santos, Harry G. *How to Attack and Defeat Zone Defenses in Basketball.* West Nyack, N.Y.: Parker Publishing Co., 1966.
A complete analysis of proven methods used in attacking zone defenses. Very helpful for coaches in designing their zone offense.

Savers, Richard J. *Basketball's Stack Offense and Defense.* West Nyack, N.Y.: Parker Publishing Co., 1973.
Presents a stack offensive system with options and drills. Good section on motivation.

Scholastic Coach. New York: Scholastic Magazines, Inc.
A monthly publication that contains numerous articles on all aspects of coaching with emphasis on the in-season sport. Basketball material is copious, current, and informative. All coaches should subscribe to this publication. The best edited of any of the coaching magazines.

Sharman, Bill. *Sharman on Basketball Shooting.* Englewood Cliffs, N.J.: Prentice-Hall, 1965.
A masterful book covering all pertinent areas of shooting. Each phase of a shot is thoroughly explained by one of the game's outstanding shooters. Corrective measures are excellent.

Shublom, Walter R. *Tips to Titles.* Wyandotte High School, Kansas City, Kan.: The Author, 1960.
An instructive coverage of high school basketball authored by one of the country's most successful coaches.

Shublom, Walter R. *The Ways of a Champion.* Kansas City, Kan.: The Author, 1964.
A complete manual for the high school coach.

Smith, Carroll. *The One-Two-Two Offense for Winning Basketball.* West Nyack, N.Y.: Parker Publishing, Co., 1976.
A description of an offensive system against man-to-man and zone defenses that includes good drills.

Spaulding, Dayton, M. *Basketball's Destroyer Offense.* West Nyack, N.Y.: Parker Publishing, Co. 1972.
The author's set pattern approach to offense is well presented. Drill coverage is deftly handled.

Sports Illustrated, eds. *Sports Illustrated Book of Basketball.* Philadelphia and New York: J. B. Lippincott Co., 1962.
An expertly illustrated book containing line drawings and accompanying text briefly outlining basic individual and team techniques.

Stack, D. H. *Basketball.* Englewood Cliffs, N.J.: Prentice-Hall, 1968.
Drills, methods, team patterns, and strategies as taught by one of the more successful college coaches.

Stevens, Steve, and Versace, Richard. *The Trident Attack for Winning Basketball.* West Nyack, N.Y.: Parker Publishing Co., 1969.
An analysis of the authors' disciplined offensive system. A fine developmental drill program is included.

Stewart, Norman E., and Scholz, George W. *Basketball: Building the Complete Program.* Marceline, Mo.: Walsworth Publishing Co., 1980.
An excellent new text applicable at all levels of play. It stresses teaching of basic skills and eight important fundamentals. This beautifully done book covers all aspects of the game completely.

Sweet, Virgil. *Specifics of Basketball Fundamentals.* Valparaiso, Ind., 1966.
Booklet on basketball's fundamental techniques as taught successfully at Valparaiso High School by the author. One of a series.

Sweet, Virgil. *Specifics of Free Throw Shooting.* Valparaiso, Ind., 1966.
Booklet on free throw shooting as taught by the author at Valparaiso High School. Experiments with hand placement on back and other theories valuable. One of a series.

Sweet, Virgil. *Specifics of V Offense.* Valparaiso, Ind., 1966.
The type of offense taught successfully and used by the author at Valparaiso High School.

Tarkanian, Jerry, and Warren, William, E. *Winning Basketball Systems*. Boston: Allyn and Bacon, 1981.
An authoritative analysis of offensive and defensive systems and styles of play by a highly successful coach.

Tarleton, Tom. *Tips and Ideas for Winning Basketball*. Englewood Cliffs, N.J.: Prentice-Hall, 1965.
Good coverage of sometimes overlooked or seemingly insignificant details. Text compiles thinking of several other coaches.

Toomasian, John. *Developing a Winning Offense for High School Basketball*. Englewood Cliffs, N.J.: Prentice-Hall, 1964.
Covers all aspects of basketball essential to the high school coach. Excellent drill and play diagrams.

Turnbull, Anne C. *Basketball for Women*. Reading Mass.: Addison-Wesley Co., 1974.
A practical manual that covers the basic aspects of the game.

U.S. Naval Institute. *Basketball*. Rev. ed. Annapolis, Md.: V-Five Association of America, 1950.
A professionally prepared document compiled by outstanding basketball coaches while in the U.S. Navy for use in the naval aviation cadet physical training program. One of the finest basketball books available for organization and instruction in basketball.

Vanatta, Bob. *Coaching Pattern Play Basketball*. Englewood Cliffs, N.J.: Prentice-Hall, 1959.
Basic play patterns are broken down and described. Such areas as pass and cut, pass and screen, and pass and drive, are set forth in clear and precise terms.

Van Ryswyk, Ron. *Ball Controll Offensive and Disciplined Defense in Basketball*. West Nyack, N.Y.: Parker Publishing Co., 1967.
Approaches team basketball from a complete control point of view, emphasizing good offensive ball control while waiting for the high-percentage shot and advocating aggressive man-to-man team defense.

Veenker, George F. *Basketball for Coaches and Players*. New York: A. S. Barnes & Co., 1930.
Still of practical value today. Coverage of fundamentals and man-to-man team play is excellent. Good source reference.

Verderame, Sal (Red). *Organization for Championship High School Basketball*. Englewood Cliffs, N.J.: Prentice-Hall, 1963.
A complete book on the organization of a high school basketball program designed for the high school coach.

Voth, Robert. *Complete Book of Basketball's Continuity Pattern Offenses*. West Nyack, N.Y.: Parker Publishing, Co., 1980.
A well-organized in-depth analysis of four popular continuity offenses—shuffle, stack, one-four, and passing game.

Wachs, Bob. *The Patterned Shuffle Attack*. West Nyack, N.Y.: Parker Publishing Co., 1974.
This book presents a simple offensive system revolving around a single post with a variety of cuts and double screens off the pivot.

Walker, A. L. "Lee." *The Option Offense for Winning Basketball*. West Nyack, N.Y.: Parker Publishing Co., 1977.
Author's version of an all-purpose offensive system that can be incorporated against any defense.

Ward, Charles R. *Basketball's Match-up Defense*. Englewood Cliffs, N.J.: Prentice-Hall, 1964.
A complete text on the defense that matches up the offensive formation used by the opponents. The offensive maneuvers to combat this unique defense are analyzed, and effective counter-moves are detailed.

Wardlaw, Charles D., and Whitelaw, R. Morrison. *Basketball: A Handbook for Coaches and Players*. New York: Charles Scribner's Sons, 1921.
Has value as a historical reference.

Warren, William. *Zone Offenses For Women's Basketball*. Boston: Allyn and Bacon, 1980.
  Step-by-step guidelines, drills, and practical suggestions for building effective zone offenses. Contains an excellent chapter on zone defenses.

Watts, Stan. *Developing an Offensive Attack in Basketball*. Englewood Cliffs, N.J.: Prentice-Hall, 1959.
  Complete coverage of all offensive individual and team techniques. Areas on shooting, coaching, and passing to the big man are very good.

Weyland, Alexander M. *The Cavalcade of Basketball*. New York: Macmillan Co., 1960.
  Traces the development of basketball and records the accomplishments of the outstanding teams yearly. An interesting reference book.

Wilkes, Glenn. *Basketball Coach's Complete Handbook*. Englewood Cliffs, N.J.: Prentice-Hall, 1963.
  Covers completely all the essentials of basketball. Very good analysis of most patterns of offensive team play being used in modern basketball.

Wilkes, Glenn. *Winning Basketball Strategy*. Englewood Cliffs, N.J.: Prentice-Hall, 1959.
  Detailed instruction for the individual player, the team, and the coach.

Williams, Carroll L. *Coach's Guide to Basketball's Simplified Shuffle*. West Nyack, N.Y.: Parker Publishing Co., 1971.
  A solid successor to Joel Eaves's classic on the shuffle offense. This approach is worthwhile for coaches with small players.

Winsor, Chuck, and Davis, Tom. *Garage-Door Basketball*. Danville, Ill.: School Aid Co., 1965.
  An excellent treatment of off-season practice essentials for the squad when formal coaching cannot be given.

Winter, Fred (Tex). *The Triple-Post Offense*. Englewood Cliffs, N.J.: Prentice-Hall, 1962.
  Carefully prepared diagrams outline implementation of triple-post offense.

Wolfe, Herman. *From Try-Outs to Championship*. Englewood Cliffs, N.J.: Prentice-Hall, 1964.
  Covers all aspects of basketball involved in developing the basketball team from the start of a season to its completion.

Women's Coaching Clinic. P.O. Box 14, West Nyack, New York 10995.
  Monthly publication (except July and August) of outstanding articles on women's basketball.

Wooden, John R. *Practical Modern Basketball*. 2d ed. Somerset, N.J.: John Wiley and Sons, 1980.
  An update of a 1966 text for the benefit of today's coaches. An excellent technical book containing the master's brilliant philosophy. Belongs in every coach's library.

Wooden, John. *Practical Modern Basketball*. New York: Ronald Press Co., 1966.
  A complete analysis of the methods and philosophy of one of the most successful college coaches of all time. The book, covering all essential phases of basketball, is clearly diagramed.

Wooden, John, and Sharman, Bill, with Seizer, Bob. *The Wooden-Sharman Method: A Guide to Winning Basketball*. New York: Macmillan Publishing Co., 1975.
  Two legends team up on an enjoyable and sound book dealing with relationships, attitude, fundamentals, and practice hints.

Yaksieh, Rudy. *Winning Basketball with the Free Lance System*. Englewood Cliffs, N.J.: Prentice-Hall, 1968.
  Describes use of two-man and three-man maneuvers as a complete pattern for team offense. Individual initiative stressed.

Zampardi, Frank. *Multiple Penetrating Attacks for Winning Basketball*. West Nyack, N.Y.: Parker Publishing Co., 1980.
  Describes four offensive sets for a multiple-pressure attack designed for teams with limited personnel.

Index

Continued

Continued

Continued